INTERPRETING
ACTS

INTERPRETING

ACTS

The Expanding Church

by

EVERETT F. HARRISON

Academie
Books Grand Rapids,
Michigan
Zondervan Publishing House

INTERPRETING ACTS

Copyright © 1975 by The Moody Bible Institute

Copyright © 1986 by Everett F. Harrison

ACADEMIE BOOKS is an imprint of
Zondervan Publishing House
1415 Lake Drive S.E.
Grand Rapids, Michigan 49506

Library of Congress Cataloging in Publication Data

Harrison, Everett Falconer, 1902–
    Interpreting Acts.

    Bibliography: p.
    1. Bible.   N.T.   Acts—Commentaries.   I. Title.
BS2625.3.H372   1986   226'.607   86–10794
ISBN 0-310-31850-5

Designed by Louise Bauer

Printed in the United States of America

86 87 88 89 90 91 92 93 / 10 9 8 7 6 5 4 3 2 1

CONTENTS

FOREWORD

Without the Book of Acts it would be hard to make sense out of the New Testament. The Gospels end with the resurrection and ascension of Jesus Christ. The Epistles, mostly by Paul, are largely doctrinal in nature, with only an occasional biographical or historical reference. So we ask all sorts of questions. What did the apostles do after the ascension? When was the church founded? Who was Paul? How were the churches established to which the New Testament letters were written? These and other questions are answered by the Book of Acts. Acts provides an account of the origin and early development of the Christian church and serves as a historical bridge between the Gospels and Epistles.

But Acts does more than merely satisfy antiquarian interests: it provides practical instruction for Christians in a twentieth-century world. It shows that the wall of partition was broken down between Jews and Gentiles and, by extension, between peoples of all races and tongues. It gives clear indications of the high spiritual standards that God has set for Christians. It provides examples of God's powerful working through His people and implies that this same power is available to believers today. It demonstrates that the gospel had the power to defeat paganism and demonism in the first century and intimates that, for meeting twentieth-century paganism and Satanic forces, its power has not waned.

THE PUBLISHER

PREFACE

My purpose in writing this commentary has been to deal adequately, though not exhaustively, with the Book of Acts. Critical problems have not been overlooked, nor have practical applications been entirely avoided; but the main thrust has been to discern the meaning of the text.

As a rule, a summary, usually brief, is provided to introduce each passage of Scripture to be treated. This enables the reader to grasp the main content of each portion before its details are examined.

The biblical text is from the New International Version (North American Edition). Occasionally, in connection with the commentary, other translations are given. Greek words are transliterated.

The footnotes omit the place, publisher, and date of publication of works that are listed in the Bibliography at the end of the book.

ABBREVIATIONS

BA	*Biblical Archaeologist*
BC	*The Beginnings of Christianity*
BS	*Bibliotheca Sacra*
ExpT	*The Expository Times*
HDB	*Hastings' Dictionary of the Bible*
IDB	*Interpreter's Dictionary of the Bible*
ISBE	*International Standard Bible Encyclopedia*
JBL	*Journal of Biblical Literature*
JTS(NS)	*Journal of Theological Studies (New Series)*
KJV	*King James Version*
LXX	*Septuagint*
NASB	*New American Standard Bible*
NEB	*New English Bible*
NIV	*New International Version*
NovTest	*Novum Testamentum*
NTS	*New Testament Studies*
RSV	*Revised Standard Version*
TDNT	*Theological Dictionary of the New Testament*

INTRODUCTORY MATTERS

TITLE

It is widely recognized that the titles of New Testament books were not provided by the writers but by the church in the course of the second century. This is demonstrated by the varying ways in which early writers refer to the same book. The manuscripts of Acts reflect considerable diversity: "Acts," "Acts of Apostles," "Acts of the Apostles," "Acts of the Holy Apostles." There is no way of knowing what Luke's own choice would have been. The contents do not support completely the suggestion that only the deeds of apostles are to be recited, nor do they carry out the suggestion that the work of all the apostles is to be described.

Some moderns have proposed the title "Acts of the Holy Spirit" as more accurately identifying the nature of this book. But, however suitable this may be, it will not displace the familiar designations "The Book of Acts" or "The Acts of the Apostles," and it fails to convey any suggestion of necessary human participation in the events that are to be recounted.

PLAN OF THE BOOK

The Great Commission of the risen Lord, as recorded in 1:8, is a key to the structure of the narrative, which reports the progress of evangelization in the same order as in that passage: Jerusalem, Judea, Samaria, the remotest part of the earth. This is true only in a representative sense, however, since there is an obvious selection of material. Omissions are evident, such as the witness in Galilee, Paul's sojourn in Arabia (Gal. 1:17), and details of his labors in Syria and Cilicia (Gal. 1:21). Jerusalem was the geographical focus for the outreach into Judea and Samaria, and it continues to have considerable influence through the remainder of the narrative. Antioch was the center from which evangelization of the Gentile world was undertaken.

Peter is the chief figure in the first half of the book, Paul in the second. Both men engaged in essentially the same kind of work: preaching, manifesting the mighty works wrought by the Spirit, and experiencing opposition to their witness, including bodily suffering and imprisonment. Sometimes these leading apostles had associates; at other times they were alone. Certain other individuals gained prominence because of their witnessing activity: Stephen and Philip in the first half of the book; Barnabas, Silas, Aquila, Priscilla, and Apollos in the latter half. A notable feature of Paul's labors is the rigorous manner in which he held to the plan of campaigning in the cities, leaving to his converts the task of bearing the message to surrounding areas.

In both halves of the book we find speeches or sermons, most of which are evangelistic in character. These are probably not intended to be verbatim reports of what was said on such occasions (they are too brief for that), nor are they imaginative creations by the writer of the book; they are, rather, digests of what was spoken.

A well-defined feature of Acts is the insertion of summaries from time to time. These serve the double purpose of generalizing the progress of the gospel on the basis of particular incidents cited (thereby suggesting that the material is only a fragment of what actually happened) and of providing a transition to new developments about to be recounted. The leading passages of this kind are 6:7; 9:31; 11:21; 12:24; 16:5; 19:20; and 28:30–31. However, there are others, such as 2:47; 5:14; 5:42; and 19:10, that seem to have something of this same summarizing character. Incidentally, there is no reason to conclude that the summaries were put into the text to cover up lack of information on the part of the writer. To give a complete account of early Christianity would require many books.

Quite naturally, the composition of Acts includes more than a mere recital of the progress of evangelism, for that story could not be fully told without mentioning the opposition that flared up in place after place. The reader receives the impression that this was the normal, expected thing. Persecution usually originated with the Jews, who were incensed at the proclamation of the resurrection of Jesus and the declaration that it was wrought by the power of God, since this exposed and condemned their own unbelieving attitude toward Jesus of Nazareth during His ministry and their determined efforts to secure His death. The Sadducees took the lead in trying to restrain the apostolic testimony, but soon the torch passed into the hands of a passionate young Pharisee named Saul.

After Saul's conversion a distinct lull in persecution is

detectable in the area of Judea, only to be revived briefly by Herod Agrippa I in his action against James and Peter. Saul's conversion, especially after his prominence in opposing the church, made many enemies for him among the Jews, so that wherever he went he found his own people prevailingly hostile to his person and his message. His very success in reaching Gentiles with the gospel rankled with his countrymen, who seldom gave him much peace in his labors. Persecution occasionally came from other sources, as at Philippi and Ephesus, where in certain quarters the success of Paul brought an economic pinch that exploded into attempts to suppress his work.

The closing chapters of Acts revolve around Paul's being seized in Jerusalem at the instigation of hostile Jews from the Ephesus area, followed by his protective detention by the Romans and a succession of hearings before Roman officials, concluding with his transfer to Rome after his appeal to Caesar.

Another element in the plan of the book is the portrayal of the life of the church. We are enabled to see it growing in numbers, following up its evangelism with regular instruction of converts (2:42); laying great store by prayer (2:42; 4:31; 9:40; 10:9; 12:5; 13:3); providing for the physical needs of its members (2:45; 4:32–37; 6:1); developing simple organization as needed, including the appointment of the seven (6:1–6), the selection of James the Lord's brother as guiding head of the Jerusalem church when the apostles turned to evangelism beyond the city (12:17; 15:13), and the appointment of elders (11:30; 14:23; 15:2; 21:18). The apostles continued to function as Christ's authoritative appointees for the direction of the church's life and work. In addition, prophets were raised up (11:27–30; 13:1), as well as teachers (13:1), for the guidance of the congregations.

Glimpses are afforded of believers partaking of fellowship meals (2:46) and observing the Lord's Supper (2:42; 20:7). Faithfulness to their own gatherings did not rule out the continued use of the temple and its services (3:1), and this very circumstance earned them the right to use the temple courts for public preaching (5:25). Again and again we read of the remarkable unity of spirit and purpose that characterized the members of the Christian community (1:14; 2:44; 4:32), a unity born of the Holy Spirit (cf. Eph 4:3). That unity was marred briefly by the Ananias and Sapphire incident (5:1–11), but that incident only served to purify the company of believers, who were shocked by this breach in their ranks.

The taking of the gospel to the Samaritans does not seem to have disturbed the church greatly, but the same cannot be said of the influx of Gentiles, especially after Paul and Barnabas had considerable success in reaching them on their first journey to Asia Minor. An element in the Jerusalem church demanded that Gentiles be subjected to circumcision. Paul, Barnabas, and others journeyed to Jerusalem to confer with the apostles and elders about this and to present the case for receiving Gentiles simply on the basis of their faith in Christ. This position was adopted by the Council, with the result that work among the Gentiles could then go forward with even greater freedom.

In summary, although the main thrust of the narrative in Acts is to accent the spread of the gospel and to note in passing the opposition that was encountered, other factors, such as the spiritual life, organizational development, and internal problems of the church, are not neglected.

AUTHORSHIP

Traces of the use of Acts by Christian writers of the late first and early second centuries have been claimed by some scholars, but no early testimonies to authorship are available. For this information it is necessary to go beyond the middle of the second century. The Canon of Muratori attributed the work to Luke. About this time Irenaeus did the same, emphasizing in his work *Against Heresies* the author's close relationship to Paul, calling him his follower. After this, many Fathers of the church, including Clement of Alexandria, Tertullian, and Origen, continued the tradition.

The question remains whether the Book of Acts itself substantiates this united testimony from the early centuries. The author did not identify himself by name, being content to note that he had written a former treatise to the man addressed in the opening words, a certain Theophilus. Yet the author's presence with Paul seems to be indicated at certain points in the narrative: the momentous venture into Europe from Asia (16:10–17), the journey from Macedonia to Jerusalem that led to Paul's arrest (20:5–21:18), and the journey to Rome (27:1–28:16). These passages are often referred to as "we" sections, because the narrative is couched in the first person plural. It is likely that

11:28 should be included also, where several Greek manuscripts of the so-called Western type, in describing the visit of Agabus to Antioch and his testimony to the church about a forthcoming famine, add the words, "when we were gathered together." This reading, if accepted, serves to make the author a probable resident of Antioch and a member of the church in that city.

A glance at the passages noted above reveals that this companion of Paul, whoever he was, made the sea trip to Rome with him. We are looking for a man, then, who not only traveled with Paul on some of his eastern campaigns but who presumably spent some time with him in Rome. By turning to the letters of Paul that in all probability were written from Rome (Ephesians, Colossians, Philemon, and Philippians) and noting the names of his associates during this period of detention, it should be possible to narrow the list of prospects and perhaps arrive at the identity of the one who wrote the "we" sections. By this process all individuals other than Luke may be set aside either because they are mentioned in the third person in Acts (in contrast to the author of the book) or because they did not make the journey to Rome with Paul. We have the apostle's statement that Luke was with him during his first imprisonment (Col. 4:14) and also during his second (2 Tim. 4:11). The aging apostle probably had need of the beloved physician's services as well as of his Christian companionship.

In the Colossians passage Luke is mentioned after Paul's helpers who belonged to the circumcision (Jewish believers). From this one may conclude that he was a Gentile. This judgment seems to be supported by an indication in his writings of a broad interest in the world of his time, as well as by his expert use of the Greek language. He did not identify with those who used the Jews' language (1:19).

But is the author of the "we" sections necessarily the author of the book as a whole? Some scholars have advanced the opinion that Luke's travel diary was taken over by another person who was responsible for the final form of Acts. But this is improbable for two reasons. If the man who was responsible for bringing together the materials of the book allowed the "we" form to remain unaltered, why did he not follow the same practice in his handling of other source material, such as is found in the early chapters, where participants presumably included themselves in the narrative? Also, the vocabulary and style of the "we" passages is thoroughly in accord with the vocabulary and style of the book as a whole. Unity of authorship is the best explanation of these phenomena.

Since Paul referred to Luke as a physician, the question may legitimately be raised as to whether Acts throws any light on this matter. In his book *The Medical Language of St. Luke* (1882) W. K. Hobart made a comparative study of the language of Luke-Acts and the works of several physicians of the ancient Greek world. He concluded that Luke did indeed use a great many medical terms, and suggested that this fact demonstrated medical training. But more recent study has shown that the vast majority of terms regarded as medical appear also in writers of antiquity who had no medical training. So the evidence of Luke-Acts does not demand that the author be a physician; yet it remains true that there are touches here and there that are highly congenial to this conclusion (see Luke 8:43 and 22:51 for Lucan distinctives).

From the fact that the "we" feature of the narrative is discontinued after the account of the founding of the church at Philippi, it is reasonable to conclude that Luke stayed in that city to shepherd the company of new believers. If so, he deserves to be thought of not only as a physician and an author, but also as a preacher and pastor. Christianity meant more to him than his chosen profession. For further discussion of authorship, see the section on the historical worth of Acts.

SOURCES

One can do no better than to cite the conclusion of a noted scholar who has delved deeply into this subject. Jacques Dupont states:

> Despite the most careful and detailed research, it has not been possible to define any of the sources used by the author of Acts in a way which will meet with widespread agreement among the critics. . . . We find traces of rewriting, cases of juxtaposition, even of insertion of different materials one in the other. There are so many indications which set us on the track of preexisting sources. We seize a link, which is very clear; we try to follow the source from which it comes and, almost immediately, it becomes lost and disappears, whereas other links present themselves, just as clear and just as disappointing. This can be explained by the literary work of the author: he is not

satisfied with transcribing his sources, he rewrites the text by putting the imprint of his vocabulary and his style everywhere.[1]

LANGUAGE

Research is demonstrating that although Luke wrote in Greek, there was considerable Semitic influence at work behind this Hellenistic medium, both in vocabulary and in syntax. The theory of C. C. Torrey, that behind the first half of Acts is an Aramaic document translated into Greek rather literally, has not found favor. All agree that there is evidence of the influence of the Septuagint (Greek translation of the Old Testament) on Acts, but if this were all, there would be no problem, for Septuagintal influence is plain in Luke's Gospel. The problem is to account for non-Septuagintal ingredients of a Semitic sort. It is beginning to be recognized that there are affinities between Luke's diction and that of the Targums and of Qumran materials. But the peculiarity is that Luke did not follow one textual tradition consistently. Wilcox notes that "he seems to have had before him 'ready-made' blocks of material, whose deviation from the Septuagint he did not choose to alter."[2] The whole subject is one of great difficulty, where special expertise is required.[3]

PURPOSE

Luke does not tell us why he wrote this book. The prologue of his Gospel deals ostensibly with the period of the life and ministry of Jesus and provides no information about the Book of Acts beyond giving assurance that the same careful investigation used in gathering data for the writing of the Gospel may be expected in connection with any further writing undertaken by the beloved physician. Luke wrote to impart truth rather than to entertain.

A comparison of Acts with the Gospel discloses an interest in the secular environment of both of these periods. Christianity

[1] Jacques Dupont, *The Sources of the Acts,* 2.

[2] Max Wilcox, *The Semitisms of Acts,* 181.

[3] Interested readers will find a profitable discussion by D. F. Payne in *Apostolic History and the Gospel,* ed. Ward Gasque and Ralph Martin, 134–50.

is viewed as a part of world history. Jewish and Roman authorities move across the pages of the narrative with considerable frequency.

The two periods are intimately related, as the wording of Acts 1:1 suggests. What Jesus began by His earthly ministry is seen as carried forward through the agency of the Holy Spirit working through the church. Luke evidently conceived of his own writing as divided into two parts, out of respect to the differing nature of the two periods, yet retaining a sense of unity throughout. That the ministry of Jesus should have no transforming effect on the world was unthinkable; that the church should spring into being without the background of that ministry was equally unthinkable. Luke undertook to provide a sense of continuity between these two phases in giving us Luke-Acts. The more the two halves are studied as a unity, the clearer will be the picture of Christian beginnings. As the gospel events were the fulfillment of Old Testament prediction, they were in turn the fountainhead of developments in the apostolic age.

With reference to Acts alone, the primary objective is doubtless to relate the story of the rise and progress of the early church—its dramatic origin in Jerusalem, the city that rejected and crucified Jesus of Nazareth; its gradual spread into Judea, impelled in part by persecution; its bold invasion of Samaria with the gospel; and its steady expansion into the Gentile world, climaxed by the bringing of the message to Rome, the heart of the empire. Just as Jesus accomplished His mission in the power of the Spirit, so believers filled with the same Spirit bore witness to Him and His saving work, not sparing themselves. Luke was especially interested in the mission to the Gentiles. He was bent on commending the Christian faith by narrating its progress in the Greco-Roman world.

But a faithful narration of the gospel's progress during the first three decades of the church's life must include some account of the rejection of the message as well as of its reception. Luke sought to show that the same spirit of unbelief and repudiation that marked the reaction of the Jews to Jesus in His lifetime (cf. 4:16-30) manifested itself in the treatment of Christian missionaries. This motif runs all the way through Acts, from chapter four on.

Interwoven in this pattern is a related strand, namely, the problem posed for the Roman authorities by the energetic propagandizing carried on by Christians. Jews were not slow in expressing their displeasure and resentment that Christians, even though they were Jews, should be allowed by Rome to enjoy the protection afforded Judaism as a permitted religion (historically based on Julius Caesar's arrangements with the Jewish nation). Luke took pains to show that whenever Jews brought accusations of disloyalty against the Nazarenes before Roman officials, they got nowhere (18:14-15; 25:25; 26:31). He quoted Paul as denying any offense on his part against the empire (25:8), to which the governor concurred (26:31).

In line with this, the closing paragraph of the book pictures Paul, a prisoner, enjoying full freedom to preach the gospel in the capital itself. By ending his account with the words, "without hindrance," Luke seems to have been making an appeal to Rome to allow this freedom to continue. It would be a mistake, however, to magnify this purpose by making it primary, for most of Luke's narrative has no direct bearing on contact between representatives of the gospel and Roman authorities.

Did the purpose of Luke include a thrust at Gnosticism, the heresy that plagued the church of the early centuries for so long? Some would argue that the author's preoccupation with history is a pointer in this direction, and this may be so, but it is rather disconcerting that he made no reference to this danger. The same might be said of the Johannine writings, but it is certainly much easier to see a warning against Gnosticism there than in the writings of Luke.

DATE

After devoting more than seven chapters to the events connected with Paul's arrest and trial, Luke strangely brought his account to a close without indicating the outcome of the case. He was content to say that Paul continued for two years in his own hired quarters and was able to witness to those who came to him (28:30-31). This leads naturally to the supposition that the author terminated his account at this point in order to publish it, probably with the hope that it would be of some help to Paul and to the Christian cause in general. It is hardly satisfactory to conclude that Luke's objective must have been simply to trace the progress of the gospel from Jerusalem to Rome, so that he could regard his task as completed. Actually, Paul was not the one who first brought the gospel to Rome, and if his mere arrival was regarded as a fitting climax to the story, why should Luke have bothered to take note of the two years that followed?

It is possible that the author ran out of room on his writing material and felt that the roll could not well be made larger lest it be too bulky for use. Yet his Gospel is somewhat longer than Acts. He may have counted on writing an additional book that would contain information on the trial and the last days of Paul. If so, this plan was not carried out. But all this is conjecture, anyway.

What we must recognize is the fact that the many references to Paul's vindication before Roman officials that stand in the book would have no real value, or would at best have antiquarian interest, if the work had been published after Nero's persecution of Christians at Rome (A.D. 64). "The only time when the picture of the Roman state's originally friendly attitude toward the Christians would have been worth recalling to people's minds was the time when it was still valid but in danger of being lost. And this means that it was the time of Paul's trial, after he had made an appeal to the court of Caesar."[4]

An early date for Acts is supported by the circumstance that nowhere in this book are there allusions to the writings of Paul. Granted, Luke would not be expected to quote from them in a work of history; yet the complete absence of even the slightest allusion to the apostle's writings suggests that those writings had not yet become the common possession of the churches.

Consideration should be given also to Paul's statement in 20:25 that the Ephesian elders would not see him again. That was his conviction at the time. Yet he did return to Ephesus after release from his first imprisonment (1 Tim. 1:3). Had Luke written after this, it is questionable that he would have allowed 20:25 to stand in the record. He was with Paul in Rome after the final visit to Ephesus (2 Tim. 4:11), and was doubtless aware of his movements prior to that time.

There have been and still are advocates of a late dating for the book. At one time a second-century setting was popular. Today the interval has been shortened by placing the origin of

[4]Johannes Munck, *The Acts of the Apostles,* liii.

Acts somewhere near the close of the first century. Support for such a position has been sought in the author's supposed dependence on Josephus, whose *Antiquities* appeared in the year 93. In this work the Jewish historian mentions the abortive revolt of Theudas and then refers to the execution of two sons of Judas the Galilean.[5] In Luke's report of Gamaliel's speech before the Sanhedrin (5:35–39) Theudas's revolt is mentioned first, and then that of Judas (which preceded it chronologically). However the order of these two events in Acts 5 is to be explained, it is incredible that a historian of the caliber of Luke would have read Josephus so carelessly as to think that Judas came after Theudas. Few scholars today hold to his dependence on Josephus's work.

Support for a late dating has been sought in Luke 21:20, where the prophetic language concerning the siege of Jerusalem is construed as a reflection of the actual event, which culminated in the destruction of the city in A.D. 70. On the assumption that Acts was written after the Gospel (Acts 1:1), the conclusion is reached that Acts must have been penned later than the fall of Jerusalem. This construction will appeal only to those who are unwilling to accept the possibility of genuine prediction.

In recent years some German scholars have advanced the theory that Luke's work was heavily influenced by the delay in the second coming of Christ. This viewpoint insists that in the earliest days of the church there was an expectancy that the Lord would return very soon, in line with His predictions, but that with the passage of time it became necessary for the church to adjust to life in the world and to see its mission of witness as lasting for a considerable time before the end would come. The bearing of this reconstruction on the supposed date of Acts is fairly obvious. Although it does not attempt to furnish a precise point for the emergence of this book, the theory requires a considerable period during which this shift operated and therefore favors a date toward the end of the first century.

While the dating of Acts around A.D. 62 seems the most likely in view of Paul's circumstances, one ought not to exclude the possibility that it appeared some years later, largely because Acts is later than the Gospel of Luke, and the Gospel seems to show the writer's knowledge of Mark. Luke would then have

[5]Josephus, *Antiquities* XX.5.1–2.

to be dated before A.D. 60, and this many find difficult to accept. But the attempt to relegate Acts to the close of the century has no compelling reason in its favor.

HISTORICAL WORTH

Luke's interest in placing the rise of Christianity in the setting of the secular world, seen in Luke 3:1–2, is continued in his second volume. He is the only New Testament writer who can be described as a historian. But in what sense is he a historian? Certainly he was not a mere annalist who chronicled names and dates and events. Nor was he a historian in the full modern sense of the word, of whom much interpretation and evaluation are expected along with the recital of facts. Rather, his interest was in setting forth sacred history, saving history, showing how the divine purpose in the world is carried out through Christ and His Spirit-filled followers.

There is an observable difference between the two portions of Acts. In the first half, which centers almost entirely in Palestine and revolves around the Jerusalem church, years of expansion are pressed into a few chapters. The record consists of highlights interspersed with summaries. It is the sort of writing one should expect from a man who was not personally present when the events occurred and was therefore dependent on written or oral sources. Sometimes the sentence structure varies considerably from passages describing events in which Luke was involved. In such instances written sources were probably involved. But Luke also had opportunities to confer with various individuals who belonged to the church in Judea. At Antioch he may have known the Hellenists who founded the congregation in that city. Later on, Barnabas, Silas, and others came from Jerusalem. He himself went to the holy city with Paul (21:17) and must have met many disciples. When Paul was kept a prisoner at Caesarea, Luke had time to consult with Philip, who made his home there (21:8). During this interval he could have interviewed many people in Palestine.

With respect to the second half of the book, the "we" sections attest his presence with Paul and others. For the events that occurred when he was not present, he had opportunity to consult with the apostle at Caesarea, on the journey to Rome, and in the imperial city. We may be sure that his visits with Paul were not taken up with discussions about the weather and politics. Luke doubtless learned much also from Timothy and Titus, Paul's trusted lieutenants. The latter may have been Luke's brother (see 2 Cor. 8:18; 12:18).[6]

Scholars who are historians have frequently noted how true to life in the first century is the whole panorama of Paul's journeys as they are unfolded in Acts. Greco-Roman culture of the day is faithfully reflected. Ease of travel attests the stability that the Roman peace had brought to the eastern Mediterranean area. Jewish penetration of this Hellenistic world accords with the observations of Jewish and Roman historians of the period concerning their dispersion and with the testimony of archaeological remains. Geographical notes are accurate, as are the references to Roman officials, who are always called by the title appropriate to their position. This would be difficult for a writer who was not contemporary; for the status of provinces, whether imperial or senatorial, sometimes changed, as with Cyprus and Achaia, carrying with the change a shift in the title of the Roman official in charge. Luke knew the correct term to apply to the rulers of Thessalonica (Acts 17:6) and to the town clerk at Ephesus (19:35). The case of the chief official on the island of Malta is of interest, for inscriptions have shown that the proper designation for this man is precisely that which Luke used (28:7).[7] (For comments on these terms see subsequent discussion on the verses indicated here.)

Important, too, is the fact that Luke did not idealize the church. Alongside the reports of bold witnessing and almost fantastic results, of devoted commitment to Christ and unselfish concern for fellow-believers, he set down the evidence of human frailty and failure (chaps. 5 and 6).

But some critics insist that despite these and other clear marks of fidelity to the historical situation, the writer of Acts failed to be convincing in other matters. His failures are used to cast doubt on the church tradition that Luke, a companion of Paul, could have written the book. Two of the more important

[6] A. T. Robertson, *Word Pictures in the New Testament* (Nashville: Broadman, 1943), 4:245; William M. Ramsay, *St. Paul the Traveler and the Roman Citizen,* 389–90.

[7] For further information on this general subject see William M. Ramsay, *The Bearing of Recent Discovery on the Trustworthiness of the New Testament* (Grand Rapids: Baker, 1953), especially chap. 3; R. P. C. Hanson, ed., *The Acts,* 2–11; and A. N. Sherwin-White, *Roman Society and Roman Law in the New Testament,* especially 172–93.

areas in question are his presentation of Paul and his reporting of the Jerusalem Council.

Involved in the first item is the assertion that the picture of Paul in Acts differs too widely from that of the Pauline Epistles to be credible. For example, Luke made practically nothing of Paul's apostleship, which Paul himself magnified, especially when involved in controversy. He was an apostle not from men nor through a man (Gal 1:1), yet Luke represented the Lord as conveying his call through Ananias (Acts 9:11-16). From Galatians, one receives the clear impression of Paul's strong antagonism toward legalism, yet in Acts he is pictured as circumcising Timothy (16:3), taking vows on himself (18:18, 21:17–26), and in his speeches after being made a prisoner as professing a continuing loyalty to the Pharisaic mode of life. In the reports of Paul's preaching in Acts, furthermore, sadly lacking is the strong emphasis on redemption through the Cross such as is found in his Epistles. From his writings it is evident that Paul had many fears and misgivings as he pursued his task, and also that there were great conflicts within the churches. Of all this the reader of Acts is given no inkling. Toward the end of his stay in the East the apostle made a great effort to rally his churches in support of a fund to be taken to Jerusalem to aid the Christian poor in that area. Luke reported the journey and named Paul's companions who represented the local congregations (20:4ff.), but did not explain the purpose of the trip. Again, whereas Paul had the intention of going to Spain (Rom. 15:24, 28), Luke said nothing about this, concentrating simply on the journey to Rome.

Many of these considerations involve Luke's silence regarding matters set forth in Paul's letters. Silence is not the same thing as disagreement. As for the mediation of Ananias, it is clear that this man did not appoint Paul to be an apostle nor did he reveal the gospel to him. Luke's account implies that when Paul was nearing Damascus, he definitely saw the risen Lord (Acts 9:7–8, 17) and therefore stood on an equal footing with those who were apostles before him (cf. 22:14; 26:16). It is with these matters that Paul was concerned in writing Galatians, where he writes more explicitly than Luke does in Acts. As to the allegation that Luke misrepresented Paul's preaching by failing to make central the saving significance of the Cross, it may suffice to point to 20:28, which Luke could have omitted if he had a prejudice against such a doctrine. Also notable is the report of Paul's preaching at Pisidian Antioch, where Jesus is called Savior (13:23), whose mission made possible a message of salvation (13:26), which is then defined in terms of forgiveness and justification (13:38–39). We can cheerfully grant that Luke did not disclose Paul's feelings or trace his difficulties in the churches he founded. This was not germane to his purpose of describing the spread of the gospel. Finally, Paul's apparent concessions to legalism in Acts were not out of line with his announced principles (1 Cor. 9:19–23).

Equally serious is the contention that whereas Luke represented the Jerusalem Council as providing a decisive answer to the circumcision party in the church, Paul's letters indicate that the legalists continued to make trouble for him in his work. Moreover, there is no little difficulty in attempting to find a place for the Council in Galatians. The Book of Acts notes three visits of Paul to Jerusalem that are pertinent to the problem (9:26–29; 11:30; 15:1–29), whereas only two are mentioned in Galatians (1:18–19; 2:1–10). There is general agreement that Acts 9:26–29 and Galatians 1:18–19 refer to the same visit.

Galatians 2 offers promise of picturing the same events as Acts 15, because many of the same persons are involved, and the issue—whether or not Gentiles must be circumcised in order to be admitted into the church—is the same. Both passages indicate that Gentiles were declared exempt from this rite (and by implication, from bondage to the Mosaic Law). Yet the accounts are not wholly harmonious in that Acts pictures a large gathering that included elders and others, whereas Galatians presents a rather private meeting between three Jerusalem apostles (though other figures representing the circumcision party are in the background) and the two representatives from Antioch: Barnabas and Paul. Furthermore, the meeting described in Acts resulted in a decision to send a letter to the Gentile churches where trouble had erupted, stating the verdict of the Council and requesting these believers to be careful to abstain from certain things that were abhorrent to faithful Jews. Of such a decree Galatians has nothing to say.

Because of these difficulties some scholars have turned to equating Galatians 2 with the Acts 11 visit of Barnabas and Paul as a possible solution. This identification would explain handily the absence of the decree from Galatians 2, for the Jerusalem Council had not yet been convened. Furthermore, it seems likely that Paul's statement in Galatians 1:20 committed him to include every visit he made to Jerusalem up to the time of writing, so the famine visit would have to be included in his narrative. Finally, this solution seems to be favored by Paul's statement that he went up to Jerusalem in accordance with revelation (Gal. 2:2), since the Acts account informs us that it was Agabus the prophet's revelation about an approaching famine that led the Antioch church to send relief to Judea by the hands of Barnabas and Paul. Perhaps Galatians 2:10 could be said to glance at the same item, for it calls attention to the needs of the poor.

To be sure, this identification has its own crop of disadvantages. The occasion of the visit had nothing to do with a doctrinal crisis, and it is not clear that the two emissaries met with any apostles (Luke mentions only elders), who were often out of the city engaged in evangelistic work.

Furthermore, chronology is against the identification. The famine visit cannot be put later than the year 46, when the famine was at its height. Subtracting 14 (Gal. 2:1) plus 3 (Gal. 1:18) from 46, one arrives at the year 29 for Paul's conversion, obviously too early. Even if both figures in Galatians are calculated on the basis that a part of a year was counted as a full year, this alters the conversion date only to 31, which is still too early, being only a year after Pentecost.

Galatians 1:20 should not be pressed to mean that Paul was solemnly swearing to record every visit he made to Jerusalem, since the issue is not Jerusalem but contact with the apostles, as is clear from his account of his first visit. Likewise the allusion to revelation is not weighty, since the kind of revelation Paul had in mind in Galatians, as chapter 1 makes clear, is not that which comes through man but directly from the Lord. Furthermore, it would be strange for the leaders in Jerusalem to make the request concerning the poor noted in Galatians 2:10 if in fact Barnabas and Paul had just brought a generous offering from Antioch for this very purpose.

Finally, the prominence of Paul in Galatians 2:1–10 does not fit well into the Acts 11 visit. Barnabas is mentioned only at the close of the passage (Gal. 2:9). It was during the first missionary journey that the leadership of Barnabas was supplanted by that of Paul. Galatians 2:1–10 clearly reflects this shift, but on the identification of this passage with the occasion of the famine visit the prominence of Paul does not ring true to the actual situation, since no missionary journey had yet been undertaken by the two men.

The problem is admittedly difficult, some would say even insoluble. But it seems that the identification of Galatians 2 and Acts 15 ought not to be abandoned. Since Paul's account has in the background the presence of those who would have liked to have Titus circumcised, a larger assembly may well be implied. Paul was content merely to emphasize the phase of the Council that brought the leading figures into conference. Omission of any reference by Paul to the decree is quite in keeping with his character. When dealing with some of the same practical issues in the Corinthian church, he chose to bypass any reference to the Council decree in favor of instructing the church on his own apostolic authority and along lines of spiritual principle.

In comparing what Paul and Luke have written, it should be borne in mind that people who agree in general outlook may still vary from one another in emphasis. In dealing with the Council, Luke was concerned with the peace and progress of the church, but Paul was more concerned with the theological issue of the truth of the gospel (Gal. 2:5). Luke did not cite further Judaizing activity against Paul, probably for the reason that such activity came after the founding of the churches rather than in connection with their establishment, so that it was outside the scope of the task that the writer had set for himself. It is fairly apparent from Acts 21:20–21 that Luke was not uninformed about the persistent propaganda of the legalists against Paul.

Admittedly the writer of Acts did not tell us all we would like to know about the early days of the church, but what he has told us is of tremendous importance. It is rather paradoxical that some scholars who approach Acts with a Christian background have been extremely critical about Luke's accuracy as a historian, whereas professional historians have tended to be high in their praise of his work. A representative of the latter group has gone on record in these words: "For Acts the confirmation of historicity is overwhelming. . .any attempt to reject its basic historicity even in matters of detail must now appear absurd. Roman historians have long taken it for granted."[8]

---

[8] Sherwin-White, *Roman Society*, 189.

One of the most notable features of the study of Acts in recent years is a lessened concern over historical matters and a growing interest in assessing Luke as a theologian. This tendency, strongly marked in the work of Dibelius, has been taken up by Conzelmann and by Haenchen (see bibliography). For a survey of this trend and an evaluation of its strengths and weaknesses, the reader would do well to consult I. Howard Marshall's volume, *Luke: Historian and Theologian*. The author points out that both aspects need to be held in balance and that a trustworthy, historical base is the necessary foundation on which to erect theological interpretation.

THEOLOGY

Since doctrinal teaching is hardly to be expected in the course of historical narrative, it is necessary to look mainly to the speeches contained in Acts for this information. Divergent views have been entertained about their nature and value, with conservative scholars maintaining that although they are not necessarily verbatim reports of what was said on the various occasions, they are nevertheless trustworthy.

However, the approach associated with the name of Martin Dibelius (*Studies in the Acts of the Apostles*) regards them as free compositions by Luke, who shaped their content and is therefore to be considered a theologian more than a historian. This means that the speeches are believed to have been directed to Luke's audience several decades after the time of the events described in the book. It is alleged that Luke was simply following the custom of those days, a practice that went back to the Greek historian Thucydides, who confessed that it was hard to retain speeches in the mind word for word, whether he had heard them himself or had a report on them from others, so he had to settle for the following procedure: "My habit has been to make the speakers say what was in my opinion demanded of them by the various occasions, of course adhering as closely as possible to the general sense of what they really said."[9]

This is rather different from relying on the imagination. Indeed, the leading Greek and Roman historians repudiated the manufacturing of speeches. Luke's proven accuracy at many

[9] Thucydides, *History of the Peloponnesian War* 1.22.

points where he can be tested gives confidence that he would have used all possible means to arrive at a faithful report of the sermons and other addresses that he included in his account. As a Christian he must have had a special concern to honor the truth. Nearly all the speeches mention the resurrection of Christ, and several of them make it the principal theme. This is understandable in the setting of the years immediately following the death and resurrection of Jesus, but it is not at all clear that it was the major topic of concern for the church near the close of the first century, when Dibelius and others assume Luke wrote. Furthermore, it is difficult to think that Luke could have been greatly influenced by Greek models since these do not include the missionary sermon, which is the principal type in the Acts.

In view of Luke's familiarity with the Septuagint, the influence of the Old Testament on his thinking and workmanship should not be overlooked or underestimated. It is probable, Bertil Gartner thinks, that Jewish historiography had a greater effect on Luke's methodology than anything of Greek origin.[10] Speeches in many Old Testament passages can be demonstrated to rest on tradition faithfully preserved and highly valued. There is no good reason for doubting that similar factors lie back of Luke's reports of sermons in Acts. In regard to the examples of early apostolic preaching after the Resurrection, Bo Reicke observes, "Because of their primitive Christology (e.g., Jesus is called *pais*), it is reasonable to look upon these speeches as conforming to a real tradition, and not as later constructions of Luke."[11]

Turning to the theology reflected in the sermons, we note that in discourses addressed to Jews the general procedure was to accent the faithfulness of God in fulfilling the promises made through the prophets by bringing Jesus the Christ into the world, by raising Him from the dead when His nation rejected Him, and by sending the Spirit. The speeches of Stephen (chap. 7) and Paul (chap. 13) are especially full in recounting the Old Testament background for the new age of the gospel. On the other hand, in addresses to Gentiles there is no specific appeal to the Old Testament but rather appeal to the creation and the

---

[10] Bertil Gartner, *The Aeropagus Speech and Natural Revelation*, 8–11, 27–30.

[11] Bo Reicke, "A Synopsis of Early Christian Preaching," in *The Root of the Vine: Essays in Biblical Theology*, 128–29.

providential care exercised by God toward His creatures (chaps. 14, 17).

Concerning the person and work of Jesus, the following items are to be noted: His humanity (2:22, 17:31; also the allusion in 10:41), His dignity as the Son of God (9:20; cf. 13:33), His position as sent of God (3:20, 26; 13:23), His anointing by the Spirit (10:38), His identity as God's Servant (3:13, 26; 4:27, 30), His position as Leader (5:31; cf. 3:15), and His fulfillment of the promise of the Christ (8:5; 17:3; 18:5; cf. 4:26). He is identified as Jesus Christ (2:38), Christ Jesus (24:24), Lord Jesus (4:33; 7:59), Lord Jesus Christ (11:17; 28:31), Lord of all (10:36), the rejected stone (4:11), Savior (5:31; 13:23; cf. 4:12; 16:31), the Deliverer from sin (3:26; 10:43; 13:38–39; cf. 20:28), the One raised from the dead (2:32; 4:10; 13:30; 17:31), the Righteous One (7:52; 22:14), the exalted One (1:10; 2:33), the returning One (1:11; 3:20), and the Judge of mankind (17:31).

Naturally one does not expect to find in a book such as Acts the same full, rich Christology that meets us in the epistles of Peter and Paul and in Hebrews. There is nothing about preexistence except what is implied in His being sent of God. The theme of Christ's redeeming work is not greatly developed, and beyond what is hinted in 9:5 there is nothing about union with Him as the portion of believers. What stands out is the exaltation of the once-rejected Savior and the revelation of His spiritual presence, energy, and authority exercised in the church through the Spirit.

The doctrine of the Holy Spirit attains great prominence in Acts, in contrast to the Gospels. There the Spirit is seen almost entirely in connection with the person of Christ (the Holy Spirit was "not yet," as far as believers were concerned), but in Acts He is the portion of the church. He was described by the risen Lord as the promise of the Father (1:4; cf. Luke 24:49), and from the very moment of His coming He revealed Himself as the Spirit of power, as in our Lord's ministry (Luke 4:14). The men whom Jesus had called and trained, who had been so timid and uncertain of themselves, were now cogent in thought and bold in speech. Provincial in their Jewish outlook, they became willing to include Gentiles in the scope of their ministry as the Spirit enlarged their vision. Jesus' prediction that He would prove to be their Counselor was abundantly fulfilled. These witnesses for Christ learned that the Spirit sustained them, giving courage to their hearts and readiness of speech to their tongues (Acts 4:13), as Jesus had promised (Luke 12:11–12). The missionary operation of the church is seen as under His control (Acts 8:29; 10:19; 13:2, 4; 16:6–7). At turning points in the story, He manifested Himself in outward and observable effects that call attention to the reality of the spiritual realm (2:2; 8:17–18; 10:44–46; 19:6).

In summary, the ingredients for a formulation of a doctrine of the Trinity are present in Acts, but none takes shape. This was not intended to be a treatise on theology.

Similarly, Luke was too busy describing the progress of the church to theologize about it. He was content to note the rise of congregations here and there. Only rarely did he use the singular form to designate the church at large (9:31; cf. 20:28). Baptism is often cited as the rite by which one is received into the church, but faith (including repentance) is the condition for salvation (2:38, 44; 16:31). The Lord's Supper is not mentioned as a rite but is probably referred to occasionally (2:42; 20:7).

Other items that characterized the life and ministry of the church (items prominent in the Gospel of Luke also) are prayer; the performing of miracles, especially healings; and the experience of angelic visitations (12:7; 27:23).

Finally, we discover that eschatology is not ignored, though it can hardly be said to have great prominence. Christ's return is put in the forefront of the book as a promise (1:11) and had a place in the preaching of Peter (3:19–20), as the Day of Judgment had in the preaching of Paul (18:31).

Despite all that the Book of Acts contains of a theological nature, it should be evident that not all of Christian truth is set forth here. It was not in the purpose of God that the total framework of theology should be communicated at the very beginning of the church's existence, but rather that it should be unfolded gradually to meet the specific needs of an expanding and experiencing organism.

QUMRAN INFLUENCE

The Qumran community, which was in existence at the time of the rise of the church in Jerusalem and was located only a few miles away near the Dead Sea, had certain features that bear sufficient resemblance to those of the early church to suggest some relationship. These "men of the new covenant" were Jews of the Essene type, who had withdrawn from the mainstream of Jewish life as a protest against its corruption. They were especially hostile toward the priestly caste who controlled the temple. At many points the Qumran community differed substantially from the early church in Jerusalem, but our concern is to evaluate the elements of possible connection.

For one thing, both groups were known as "the Way," a term that occurs in Acts 9:2 and several other passages. The problem is to know whether both strands go back independently to Isaiah 40:3 for the usage of this term, or whether the Christian use goes back to Qumran influence. Another point of comparison is the communal type of life found in both groups, represented in meals and the pooling of possessions. There is considerable similarity here, though the right of private ownership of property and goods was denied to Qumran members, whereas the sharing in the Jerusalem church was on a voluntary basis and was exercised as need arose. Of special interest is the use of the term *the multitude* as descriptive of the congregation (Acts 6:2, 5). That this usage should appear also in the Qumran literature as a technical term for the group as convened is a striking phenomenon.

It is quite possible that in these and in some other respects an influence on Jewish Christianity in its earlier stages is to be traced. But this influence was largely peripheral. Faith in Christ as the fulfillment of the hopes of Israel differentiated the church sharply from this sect of current Judaism that centered its attention on the Mosaic Law.

THE TEXT

It is in Acts that the so-called Western text comes into special prominence. This type of text is old and widespread, making the term *Western* rather inappropriate. Its chief feature is the inclusion of traditional material, some of which may provide valuable information. At times this text type is guilty of omissions also. These features are best explained on the theory that the Western text came into being at any early time, when there was little attempt at regulation or the fixing of a standard text. The chief witness for this type of text are Codex Bezae (D) and several manuscripts of the Old Latin Version. Some of the more interesting of the Western readings will be noted in the commentary. The King James Version has a few Western readings (8:37; 9:5b–6a; 24:6b–8a; 28:16 in part; 28:29), but modern translations are free from these additions, since they render a text superior to that which was available to the 1611 translators.

Although J. H. Ropes, in an extensive study of the text of Acts, found little to convince him that there was any theological point of view reflected in the distinctive readings of the Western text in this book,[12] a later investigator, Eldon J. Epp, has found considerable evidence of an anti-Jewish bias in such readings, since they come down heavily on Jewish guilt in rejecting Jesus, in opposing the apostles, and in failing to receive the gospel.[13] Agreeing basically with this analysis, C. K. Barrett nevertheless finds in the Western text something that is even more characteristic—its tendency to exaggerate. "The editor does not so much introduce new tendencies into Acts as make clearer and more emphatic tendencies that were already there."[14]

CHRONOLOGY

Luke furnished little help for dating the events he described, though occasional time notices are given, especially in relation to Paul's activities. The generally accepted date for the beginning of the church is A.D. 30. Certain events can be dated with some precision by means of information from secular sources of the period. One such is the death of Herod Agrippa I in the year 44; another is the proconsulship of Gallio in Achaia, which apparently began in the summer of 51; a third is the ascension of Festus as governor of Judea (ancient testimony about the exact time is somewhat conflicting, but it was probably in 59). By using the data of Acts and the Pauline Epistles, it is possible to proceed from these fixed points and achieve at least approximate results for the time of Paul's conversion and missionary journeys, the council at Jerusalem, Paul's arrest and arrival at Rome, and other events.

Acts 18:12 seems to imply that shortly after the coming of Gallio to Corinth the Jews appeared before him to accuse Paul. Since 18:11 indicates that the apostle had been in the city for eighteen months, his arrival can be safely put at the end of 49 or

---

[12]J. H. Ropes, ed., *BC*, 3.

[13]Eldon J. Epp, *The Theological Tendency of Codex Bezae Cantabrigiensis in Acts*.

[14]C. K. Barrett, *New Testament Essays* (Naperville, Ill.: Allenson, 1972), 104.

the beginning of 50. This accords with the information that on his arrival at Corinth the apostle took up residence with Aquila and Priscilla, who had recently come from Rome because of the expulsion of Jews by the emperor Claudius, an event known to have occurred in 49. The apostle's sojourn in Philippi, Thessalonica, Berea, and Athens was brief, so the last few months of 49 probably sufficed for these ministries. Prior to that he was in Asia Minor (Acts 16) for the spring and summer of that year (on the presumption that he commenced his second missionary journey in the spring, the natural time for starting a campaign).

Prior to this journey the apostle attended the council at Jerusalem, which may tentatively be placed early in 49. Before going to Jerusalem he was occupied, along with Barnabas, in evangelizing Cyprus and southern Galatia, a journey that may well have covered most of 47 and 48. Earlier he spent a year in Antioch ministering to the church (Acts 11:26), and this accounts for the year 46. Lying behind that is a period of undetermined length spent in the regions of Syria and Cilicia (9:30; 11:25; cf. Gal. 1:21). Its duration can be estimated only after an attempt is made to fix the date of Paul's conversion.

Paul's own account includes two time notices (Gal. 1:18; 2:1). On the assumptions that the periods of three and fourteen years are intended to be sequential and that the second visit to Jerusalem is to be identified with the Jerusalem Council meeting of Acts 15, which has been assigned to the year 49, one arrives at a date of 32 (49 minus 17) for Paul's conversion. It is impossible to check this by the data in the early chapters of Acts, as time notices are lacking, but the impression made by the narrative on many students (e.g., T. W. Manson and George Ogg) is that the interval from Pentecost to the death of Stephen was rather brief. Some, however, prefer to date the conversion a year or two later. This variation affects in turn the determination of the time spent by Paul in Tarsus and vicinity before going to Antioch, but that period can be roughly estimated as covering eight to ten years.

Now it is expedient to return to the Gallio date and use it as a point of departure for dating events in the latter part of Paul's life. Luke tells us that following the Gallio incident Paul remained in Corinth for many days (Acts 18:18). This rather indefinite expression may mean no more than that he stayed long enough to avoid suspicion that he was running away from the possibility of further persecution. A brief stop in Ephesus followed, then what appears to have been a somewhat hurried journey to the south, including Caesarea and Jerusalem, ending with a return to Antioch. Again the Lucan narrative is indefinite, stating that Paul spent some time there before making his way back to Ephesus by way of interior Asia Minor. Possibly he spent the winter of 52 in Antioch, arriving at Ephesus in the spring of 53 to begin his longest ministry in one place. The apostle spoke of it as spanning three years (20:31). This figure embraces three months spent in the synagogue (19:8), two years at the school of Tyrannus (19:10) and "a while" (19:22) between this period and his departure from the city.

Presumably it was late in 56 when he arrived in Corinth to spend the winter (1 Cor. 16:6), and this would place his final visit to Jerusalem and his arrest in the spring of 57. The period of detention under Felix lasted two years (Acts 24:27). Since the journey to Rome fell in the winter, Paul's arrival at Rome presumably occurred in the spring of 60. Luke observed that he was kept under house arrest for two more years (28:30), bringing the conclusion of the narrative to the year 62.

The question of the apostle's release and subsequent labor, possibly in the East as well as in Spain, is much debated, but there is general agreement as to his martyrdom in 64, the year of the great fire in Rome, even though Eusebius in his *Chronicon* put it in the thirteenth year of Nero (67) and Jerome in his *De Viris Illustribus* still later (68), near the end of Nero's reign. The date of 64 is based in part on the testimony of Clement of Rome who placed the death of Peter and Paul in the imperial city at a time when many other believers were martyred.[15] The only time known prior to Clement when this could have taken place is in the reign of Nero. Clinching testimony comes from Tacitus, who told of the great fire that swept Rome in the summer of 64 and the suspicion that Nero himself had set it.[16] To avert suspicion, the emperor blamed the Christians and had many of them put to death. The close agreement between Clement and Tacitus makes it reasonably certain that the year 64 marked the close of the life of Paul.

[15] 1 Clement 5–6.
[16] Tacitus, *Annals.*

VALUE

This book serves as a bridge between the Gospels and the Epistles. In the Gospels the church is present only as a prediction made by the Savior. In the Epistles the church is an accomplished fact, having become fairly widely distributed around the eastern Mediterranean basin. It is from Acts that we acquire needed information on how the church arose and grew and spread.

In a narrower sense, Acts constitutes a helpful introduction to the Epistles of Paul, telling us the circumstances surrounding the founding of most of the churches to which he wrote letters.

Acts is especially pertinent to the present day, for the church in our time is faced with somewhat the same conditions as those that confronted the infant Christian community. In the Western world Christians are becoming more and more a minority in the population and are subject to pressures because of unwillingness to conform to some features of modern secular life. Less and less is the church able to claim government patronage or protection. Under such circumstances the church cannot afford to neglect the message of this book.

From start to finish the thrust of Acts is missionary. Significantly, its close is abrupt, as though to tell the reader that what Paul was doing in Rome, under conditions not wholly ideal, continues to be the task of all later generations of believers. The unfinished book underscores the unfinished task.

Part I

THE CHURCH AT JERUSALEM
1:1–8:3

In this section Luke was intent on describing the origin of the church, relating it to Jesus' ministry and the work of the Holy Spirit. The apostles are the principal human figures. The early phase is restricted to primitive Jewish Christianity and developments in the Jerusalem area. Its content includes sermons, summary statements of the growth of the Christian community, glimpses of spiritual and social life, and intimations of the opposition stirred up in official Jewish circles by the apostolic proclamation that Jesus of Nazareth had been raised from the dead by the power of God.

1

PREPARATION
1:1–26

Instead of plunging into the history of the church immediately by describing what occurred on the day of Pentecost, Luke sketched the background for that event. He had constructed his Gospel in somewhat the same way, not starting directly with the birth of Jesus but dealing with the story of John the Baptist as an introduction.

JESUS' MINISTRY AND ASCENSION (1:1–11)

In this period the risen Lord had contact only with His followers (cf. Matt. 23:29). It was a time of fellowship, of instruction, and of adjustment on the part of the disciples for the work that lay ahead of them.

1:1. "My former book" (literally "first" in Greek) is a reference to the Gospel according to Luke. Similarly the Jewish historian Josephus, in Book 2 of his work *Against Apion,* made reference to "the former book" (Book 1). Since the ancients used *first* at times when strict grammatical usage called for *former,* Luke's wording is hardly a sufficient basis for assuming that he planned to write a third volume.

It is reasonably certain, in line with the dedicatory custom of the time, that a real person is intended by the name "Theophilus." In view of the title "most excellent" given to him in Luke 1:3, it is probable that he belonged to the nobility. Possibly he was a Roman official (cf. Acts 26:25). Whether he was a confessed believer is not certain. Luke 1:4 seems to favor this verdict, especially if Luke meant to say that he was instructed, or even catechized, concerning Christian truth. On the other hand, the verb can be rendered "informed," but this does not necessarily indicate that he was a believer. The title is dropped at the beginning of Acts, and some interpret this as an indication that in the interval between the writing of the two books he became a Christian, warranting a more informal approach by the writer.

"All that Jesus began to do and to teach" is Luke's way of summarizing the main lines of Jesus' earthly ministry as enshrined in his Gospel. "Began" is the troublesome word here. While it could mean that He acted and taught "from the beginning," more likely it is intended to suggest the thought that after His ascension the Lord continued to make His power felt on earth by these means. This is agreeable to certain passages in the Gospels (Matt. 28:18–20; John 14:12–14). It finds support also in Acts, where the Lord Jesus is represented as intervening in developments on earth such as the coming of the Holy Spirit (2:33; see John 16:7); in Peter's use of the keys of the kingdom (Acts 2:14–40; see Matt. 16:18–19); and in the conversion of Saul (Acts 9:15) and visions granted to him (18:9; 23:11). Paul expressly attributed the miracles of his missionary career to Christ (Rom. 15:18–19).

That Jesus continued to "teach" presents a difficulty in that His ethical teaching, such as is contained in the Sermon on the Mount, is not reproduced in Acts. However, the teaching that He gave to His disciples about His death and resurrection has a prominent place in most of the sermons Luke reports. The ethical teaching may have been shared with converts (Acts 2:42).

1:2. Luke used the same verb, "taken up," in verses 11 and 22, and the noun form in Luke 9:51. The Ascension is noted here as the event that terminated the Savior's earthly ministry, but the description of it is reserved for verse 9. "Instructions" is similarly an anticipation of verse 8 (cf. Luke 24:47–48) and doubtless of verse 4 also. The choosing of "the apostles" (Luke 6:12–16) had momentous consequences for the future. These men had authority from Jesus to preach and teach, to perform miracles, and to guide converts. It was "through the Holy Spirit" that the Lord now outlined their task more specifically. Although the Spirit had not yet been bestowed publicly (v. 5), He had been communicated to this select company on the evening of Resurrection Day (John 20:22). Because of this the words of Jesus were more meaningful and powerful in their impact than in the precrucifixion period, when the disciples had been prone to argue and to doubt.

1:3. This is our one source of information concerning the interval between the Resurrection and the Ascension. No such interval is stated in Luke 24, but it would be precarious to assume that when Luke wrote his Gospel he thought the Resurrection and Ascension had taken place on the same day. He probably had Mark's account for reference, where the promise is given of appearances in Galilee (Mark 16:7). Acts 1 seems intended to enlarge and clarify the rather summary narrative of Luke 24, and this in several particulars. We know from the Gospels that the post-Resurrection appearances were sporadic. Jesus came and went during this period.

In his Gospel, Luke included "many . . . proofs"—Jesus' self-disclosure to the Emmaus pair (Luke 24:31); to Simon (Luke 24:34); and to the Eleven, when He showed His hands and feet, invited touch, and proceeded to eat in their presence (Luke 24:36–43).

That Jesus "spoke about the kingdom of God" summarizes His verbal communication to His followers. Judging from verse 6, the teaching did not deal with the future aspect of the kingdom; otherwise the disciples would not have queried Him with the kind of question they posed. Once again, Luke 24 provides necessary guidance, informing us that after the Resurrection Jesus was primarily occupied with explaining His mission in the light of the Old Testament (Luke 24:25, 44–47). The kingdom, or rule, of God, as used in Acts, seems virtually to be a term for the gospel viewed in relation to the overall plan of God (8:12; 19:8; 20:25; 28:23, 31). Only in 14:22 is the eschatological aspect given any specific prominence. One has only to refer to Matthew 16:18–19 to realize how closely intertwined are the church and the kingdom.

It is notable that the teaching of Jesus here is not described in detail. If Luke had been interested in using his imagination, he could, for example, have inserted a statement about the divine purpose regarding the Gentiles—something that could in turn have helped the church in dealing with this problem later on (chaps. 10–11, 15), or he could have given instructions on church organization. The sacred historian needs to be judged by what he did not say as well as by what he included.[1]

1:4. There is considerable uncertainty regarding the translation of the phrase "while he was eating with them." The expression in the Greek language would ordinarily mean to assemble or congregate, referring to the action of a group, whereas here the action is attributed to Jesus. The NIV translation, "eating with them," is based on the supposition that embedded in the word is the Greek term for salt. The etymology is precarious, but some favor this translation because in two other passages Luke refers to the fact that Jesus ate with his disciples following the Resurrection (Luke 24:43; Acts 10:41). A few manuscripts have a form that differs in only one letter from that which most of the others attest. This reading yields the rendering "staying with them," without implying permanence in the relationship. Everything considered, this may well be the most satisfactory solution of a problem that is widely acknowledged to be very difficult.

It was during the period that Jesus was staying (if only intermittently) with His disciples that He commanded them not to leave Jerusalem but to await "the gift [His] Father promised" (see Luke 24:49). We can understand why the disciples would be inclined to leave Jerusalem, for this was the city that had slain their leader. Besides, their homes were far away in Galilee. In fact, their presence in the city at this time cannot be understood apart from obedience to the command of the Lord.[2] In the wisdom of God, the Spirit was to manifest Himself at the very place where Jesus was rejected. If the gospel could make its way there in the power of the Spirit, it could go anywhere in triumph.

Jesus' description of the Spirit as "the gift my Father promised" goes back to Luke 24:49 and also finds its rationale in the teaching of Jesus on the eve of His crucifixion (John 14:16, 26; 15:26). Clearly it was not enough that the disciples had spent three years with Jesus and had been under His instruction. They needed the wisdom and power of the Spirit of God and were sufficiently chastened by past failures to recognize their need.

1:5. The truth contained here is a decisive one for the Christian era. Up to this time, baptism both with water at the

---

[1] F. C. Burkitt, *Christian Beginnings,* 96.

[2] Bo Reicke, *Glaube und Leben der Urgemeinde,* 14.

hands of John and with the Holy Spirit had been the experience only of Jesus, not of the Eleven (Luke 3:21–22). Although their baptism by John is not recorded, it may be assumed, since many of them had been John's disciples. Now Jesus indicated that these men would share in the Spirit. He did not add that He himself would baptize them with the Spirit, as the Baptist had affirmed (Luke 3:16 and parallels), but this may well be implied in the passive form of the verb. The apostles were the nucleus of the church and as such had to possess the Spirit, for this is the indispensable token of belonging to Christ (Rom. 8:9; 1 Cor. 12:13). What the effect would be on the lives of the disciples is not stated, but it comes out in verse 8 (cf. Luke 4:1, 14). For an echo of verse 5 in the experience of Peter, see Acts 11:16.

Just as water baptism is a once-for-all matter, so is baptism with the Spirit. Because of the peculiar historical position of the Eleven, they were believers for some time before being baptized with the Spirit; but this is not the norm for this age. Only very special considerations in the life of the early church dictated delay in the giving of the Spirit (8:12, 15–16).

1:6. "So when they met together" implies a somewhat later occasion and confirms what the Gospels make clear—that the Lord's post-Resurrection appearances were followed by disappearances. The meeting now to be considered was the final one, on which the Ascension occurred, and the place was near Bethany (Luke 24:50–51).

Instead of questioning the Lord about the Spirit and what His coming would mean for them, the disciples revived the viewpoint that had been rampant among them even when Jesus was going up to Jerusalem to suffer. The popular expectation and hope was that He would institute the kingdom at that time (Luke 19:11). In this expectation the disciples shared, despite several intimations from Jesus that He was going to Jerusalem to suffer and die (Mark 10:32–40). To them the thought of death for the Messiah was intolerable, so the words of Jesus were not taken literally. But now that He had risen from the dead, surely that display of power (so they thought) warranted the conclusion that He could restore the kingdom to Israel. It seemed to them altogether natural. God's chosen people had been trodden down by alien nations for too long. "Restoring," to them, meant the reviving of Israel's independence and glory, with the period of David and Solomon as the model. It is possible that the disciples misunderstood the significance of "the gift" the Father had promised, thinking it applied to the Davidic covenant (cf. Luke 1:32–33).

1:7. Jesus' response questioned the timeliness of this hope. Its realization belongs to the secret, hidden things that are the property of the Father alone (cf. Mark 13:32). "Times" is a strictly chronological word, whereas "dates" (better, "epochs") includes the character and circumstances of the times. The two terms are combined again in 1 Thessalonians 5:1.

1:8. But there was something that the disciples could know, and this belonged to the present rather than to some uncertain time in the future. As already indicated, only a few days would elapse before the Spirit would come on them (v. 5), with resultant "power" to make them effective witnesses for their Master. This would mark the final phase of their preparation for service in His name. The power lay in the person of the Spirit rather than in some sort of spiritual energy He might release to them. The correlation of Spirit and power was notable in the ministry of John the Baptist (Luke 1:15–17) and of Jesus (Luke 4:14; cf. Acts 10:38). That this enduement was not confined to the apostles is apparent from what is said later on of Stephen (Acts 6:5, 8).

"Witness" is related to the old verb *to wit,* that is, "to know." Consequently, a witness is one who is able to give testimony based on knowledge (cf. Isa. 43:10–12). One must know Christ in order to bear witness to Him. An unbeliever, no matter how much he might have seen and heard Him, cannot qualify. The Resurrection was a key element in this testimony (Acts 1:22), and only believers had seen the risen Lord.

Was "you will be my witnesses" prophecy or command? Surely both. As prophecy the disciples could count on its realization; as command they were bound to sense their responsibility to make themselves obediently available. Implied in our Lord's words is the duty to make Him their message. To preach the good news of the gospel and to preach Christ amount to the same thing (see 8:5, 12).

The place where the witness was to be exercised is comprehended in four terms that represent more specific direction than that given in Luke 24:47, terms that denote moving out geographically from a center to the circumference, as ripples from a pebble dropped into a pond. The same terms may be viewed according to the degree of spiritual preparation found in these places. Judaism held sway in Jerusalem and Judea and rested on the revealed religion of the Old Testament. Samaria enshrined a religion partly true and partly false, a confused mixture (John 4:22). "The ends of the earth" speaks of the unenlightened condition of paganism, with false notions of God corrupting the ideals and life of society.

Each of these four areas contained its peculiar challenge to the disciples. Jerusalem had the blood of prophets on its hands (Matt. 23:37), and now it had added the blood of Jesus of Nazareth. Would the disciples be expected to follow in His train (Matt. 16:21, 24–25)? Judea was the home of Judas Iscariot, the man of Kerioth, the betrayer. The prospect of going there was not a welcome one. Samaria, with its traditional hostility toward Jews, was not likely to be hospitable to the followers of One to whom it had refused the rights of a traveler (Luke 9:51–56). The remotest part of the earth was the home of the Gentiles (Isa. 49:6), whose spiritual and moral uncleanness drew from Jews the epithet "dogs."

But the disciples were now to be the witnesses of One who had wept over Jerusalem. This One had already taught in all Judea (Luke 23:5), had felt that He must pass through Samaria rather than avoid it (John 4:4), had welcomed the faith of Gentiles and responded to it (Matt. 8:5–13; 15:21–28). "The ends of the earth" answers to "all the nations" (Luke 24:47; cf. Isa. 49:6).

Notable is the absence of Galilee from the places indicated by our Lord. He evidently counted on the willingness of His disciples to spread the good tidings in their native places, and so it happened (Acts 9:31). However, there is a possibility that "all Judea" is an expression intended to include Galilee, since there are examples where Judea seems to have this comprehensive meaning, notably in the Lucan writings. Especially significant are Luke 23:5 and Acts 10:37.

1:9. With the giving of this final charge, Jesus was ready to be "taken up." This is one of several terms used for the ascension. In Luke 24:50 it is used of the raising of the hands of the Lord in blessing as He departed from His own. The disciples "were looking intently up into the sky" (v. 10). At other appearances the risen Lord had slipped away after disclosing Himself (Luke 24:31), but this time there was a gradual, stately departure from the earthly scene. The "cloud" is often associated in Scripture with revelations of the Deity, serving to emphasize the dignity and mystery of the divine person (Exod. 19:16; Dan. 7:13; Luke 9:34).

The Ascension has very little place in the Gospel records, leading to this observation: "The ascension apparently did not lie within the proper scope of the gospels, as seen in their genuine texts: its true place was at the head of the Acts of the Apostles, as the preparation for the Day of Penetecost, and thus the beginning of the history of the Church."[3] This event was the logical sequel to the resurrection of the heavenly Man. It provided the basis for the presentation of the present life and ministry He carries on in heaven, as set forth in the epistle to the Hebrews; and it accorded with the promise of His return, in line with Acts 1:11. It is the exalted Christ who sends the Spirit, and by that same Spirit He, though physically absent, is present dynamically in the lives of His own.

1:10. Straining to keep the Lord in their vision as long as possible, the disciples kept their eyes riveted on Him. The spell was broken by the sudden appearance of "two men" in white. That they were angels is evident both from their appearance and from their message. Other passages describe angels as men (Acts 10:30; Rev 21:17). Such messengers of God are represented as serving also at the annunication of the Incarnation (Luke 1:26), at the birth of Jesus (Luke 2:9, 13), at the Temptation (Matt. 4:11), and at the Resurrection (Luke 24:4).

1:11. "Men of Galilee" agrees with the Gospel records. The only problable exception, Judas, was no longer one of their company. If there was a gentle rebuke in the question addressed to them, it merely prepared the way for a message of comforting assurance to the effect that the departing Savior would someday return. "This same Jesus"—the human name, serving to emphasize the abiding humanity of the One who had taken to Himself human nature—"will come back in the same way. . . ." This cannot be a reference to the occurrence at Pentecost, the Lord's coming through the Spirit. A personal, visible return was promised, but there was no word added to indicate that these men would be alive to see Him. This event will complete the Lord's relationship to earth; His birth called for His death, His death for His resurrection, His resurrection for His ascension, and His ascension for His return. Can there be any doubt that the earth is the divinely intended center of the universe? The Ascension was the acknowledgment by the

---

[3] B. F. Westcott and F. J. A. Hort, *The New Testament in the Original Greek* (New York: Harper, 1882), Appendix, 73.

Father of the finished work of the Son. It set the stage for the sending of the Spirit. Taken with the truth set forth in 1:1, it implies a continuing concern for this world, which is made explicit by 1:11.

DAYS OF WAITING (1:12–14)

This was a period of ten days, since forty days had passed (*Pentecost* means "fifty"). It was a time of waiting but not of inactivity, for the group was much in prayer.

1:12. The site of the Ascension was apparently the ridge of "the mount of Olives," famous for its olive groves. "A Sabbath day's walk" was the limit allowed by Jewish custom for travel on the Sabbath—a little over half a mile. Luke did not say that the disciples made this short trip on the Sabbath; he was merely noting the distance. According to Luke 24:52 the return to the city was made with great joy, inspired doubtless by the promise of the Lord's return.

1:13. The disciples' destination was the "upper room." Since the definite article is used, this suggests a well-known place, one that they had occupied before. A possibility is the large upper room where Jesus had kept the Passover with His disciples (Luke 22:12), even though a different Greek word (meaning "above the ground level") is used in the latter passage. "Staying" is sometimes used of temporary residence, which fits the present situation.

Luke 24:53 makes no mention of the upper room but concentrates on the public worship in which the disciples participated in the Temple. In Acts 1:13–14 the concern is to picture the activity of Jesus' followers when they were in their own company. Similar alternation between public and private activities is noted in later passages (2:46; 5:42).

The eleven disciples are named at this point (each of the synoptic Gospels has a list also). Peter's name stands first, as in all the other accounts. Of considerable interest is the fact that Luke put John next, whereas in his Gospel he assigned him fourth place. The shift prepares the reader for the several occasions in Acts when John appears as Peter's partner in the work (3:1; 4:13; 8:14).

1:14. In the relative seclusion of the Upper Room the apostles were joined by certain "women," no doubt those who had accompanied Jesus from Galilee and were present at the

Crucifixion and at the empty tomb (Mark 15:40–41; 16:1). Special note is taken of the presence of "Mary the mother of Jesus" and "his brothers." Their names are given in Matthew 13:55. The Lord's appearance to James (1 Cor. 15:7) may have been influential in bringing the rest of the family to faith (cf. John 7:5). Without straining, the word "brothers" (brethren is only an alternative rendering) is broad enough to include the sisters. There were at least three of them, all unnamed (Matt. 13:56). The presence of Mary and of other women makes this the more plausible.

It was important that the family of Jesus should be found in the company of believers from the start. As descendants of David, their participation and leadership "was a visible sign of the connection between the new community and the old."[4] The apostle Paul testified to their activity in Christian witness at a later time (1 Cor. 9:5). There is little ground for seeing a reference to them in John 20:17, where the disciples are naturally in view.

The entire company, united as never before by a common devotion to Jesus the Christ, gave themselves to "prayer." Did they remember that Jesus was in prayer when the Spirit came on Him (Luke 3:21–22)? Perhaps they recalled the promise that the Father would give the Spirit to those who ask Him (Luke 11:13), but they were under no command to pray thus. Jesus had announced the coming of the Spirit, in emphatic terms, as near at hand. However, the events of recent days had been so momentous that the thought of being caught up into the plan of God at this strategic juncture of history was overwhelming. Who was sufficient for these things? They turned instinctively to God in prayer.

APPOINTMENT OF MATTHIAS (1:15–26)

The group did not remain in prayer continuously, for this spiritual exercise made them aware of practical needs that had to be met. Prayer gave them insight concerning a specific problem within their ranks.

1:15. During the ten-day period others joined the small

[4] A. Schlatter, *The Church in the New Testament Period,* 13.

group until it increased to around "a hundred and twenty" persons.[5] Nicodemus and Joseph of Arimathea may have cast in their lot with them. The Emmaus pair are possibilities, as are some if not all of the seventy whom the Lord had sent before Him on the final journey to Jerusalem (Luke 10:1). Could Martha, Mary, and Lazarus have remained aloof? Even so the number is not as great as the five hundred to whom the Lord appeared at one time (1 Cor. 15:6).

Who was to take the leadership of this company? There was no immediate need for supervising corporate prayer, but now the group faced a problem requiring deliberation. The twelve had suffered a loss through the defection of Judas, and a replacement had to be found for him.

"Peter stood up." He was a man of ready speech and bold action, but after his denial of his Lord he could assert himself only because of forgiveness (as indicated in Luke 24:34) and reinstatement graciously granted to him in the presence of his brethren (John 21:15–19). He began at once to exercise his authority to shepherd the flock, even as in due course he would be ready to open the door of faith to unbelievers at Pentecost (see Matt. 16:19). "Among the believers" is a reference to the whole company. Jesus had anticipated the unity of believers by His own usage (Matt. 12:50; John 20:17).

1:16–17. Peter indicated at once that he had been to school with the risen Lord, who had talked much about the fulfillment of Scripture in connection with His death and resurrection. One can almost imagine hearing Jesus speak in Peter's words, "the Scripture had to be fulfilled" (cf. Luke 24:44). Peter had learned also to give the Holy Spirit recognition as the ultimate Author, the One who spoke through David (cf. 2 Peter 1:21). Moreover, his ability to find Judas alluded to in the Old Testament was no doubt prompted by the fact that on two occasions when our Lord spoke of Judas' failure, He had noted that thereby Scripture had been fulfilled (John 13:18; 17:12). But Peter's choice of Scripture passages was not the same as that of his Master, since he was concerned most of all with the position

---

[5] Bo Riecke calls attention to the fact that in Jewish practice a town congregation had to have this many persons in order to be able to elect members to the Sanhedrin ('The Constitution of the Primitive church in the Light of Jewish Documents," in *The Scrolls and the New Testament,* ed. Krister Stendahl, 145–46). Since Acts 1 is concerned with an election, Luke may have been intent on making clear that the procedure followed was regular.

that Judas had abdicated by his betrayal of the Lord (see Acts 1:20).

Before quoting Scripture he made a simple identifying comment about this man, calling him "a guide to those who arrested Jesus." It would have been in order to call attention to his sin more directly, but Peter seems to have been anxious to avoid harsh, judgmental language. After all, he himself had failed the Lord miserably that same night and had been humbled by his failure. One can detect a tinge of sadness and nostalgia in his further comment about this man. The betrayer had shared in the apostolic office, yet had proved unworthy of it.

1:18–19. This portion is properly set apart by a parenthesis, for it was not a part of Peter's speech but rather Luke's own account of what happened to Judas following the betrayal. The inclusion of this material is the more appropriate because Luke's Gospel has nothing about Judas after his part in the arrest of Jesus. Likely he gleaned this information through contact with one or more persons from the Jerusalem church.

Some difficulties appear as this account is compared with that in Matthew 27:3–10. Luke says that Judas bought a field with his ill-gotten gain, whereas Matthew indicates that the Sanhedrin bought it as a place in which to bury strangers. If they bought it in his name, seeing the money was his, both accounts become reasonably harmonious. The other problem is that Matthew's account states that Judas took his own life by hanging himself, whereas Luke pictures a fall resulting in a rupture of Judas's body at the middle. The standard explanation of this apparent discrepancy is the assumption that the noose used by Judas broke, resulting in a fatal fall, perhaps on a sharp object such as a stake or jagged stone. The incident accounts for the name given to the plot of ground, namely, "Field of Blood." Thus Luke made clear the meaning of the Aramaic *Hakeldama* for the benefit of Gentile readers.

Now we come to the two citations from the Psalms that Peter makes use of in connection with Judas.

1:20. Among the psalms regarded by the early church as messianic is the sixty-ninth, which is ascribed to David and recites a series of afflictions at the hands of his enemies, and his prayers to God for aid. Its applicability to the sufferings of Christ (e.g., v. 21, in light of John 19:28–30) may go back to our Lord's teaching after the resurrection (Luke 24:44). Quoted from the LXX with minor changes, Psalm 69:25 is here applied to Judas. The traitor's place was left empty. This was both a judgment on him and a tacit acknowledgment that the vacancy cried out for someone to fill it.

The warrant for replacement is found is Psalm 109:8, quoted from the LXX: "May another take his place of leadership." Even apart from Scripture's sanction, the body of believers must have felt the logical necessity for a successor to Judas. The number twelve was highly symbolic, because of its correspondence to the number of the tribes of Israel, and consequently served to express the idea of the church as the new Israel, or people of God, the faithful remnant of a largely unbelieving nation. "Place of leadership" is literally "bishopric," but there is no warrant for concluding that a term used in a quotation was intended to point to an episcopal structure in the organization of the early church. Also, it is patent that the reason for choosing a replacement for Judas was not his death but his defection. There is no support here for the doctrine of apostolic succession.

1:21–22. Here Peter laid down the qualifications for the man who was to succeed Judas in the apostolate. The main objective was to have someone who would be "a witness . . . of his resurrection." Already there was an awareness that the proclamation of the Twelve would magnify the Resurrection, and the sermons in Acts reveal the correctness of this appraisal. To be a witness of the Resurrection did not mean that one must have seen Jesus emerge from the tomb, for no human eye saw Him at that moment, but rather that one must have seen Him alive from the dead and enjoyed fellowship with Him.

But it was also deemed important that this person should have been among the followers of Jesus from the beginning of His ministry, which was marked in a general way by "the baptism of John." According to Mark 1:1–15 this was the beginning of the gospel. This qualification meant that such a man would have the advantage of having heard the Lord speak on many occasions and having watched Him perform His mighty works of help and healing. In short, he would have all the qualifications of the Eleven, apart from actual call to apostleship by the Lord and the special instruction Jesus had given to this restricted group. This passage confirms the accuracy of the presentation in John 1, where initial contact between Jesus and certain of His disciples is tied in with the ministry of John the Baptist.

1:23–26. In the phrase "So they proposed two men," some manuscripts of the Western text have "he" (Peter) instead of "they." But the latter reading is more likely, especially since exactly this procedure was followed in choosing the seven (6:3). The church made the selection. In the case before us, only one man was to be chosen, and there were two who possessed the necessary qualifications. The brothers of Jesus were present, but they had been unbelievers during His ministry.

It was a solemn occasion, a time for seeking divine wisdom. The brethren knew the men involved, but only the Lord knew their "hearts." His wisdom was needed, so His help was invoked. "Lord" could be God the Father here, in agreement with 2:39; 3:19 and other passages. It is probably a reference to the Lord Jesus, however, because the words "You have chosen" recall the fact that it was He who had chosen the Twelve. The man chosen would fulfill Judas's abandoned "apostolic ministry" (v. 25). The order of events suggests that the actual service involved, with the sacrifices that would be entailed, was given primary consideration, while honorific position was secondary. The final mention of Judas agrees with Christ's verdict—"the one doomed to destruction" (John 17:12). He was never a regenerated man (John 13:10–11). Membership in a Christian group and even active service therein (Judas was treasurer) do not guarantee that one truly belongs to Christ.

"They cast lots." Of the various methods of casting lots, the one probably used on this occasion was to mark stones for identification, then shake them in a vessel before shaking them out. Matthias was the choice, and he was then and there "added to the eleven apostles."

Various objections to this incident have been raised by those who judge that a mistake was made. For one thing, was it right to use the lot, an Old Testament practice, when the new age of the gospel had dawned? The practice, however, was not regarded in Old Testament days as a matter of luck or magic. Men might propose, but only God could dispose (cf. Prov. 16:33). It should be noted that the Holy Spirit had not yet come, so resort to the ancient method is quite understandable. The brethren themselves had no doubt that the Lord had revealed His will. A second objection, that Matthias is not heard of again, while true enough, does not mean that God refused to honor the choice, for silence cloaks the personal activities of almost all the apostles in the ensuing history. Again, fault is found on the ground that the divine choice was Saul of Tarsus. It is quite apparent, however, that Saul could not meet the qualifications laid down. In addition, his apostleship, which was not from men nor through a man (Gal. 1:1), was of a special, independent type. He knew he was of equal rank with the original apostles, but he did not classify himself with them (1 Cor. 15:11).

One should observe that the selection of Matthias was made after prayer. The will of God was earnestly sought. To rule out Matthias is to call in question the efficacy of divine guidance through waiting on God. There is a possibility that some who were not present could have met the qualifications (1 Cor. 15:6), but if so, their failure to be present on these crucial days of waiting ruled them out.

2

BIRTH
(2:1–47)

The materials of Acts 2 fall readily into three parts: (1) the coming of the Spirit, with powerful effects on the disciples, bringing in turn excitement and bewilderment to the inhabitants of Jerusalem; (2) the sermon of Peter, which began with an explanation of the strange phenomena just witnessed by the people, continued with an exposition of what God had done through Jesus of Nazareth, and concluded with an appeal for repentance and a promise of acceptance with God sealed by the reception of the Spirit; (3) and a statement of the results of Pentecost in terms of the growth of the church, its daily activities, and the effect on the people.

THE SPIRIT'S MANIFESTATION (2:1–13)

Jesus' word about the promise of the Father (1:4–5) was now fulfilled. The coming of the Spirit to His followers was the necessary condition for reaching those who were not yet believers (John 16:7–8).

2:1. "The day of Pentecost" marked one of the three major festivals of the Jews (the other two being Passover and the Feast of Tabernacles). It had the name *Pentecost* (the Greek word for *fiftieth*) because it fell on the fiftieth day after the Sabbath of Passover (Lev. 23:15). Occasionally the word appears in the intertestamental literature (2 Macc. 12:32; Tobit 2:1), but the usual Old Testament term is "Feast of Weeks" (Exod. 34:22, where it is called also "the firstfruits of the wheat harvest"). The term "firstfruits" is especially significant, for it hints at the truth that the thousands who came to Christ on that day are to be viewed as the firstfruits of a much greater harvest. A Jew could hardly avoid making such an association. On the basis of Leviticus 23:15, which states that the seven full weeks were to be counted after the Sabbath, Pentecost fell on the first day of the week, providing a link with the resurrection of Christ, which also occurred on the first day of the week (Luke 24:1–7).

It seems strange that there is no explanation of Pentecost in the Epistles. However, the sole reference (1 Cor. 16:8) may be significant, for the very fact that Paul was writing to Gentiles and used a term for a Jewish feast without a word of explanation seems to indicate that his readers had been instructed in its theological importance.

"They were all together." It is not clear whether the "all" is intended to refer to the total number of 120 (1:15) or to the twelve apostles. Since the latter group has just been mentioned in the preceding verse, and since the apostles alone are mentioned in the following narrative (2:14, 42), it may well be that they are in view here. On the other hand, it is difficult to think of the remainder of the whole company as passed by in the Spirit's visitation, since they were believers. If those who responded to Peter's message received the Spirit (2:38), surely the same would be true of those who had been waiting for His coming. Yet reception of the Spirit did not necessarily involve the special manifestations that are mentioned in connection with the Twelve.

"In one place" is made more precise in verse 2, where the "house" is mentioned (cf. 1:13). Presumably the group moved from the house to some larger area when people began to be attracted to the spot. The temple offered adequate space, and its consecrated status made it the appropriate setting for explaining what had happened.

2:2. Luke was careful to say that the "sound" was like that of a strong wind, but he avoided saying that a wind was blowing. The word more often means "breath" than "wind." It was the sound that filled the house, not wind. A connection may be seen here with Ezekiel 37:1–14, the episode of the dry bones, where the Spirit is mentioned along with a noise and breath. The symbolism fits well into the concept of the new creation (cf. John 3:7–8, where wind illustrates the mysterious operation of the Spirit in effecting the new birth).

2:3. A second token of the Spirit's presence was the

appearance of tongues, distributed so as to rest on each of those present, which most naturally includes the others as well as the Twelve (cf. 1:15; 2:17–18). In some way these resembled fire and as such could be intended to express the presence and involvement of God (cf. Exod. 3:2; 19:18; 1 Kings 18:38–39; Ezek. 1:27). More than that, the fire can be considered the fulfillment of the prediction of John the Baptist that Jesus would baptize with the Holy Spirit and fire (Luke 3:16).

But why the tongues? The most natural explanation is that they symbolized the element of speech, of communication of the gospel. By the Spirit's impulsion the apostles would be able to make known the message of salvation. The tongues had their unity in the one Spirit, but as "separated" they pointed to the individualizing of the Spirit's bestowal (cf. 1 Cor. 12:11). They "came to rest on each of them." This agrees with our Lord's advance announcements about the Spirit's relation to the disciples—an abiding presence (John 14:16–17).

The two signs—one of sound for the ear, the other of sight for the eye—recall the scene of Jesus' baptism, when the voice came from heaven and the Spirit was manifested in bodily form (Luke 3:22). The immediate effect of the two phenomena was to make clear to the Twelve that God was beginning to work. What had been promised by the Father was being realized. The fulfillment was too external, too realistic to be discounted and written off as imagination. They all had seen and heard.

2:4. Following the outward tokens came the inward reality: "All of them were filled with the Holy Spirit." This was something new in Israel, for until now visitations of the Spirit had been selective (cf. Num. 11:26–29). There was no suggestion at Pentecost that the objective of the experience was mystic contemplation; it was utterance. The Spirit has many functions, but the Pentecostal emphasis fell on communication. Jesus had promised a baptism with the Spirit (Acts 1:5).

In reporting the event, Luke used the term "filled" rather than baptized, for this was the actual effect. *Baptism* is the objective term, the theological reality, the Godward aspect of the matter. *Filling* is the manward, subjective aspect. Filling and baptism are not completely synonymous terms. Baptism is appropriate for the initial gift of the Spirit (1:5; 11:16-17), for it marks the beginning of a new relationship. Like water baptism, it belongs to Christian beginnings and is not repeatable (cf. 1 Cor. 12:13; see also the discussion of the apostles' situation regarding baptism, under Acts 1:5). One who has been baptized with the Spirit may be filled, not merely once (4:8) but again and again (4:31; Eph. 5:18). But no one is reported to have been baptized with the Spirit more than once.

They "began to speak in other tongues." This is declared to be a supernatural phenomenon, for it was done "as the Spirit enabled them." The sort of thing that took place in the congregation at Corinth is called glossolalia (speaking in a tongue) and refers to ecstatic utterance that required another gift of the Spirit, interpretation of the tongue, in order to make it intelligible to others. Since it could be exercised privately (1 Cor. 14:28) and in connection with prayer (1 Cor. 14:14), it was related to the worship of God. But at Pentecost there was no interpretation by the apostles or others. The tongues were not ecstatic utterances but the languages of people (Acts 2:6, 11; cf. 1 Cor. 13:1). The charge of drunkenness (2:13) need not connote an ecstatic state but rather indicates the joy and freedom of speech that the participants felt.

The hearers understood that the apostles were uttering the mighty deeds of God (v. 11). This special feature of under-standable speech in relation to the tongues at Pentecost is apparently connected with the presence of people from many nations (v. 5). It was to a certain extent a prophecy that the gospel would be made known to people everywhere by the enablement of the Spirit (cf. 1:8). This makes irrelevant the claim that Aramaic and Greek would have been sufficient for communicating with the audience on this occasion, so that other languages were unnecessary.

In the other two instances of speaking in tongues reported by Luke (10:46; 19:6) this feature of intelligible speech is not present. Speaking in tongues, in the technical sense of glossola-lia, is said to be concomitant with a highly emotional state; yet the curious thing is that at Pentecost, with the promise of the Spirit's coming followed by the days of waiting and praying as a background, Spirit-filled men spoke in intelligible speech. At Caesarea, on the other hand, there seems to have been much less emotional build-up, yet there was glossolalia, and at Ephesus there was probably even less excitement, yet there was glossolalia again. The element of mystery connected with the Spirit's operations is ever to be reckoned with.

2:5. Two questions must be raised here. One is a problem of text, for some manuscript testimony omits the word "Jews."

Could this word be a scribal addition based on its occurrence in verse 14 (somewhat disguised when translated "men of Judea")? And would it be justified to go a step further and take the following phrase ("God-fearing Jews from every nation under heaven") as including Gentiles who were showing their interest in the Jewish religion by the attendance at the feast? Unquestionably Gentiles could attend (John 12:20); however, proselytes are mentioned in verse 11, strongly suggesting that the rest were not Gentiles. Furthermore, the Greek word for "God-fearing" (used again in 8:2; 22:12) is not the term for Gentiles who had adopted the Jewish faith but describes people who were pious and reverent. The conclusion to be drawn, then, is that the vast majority of those present were Jews by race as well as by religion.

But a second question arises. Were these people permanent residents of Jerusalem, or were they in the city for a limited time, after which they expected to return to their places of residence in the Dispersion? The evidence seems somewhat conflicting, for the list includes "visitors from Rome" (v. 10) and yet the Greek word *katoikeō*, translated "staying" and "are in" (vv. 5, 14), suggests permanent abode. Many times in Acts Luke used it of residents of a community (1:19–20; 2:9; 4:16; 13:27). Presumably he was thoroughly familiar with the difference between this word and the Greek term meaning "sojourner" (Luke 24:18). The safest way to handle this difficult question is to conclude that at the very least these men had spent some time in Jerusalem, probably having come for the Passover and remaining for the Feast of Weeks. That the converts of that day continued in Jerusalem for a considerable period thereafter appears decisively settled by Acts 2:42. Possibly some of Peter's audience had returned to Jerusalem from the Dispersion in order to spend their last days on the beloved soil of the Holy Land. Some may have resorted there for study (cf. 22:3).

They were a group providentially prepared for the hearing of the gospel, for they were familiar with the ministry of Jesus (2:22) and presumably had been in Jerusalem at the time of the Crucifixion and had heard reports about the Resurrection. Furthermore, being devout men, they could be appealed to on the basis of the Scriptures.

The sweeping nature of Luke's language, "every nation under heaven," could be intended to suggest, when taken with the mention of tongues, that Pentecost represented a reversal of the confusion of tongues experienced at Babel (Gen. 11:1–9).

Though diverse languages continue to exist, those who speak them can find their unity and harmony in Christ.

Some scholars allege that Pentecost was observed as a memorial of the giving of the Law at Sinai. In this case, the birthday of the church may be thought of as marked by a new and gracious revelation of God, with emphasis on His saving act in Christ. Rabbinic testimony to this conception of Pentecost in late Judaism begins early in the second century A.D. There is some evidence, however, that both in Jewish circles represented by the Book of Jubilees and in the Qumran community the association of Pentecost with the giving of the Law is pre-Christian.[1]

2:6. As a siren attracts a crowd on a busy street, the sound of many voices brought the milling crowd together. By this time, presumably, the disciples had left the Upper Room and were making their way to the temple. "Bewilderment" suggests in the original a combination of confusion and excitement. The content of the speaking is not stated here, but is reserved to verse 11.

2:7-8. The amazement was due to the fact that they were hearing "Galileans" speak in their own languages. It is hazardous to conclude that, since the word for "language" (v. 6) is literally "dialect," the amazement stemmed from the ability to reproduce even local linguistic peculiarities. Luke previously used the word in connection with Aramaic (1:19). The *koinē,* or Hellenistic type of Greek, in its full designation, is the *koinē* dialect, which shows how broad the use of the term *dialect* could be in the Greek tongue. "Language" is the proper translation in our passage.

2:9-11. Jerusalem, mother of all Jewry, drew her sons from around the civilized world, where they had been dispersed because of the captivity of their ancestors or voluntary emigration for economic advantage. In a general way the list proceeds from east to west, though Cretans and Arabians disturb this pattern.[2] Mesopotamia, Asia (the province), Egypt, and Rome

---

[1] Bent Noack, "The Day of Pentecost in Jubilees, Qumran, and Acts," in *Annual of the Swedish Theological Institute* 1 (1962): 73-95.

[2] Bruce M. Metzger notes that it was not uncommon among the ancients to regard lands and regions as placed under the dominion of heavenly bodies. But his comparisons of Luke's catalog with that of Paul Alexandrinus reveals such disparity as to raise serious doubts in his mind that Luke shared this conception ("Ancient Astrological Geography and Acts 2:9-11," in *Apostolic History and the Gospel,* ed. W. Ward Gasque and R. P. Martin, 123-33).

had large concentrations of Jewish residents. Rather strangely, Greece and Syria are not included.

Especially vexing is the inclusion of Judea, since it is out of place geographically. Various suggestions have been made as to what the original wording may have been (e.g., "Armenia," "Syria," or "India"). Perhaps "Judea" was introduced into the text by an early scribe who was influenced by the opening words of Peter's speech (v. 14). On the other hand, it may refer to a district north of Antioch that has recently become known through a few inscriptions in Phoenician with some Aramaic mixture.

"Visitors from Rome" is ambiguous since the word *Rome* does not occur here, but rather *Romans,* which elsewhere in Acts means Roman citizens. If the above rendering is accepted, it opens the possibility that these visitors eventually returned to Rome and became the founders of the church there. It is uncertain whether "Jews and converts to Judaism" is intended to apply only to Romans or whether it should be referred to the entire list. Since proselytes (Gentile converts to Judaism) were certainly to be found in many places, the latter view is the more probable.

"The wonders of God" (cf. Luke 1:49) are not defined. Luke's source of information may not have included anything precise at this point. But it is wholly natural to conclude that the gift of the Messiah and the succeeding gift of the Holy Spirit occupied a central place among these works.

2:12–13. The mood of amazement continued (cf. v. 7), with the sense of wonder gradually shifting to perplexity. Such strange things cried out for an explanation.

Some went beyond questioning and ventured an answer. These men must be intoxicated, they thought: "They have had too much wine." (The KJV has "new wine," but the more strict rendering is "sweet wine"; the grape harvest, which would provide new wine, came later in the year, associated with the Feast of Tabernacles). The verdict was given in a jesting spirit, but it revealed an underlying attitude of unbelief, for the apostles were speaking of the mighty deeds of God. Luke caught the frame of mind by using the word "mocking" (NASB). It would be difficult to say whether the reaction of this portion of the crowd was called forth by the joyous bearing of the apostles or by their readiness of speech or both. One wonders also if the claim of drunkenness was associated with a similar jibe at Jesus (Luke 7:34).

PETER'S SERMON (2:14-40)

The sermon of Peter consisted of explanation of the apostles' conduct, first negatively, and then positively (vv. 14-21); proclamation of the Christ-event by touching lightly on Jesus' ministry and death, and dwelling at length on His resurrection and exaltation to God's right hand as Lord and Christ (vv. 22-36); and exhortation, calling for a response to the preaching in terms of repentance and reception of Christ, a response that would in turn bring the gift of the Spirit (vv. 37-40).

2:14-15. Peter's leadership, already demonstrated in the company of believers (1:15), was now exhibited in a public situation. The apostles were not scattered through the crowd, but remained together as a unit, conscious that they were a chosen band with a mission to their own people. "To stand" was a favorite verb with Luke, used to express the grasping of a strategic moment for addressing others (Luke 19:8; Acts 17:22; 27:21). As this word portrays the manner of a speaker, the word "addressed" suggests weighty utterance rather than a speech of trivialities (cf. 26:25).

There is no suggestion here of the continued use of tongues. As to whether Peter spoke in Aramaic or Greek, a study of the text for clues is rather decisive: it can be determined by the length of time the hearers had been in Jerusalem. Recent arrivals would probably have been more familiar with Greek than with the language of their fathers, but the longer their stay, the greater would be their familiarity with Aramaic. It is worth recalling that when Paul addressed the mob in the temple area, also at the time of Pentecost (20:16), he spoke in the national language (22:2, where Paul is asid to have spoken in Aramaic, which was in common use at the time in Palestine).

Peter's initial task was to refute the slanderous charge that the apostles were "drunk." That was comparatively easy, since "nine in the morning" was not the time people became inebriated (cf. 1 Thess. 5:7). It was a case of spiritual intoxication, as he went on to explain (v. 17). Three times in Scripture a contrast is stated between using wine and being filled with the Spirit. The other two instances are Luke 1:15 and Ephesians 5:18. There is a certain similarity between a drunken person and a Spirit-filled person, for both are carried out of themselves into an abnormal sense of freedom and expressiveness. But beyond this all is contrast, for the results in one case are not fruitful of good as they are when the Spirit is in control.

2:16–21. Since Peter's audience was made up of Jews and proselytes, it was useful to quote Scripture to establish the meaning of what had just happened. While the quotation from Joel 2:28–32 is essentially the LXX text, there are certain changes, the most important being "in the last days" as a substitution for "afterward," to make clear the eschatological bearing of the passage, its applicability to the beginning of the messianic age (cf. Heb. 1:2). "This is what was spoken of by the prophet Joel" is a correlating of prediction with event, a practice learned at Jesus' feet (Luke 24:44–46) and used by Him in His preaching (Luke 4:16–30). The word "this" picks up the "this" in the question of the crowd (v. 12). The people of Israel should not have been wholly taken aback by the phenomenon of Pentecost, seeing this event had been predicted by one of their own prophets.

"I will pour out my Spirit" uses the language of effusion common in reference to the Spirit (v. 33; Isa. 32:15; Rom. 5:5) and prepares one for the concept of the fullness of the Spirit.

"All people" seems to be defined by what follows: old and young, women as well as men. This makes it reasonably certain that the whole company of 120, which included women, received the Spirit at Pentecost.

"Will prophesy" means not "to predict" but "to declare the counsel of God" under the immediate influence of the Spirit. Where glossolalia was involved, prophecy was sharply distinguished from it (1 Cor. 14:2–5). But at Pentecost, where the apostles spoke in languages that were known, they could be said to have prophesied (Acts 2:11). "Visions" and "dreams" were common means of communicating revelation, especially in the Old Testament. Visions are referred to rather frequently in Acts (9:10; 10:3, 17; 16:9; 18:9; cf. 23:11). In each case the vision had a definite bearing on the progress of the divine program.

It cannot be ascertained whether those "wonders . . . and signs" noted in the text were thought to have some relation to the portents that occurred at the Crucifixion (Matt. 27:45, 51–53). The sequence given in the Olivet discourse is the proclamation of the gospel; the Tribulation; and the return of the Son of Man, preceded by upheavals in the realm of nature (Matt. 24:14, 21, 29–30). It was taught in the prophets that the "day of the Lord" was a time of judgment and also of deliverance. In fact, in the Joel passage, the word "saved" (Acts 2:21) could well be translated "delivered" when its original setting is regarded. In the context of Pentecost it referred to salvation to eternal life (cf. Rom. 10:13), though it included salvation from the threat of judgment (cf. 2:40).

In summary, prophecy had indicated the outpouring of the Spirit in connection with the Day of the Lord, the time of divine manifestation. Pentecost was a clear indication that the messianic age had dawned. Its consummation, whether near or remote, was rendered certain. Peter did not enlarge on this phase of prophecy. As H. N. Ridderbos says, with reference to the early Christians in general: "It was simply because what had already happened was of such immense importance to them that their attention was focused less upon the expected consummation than upon the fulfillment which had already begun."[3]

2:22–23. "Men of Israel" confirms what has already been noted, that Peter's audience was made up of Jews (cf. v. 14). It is at this point that the sermon proper begins, hence the renewed address.

Nothing had been said about "Jesus of Nazareth" up to this time, but here He, rather than the Spirit, was immediately placed in the forefront. Peter began by calling Jesus a "man" (v. 22) and concluded by calling Him Lord and Christ (v. 36). By using the word "accredited," the speaker made it plain that this was no ordinary Man; He had been sent of God. Since Jesus Himself had not shied away from certifying His divine mission by His works (Luke 4:18–21; John 5:36), Peter could the more boldly call attention to the "miracles, wonders and signs."

The first word calls attention to the power of God at work. The second term views the miracles as demonstrations that appeal to the senses, creating wonder and awe. As signs, the works underline the message that is communicated to the discerning through what occurs. It is the spiritual interpretation of the occurrence and as such makes appeal to faith. In view of the fact that the audience was made up largely of people of Judea and Jerusalem, the observation "among you" tends to confirm what the fourth Gospel maintains, namely, that Jesus performed mighty works in that area (John 2:23; 5:1–9; 9:1–7; 11:1–44). "As you yourselves know" makes clear that even the

[3]H. N. Ridderbos, *The Speeches of Peter in the Acts of the Apostles*, 16.

enemies of our Lord were obliged to acknowledge that He did mighty works (Mark 3:22; John 11:47). It is notable that Peter did not call attention to what Jesus said. This would be more appropriate for converts to the faith. Salvation comes not through what Jesus said but through what He did. Peter quickly passed to this, calling attention to His death (v. 23). Statements of the *kerygma,* or gospel message, often enough having nothing to say about the ministry, but begin with a reference to the death of Christ (5:30–32; 1 Cor. 15:1–8).

"Handed over . . . by God's set purpose, you . . . put him to death" tersely summarizes the Godward and manward aspects of the Crucifixion. God's purpose was declared in the prophetic Scriptures (Isa. 53:10), accepted by Jesus as His role (Mark 10:45), and is maintained in the teaching of the church. It was understood by the Christian community at Jerusalem (Acts 4:28), but Jews had found it hard to accept before the event (Matt. 16:21–23; John 12:34). The Romans had put Jesus to death, but the major share of blame rested with the Jewish nation. By their refusal to accept Him (John 1:11) and by their acquiescence in the scheming of their leaders to turn Him over to the Roman governor, they had condemned Him to this shameful death. Peter continued to level the accusation "You . . . put him to death" at his audiences (3:15; 4:10; 5:30; 10:39) and found no one able to offer a rebuttal (5:28). Full recognition was given to the part played by the Romans—"wicked men"— but the very description of them implies deeper guilt for the Jews, because they had the Law of God, which made known His sovereign will.

2:24–32. The God who was active in the ministry of Jesus (v. 22) and proceeded according to plan in the death of His Son, asserted Himself also in the next step of redemption history. "God raised him from the dead," a grand reversal of the human verdict regarding Jesus (cf. Luke 3:22). "Freeing him from the agony of death," curiously, uses the word for the pains of a woman in travail. Jesus indeed had experienced pain in anticipation of His death, since He had predicted it, and He had had the terrible pain and distress of crucifixion. But these pains came to an end and were succeeded by resurrection life (paralleling birth in human experience).

"It was impossible for death to keep its hold on him." Why was it impossible? Because Jesus had no personal sin that would warrant a continuation under the power of death, the executor of sin. Once He had met the judgment of a righteous God against a sinful race by laying down His own infinitely valuable life, there was no basis on which He could rightly be held by death. Furthermore, the Resurrection was the clear demonstration that His sacrificial death on behalf of sinners had been accepted by God. The whole plan of redemption called for His risen life to be imparted to those who come to Him by faith. Finally, Scripture had to be fulfilled. David had foretold the Resurrection in Psalm 16, from which Peter proceeded to quote. The psalmist had spoken better than he knew. His own desires to escape the hold of death ("Hades" means the unseen realm) prophetically guaranteed the deliverance of God's Anointed. Whatever desire to escape death David may have had, this was not his fortune. But David's greater Son triumphed over the grave; His flesh did not suffer "decay." He is now in the presence of God.

In Acts 13:35–36 we find Paul using a portion of the same psalm and applying it to Jesus as Peter did. David died, but Jesus the Christ survived death. Evidently the use of the psalm early became a part of the Christian arsenal of Old Testament proof texts that could be applied to the Lord Jesus (recall Paul's teaching that the resurrection was according to Scripture [1 Cor. 15:4]). This is readily understandable if the Savior, after His resurrection, directed His disciples to this psalm (see Luke 24:44).

Peter went on to point out that whereas the casual reader might assume that David had been speaking of himself, his death voided any such simple conclusion. It must be understood that he was a "prophet." One would not readily gather this from the Old Testament, for David depended on prophets for counsel. God did not give the so-called Davidic covenant to David directly but through Nathan the prophet (2 Sam. 7). His prophetic powers came out, however, in the psalms, where from time to time he spoke of the future and of God's Annointed.

An example of this is Psalm 16. It was recognized in Israel that "God had promised him on oath" (Acts 2:30; Ps. 132:11) concerning the perpetuity of his house. His "throne" would not lack one to sit on it. Had not God reiterated His promise in recent days (Luke 1:32–33)? In the last analysis, an enduring throne called for a deathless occupant. So David saw what was ahead and "spoke of the resurrection of the Christ." Only

Christ has a truly indestructible life (Heb 7:16). He was in the tomb, but his flesh did not suffer decay. In support of the argument from fulfilled prophecy, Peter adduced the personal witness of the apostles and possibly others who had seen Jesus alive from the dead (cf. Acts 3:15; 4:20; 5:32; 10:39, 41).

Looking back for a moment, one can readily see that Peter devoted far more attention to the resurrection of Christ than to His death, and in dealing with the latter he did not state its purpose. His main thrust was to convince his hearers of the Resurrection. The sin problem could be dealt with later (v. 38).

2:33–35. Being "exalted to the right hand of God" notes a major result of the Resurrection. In His risen state, the Lord Jesus did not belong any longer in this sin-ridden world. His place was at the right hand of the Majesty on high. This was one of the glories that belonged to Him as a result of His humiliation and suffering (1 Peter 1:11).

Peter's hearers had not seen the Ascension any more than they had seen the Lord after His resurrection. How then could they be convinced that He was not only risen but also was now in glory? First, by the gift of the Spirit that came from Him. Could a dead man do that? The people had seen the powerful manifestations of the Spirit that very day. Jesus the Lord had the authority to dispense the Spirit. But further, Scripture had anticipated the exaltation as well as the Resurrection. David was appealed to once more. David did not ascend to heaven, as surely as he had not risen from the dead, so what he said on this point in Psalm 110:1 must apply to another. The discussion between Jesus and the Pharisees on this psalm indicates that both parties took it to be messianic (Matt. 22:41–46). There is an obvious distinction between the persons called "Lord," for one speaks to the other. The two words for Lord are different in the Hebrew, the first pointing to the Lord God, the second to God's Anointed, the One who is called His Son in Psalm 2:7.

"Sit at my right hand" marks the completion of Jesus' mission on earth and is the divine recognition of it (Heb 1:3). It also points forward to the return in glory, as the "until" of verse 35 indicates (cf. 3:21). There is a work of judgment reserved for that future day. Meanwhile the Son of God will be reaping the fruit of His redemptive mission through the working of His Spirit in the world from which He has departed.

2:36. By virtue of resurrection and exaltation, God has made the very Jesus whom the nation had crucified "both Lord and Christ." This raises the question whether Jesus is properly viewed as Lord and Christ prior to His resurrection. It is clear that Peter did not intend to restrict the use of the titles in this fashion, for according to his own statement a bit later, it was the Christ of God who suffered (3:18), and this was in line with Jesus' teaching (Luke 24:46), with Peter's confession and Jesus' acceptance of it (Matt. 16:16–17), and with the Savior's affirmation before the high priest and the Council (Mark 14:62). So it was reasonable to conclude that Jesus was Lord and Christ during the ministry, but that the Resurrection and Ascension put the application of these titles to His person beyond dispute. Before this time they were used sparingly. The marvel of the Son of God among the sons of men was too great, too mysterious, too overwhelming to be flashed on the scene at once. The awareness had to come gradually. So it was that the title Lord was used only occasionally of Jesus in the Gospels until the Resurrection. Help on this problem can be derived also from Romans 1:4, where it is stated that this same Person was marked off as Son of God with power by the Resurrection. The preceding verse makes it clear that He was the Son of God prior to the Resurrection, but that event lent a powerful attestation to his Sonship. Doubtless Acts 2:36 should be understood in the same way. What was true of His person essentially, but was only dimly perceived before, was now known demonstrably.

2:37. Peter's speech revealed how thoroughly the word of Jesus was fulfilled in respect to the the teaching ministry of the Spirit in the lives of the apostles (John 16:12–13). Now it was to be seen also how His prediction about the Spirit's ministry in convicting the world of sin, righteousness, and judgment (John 16:8–10) was vindicated. This was apparent in the sphere of sin. The audience had previously not believed in Jesus as their Messiah, and this was their chief sin. Peter accused them of the sin of crucifying the One who fulfilled the promises. Jesus' word regarding righteousness was fulfilled also, and in line with it we find Peter placing great emphasis on the return of the Son to the Father. The judgment aspect of which Jesus spoke is reflected here in the warning to the hearers that they should save themselves from a nation displeasing to God and ripe for judgment (v. 40).

"They were cut to the heart": the conviction went deep. To think that they had been guilty of rejecting their Messiah! It is difficult for a Gentile to appreciate how great must have been the sense of shame and sorrow. What a blunder! (See Isa. 53; Zech. 12:10; and 1 Tim. 1:13, 15 taken with Acts 9:4.) Hence the outcry, "What shall we do?" (cf. Acts 16:30).

2:38. "Repent, and be baptized, every one of you" sounds like a repetition of the summons of John the Baptist to his audiences (Luke 3:3). But something distinctly new was added—"in the name of Jesus Christ." It was on the basis of the name (the person and the worth) of Christ, as already expounded by Peter and acknowledged in baptism, that people could expect forgiveness of sins. As the sign and seal of their acceptance before God in His Son, they would receive "the gift of the Holy Spirit" (cf. Eph. 1:13–14). Nothing is said here about the gifts of the Spirit. The Spirit Himself is the great gift in which all lesser gifts are contained.

It would be a mistake to conclude that the Spirit was automatically bestowed when people submitted to baptism. This rite was administered in response to repentance, which includes faith (Acts 2:41, 44). Baptism is a means of making confession of allegiance to Christ (Rom. 10:9–10). It is clear from Acts 8:15–16 that water baptism was not in itself the key to receiving the Spirit. Repentance and a believing heart provided the necessary preparation. One might insist that Acts 1:5 does not make room for water baptism at all. This was true in the case of the apostles, but they were a special class. Having received the baptism of John, in all likelihood, and having the qualification of faith, plus years spent in following Jesus, they were fit candidates for the reception of the Spirit. Acts 2:38 presents the normal pattern for obtaining the Spirit (10:44–48 involves a special situation that, together with the Samaritan episode, must be left for later examination).

2:39. "The promise" presumably refers to the gift of the Holy Spirit, but this as conditioned on repentance and faith. Its blessings are not withheld from the "children." This is in line with the covenant promise to Abraham (Gen. 17:7).

"All who are far off" could refer to other Jews in the Dispersion, perhaps with a glance at Isaiah 57:19. But a few years later Paul used the phrase of Gentiles, who are contrasted with those who are near, namely, the Jewish people (Eph. 2:17), and Peter may have used it in the same way. The question is bound up with the early Christian understanding of the Joel prophecy. Since Paul quoted Joel 2:32 as applicable to Gentiles as well as to Jews (Rom. 10:13), it is possible that Peter understood it in the same way. He may have universalized "all people" also, in which case "all who are far off" could readily be assumed to be Gentiles.

The promise is related to the divine "call," which was a familiar thought to Peter's audience from its frequent use in the Old Testament. Israel was a called, i.e., chosen, nation, the peculiar people of God. Now, there seems to be a hint of an extended family in terms of the New Covenant, embracing Gentiles as well as the children of Israel. Its application would appear presently as the gospel was taken to Caesarea, Antioch, and other Gentile communities.

2:40. It is made plain here that Peter had more to say on this occasion than is reported. "Warned" suggests a further witness of a strong and penetrating nature, whereas "pleaded" indicates repeated appeals to come to the point of decision. That decision involved separation from a "corrupt generation" (cf. Luke 11:29) that had taken upon itself the blood of the Crucified (Matt. 27:25). It involved identification with the new people of God, who called on Him through the name of Jesus Christ.

CONVERTS (2:41–47)

A brief summary of the life of the Christian community following Pentecost is provided. The little band found its numbers swelled immediately by the response to Peter's preaching. Wonders and signs brought favor with the people throughout the city, and among believers there was instruction and growth, the sharing of possessions, and continual praise to God.

2:41. "Three thousand" people were "baptized" that day and took their places among the disciples as believers. The number may well exceed the total number of Jesus' true disciples during the days of His flesh (cf. 1 Cor. 15:6). The temple area, especially the court of the Gentiles, was commodious, able to contain around 200,000 people. If only a quarter of this total constituted Peter's audience (more would have made hearing very difficult), the figure of three thousand is not astonishing, for, as noted earlier, this was a prepared audience consisting of devout people who were familiar with the Scriptures and who had been in the city during the agonizing period of the Crucifixion. Added to all this was the power of the Spirit at work in Peter's message.

A question could be ventured here as to whether such success does not tend to give the Spirit greater stature than Christ Himself possesses. This possibility is negated by the very nature of the Spirit's work, which is intended to glorify the Son by bearing testimony to Him (we have observed that Peter made only passing reference to the Spirit at the beginning and the end of his address, but made Christ his theme). Furthermore, Acts 1:1 is a warning not to forget that the Spirit's activity is to be viewed as the continuing work of the Lord Jesus.

2:42. The converts were continually devoting themselves to the apostles' teaching. What a large church to shepherd! Yet it had twelve pastors and teachers. If some of the people returned to the lands of their birth, they did not do so immediately. They needed instruction. There is general agreement today that the early church had not only a kerygma, or gospel proclamation to the unsaved (most of the ingredients of which can be gleaned from the Pentecost sermon), but also a rather well-defined pattern of instruction for new converts. This is in view in the word "teaching," which is a synonym for the apostolic tradition handed down in the church.

Unfortunately Luke did not provide information about its contents. But this may be reconstructed with a fair degree of probability. It must have included the high points of Jesus' life and work; His ethical teaching, such as is epitomized in the Sermon on the Mount; an appreciation of the Old Testament prophetic background for His ministry, such as He imparted to the Eleven after the Resurrection; a digest of obligations toward one another, especially in the family relationship, and toward those outside the fold; and a warning about the possibility of persecution and the inroads of false teaching. Since these converts were Jews, much could be assumed from their background. What they needed was insight into the epochal character of the new age into which they had entered because of Christ's finished work and the advent of the Spirit. The commandments of Jesus must have been given special prominence (Matt. 28:20). Later, catechetical instruction preceded baptism as a condition for acceptance into the church. It was especially necessary for those who came out of paganism.[4]

---

[4]For additional information, see Philip Carrington, *The Primtive Christian Catechism* (Cambridge: Cambridge University Press, 1951); C. H. Dodd, *Gospel*

"Fellowship" is hardly to be thought of as a substitute for church, or even as a reference to the sharing of goods (v. 44). Rather, the act of sharing possessions was a practical demonstration of a more fundamental fellowship of a spiritual nature. Fellowship was the reality of the unity of faith and love and joy that characterized these early believers. In the structure of the sentence the word is not intended to imply that this was the apostles' fellowship to which others were admitted. It was instead the fellowship of the Spirit in which all alike participate (cf. 2 Cor. 13:14). Since converts had formerly lived in diverse parts of the earth, their genuine fellowship augured well for the unity of the church in days to come, when still greater diversity would prove no bar to oneness in Christ.

"The breaking of bread" is probably something different from what is mentioned in verse 46. In that verse ordinary meals are in view, whereas in this instance the close association with prayers suggests a sacramental function. But if the Lord's Supper is intended, why does the terminology not include the wine, as in the account of the Last Supper in the Upper Room? Probably because the renewed association with the Savior after His resurrection involved the breaking of bread (Luke 24:30). It became a kind of shorthand way of speaking of the Lord's Supper (cf. Acts 20:7), as is true today in some circles. Possibly there was a common meal that preceded the solemn observance of the sacrament. At least we have evidence for this in the Corinthian church (1 Cor. 11:20–34). *Agapē* is the term given to this common meal, since it was thought of as a love-feast (see Jude 12).

The word "prayer" almost certainly refers to seasons of prayer in which believers alone participated, and so is to be distinguished from attendance on the hours of prayer in the temple (cf. 3:1). The apostles and their associates had already discovered the importance of waiting on God together (1:14).

2:43. Jesus had promised that the disciples would do the works that He had done (John 14:12). Luke was content to note that the apostles wrought "many wonders and miracles." One of these was especially notable in its results and is therefore

and Law (New York: Columbia University Press, 1951); E. F. Harrison, "Some Patterns of the New Testament Didache," in *BS*, 119:118–28; E. G. Selwyn, "Essay II; Appended Note," in *The First Epistle of St. Peter* (New York: Macmillan, 1964), 363–488.

related in detail (3:1–8), but the continuing occurrence of such things helped to maintain an atmosphere of fear, or "awe," among the people. That God was at work could not be doubted. Was the Day of the Lord about to break upon them? The manifestation of the Spirit and the substantial number of converts made at Pentecost must have brought considerable soul searching to the population of Jerusalem.

2:44–45. "All the believers were together." This does not mean that the saints lived in the same quarter of Jerusalem. They were not a separate community in that sense. However, they were together as much as possible for instruction, fellowship, and worship. This togetherness prompted the result stated, namely, that they "had everything in common." This was not a forsaking of the principle of private ownership, since the disposal and distribution of their possessions was directed "to anyone as he had need." When the need became known, action was taken based on loving concern (cf. 1 John 3:17). So the Christian society differed from that of Qumran, where the pooling of resources was obligatory when one was accepted into the group.

The assumption of some scholars, that this picture presented by Luke is not historical but rather based on his own concern for the poor (judging from the prominence given to them in his Gospel), is ill-founded. If Luke inserted this element into his record of the early Jerusalem church, he could be expected to have mentioned it in connection with other churches, but this he did not do. Cessation of the practice of a community of goods was probably due to the gradual diminution of resources, a process hastened by persecution. It also received a jolt due to flagrant perversion of its whole spirit and purpose (chap. 5).

2:46–47. By frequenting the temple and mingling with other worshipers, the believers made it plain that they were not seeking a break with the religion of the Jews. It should be recalled here that our Lord, despite His differences with the spiritual leaders of the nation, did not forsake the temple, which He spoke of as His Father's house. Judaism had several sects, each with its special emphasis, and all were free to use the temple. Even Gentiles could use it in part. If the Christians had withdrawn from the temple, the task of reaching their Jewish brethren with the gospel would have been made difficult if not impossible. But as it was, they continued "enjoying the favor of all the people." It is likely that a favorite spot for coming together was Solomon's Colonnade (3:11).

Believers alternated between the temple and their homes, where they took their meals in an atmosphere of joy and mutual helpfulness, grateful to God for His blessings. The Mosaic Law had directed that Pentecost should be a time of gladness and sharing the bounty God had bestowed on His people (Deut. 16:10–11). It is not surprising that the inhabitants of Jerusalem were impressed. Such a lifestyle was contagious, possessing evangelizing power. People continued to be "saved" daily (note the correlation between vv. 46 and 47 on the basis of the phrase "every day"). When the church is truly Christian in its day-to-day life and activity, it is a growing church.

Since those who were healed of physical ills could be said to be saved, or made whole (see 4:9, the case of the lame man), the question may be raised whether "those who were being saved" were the beneficiaries of healing, since the wonders and signs noted in verse 43 must have included many such cases. But with regard to joining the Christian community, being saved would much more naturally relate to their spiritual than to their physical condition, especially since "the Lord was adding" these people. After all, the three thousand who responded at Pentecost are noted for their faith rather than for being the recipients of healing, about which the record is silent.

There is nothing here to suggest that the increase was due to more public preaching. While the possibility of such preaching must be granted, the most likely explanation for the growth of the church at this stage was the transformation observable in the three thousand. The impact of the few at Pentecost had broadened and become the impact of the many.

3

GROWTH OF THE CHURCH
(3:1—4:37)

This growth began on the Day of Pentecost, but it continued without abatement for some time, spurred on especially by the notable miracle of the healing of the lame man (4:3–4, 21–22) and aided by the boldness of the apostles (4:13, 31) and the healthy, happy condition of the church in general (4:32–35). The authorities' attempt to curb the testimony only made believers more determined to fulfill their task.

MIRACLE (3:1–10)

The story follows closely the pattern of the accounts of healing miracles in the Gospels—a description of the circumstances surrounding the contact between healer and healed, the nature of the infirmity, the request for help, the act of healing, the demonstration of bodily (or mental) soundness, and the impression made on bystanders.

3:1–3. "Peter and John" had a friendship that reached back several years and continued through these days in Jerusalem. The two men, along with their brothers, had been partners in the fishing business (Luke 5:10). They had belonged to the inner circle of three among the disciples of Jesus (Luke 9:28), who entrusted to them the preparation of the feast in the Upper Room (Luke 22:8). They had shared the agony of Peter's denial of the Lord (John 18:15–17) and the marvel of the empty tomb (John 20:2–8). For them the risen Lord had had a special word regarding the future (John 21:18–22). By going about together they honored the two-by-two procedure set by Jesus for His disciples (Mark 6:7; cf. Luke 10:1). Here in the book of Acts John maintains a role that is secondary and silent except for some corroboration of Peter's testimony (4:13, 19; 8:14–23).

"Going up to the temple" is in line with the previous notice that believers frequented this spot (2:46). Three o'clock in the afternoon (Greek, "the ninth [hour]") is designated as "the time of prayer." The principal feature of the daily routine of the temple was the offering of the morning and evening sacrifice, at which time incense was burned to symbolize the ascending prayers of the gathered worshipers (cf. Luke 1:9–10). These two periods of prayer, the one shortly after dawn and the other in mid-afternoon, were kept by godly Jews and even by God-fearing Gentiles far from the holy city, as in the case of Cornelius (10:30). A third period for prayer at the temple was observed at sunset, but the other two occasions were more prominent (Dan. 6:10 does not fit into this pattern, for it is not related to the temple worship).

The central figure in this episode was a man "crippled from birth." He was somewhat more fortunate than the invalid whom our Lord healed in Jerusalem (John 5:7) in that he had friends to place him daily before one of the gates of the inner temple area. Possibly he had heard the Lord teach during holy week in Solomon's Colonnade, which was not far from the gate called Beautiful, the scene of the miracle. It is thought that this gate opened onto the court of the women, which in turn led to the inner court surrounding the temple building proper. Less likely is the identification with the Golden Gate in the outer wall near the northeastern corner of the temple area. It was to the court of the women that worshipers made their way morning and afternoon for the seasons of prayer.

The man was there "to beg." Ideally there should have been no poverty in the land of Israel (Deut. 15:4), since obedience to God's will carried with it assurance of the supply of temporal needs; but realistically, the poor were a factor in the society at all periods (Deut. 15:11; Mark 14:7). It is hard to think of this lame man as already a member of the Christian community, since his needs would have been cared for (2:45).

He was shrewd enough to know where to take up his post, for people could not worship God restfully if they carried with them into the temple the image of a helpless man whom they had passed by. As friends were in the process of placing him in his accustomed spot, Peter and John came along on their way to prayer.

3:4. Peter "looked straight at him." The idea conveyed is that he looked with fixity and intensity at him (cf. 1:10; 23:1). His attentiveness may have been in unconscious imitation of his Lord, who on one occasion had spotted a lame man and proceeded to minister to him (John 5:6). The command, "Look at us!" seems to have been designed to awaken a sense of expectation.

3:5–6. Responding with fixed "attention," the lame man showed his hope that some unusual generosity might be extended to him. Cruel disappointment would have followed had Peter stopped with the words "Silver or gold I do not have." The truth was, he had something infinitely better to give—a soundness of limb that the unfortunate man had never known. There is a discernible tension between "Look at us!" and "in the name of Jesus Christ of Nazareth." In himself Peter had no more power to bestow healing than he had money in his wallet.

Incidentally, it is to Peter's credit that he had no money, for it shows that he had not dipped into the common treasury that had been established (2:44). In view of the sin of Judas, those who had been his associates could only have looked on such an act of pilfering with horror. Another aspect of the story is that Peter was going into the house of God for worship without any money (the court of the women, whither he was bound, contained the temple treasury). He seemed to know that true worship is not identical with the presentation of gifts (cf. Matt. 2:11).

The moment had come for action, and "the name of Jesus Christ" proved efficacious for the miracle that was needed. It was by His authority that the good deed was accomplished (cf. Luke 10:17). Was there any special significance in linking Jesus with Nazareth? It was sufficiently well-known that this was His home, so such information was hardly needed. Noting the frequent use of this appendage in post-Resurrection settings, C.F.D. Moule suggests, "This seems to reflect an awareness of his continuity with the Jesus of history."[1]

3:7–8. To encourage the lame man to act on his command to walk, Peter extended his "right hand" and lifted him to his feet. Luke the physician was interested in calling attention to the

---

[1] C. F. D. Moule, "The Christology of Acts" in *Studies in Luke-Acts,* 166.

instantaneous impartation of strength provided for the portions of the body that needed it. With a leaping motion the man tested his feet and found them able to sustain his weight, whereupon he began to take steps and entered the temple with his benefactors, unable to restrain his exhilaration. He expressed his elation by jumping about as he gave praise to God for the deliverance from his infirmity. He recognized that Peter and John were only instruments in the hand of God to effect his healing. That he became a believer through this experience may safely be assumed.

3:9–10. There could be no question in the minds of the people as to the reality of the miracle, for they recognized the familiar figure who had sat for so long in the same spot. Verification was much easier than in the case of the man born blind, whose recovered sight seemed to transform his appearance completely (John 9:9). The popular reaction to the lame man's restoration was "wonder and amazement." What seemingly could never have happened had occurred, and the credit was to be ascribed to Jesus of Nazareth, the despised and rejected One. Surely there was food for thought here.

MESSAGE (3:11–26)

Whereas in the Pentecost sermon the great proof of the claims of Jesus was His resurrection, here the emphasis falls on the demonstration of His person through a miracle that, wrought in His name, revealed the power of His risen life. Peter's first task in addressing the gathered multitude was to provide sufficient background concerning Him to give an explanation for the miracle. With this established, he proceeded to explain what the mission of the Christ could mean to Israel if only the people would respond to Him in faith.

3:11–12. Even after they emerged from the temple service the healed man clung to the apostles out of sheer joy and gratitude. By this time the people were in a mood of excitement as they moved toward that portion of the outer court, on the eastern side, known as Solomon's Colonnade. It is likely that prior to this time believers had become accustomed to congregating in this area. Probably most of the people who had observed the hour of prayer stayed for a time to hear what the apostles would say about the miracle. To this astounded assembly Peter addressed first of all a rebuke, for the crowd was staring at the apostles as though the two had some hidden source of magic or some inherent power that enabled them to perform miracles. (Paul encountered a somewhat similar reaction after healing a cripple at Lystra [14:11–18].) But neither their power nor their piety was the true explanation.

3:13–16. Instead of simply stating that God had performed the miracle, Peter prefaced his explanation (v. 16) with the background for the release of divine power (vv. 13–15). For such an audience it was wise to begin with God, whom Peter identified as "the God of Abraham, Isaac and Jacob." The title goes back to Exodus 3:6 and emerges on especially solemn or important occasions (1 Kings 18:36; 1 Chron. 29:18). Its thrust is to underscore the covenant faithfulness of God. In line with the promises that He made to the fathers, God "glorified his servant Jesus."

"Servant" is the first of several distinctive terms for the Lord Jesus Christ that appear in this sermon. The Greek word is *pais,* which is used in the LXX in Isaiah 52:13 to render the Hebrew ʿ *ebed* at the commencement of a passage that runs through chapter 53. The LXX translators should have used it also in 53:11, where the word occurs again in the Hebrew, but they misconstrued the meaning. Since Peter at this point stressed the glorification, then went on immediately to speak of Jesus' death, and since glorification as well as death is part of the presentation in Isaiah (52:13; 53:12), the concept of the suffering Servant was likely in his thought. What renders this more certain is the identification of the Servant with Jesus by Philip, another member of the Jerusalem church, when he dealt with the Ethiopian eunuch (8:30–35). Evidently this interpretation of Isaiah 53 was held by the Jerusalem church and in fact seems not to have taken hold elsewhere. At any rate, the only other occurrences of *pais* in referring to the Lord Jesus are found in the early chapters of Acts (3:26; 4:27, 30). It is not surprising, however, that in his first Epistle, especially in 2:23–24, the apostle Peter should again make use of the Servant motif.

God's appraisal of His Servant was vastly different from that of the nation that "handed over" the One whom He had sent. This term " delivered up" is used twice in the LXX text of Isaiah 53:12. In the New Testament it serves to describe the act of the Father in giving His Son to die for the sins of people (Rom. 8:32), of the Son in giving Himself (Gal. 2:20), of Judas in betraying Him (Luke 22:21), of the Council in handing Him over to Pilate (Mark 15:1), and of Pilate in surrendering Him to the will of His accusers (Luke 23:35). Similarity of action may conceal a great difference in motive. Peter charged his audience with complicity in the death of Jesus, for although the Sanhedrin had delivered Him to Pilate, the representatives of the people supported the demand for His death. Theirs was the special responsibility for having put pressure on Pilate when he had been inclined to release the prisoner (Luke 23:4, 15–16, 20, 22). They had denied Jesus in the presence of the governor, preferring that a murderer be released to them (Luke 23:18). They would not have Him as their King (John 19:15).

Peter could hardly take on his lips the word "disowned," in reference to their sin, without feeling pain over his own, even though his denial had involved, not rejection, but disloyalty. Peter had claimed that he did not know Jesus; the Jews had refused to acknowledge Him as their Messiah. One may deny a statement and think little of it, but to deny a Person who claimed, with the proper credentials, to be sent of God as the Savior and Lord of mankind involves a sin of inestimable magnitude (Matt. 10:33). It amounts to making God a liar (1 John 2:22; 5:10).

Peter used a double title here for Jesus, one that presented a strong contrast to "murderer"—"the Holy and Righteous One." This description was clearly intended as a messianic title. Neither term appears to have been much used outside the early Jerusalem church. "Holy" may owe something here to its occurrence in Psalm 16, which Peter had quoted in his Pentecost message (2:27), but this was not the first time he had used it of his Lord (cf. John 6:69). The term "Righteous One" emerges again on the lips of Stephen in a context similar to that of 3:14, when he spoke of an unjust and murderous throng taking the life of Jesus (7:52). The remaining example is Ananias's use of the term in speaking of Jesus to Saul of Tarsus (22:14).

If it is correct to assign to Isaiah 53 the source of the use of "Servant" in this sermon, the possibility is strong that the same Old Testament influence may account for the use of "Righteous One" (Isa. 53:11). Its use by the centurion at the cross (Luke 23:47), however gratifying, is not sufficient basis for the adoption of the title by the church.

Peter achieved a startling contrast when he charged his audience with having killed "the author of life" (v. 15). How incongruous! It is improbable that the thought behind this title is the initial communication of life to mankind (John 1:3–4), since the association is rather with the resurrection life of Jesus (cf. John 14:19), as indeed the present verse suggests as it continues, "but God raised him from the dead."

The word translated "author" is found in three other passages (Acts 5:31; Heb. 2:10; 12:2), and it has also been translated "prince," "leader," "pioneer," and "originator." Its use in Hebrews raises the question of relationship and suggests the distinct possibility that the writer of that Epistle may have been rather well acquainted with the outlook of the early Palestinian church. The idea conveyed by the word is that of a champion whose victory involves those whom he represents (cf. 1 Sam. 17:8–9). C. F. D. Moule makes the observation that this is one place at which the early Jerusalem church possessed a concept of Christology somewhat akin to that of Paul, who emphasized so much the corporate relationship between Christ and those who belong to Him.[2] Peter and his associates were "witnesses" (v. 15), not of the resurrection event itself (seen by no mortal) but of the resurrection fact (cf. 10:41).

Finally Peter was ready to speak of the miracle that had his audience agog with excitement. The ultimate explanation for the cure lay in the "name" of Jesus, which is full of power—not in a magical sense, but as summing up who and what He is. But even this reservoir of power flows into human life only as it is tapped by "faith in his name." This involves trusting in Jesus as the Son of God and Savior of men (cf. John 1:12). If the lame man had not exercised faith in Jesus and had instead resisted the use of His name by Peter (v. 6), he would not have been healed. To call upon the name of the Lord brings salvation, for it means calling upon the Lord Himself (Rom. 10:13).

3:17–21. Peter handled his audience with gentleness, his opening word, "brothers," being an indication of that gentleness. Having charged them in strong language with the death of Jesus, he now sought to mitigate their wrong as much as he could. The crime was committed "in ignorance" (cf. 13:27; John 8:19; 1 Cor. 2:8). Here we are probably confronted with an Old Testament conception, for in Israel sins were classified as done in ignorance or done with a high hand (Num. 15:27–31). The man who gathered sticks on the Sabbath

---

[2] Ibid., 180–81.

flaunted the law and found no mercy (Num. 15:32–36). Proof that the term *ignorance* was interpreted liberally may be seen in the case of David's sin (2 Sam. 12:13–14). Saul of Tarsus received mercy because he acted ignorantly in unbelief when he persecuted the church (1 Tim. 1:13).

The Jews should have known that God was sending them a Messiah who would "suffer," since He had foretold it through "all the prophets." As Jesus said on more than one occasion, the leaders of His people did not know the Scriptures (John 5:39; Matt. 22:29). Peter himself had not been able to accept the idea of a suffering Messiah, even from the lips of the Master (Matt. 16:21–22), and on this very account he felt compassion for his hearers and desired for them the insight he had come to possess concerning the prophetic word (cf. 1 Peter 1:11).

It is somewhat disconcerting to read that "all the prophets" foretold a suffering Messiah. True, the prophets are referred to in Luke 24:44–46 as predicting a suffering Messiah. But it is hard for us to find this strain in many places as we read the prophets today. The clearest pronouncement on the suffering aspect is found in the Servant passages of Isaiah. Since these found their fulfillment in the person of One who was also the Christ, Luke took the liberty to speak of a suffering Messiah (and not simply of a suffering Servant). The word "all" remains as a stumbling block. Is this a case of hyperbole, or is there more in the prophets than we have been able to see? "This is how God fulfilled," that is to say, God brought to pass the death of Jesus in the manner indicated, through suffering wrought by the action of men. One pathway of hope lay before the guilty ones, and Peter was quick to point it out.

Peter exhorted his audience, "Repent therefore and turn to God." If repentance was in order in the preaching of John the Baptist and of Jesus, how much more now, in view of a crucifixion inflicted by human passion and unbelief. The Lord's word to Peter, that he would turn back after his denial (Luke 22:32), was now held out by the apostle to those who may yet find mercy with God. Their "sins"—not only of rejection and crucifixion, but all others—"may be wiped out" (cf. Isa. 43:25; 44:22). The figure of speech involves the erasure of a writing, in this case as a record of sins committed (cf. Col. 2:14).

Repentance and forgiveness would clear the way for "times of refreshing." Seasons of refreshing and renewal are not to be thought of as a present respite from the labors and sorrows of life, as in Matthew 11:28–30, but as the hoped-for day of the return of the Messiah (cf. Matt. 23:37–39). The source of the refreshing is the presence of the Lord, who in this passage is God the Father. The ascended Lord Jesus is with Him in glory, whence He will return. The Lucan writings afford many examples of *Lord* being used of the Lord God (e.g., Luke 1:46, 66; 2:15; Acts 1:24; 4:24). Jesus will bring from the Father's presence the time of renewal and blessing when He returns.

He is the Christ "appointed" for His people. More may be involved here than meets the eye, for the word "appointed" has a prefix, a preposition meaning "beforehand," which appears also in verse 18. This raises the possibility that we have here a hint of the preexistence of the One whose first coming is history and whose second coming is being seen in prospect.

"Heaven" has been the abode of the Messiah since the Ascension, but "until" is a reminder of the promise of His return (cf. 1:11), which is the time "for God to restore everything" in accordance with what has been prophesied. The pattern of thought here bears a close resemblance to what our Lord talked about when He anticipated the *palingenesia,* or regeneration, of the present order in connection with His return in glory (Matt. 19:28). This theme looms large indeed in the writings of the prophets.

3:22–23. Having spoken of the prophets, Peter then went back to cite the testimony of Moses, regarded by the Jews as the greatest of the prophets.[3] He was the one who had foretold the coming of a prophet like himself who would speak the words of God and who must be heeded (Deut. 18:15, 18). While Peter did not in so many words identify this Prophet with Jesus, his intention is evident from the movement of thought and also from verse 26, where "raised up" looks back to the same expression in verse 22. In this context the verb "raise up" does not allude to resurrection but to emergence on the plane of history (other examples in Acts occur at 5:36–37; 7:18; 20:30).

---

[3]Philo not only calls him "the greatest and most perfect of men" (*De Vita Mosis* 1:1), but in dealing with him as a prophet, in the words of H. A. Wolfson, makes him "a prophet according to the wider sense which that term has in Scripture, namely, a prophet who by virtue of his being a prophet is also priest and lawgiver" (*Philo* [Cambridge, Mass.: Harvard University Press, 1948], 2:18). The Samaritans believed "Moses' soul returned to God at his death and he wants to be reborn as Taheb for the restoration" (John Macdonald, *The Theology of the Samaritans,* 443).

The fact that Stephen alluded to the same passage in Deuteronomy (Acts 7:37) makes it clear that the early church was aware of this prediction as pointing to Christ. That Judaism looked for a prophet like Moses can be seen from John 1:21; 6:14. This was a strong feature of the Samaritan religion also. A trace of the Samaritan expectation seems to emerge in John 4:25. In recent times it has been learned that the Qumran community also had such an expectation of an eschatological prophet based on the Deuteronomy passage. Luke's point is not that Jesus was a prophet (this was freely granted on all sides during His ministry) but that He was that particular Prophet for whom many were looking in that day as the One whose appearance would herald the consummation. The ancient prophecy had warned that unwillingness to heed this Prophet would mean destruction (Acts 3:23). As a sidelight, we should recall that at the Transfiguration the heavenly voice bade the disciples give heed to the Son (Luke 9:35). He is the Prophet par excellence.

3:24. Not only the unique prophet Moses but the whole order of prophets, beginning with Samuel, who was both judge and prophet, "foretold these days." The reference seems to be to the times of refreshing mentioned in verse 19, and this agrees with the fact that the great burden of the prophets was the proclamation of the messianic kingdom.

3:25–26. The conclusion of the address was intended to bring encouragement, for the hearers were descendants of the prophets and should have taken seriously their predictions. They were also the beneficiaries of the covenant God had made with Abraham. As his posterity, they could enter into the blessing of the covenant for themselves and receive forgiveness of their "wicked ways." God had "raised up" (sent) His Servant Jesus "first" to Israel. This was to be expected, for God could not ignore His covenant (cf. Rom. 1:16). It agrees with our Lord's insistence on restricting His ministry to His own people Israel (Matt. 15:24). Yet His openness to the needs of Gentiles and His responsiveness to their faith (Matt. 8:13; 15:28) demonstrated that there was room for Gentiles in the divine plan. Scripture presents the prospect that through a believing Israel "all peoples on earth" can and will be blessed (Gen. 12:3). This, to a degree, actually took place as the history in the book of Acts unfolds, for it was through believing Jews that Gentiles heard of the Lord Jesus and entered into the blessings of the covenant. Paul foresaw a day when this divine purpose will be fully realized (Rom. 11:11–12).

Anton Fridrichsen summarizes the thrust of the sermon as a whole by saying,

> Peter interprets the significance of the resurrection of Jesus from a Jewish point of view: "God, having raised up his servant, sent him to you first" (3:26). The resurrection of Jesus from the dead means that he is now, as the heavenly Messiah of Israel, ruling over the new-covenant people consisting of those Jews who believed in him. The way of salvation is open to all children of Abraham; one has only to believe in Jesus as the crucified and exalted Messiah. This form of gospel is all through based upon the priority of Israel as the covenant people of the world; they are the people of prophecy now experiencing its fulfillment. It is a typical gospel of the circumcision.[4]

One need only add that it is not exclusively Jewish, for all the families of the earth are seen as the ultimate recipients of blessing.

OPPOSITION (4:1–22)

This section has three successive developments: the arrest of Peter and John by Jewish authorities and their overnight imprisonment (vv. 1–4); the hearing before the Sanhedrin the following morning, featuring Peter's speech (vv. 5–12); and the deliberations of the Council, leading to the decision to release the apostles but also to forbid further preaching in the name of Jesus (vv. 13–22).

4:1–2. The phrase "While they were speaking to the people" leads to two conclusions: John joined Peter in addressing the throng that had gathered, and much more was said on this occasion than is contained in 3:12–26.

The apostles were interrupted by the arrival of certain dignitaries from the Sanhedrin. Luke delighted to use the verb meaning "to come up to," especially in the sense of a sudden and unexpected arrival (cf. Luke 2:9; Acts 17:5). Drawn by the report of a large concourse of people in the temple area, this

---

[4] Anton Fridrichsen, *The Apostle and His Message* (Uppsala: Uppsala Universitets Arsskrift, 1947), 9.

investigating group consisted of "priests" and "Sadducees," accompanied by "the captain of the temple guard." This officer was second only to the high priest in authority. Under him were men who supervised the guards of the temple treasures and the gatemen. In other words, he commanded the temple police force. His presence on this occasion heralded an arrest.

The priests were likely chief priests (some manuscripts say this), since they, rather than ordinary priests, had a place in the Council. However, it is possible that some of the officiating priests joined the investigating party because of concern that the afternoon worship period had been somewhat disturbed.

The Sadducees constituted one of the sects into which current Judaism was divided. Differing from the Pharisees in that they refused to sanction the oral traditions that had grown up around the interpretation of the Mosaic Law, these men jealously guarded the ancient right of the priests to teach the Law as well as to supervise the worship in the house of God. Due to historical trends during the intertestamental period, they were drawn increasingly into the political arena, since there was no king in Israel, and by the time of Christ they had found it expedient to keep on good terms with the Romans (John 11:48). They manifested little interest in Jesus until it appeared that He might turn out to be a revolutionary leader whose movement would bring reprisal from Rome. Joining hands with the opposition party, the Pharisees, they engineered the death of Jesus.

Their reason for visiting the temple courts on this day was that they were "greatly disturbed" over two things. For one, the apostles "were teaching the people." After all, these were rude Galileans, unschooled in the Law. To be sure, Jesus had taught there, but He had had such ability that men instinctively called him Rabbi. It was galling to have to put up with the attempt of His disciples to assume a similar role.

But more than that, the Sadducees were inflamed because the two men were "proclaiming in Jesus the resurrection of the dead." It was bad enough to have people preaching the doctrine of resurrection, something the Sadducees did not accept (23:8), presumably because it did not seem to be in the Pentateuch, which they ranked higher than the rest of the Old Testament as the foundation of all else. But to preach resurrection in the case of Jesus, whom they had condemned to death, was doubly offensive. Months before, it had been the resurrection of

Lazarus that had stirred them up against Jesus (John 11:45–53; 12:9–11). Now the report of the resurrection of Jesus Himself was beginning to haunt them and make them uneasy. But it is reasonably certain that their religious views, even on resurrection, were less vital to them than their political well-being. They feared any disturbance among the people that threatened to upset the status quo and bring Roman intervention.

4:3–4. "They seized Peter and John." No delay is indicated, nor is there any evidence of resistance either by the apostles or by the people on their behalf. An attempt to arrest Jesus in the temple had failed when the officers had been overawed by His teaching (John 7:32, 45–46), but on this occasion their superiors were in action, men who would not be denied. Because it was now "evening," probably three hours or so after the hour of prayer, it was not possible to have a meeting of the Council; so the prisoners were placed in custody overnight with a view to placing them before that body the next morning. The crowd could readily be persuaded to leave, for it was time to close the temple gates anyway.

Then, or later on, the apostles learned that their testimony in the temple had not been in vain, for many in their audience believed. These additions brought the total of believing "men" (there were women also) to "about five thousand." This does not mean that an additional two thousand were converted that afternoon, for believers were being added from day to day ever since Pentecost (2:47). It is not possible to know how many days had intervened.

This figure of five thousand has been questioned on the ground that Paul had no such success in his efforts to evangelize his own people. But the conditions were by no means the same. By the time Paul was carrying on his work, official Judaism had arrayed itself against the sect of the Nazarenes; but at this early period in Jerusalem no official action had been taken, and there was a great wave of popular support for the apostles, aided by their works of mercy among the masses (cf. 2:43). All this was changed after the death of Stephen.

4:5–6. During the night, while Peter and John were kept in prison, word went out to the members of the Sanhedrin to be ready to meet "on the next day." This was the highest court in the land, having had its origin, so far as is known, in the Gerousia, or senate, which functioned in Maccabean times. Its membership was drawn from the two leading parties—the

Sadducees and the Pharisees—and totaled seventy men (cf. Num 11:16–17) in addition to the high priest, who presided over the body.

Luke's description of the court has some interesting features. He revealed his detachment as a Gentile by speaking of "their" rulers (cf. "their" language in 1:19). Three elements among the members are noted: "rulers and elders and teachers of the law." The first group can safely be identified with the chief priests or ex–high priests. Elders were representatives of the people and were probably for the most part Pharisees. Teachers of the law were men with rabbinical training who attached themselves both to the Pharisees and to the Sadducees as experts in the Law.

Certain individuals are mentioned also because of their prominence. Annas is called "the high priest." He had been high priest for several years but was removed by the Roman procurator in A.D. 15. It is likely that the Jewish people still regarded him as the legitimate holder of the office, which according to the Law, was for life. In addition, he continued to exert influence through five sons, one grandson, and his son-in-law Caiaphas, who was the actual incumbent at the time. In Luke's Gospel the two men, probably out of deference to popular sentiment, are presented as sharing the office (Luke 3:2; cf. John 18:13). "John" may be Jonathan, one of the sons of Annas (Codex Bezae has this reading). Of Alexander nothing is known. "All who were of high-priestly descent" (NASB) included five or six families, the priestly aristocracy from which high priests were selected in this period.

Luke's source of information for this narrative could have been the apostle John, provided he can be identified with "the other disciple" who was known to the high priest (John 18:16).

4:7–12. The two apostles were placed "before them," where they could be readily seen and heard (the Sanhedrin sat in a semicircle). This was the first occasion when the prediction of Jesus that His followers would be delivered up to councils (Mark 13:9) was fulfilled. Perhaps they recalled His further remark that the purpose behind such a situation was that they might bear testimony before them. At any rate, when the two were interrogated as to the "power" and the "name" (authority) by which they had been acting (cf. Luke 20:1–2), Peter was enabled to reply because he was "filled with the Holy Spirit," as Jesus had promised (Mark 13:11).

There was no thought of using guarded language that might make their lot easier. Peter came right to the point, appearing to rejoice that he had such an audience through which, in a sense, he was making his message known to all the people of Israel (cf. Paul's attitude in a similar situation, which gave him a sounding board for reaching the Gentiles [2 Tim. 4:17]). As to the miracle itself, he was content to remind his hearers that it was an "act of kindness," so there should have been no ground for complaint. As to the source of the power behind the miracle, the answer was Jesus Christ of Nazareth, for the One who went about doing good was still at work through His people (Acts 1:1).

Peter could have stopped there and received only a mild reaction to his testimony, for other miracles had been wrought in recent days in Jerusalem without inciting the wrath of the authorities (2:43). But the urge to bear a testimony to his Lord before the rulers of his people was irresistible. He might not have another opportunity. So on he went, disregarding the consequences to himself. His judges had "crucified" the Savior, but they had not thereby brought His career to an ignominious close, as they had supposed, for God had "raised" Him "from the dead." Neither here nor in the Pentecost address did Peter mention the empty tomb. As a mere fact, this phenomenon was open to more than one possible interpretation. What mattered supremely was the confidence that Jesus was alive, to which the apostles could bear witness because of their contact with Him. The healing of the cripple was a demonstration of the reality and power of His risen life.

But rather than continue to talk about the man who had been healed, Peter returned to the themes of the death and resurrection of Jesus. For this purpose he made use of Psalm 118:22. The form of the quotation is notable in two respects. First, it differs from the LXX, to which Luke usually adhered rather closely in his quotations. "Stone" stands here in the nominative rather than in the accusative case, which may indicate that Luke was drawing on *testimonia,* that is, groupings of Scripture passages to serve as proof texts for various Christian themes, especially in relation to Jesus as the Messiah. Such *testimonia* would naturally use the nominative. Second, Peter identified the builders as "you," the men in front of him, making an addition to the passage.

The thrust of the verse used by Peter is clear It contains on the one hand an indictment of Israel's leaders as rejecters of the Lord Jesus and on the other hand a vindication of His claims by God's action in raising Him from the dead. The leaders are viewed as builders looking for just the right stone with which to complete the edifice of Judaism by satisfying the nation's messianic hopes. They had scornfully rejected God's Man as not meeting their requirements, and did it by inflicting on Him a shameful and violent death. God has answered by raising up His Son and making Him the "cornerstone" or "capstone." This truth renders futile all attempts to find the origin of the church at some point in the pre-Cross ministry of Jesus (except by way of prediction), for the church was founded on a rejected and resurrected Savior.

"Cornerstone" is somewhat hard to define. Literally it is "head of the corner," and was applied by Jesus to Himself in a parabolic setting of rejection (Luke 20:17) and implied vindication. The term is certainly intended to suggest importance and honor. "The Crucified is the rejected stone which in the resurrection is made by God the chief corner-stone in the heavenly sanctuary (Acts 4:11), to be manifested as such in the *parousia*."[5]

Peter did not pursue the line of thought expressed by Jesus in Luke 20:18, with its threat of judgment, though he touched on it in 1 Peter 2:7–8. The reason for his reserve is hardly timidity or fear, but rather his desire to stress the positive value of Christ the stone, as the One in whom salvation is to be found (v. 12).

Salvation in the Lord God is set forth in a refrain that occurs three times in the very psalm Peter was using (Ps. 118:14, 21, 28 in the LXX). Salvation was the supreme concern of this prince of apostles (Acts 2:40; 5:31; 15:11; cf. 1 Peter 1:5, 9–10). It is found exclusively in Christ and "no one else," and it is an imperative need for sinful people (they "must be saved"). What had happened to the physical condition of the cripple, in that he had been made whole (literally, saved) was a parable for the healing of the whole person by the power of Christ.

4:13. It is likely that Peter's words were seconded, if not supplemented, by John. As they listened, the members of the Sanhedrin took note of the "courage" of the two men. The

---

[5]Joachim Jeremias, in *TDNT*, 1:793.

word carries the idea of expressing oneself without holding anything back (and this has an interesting implication in such a passage as Hebrews 4:16). When the Council coupled this observation with another, the fact that the two men before them were "unschooled" and "ordinary," the result was astonishment. The two things did not seem to hang together—the apostles' utter freedom in speaking and their lack of schooling (not general education so much as that which the scribes enjoyed [John 7:15]); plus their provincial character, lacking through inexperience the urbanity and poise necessary to command the attention of this august body.

Gradually the truth dawned on them. They "took note" of them as having been with Jesus. There is no thought here to the effect that the disciples had been waiting on the Lord Jesus in prayer and had thereby gained in boldness, however true that may have been. Rather, the dignitaries of the Council finally recalled having seen them before, possibly in the court of the high priest's house after the arrest of the Master in the garden (John 18:15) if not during Jesus' daily teaching in the temple (Luke 22:53). That night Peter had been the target of jesting by guards and maids, so that he had ended up in confusion and denial, leaving the premises in tears. John had remained silent on that occasion. Now these two were fearless in the presence of national leaders, refusing to be browbeaten. How could this be?

The unwelcome truth began to steal over the minds of the judges. Jesus also had been uneducated (John 7:15) but was adept in handling Scripture. He, too, had belonged to the backwoods country of Galilee (cf. John 1:46), yet He had won the favor of the people. This thorn in their sides had finally been removed, to their great relief. But now it appeared that Jesus had succeeded in reproducing Himself in His disciples. Could they ever truly be rid of Him?

4:14. For the moment the Council was nonplussed. No objection could be raised against the miracle, for the formerly lame man had accompanied the apostles into the council chamber, a silent testimony to the power of God and the efficacy of the name of Jesus.

4:15–17. What was needed was time and privacy for consultation. To that end the apostles were removed while the members conferred with one another. The sentiment commonly expressed was one of frustration, strikingly similar to the mood shown by the same body after the resurrection of Lazarus (John 11:47–48). They were not prepared to make themselves appear foolish in the eyes of the people by denying the miracle. But they had to do something "to stop this thing from spreading any further."

What was "this thing" that could not be voiced by troubled men? Grammar may dictate that the referent is "sign" (v. 16), but by this time virtually the entire city had heard about the healing. Clearly what the Council had in mind was to block further teaching about Jesus and the Resurrection. It was the speaking that was considered dangerous. Nothing was said about curtailing the working of miracles.

4:18–22. The restriction covered both preaching and teaching—all public utterance similar to what the apostles had been giving since Pentecost. Actually, if the language be pressed, even personal conversation on the subject was ruled out (v. 17).

If the Council had hoped to shut the mouths of these simple but eloquent men, they were immediately disillusioned. The answer of Peter and John was polite but firm. These men who had pronounced the dictum were judges. Appropriately, the apostles asked them to "judge" whether it would be right before God for them to obey the prohibition or to heed the command of God, which was the basis for their insistence on declaring what they had "seen and heard" (the risen and exalted Lord, the descending Spirit, and the power of God at work in the bodies and souls of men and women).

It was an embarrassing moment. No wonder the Council made no attempt to answer beyond repeating the warning to maintain silence, adding threats should the ban be ignored. This gave them an excuse to apprehend the apostles again in case their edict was disobeyed. There the matter rested, and since there was no ground on which Peter and John could rightly be detained, and in view of the popular sentiment in their favor, they were allowed to depart. Jerusalem was filled with praise to God for the manifestation of His goodness and power in the healing of the cripple who had endured over forty years of handicap and deprivation.

CONFIRMATION (4:23–31)

Released from custody, Peter and John sought the fellowship and counsel of the apostolic company. Through united prayer and a fresh visitation of the Spirit, all were reinforced in their purpose to continue their witness despite the warning of the Sanhedrin.

4:23. They "went back to their own people." The Greek simply has "to their own" (cf. 24:23). John 13:1 represents a close parallel since it involves the Twelve. Clearly a small company is in view here, in contrast to the larger circle of believers in verse 32. The new policy adopted by the Sanhedrin would affect these leaders in a special way. They would be under close observation. So it was important that they should confer and pray and present a solid front to the authorities, indicated as "the chief priests and elders."

This is the first time chief priests are mentioned in Acts (although some manuscripts have the word in 4:1), but the expression is well-known from its use in the Gospels. It creates difficulty, however, for the word "chief priest" in the original is identical with "high priest." It would only add to the confusion if the plural form were translated "high priests" wherever it occurs. After considerable research, J. Jeremias concluded that these men must be differentiated from the ordinary priests who ministered in the temple. "The chief priests permanently employed at the temple formed a definite body who had jurisdiction over the priesthood and whose members had seats and votes on the council."[6] This group included the current high priest, the captain of the temple (4:1), the temple overseer, and several treasurers.[7] As Acts 4:6 suggests, these men belonged to the priestly aristocracy. The older view, set forth by E. Schurer,[8] that "chief priests" indicated members of the high-priestly families, is no longer widely accepted as adequate.[9]

No mention is made here in verse 23 of teachers of the law (in contrast to v. 5). They probably did not take an active part, since the case did not involve interpretation of the Law.

---

[6]Joachim Jeremias, *Jerusalem in the Time of Jesus,* 180.

[7]Ibid., 179.

[8]Emil Schürer, *A History of the Jewish People in the Time of Jesus Christ* (Edinburgh: T. & T. Clark, 1890), 2:204–5.

[9]Gottlob Schrenk *TDNT,* 3:271.

4:24–26. Luke does not report any discussion among the apostles, but seems to say that the account of Peter and John led to a spontaneous outburst of united prayer. "Sovereign Lord" translates a word used also at the opening of Simeon's prayer (Luke 2:29). It is sometimes rendered "Master" (2 Tim. 2:21; Jude 4). Here it is followed by praise of God for His creative majesty (v. 24) and also for His activity in human affairs (vv. 25–26). "He does as he pleases with the powers of heaven and the peoples of the earth" (Dan. 4:35). Having been made keenly aware in recent days of the relevance of certain Scriptures to their own time, the apostolic company turned readily to Psalm 2 as fitting their circumstances. The portion quoted emphasizes the vanity of the effort of the Gentile nations to free themselves from divine control, and the futility of their rebellion "against the Lord and against his Anointed One"—the Messiah.

This is an instance in which "Lord" refers to God the Father. The distinction of persons (cf. Ps. 110:1) was readily seized on by the early Church, no doubt under the direct tutelage of the risen Lord (Luke 24:44) as warranting the identification of the anointed One with their Lord and Master. The expression "his Anointed One" is a pointed reminder that at this early stage in the life of the church "Christ" was not yet used as a name (as it is frequently in the Epistles) but was still a title.

4:27–28. Tokens of the fulfillment of the psalm are now spelled out. Here Jesus is spoken of as God's "holy servant." Peter had already used the expression in his second sermon (3:13, 26), but now we are made aware that this was a familiar way of speaking of Jesus, one in which others shared.

Noting the close conjunction of "servant" and "Christ" in 4:26–27, Richard Longenecker writes:

> [This] indicates that the earliest appreciation of Jesus as the Suffering Servant was inextricably tied up with the conviction regarding Jesus as the Messiah. While, therefore, a suffering servant interpretation of Jesus' ministry ultimately stemmed from Jesus himself, it seems to have been only established in the church's consciousness on the basis of conviction regarding his messiahship.[10]

[10] Richard N. Longenecker, *The Christology of Early Jewish Christianity,* 107.

"Whom you anointed" probably means the same as in 10:38, where the baptism of Jesus is indicated, the occasion when He received the endorsement of the Father and the enduement with the Spirit. As the anointed One, Jesus is the Messiah; as the Servant, He is the Savior. In this spontaneous expression of the apostles' awareness of the dignity of their Lord there is recognition both of His office and of His redeeming work.

Now the rulers who opposed God and His program, indefinite in the psalm, were specified in terms of recent events. Herod Antipas, though technically a tetrarch, could be called king by courtesy (Mark 6:14), answering to the language of the psalm. Luke was the only Gospel writer to mention Herod in connection with the trial of Jesus (Luke 23:6–12). He seemed to have had special information regarding his court (Luke 8:3; Acts 13:1). In the person of Pilate the church found a fulfillment of the reference to "rulers." In terms of the Roman soldiers, "Gentiles" were present and involved, as were "the people of Israel" through their various tribal representatives at Jerusalem during the Passover. What had been done in concert by the will of man was not understood as a working out of the divine purpose (cf. 2:23). The futility of human opposition to God is never seen to better advantage than when it serves to implement His plan.

4:29–30. The prayer turned to the present situation of the church—"Lord, consider their threats." These "threats" must be related to the warning given by the Sanhedrin (v. 18). Although Psalm 2 warned of wrath and destruction on the enemies of God and His Anointed, in this prayer there was no petition for reprisal, nor even a request to be spared the rigors of persecution. The servant is not greater than his Lord (John 15:20). All that was sought was divine restraint so that testimony to the Savior could continue. For themselves, the followers of the Lord asked for "confidence," or "boldness," such as Peter and John had displayed (Acts 4:13) in proclaiming the Word.

One other petition was voiced, the plea that God would continue to show forth His "signs and wonders," especially the manifestation of His power to heal. The two things—boldness in preaching and the divine working through healing—had been the pattern thus far (chap 3). If the human boldness alone were to remain visible, the impression could be created that God was withholding His blessing (cf. Heb 2:3–4).

97

4:31. The answer came quickly, first in the form of a physical sign, the shaking of the building where the company was gathered (cf. 16:25–26), and then in a renewed filling with the Spirit as the means of boldness in testimony (cf. 4:8, 13; John 15:26–27). The group lost no time in acting on this fresh manifestation of divine power by bearing effective witness to the Lord Jesus.

STATE OF THE CHURCH (4:32–37)

Here emphasis rests on the spiritual accord and mutual consideration that prompted to unusual generosity in providing for the material needs of the church.

4:32–35. Luke makes it clear that the willingness to share possessions was based on a powerful sense of unity ("one heart and mind"). This provided the inspiration for refusing to insist on the right to retain what one had received by inheritance or toil. It was not a matter of legislation, as in the Qumran community, where sharing of goods was imposed on its members. According to the Qumran sect, such renunciation was necessary in order to purify the mind in the truth of God.[11] With the Christian community, however, the sharing was not a means to the end of personal edification, but rather the expression of the love of the Spirit, to use Paul's phrase (Rom. 15:30; cf. Gal. 5:22). It was also in line with the teaching of Jesus (Mark 10:21).

Right in the midst of this description, as though to emphasize that the maintenance of the group was not the primary consideration, attention is called to the public witness borne by the apostles to "the resurrection of the Lord Jesus." Above all, this was a witnessing community, and for this reason they enjoyed "much grace" from the Lord.

Returning to a description of the community of goods, Luke adds the information that the common fund, out of which means were provided for the needy, was built up by the voluntary sale of "lands" and "houses." This meant that eventually the resources of the more affluent members would be drained, and the common fund would have to be replenished from other sources or be abandoned. But the church, caught up

[11] *Manual of Discipline* 1:11–13.

in the enthusiasm of sacrificial giving, was content to leave the future with God. The poverty of the Jerusalem congregation is noted a few years later (Gal. 2:10). This condition existed not only in time of famine (11:27–30) but also as a chronic state calling for help from the Gentile churches (24:17; cf. Rom. 15:26).

The very fact that benefactors brought the proceeds of their sales and deposited them with the apostles demonstrates the comprehensive role of leadership maintained by these men. Besides preaching to the unsaved and teaching believers, they assumed general oversight of the church's affairs. As the saints increased in number, the responsibility of supervising the common fund became too great, and a change had to be made (6:1–6). But for the present the apostles continued to oversee the distribution of relief, which was a daily responsibility (6:1).

4:36–37. Unexpectedly, in the midst of this general description of the church's means of subsistence, Luke introduces an individual and furnishes certain items of information about him. This is the historian's way of alerting the reader to the fact that this man, Barnabas, was destined to play a large part in the unfolding story of the spread of the Christian faith. There are two dozen references to him in Acts alone. He is described as a good man, full of the Holy Spirit and faith (11:24). That goodness included generosity. Barnabas was eager to help the church on a later occasion also (11:27–30). When his own resources were largely depleted, he was ready cheerfully to work for his living while preaching the gospel rather than depend on others; he may even have inspired Paul to adopt the same pattern (1 Cor. 9:6). He lived by the principle of the name he bore (Barnabas means "encouragement"). Luke notes that this name was given him by the apostles, indicating the esteem in which he was held.

Barnabas's possession of a piece of property seems to violate the ancient prohibition affecting Levites (Num. 18:24) and priests (Num. 18:20). But even by the time of Jeremiah this was not strictly maintained (Jer. 1:1; 32:6–15).

Being a native of Cyprus, Barnabas was a Hellenistic Jew, as was Paul, so it is not surprising that later he took a leading role in missionary endeavor beyond the borders of Palestine.

16572

4

PROBLEMS
5:1–8:3

The problems of the church were both internal and external. Within the church distress was occasioned by the dishonesty of two people (5:1–11) and by the growing difficulty of caring for the needy (6:1–7). From the outside, pressure was mounting in the form of persecution directed at the apostles (5:12–42) and then at the church (8:1–3). This persecution grew out of Stephen's preaching and martyrdom (6:8–7:60).

ANANIAS AND SAPPHIRA (5:1–11)

The connection with the previous paragraph is close, for the subject is the same, but there is also sharp contrast. Unity was temporarily disturbed, and joy was dimmed as divine judgment was meted out to a husband and wife.

5:1–4. Even this flourishing congregation became marred by human failure. Ananias was of a different caliber than Barnabas. Probably it was the desire for recognition from the apostles and the church that led to the concocting of a plan, shared by his wife Sapphira, whereby Ananias hoped to gain a reputation as a generous man. The plan was simple, namely, to sell a piece of property and ostensibly bring the amount received to the apostles, but in actuality to hold back a portion of the total for personal use. Ananias would not have been wrong to bring part of the sale price rather than the whole amount if that fact had been made known; but he made it appear that, like Barnabas, he was giving the entire amount.

There was an intention to make the element of sacrifice appear greater than it actually was. That was hypocrisy.

Peter's question "Why has Satan filled your heart to lie to the Holy Spirit?" (NASB) clearly implies that it was the responsibility of Ananias to resist the solicitation of the Evil One (cf. Peter 5:8–9). Most New Testament references to Satan's activity relate to saints rather than to the unbelieving world. Peter himself had become the tool of Satan on one occasion (Matt. 16:23). It was a source of grief to him that so early in the life of the church Satan had been successful in making damaging inroads. Presumably Ananias was not conscious of having lied to the Holy Spirit; but this was what he did, since the Spirit was in actual control of the church, empowering its witness and fostering its loving benevolence. Both witness and loving concern were now endangered by this sin of dishonesty, for the Spirit was grieved (Eph. 4:30) and unable to grant His blessing until this affair was cleared up.

What is involved here in lying to the Holy Spirit? No help can be gained by referring to the unpardonable sin (described as blasphemy against the Spirit [Mark 3:29]) and assuming from the death of these offenders that they must have been unsaved people masquerading as saints. This was not a case of blasphemy, but of lying. There is no sound reason for questioning the redeemed status of the pair. Believers are capable of lying (Col. 3:9). Chastening of God's people can be unto death (1 Cor. 11:30, and possibly 5:5). The lie to God the Spirit was so much greater than the attempted deception of the church that Peter could say, "You have not lied to men but to God." Yet the whole affair had been motivated by a desire to appear in a good light before people! Relation to God must be kept in its primary place as the key to right relations with people.

5:5–6. Peter's words were the death knell for Ananias. The suddenness and severity of the punishment brought "fear" on everyone who learned of the episode. God had revealed Himself as a consuming fire (Heb. 12:29). Burial was immediately carried out by certain "young men" who were available for service but were not an official body within the church (cf. 1 Peter 5:5). If we ask why the penalty was so severe, surely the explanation lies at least partially in the necessity of reminding the church that believers were not to trifle with the things of God. A rough parallel may be seen in the death of Achan (Josh. 7), whose death was also occasioned by involvement in financial scandal.

5:7–11. Unaware of what had overtaken her husband, Sapphira came home (had she been out spending some of the money kept back from the sale?) only to discover that she was a widow. Worse than that, her complicity in the plot to deceive the church was about to bring her to the grave along with her husband, as Peter's searching examination brought to light her guilt. The amount of space devoted to this incident is impressive. Perhaps a key to the understanding of its importance lies in Luke's repeated observation that "fear" came on everyone, including "the whole church." God was teaching His people that sin among the saints is no light matter. He can use only those who are honest with Him as well as with the brethren.

The drastic nature of the divine intervention is in contrast to the milder treatment of offenders at Qumran: "If there be found in the community a man who consciously lies in the matter of (his) wealth, he is to be regarded as outside the state of purity entailed by membership, and he is to be mulcted of one fourth of his food ration."[1] After the death of Ananias and Sapphira, a Jerusalemite would think twice before professing faith in Christ in order to share in the common fund of the church.

Two lessons emerge from this incident. One is the fact that the church is not perfect, not even when it is standing in the shadow of Pentecostal blessing. Spurgeon is reputed to have counseled a man seeking his help in finding a perfect group of God's people that if he found one he should not join it, for if he did, it would no longer be perfect. The other lesson is the reminder that the God of the Bible intends to judge sin. He has done it at the Cross; He does it among His people; and He will do it at the last day when unbelievers stand before Him.

In bringing this story to a close Luke mentions the "church" for the first time, having been content up to this point to indicate the group as believers (2:44; 4:4, 32). The freer use of the word *church* from this point on (there are twenty-three occurrences in Acts) may indicate a growing self-consciousness on the part of the Christian community as to its distinctive nature and place in the world.

---

[1] *Manual of Discipline* (trans. Gaster) 6:24–25.

PERSECUTION OF THE APOSTLES (5:12–42)

The first paragraph is transitional, summarizing the aggressive ministry of preaching and healing that brought the leaders of the Jerusalem church to the attention of the authorities once more. Luke's method in the early chapters of Acts is to present alternating pictures of the church as a fellowship of believers and of the church in contact with the world of unbelievers. The scheme is quite apparent: the focus is on believers in chapter 1, followed by Peter's challenge to the Pentecost throng in 2:1–41; believers are noted again in 2:42–47, then further confrontation with unbelievers as a result of the miracle of the healing of the lame man in 3:1–4:22; once more there is a section depicting the life of the church in 4:23–5:11, followed by an account of further contact with those outside and the opposition that developed in 5:12–42. The same twofold pattern persists into Acts 6.

5:12–16. In these verses the continued growth of the church is noted. Here the emphasis is on the mighty works of the apostles rather than on preaching, although public testimony must have accompanied the miracles by way of explanation. Purged of sin within its ranks, the church once more enjoyed the prospering of God.

With a grievous offense judged and the church purified, God was once more pleased to grant various "signs and wonders" in abundance through the apostles. This was one of the distinctives of the men appointed and trained by the Savior (John 14:12), and in the early days of the church's life miracles seem to have been performed by them alone (2:43; 4:22, 30; 5:12); but with the appointment of the seven the privilege became shared with this group, at least with Stephen (6:8) and Philip (8:6, 13). Later still, Paul and Barnabas exercised this function (14:3; 15:12). It would be hazardous to insist that no others participated, but from Luke's account it is evident that the working of miracles was vested mainly in the leaders of the church and helped to accredit them as Christ's representatives. Paul could refer to signs as marking him off from others as a true apostle of Jesus Christ (2 Cor. 12:12). It seems that the healings took place in the temple, for Luke informs us that the apostles were frequenting Solomon's Colonnade, an area along the east side of the enclosure, where Jesus had resorted for teaching (John 10:23).

What follows appears to involve a contradiction, namely, that the people kept their distance out of fear, unwilling to identify with them, yet "multitudes" were added to the Lord. But those who were moved by fear need not be thought of as the people, but rather the saints. According to some scholars, only the apostles were in Solomon's Colonnade. "The rest," who held back from joining them, could be a reference to believers who had been awed by what had happened through the instrumentality of Peter in the Ananias incident (in Acts 17:9 "the others" indicates believers rather than outsiders). Then follows Luke's comment that the people in general "highly regarded" the apostles. This is understandable in the light of the miracles that were taking place (v. 12; cf. 4:21). So the group was made up of apostles, the rest of the believers, the admiring people, and the new converts made at this time. These included "women," some of whom would soon have to pay a price for their adherence to the faith.

The healing activity of the apostles was not confined to the temple but took place here and there throughout the city. Luke seems to say that it was the new believers who desired help for their loved ones and brought them into the streets in the hope that Peter's shadow might fall on them and bring relief (cf. Luke 8:43–44; Acts 19:12). Public interest was mounting to a high pitch. For the first time notice was taken of the arrival of people from outside the city, bringing their loved ones for healing. History was repeating itself (Matt. 4:24), and the way was being prepared for the advance of the gospel into Judea (Acts 9:31; cf. 1:8).

The summary that concludes here does not contain any mention of apostolic proclamation of the gospel, concentrating as it does on the healing ministry; yet the addition of multitudes to the church certainly implies fidelity in preaching the Word.

Verses 17–32. The reaction of official Judaism to all this activity of the apostles is strikingly similar to what has been noted in regard to Acts 3 and 4. One can retrace the same cycle—healing, preaching, popular response, then the attempt of the authorities to intervene by suppression, leading in turn to the apostles' further testimony to the religious hierarchy.

5:17–21a. This new wave of opposition, like the former (4:1), stemmed from the Sadducees, who were dominant in the Sanhedrin and operated in response to the high priest, who was one of themselves. Anger at the preaching of the resurrection of

Christ had previously spurred them to try to curtail the Christian movement, but now an additional factor is mentioned, their "jealousy" of the apostles. To think that these common men had the temerity to ignore the orders of their superiors and were enjoying ever greater support from the people! This was getting to be unbearable. One senses here an echo of the frustration of these leaders at an earlier time, when the resurrection of Lazarus had created great enthusiasm on behalf of Jesus (John 11:47–48). The fear of a revolutionary movement at that time may now have been revived. If so, it only demonstrated how completely the Sadducees misunderstood both Jesus and His followers.

Formerly they had arrested Peter and John; now they put the whole apostolic company in prison overnight. But "an angel of the Lord" proved to be their deliverer (cf. Heb 1:14). Peter could look back on this as a dress rehearsal for his own escape at a later time (12:7–11). Luke the historian has much to relate about angels in connection with Christ and His church, evidently accepting at face value this element of early Christian tradition and giving it a prominent place. While it is true that the word for "angel" can also mean "messenger" and can indicate a human being, this is rare; it is wholly unlikely in the present instance, where the full description "angel of the Lord" emphasizes a celestial origin and dignity.

Acting in the Lord's name, the angel directed the apostles to resume their preaching in the temple. When God sets before His servants an open door, no one can shut it (Rev 3:8). The message to be given concerned "this new life," a suitable term for salvation in Christ, the author of life (Acts 3:15). It bears comparison with "this Way" in 22:4.

5:21b–26. The design of God was totally different from that of the Sanhedrin. Whereas the latter planned by prison and further threatening to intimidate the followers of the Lord Jesus, God wrought to discomfit the rulers and to show them that the proclamation was to continue with His blessing.

The situation called for a meeting of the nation's highest tribunal, and the high priest duly summoned the Council and all the Senate of the people. At first glance this seems to indicate two separate bodies meeting in combined session. But the Senate, or Gerousia, was the original title of Israel's council of elders in the intertestamental period (cf. Exod. 12:21, LXX), and Luke may have been intent simply on identifying the two.

106

This is feasible grammatically, since the conjunction often translated "and" can also be rendered "even," or, as here, a dash may be used, when the context makes this suitable (cf. "that is, the full senate of the Israelite nation," NEB).

Officers were sent to fetch the imprisoned apostles (cf. John 7:32). They returned empty-handed, reporting that the prison was empty despite the presence of guards in their usual positions. There are unanswered questions here. Were no other prisoners being kept at this time? Had the crime rate dropped to nothing because of the preaching of the gospel? Or had other prisoners gone out along with the apostles? Or had the apostles been kept in a separate area?

The situation was naturally disquieting to the Council, now thoroughly bewildered by this fresh turn of events. Especially concerned was "the captain of the temple guard." This man was no petty officer. He belonged to the priestly aristocracy; he was second in authority to the high priest, and could minister on the Day of Atonement in his place if necessary. As chief of police in the temple area, he had power to make arrests by means of the Levite police under his jurisdiction.[2] When word reached the Sanhedrin that the missing prisoners were only a short distance away in the temple, engaged in teaching the people, the captain joined his subordinates in seeking out their quarry. The popular esteem enjoyed by the apostles dictated persuasion rather than force, but there was no resistance of any kind on the part of those who trusted God to work out their predicament to His glory.

5:27–32. When brought before the Council for questioning, the apostles were content to state their defense in terms of fidelity to God. They were merely doing what He had commanded them.

The high priest opened the questioning with a reminder that the Sanhedrin had issued strict orders not to teach in this name, a reference to the ban placed on Peter and John (4:18). His complaint that the apostles had so completely ignored the order as to fill Jerusalem with their teaching is an unwilling confession of the widespread impact of Christian testimony on the city during a brief period. In the high priest's remarks no more respect is shown to the Lord Jesus than was accorded Him

[2]Joachim Jeremias, *Jerusalem in the Time of Jesus,* 160–63, 180.

during His ministry. By avoiding direct reference to Him, choosing to speak of "this name," "this man," he was perpetuating the practice attested by the Gospels (John 9:16, 24, 29; 11:47; 18:30, 40; 19:12; cf. Matt. 27:63), a practice largely followed by Jews in later centuries. The reference to the "blood" of Jesus finds its explanation in Matthew 27:24–25. It is quite apparent from the high priest's complaint that he was on the defensive, not knowing how to deal with a situation that was getting out of hand.

Seconded by the other apostles, Peter took exactly the same position he had voiced on the earlier occasion (4:19–20). When one is under orders from God, he cannot obey contrary orders from men. This principle was so deeply imbedded in the history of Israel (e.g., Moses versus Pharaoh, Daniel versus the king of Babylon) that the Council could not question its validity. With this in view, it is no surprise that obedience should hold an important place in the teaching of Peter's first epistle (1:2, 14, 22; 3:1, 6; 4:17).

By referring to God as "the God of our fathers," Peter seemed intent on suggesting that the great interventions the Almighty made during Old Testament days had simply prepared the way for this climactic development of the sending of the Lord Jesus as Savior of His people. In fact, the same terms "raised" and "Savior" are used in the LXX translation of Judges 2:18; 3:9. This leads to the likely conclusion that "raised up" (v. 30) is not an allusion to resurrection, which Peter was apparently including in the exaltation of Jesus, but to the emergence of Jesus in the arena of history (he used the same approach in 3:26, in line with 3:22).

Peter followed his characteristic method of contrasting the adverse human reception of Jesus with God's vindication of Him. The word "tree" symbolizes the cross, another Petrine feature (10:39; 1 Peter 2:24). As exalted to the right hand of God, the Lord Jesus is described as "Prince," or Leader (*archēgos*), and "Savior." The former term occurs also in 3:15. Christ has opened the door of salvation, making full provision for those who follow Him by faith. "Savior," as a term, is little used in the Gospels (Luke 2:11; John 4:42), but Jesus Himself was fully aware of His saving mission (Luke 19:10).

Only after His resurrection did the awareness of His Saviorhood blossom forth into full recognition, for only then did the whole sweep of the divine purpose that centered in Him come into focus. Peter summed up what His saving work was intended to mean for Israel: "repentance" and "forgiveness of sins." These had been coupled in Peter's public preaching (2:38; 3:19). The sin that especially called for repentance was the rejection of Jesus as God's appointed Savior.

The apostle concluded by saying, "And we are witnesses of these things." He and his companions were not expounding some new philosophy of their own devising. On the contrary, they were simply passing on to others what they knew to be true.

The Greek for "things" can also mean "message" (it is so used in 5:20), but here the term is employed with reference to the death and resurrection of the Lord Jesus. The apostles' witness was aided by that of the Holy Spirit, hence the boldness with which they had been able to speak (cf. John 15:25–27).

Verses 33–42. Just when it seemed that the apostles' boldness in addressing the Sanhedrin might cost them their lives, God brought to their aid an unexpected advocate, from within the ranks of the Council itself, who pleaded successfully for a policy of moderation.

5:33–39. The threat of the use of violent measures against the apostles was very real when Peter finished speaking, but a more moderate attitude was taken after hearing Gamaliel's counsel.

The Council members were furious (literally, "sawn through") and ready to kill the apostles. This is psychologically understandable, for the high priest had alluded to the death of Jesus in such a way as to intimate that leaders of the Jews were highly sensitive to the charge that they were responsible for that death. For Peter to ignore the protest and reiterate his charge (v. 30) was more than they could bear. Their strong reaction may be taken as an indirect admission of guilt.

At this juncture the providence of God brought forward a Pharisee to quiet the rage of the Sadducees and throttle their murderous intent. (Later on, the same tension between the two parties was a means of deliverance for Paul [23:6–10].) Gamaliel, a distinguished teacher, was the man under whom Paul studied in his early days (22:3). Ordering the removal of the apostles, he talked very frankly with his associates, urging caution and moderation and warning against usurping the prerogative of God Himself by passing hasty judgment on a movement that, for all they knew, might be an instrument in the hands of the Almighty.

His counsel was typically Pharisaic. The same scrupulosity that led the Pharisees to almost fanatical devotion to Levitical purity (in order to be sure they had done enough, they felt they should do more than enough in order to be on the safe side) caused them to be careful in the administration of justice. For instance, instead of giving forty lashes in a beating, they would settle for thirty-nine lest by miscount they should happen to give too many and so become guilty of undue severity (2 Cor. 11:24).

Gamaliel's thesis was that movements of a revolutionary nature, when inspired by human desire and effort, have a way of coming to nought. He offered two illustrations, and doubtless could have furnished more (cf. 21:38). It was a restless age, with many messianic pretenders seeking a following. The first case was that of a certain Theudas, whose small force of four hundred men was readily dispersed when he himself lost his life. Josephus mentions a man of this name,[3] an imposter who persuaded many to take their possessions and follow him to the Jordan, evidently posing as a second Moses who would part the waters and lead them out to a place where they would be free from Roman domination. By acting quickly, the procurator Fadus intercepted the people, killed many, and took numerous prisoners. Theudas himself was executed.

Was this the same man to whom Gamaliel was referring? It is doubtful, for the regime of Fadus belonged to a period approximately a decade later than the time of Gamaliel's speech. Furthermore, to assume that Luke got his information from Josephus rather than from some source contemporary with the events of this chapter is precarious; the Jewish historian indicated that many people were involved, as well as their possessions, whereas Luke stated that a relatively small number were with Theudas. Also, Luke was precise in saying that this man was prior to Judas, whom he cited as Gamaliel's second illustration. It is hard to believe that a historian of Luke's stature would reverse the order of two events that had happened a generation removed from each other. So, even though Theudas was not a common name (Josephus has no other in his history), it is probable that the Theudas of Luke's account was a different person than the one named by Josephus.

---

[3] Josephus, *Antiquities* XX.5.1.

The second example was not as felicitous as the first in supporting Gamaliel's thesis, for the truth of the matter is that, whereas Judas the Galilean was killed, the Zealot movement that he had spawned was growing all the time, and in another generation would lead the nation over the precipice in a disastrous war with Rome. The revolt of Judas stemmed from his opposition to the "census," which gave the Romans information on the wealth of their subjects and led to the imposition of burdensome taxes. To hold, as some scholars do, that Luke was merely putting words in the mouth of Gamaliel, since he had no way of knowing what the rabbin actually said, runs into a snag by the very fact that when Luke wrote Acts, around thirty years after this gathering of the Council, it would have been perfectly clear to him and to everybody else that the Zealot movement had not come to nothing—it was growing in strength.

Despite some deficiency in his presentation, Gamaliel had a restraining effect on his peers, especially by his parting observation that in dealing harshly with the apostles they might be found "fighting against God." This possibility was frightening to a pious Israelite. When Saul of Tarsus found that in his case it was an actuality (because of his persecuting the church of God), he was broken and repentant (26:14; 1 Tim. 1:13–15).

The fact that Gamaliel successfully resisted the policy of the Sadducees meant that the Jewish leadership was divided on the issue of persecuting the church, for the Pharisees naturally lined up behind Gamaliel. This guaranteed a period of freedom from pressure for the growing church until new issues were raised by the preaching of Stephen (chaps. 6–7).

5:40–42 The Council did not see fit to follow Gamaliel's advice completely, for he counseled that they let the apostles alone. But they worked off their anger and frustration toward God's servants by beating them and sternly warning them to stop their public speaking in the name of Jesus. The apostles went forth nursing their bruises but rejoicing at the privilege of suffering for the name of Christ. This was in line with the teaching of the Lord Jesus (Matt. 5:11–12), and it must have been experienced over and over in the days of the early church (e.g., Acts 16:23–25; cf. 1 Peter 4:12–16).

Unconcerned about what might happen to them for disobeying the orders of the Sanhedrin, the apostles went right back to their work of teaching and preaching, making it known that Jesus was the Christ (cf. Acts 2:36). They had already received a demonstration of God's protection, and they realized that their support from the people would make it difficult for the Sanhedrin to carry out any official persecution on a major scale.

The construction of the closing verse of the chapter should be noted. In all probability the order of the words "teaching" and "proclaiming" is reversed from the normal order (teaching being more appropriate for the ministry "from house to house," and preaching for the proclamation "in the temple" (cf. 2:46). The gatherings in the temple would naturally have been addressed by the apostles, with believers supporting them by their presence and personal work among the listeners as opportunity afforded. The meetings at home set the pattern found both in Acts and in the Epistles, namely, the church in the house. Here Christian fellowship found expression, and instruction in the things of God was carried forward on a more or less methodical basis (cf. 2:42). Doubtless such gatherings were open to interested neighbors (cf. 1 Cor. 14:23) and became an instrument for evangelism. The children of believers also would be welcome.

CARE OF THE NEEDY (6:1–7)

In this picture of the church at Jerusalem there is described an important administrative development that averted a breach in the unity of the Lord's people and actually contributed to the further growth of the Christian community.

6:1. "In those days" establishes only a loose connection with the foregoing events. Luke provided no precise time notices in this portion of his narrative, but the interval between Pentecost and this episode was probably quite brief.

The increase in the number of disciples posed a problem, since some were not self-supporting. Particularly acute was the need of the "widows." Historically, Israel had to be reminded from time to time of its obligation to care for these, along with orphans (Deut. 14:29; 24:19; 26:12; Isa. 1:17; Zech. 7:10). It was a blemish on the record of some Pharisees that they took advantage of the destitute and dispossessed them (Luke 20:47). The early church's concern for this group was confirmed by James, who included in his definition of true religion the care of widows and orphans (James 1:27). In time, within the church an order of widows developed, consisting of the more elderly, who were cared for by the congregation and in turn performed various services according to their abilities (1 Tim. 5:3–10).

Theoretically, Christian widows might have been eligible for help by the Jewish authorities, but this was probably increasingly difficult to receive, as the gulf between Christian and non-Christian Jews widened. Furthermore, the church itself would not encourage this practice, for failure to care for its own members would place a stigma on this new movement in Israel.

A "daily distribution" is mentioned, undoubtedly of food, in view of the mention of tables. Probably the apostles took the funds brought to them (4:35) and in person or through helpers bought the provisions that were distributed. With the increase in numbers, the arrangement became steadily more unwieldly, with the result that some of the widows, especially those of the Hellenists, "were being overlooked." There is nothing to suggest that the neglect was intentional. As noted under 2:42, this sharing was a practical application of the spiritual fellowship of the church, so that any breakdown of the material aspect would be likely to have unfortunate effects on spiritual rapport. So the apostles were doubly concerned.

How were the "Grecian Jews" (simply "Hellenists" in the original) and the Hebrews to be distinguished? Luke gives no explanation. The most obvious distinction lies in the terms themselves—a difference in language. The one group used Greek, the other Hebrew or Aramaic. Both groups were Israelites rather than Gentiles. If the Hellenists were Gentiles, they must have been proselytes to the Jewish faith before becoming believers in Jesus (cf. v. 5). Otherwise there would have been added antagonism from the synagogue toward the Nazarenes, but Luke says nothing of such antagonism. Furthermore, the difficulty felt by many in the Jerusalem church over admitting Gentiles without circumcision (11:1–18; 15:5) would be strange indeed if that congregation had already received a company of Gentiles into its fellowship.

For understanding the status of the Hellenists it is well to look back to Pentecost. Many of those who listened to Peter and became believers had come to Jerusalem from areas of the Dispersion where Greek was spoken. These Jews had their own synagogue arrangements (6:9). It would be wholly natural for such people, after becoming disciples, to maintain a special relationship with one another within the unity of the whole church. "They most probably established their own house-congregations in which they made use of the Greek language, the LXX, and the traditions related to it as they once did in the Diaspora synagogue."[4]

The notion that the "Hebrews" were of Samaritan stock and were a minority group in the church as well as the Hellenists is improbable, for in that case the assumption would have to be made that the Hebrews were in charge of the distribution, for the murmuring was against them, whereas actually the operation was carried on under the direction of the Twelve.

Language was not the only distinguishing factor of the two groups, for if Stephen was truly representative of the Hellenists' viewpoint, they had reservations about the temple that were not shared by the Hebrew brethren. As a result they became the target of a violent persecution following Stephen's death. But we need not conclude that the Hellenists were influenced by Qumran and its estrangement from the temple.[5]

6:2–4. To meet the crisis concerning the widows, the apostles summoned the congregation. It was an indication of the church's spiritual soundness that the situation was faced publicly and immediately with a view to removing the grievance. The apostles suggested that the smoother operation of the current system would require them to give more time and attention to it, and this would mean that they could not properly fulfill their primary task of preaching and teaching "the word of God." This was a sacrifice they were not prepared to make; it would mean putting secondary things first. As appointees of the Head of the church, they took the initiative in directing the congregation to a solution, namely, to select seven men to supervise the distribution. Congregational participation was honored within the framework of apostolic administration.

It was expedient to remind the people that certain qualifications ought to be kept in mind in selecting those who were to serve. These were of three kinds: ethical, having a good testimony because of sterling character and conduct; spiritual, full of the Spirit; and practical, possessing the wisdom to manage this operation.

---

[4]Leonhard Goppelt, *Apostolic and Post-apostolic Times*, 53.

[5]Reginald H. Fuller, *The New Testament in Current Study* (New York: Scribner, 1971), 127–28; J. A. Fitzmyer, "Jewish Christianity in Acts in Light of the Qumran Scrolls," in *Studies in Luke-Acts*, ed. Keck and Martyn, 238.

The apostles were relieved at the prospect that they could thenceforth devote themselves "to prayer and the ministry of the word." For them, the trouble in the church became a blessing in disguise. By including prayer, they hinted that this was a time-consuming exercise and one that was indispensable to effective ministry.

It is of some interest that the same word for "ministry" (*diakonia*) is applied both to the care of physical needs (v. 1) and to the communication of God's truth (v. 4). Both elements had an important place in the ministry of Jesus. A church dedicated to the continuation of that ministry (1:1) could not afford to slight either aspect.

6:5–6. In listing the seven men, Luke anticipated Stephen's prominence in the continuing narrative by naming him first and adding the description, "full of faith and of the Holy Spirit" (cf. 6:10; 7:55). Stephen had the supernatural equipment for miraculous works and for dynamic preaching; again Luke seemed to be anticipating Stephen's service beyond his duties as one of the seven.

Philip is named next, and he too figured in gospel outreach as the one who brought the message to Samaria (8:5). Next to nothing is known of the other men. Nicolas was thought by some of the early Fathers to have been the founder of the Nicolaitans (Rev 2:6, 15), but the supposition is tenuous. By noting that he was a proselyte of Antioch, Luke, with an eye on later missionary developments, may have been hinting at the prominence to be achieved by Antioch, and the part of the Hellenists in bringing the gospel to that area (11:19–20). There may also be a hint that Luke himself belonged to Antioch (see comment on 11:28).

It should be observed that all of the seven bore Greek names. While this does not prove all were Hellenists, members of the complaining group (for the apostles Andrew and Philip had Greek names and were Hebraists), yet this conclusion is quite possible. If this was the case, the Hebrew segment showed real grace in selecting men to serve who belonged to the aggrieved minority. Luke did not call them deacons, a term that came into use at a somewhat later time (Phil. 1:1; 1 Tim. 3:8–13).

The NASB rendering of verse 6 is ambiguous: "And these they brought before the apostles; and, after praying, they laid their hands on them." The identity of the second "they" becomes unclear, but there is no doubt that those who prayed and laid their hands on the appointees were the apostles. The decisive factor appears to be the word of the apostles to the effect that they themselves would set the appointees over this task.[6] If the men chosen were set apart by the apostles, the laying on of hands would signify that the seven would be doing their work under the authority of the apostles. Implied also is the pledge of the apostles to stand behind the appointees and support them in every possible way (cf. 13:3). Clearly the purpose of the rite in this instance was not the communication of the Holy Spirit (8:17), for the possession of the Spirit in fullness was a qualification for the selection of the seven (6:3) and is explicitly noted in the case of Stephen (v. 5).

Nothing more is reported about the seven as a group. Presumably their task was taken over by the elders (11:30) after the Hellenists were driven out in the coming persecution (8:1).

6:7. This summary statement seems intended to suggest that the adjustment of the problem of the widows brought renewed blessing to the believing community. "So the word of God spread" is a shorthand way of saying that the influence of the gospel was expanding (cf. 12:24; 19:20). As a result, the number of disciples in Jerusalem was greatly augmented. The three thousand converts (2:41) had increased to five thousand men (4:4). Luke's further statements (5:14; 6:7) are not specific, but in a general way indicate further growth.

J. Jeremias has carefully estimated the population of Jerusalem at this period between twenty-five thousand and thirty thousand, not counting some eighteen thousand priests and Levites.[7] At festival times the number of people in and around the city was greatly increased. It is probable that believers in Jesus represented about one-fifth of the population of the city at the time of Stephen, only to be diminished by persecution shortly after. This shrinkage was balanced by increase in other places (9:31).

The "priests" who were identifying with the faith at this time were not of the Sadducean aristocracy (we have no record of a Sadducee becoming a believer) but were ordinary priests of a truly pious spirit, such as the father of John the Baptist (Luke 1:6). Doubtless they had heard Peter and others bearing witness

---

[6] See a good discussion of the problem in R. P. C. Hanson, *The Acts,* 91–92.
[7] Jeremias, *Jerusalem,* 252.

in the temple courts and were greatly impressed. They must have known of the attempts of the Sanhedrin to stop the apostolic testimony and were aware of their ineffectiveness. They saw the hand of God at work in their midst. Since believers were permitted to use the temple, there is no reason to think that these converted priests were excluded from the priesthood. However, if Luke's notice of them is intended to suggest that they were influenced by Stephen, who is mentioned next, these priests would likely have been prepared to give up their priestly service voluntarily.

PERSECUTION OF STEPHEN (6:8–7:60)

The summary account of Stephen's public ministry of preaching and debating reveals a man peculiarly gifted and empowered. His very success prompted his opponents to instigate false charges against him supported by false witnesses. Even in the presence of the Council Stephen maintained his fearless, searching exposure of the unbelief of Judaism, resulting in his martyrdom.

Verses 8–15. The background for Stephen's speech before the Council is presented by Luke in terms of both miracle and the spoken word. In the various factors involved—the dual ministry, the inability of his adversaries to match him in debate, the resort to false witnesses, the arrest and appearance before the Sanhedrin—one notices a striking parallel to the experience of our Lord.

6:8–10. In addition to his service on behalf of the needy, about which nothing specific is said, Stephen went on to engage in a dual ministry of miracle-working and witnessing. Many today have reversed the pattern by diminishing their emphasis on gospel testimony in favor of social service.

It would be totally wrong to hold that the seven were emerging as a rival group to the apostles and that miracles were counted on as substantiating their right to leadership on a par with the men chosen by the Lord in the days of His flesh. There is no evidence of any such tension (cf. 8:14). "Grace and power" are coupled here as in the ministry of the apostles (4:33).

The general description of Stephen resembles that of Jesus in Luke 24:19. His faith (v. 5) enabled him to lay hold of divine grace, which in turn released the power of God in the performance of mighty works. This brought him to the attention of Hellenists who were not believers but were passionately devoted to Judaism.

Nothing precise is indicated as to the substance of the debates that followed in the synagogue. Whereas the temple was devoted to worship (though teaching could be carried on in its courts) the synagogue was dedicated to instruction, and this often led to discussion. There is some uncertainty about Luke's reference to the synagogue in this instance. Did he mean that all the groups named shared one building, or that each of the five groups had its own, or that the number of buildings lay somewhere between these extremes?

The first option is the most probable. Jeremias identifies this synagogue with one discovered on Ophel, the southern portion of the temple mount, early in this century.[8] He notes that a guesthouse and baths were attached. Jews of the Dispersion gathered here, their diverse geographical origins proving no hindrance to the cultivation of their common interests. The Freedmen have often been identified as descendants of the Jews who were taken to Rome by Pompey as captives of war about 60 B.C., but Sherwin-White doubts that after such a long interval their descendants would be thus classified.[9]

Especially interesting is the mention of those Hellenists who came from Cilicia. There is a possibility that Saul of Tarsus (21:39) may have been one of those who confronted Stephen and, like his fellows, found himself unable to withstand the "wisdom" of this Spirit-filled man. Stephen's capability fits in remarkably with a prediction of Jesus regarding His persecuted followers. "This will result in your being witnesses to them. But make up your mind not to worry beforehand how you will defend yourselves. For I will give you words and wisdom that none of your adversaries will be able to resist or contradict" (Luke 21:13–15; cf. Matt.. 10:19–20). The spiritual gifts exercised by Stephen agree closely with those enumerated in 1 Corinthians 12:8–9.

6:11–15. Defeated in argument, the unbelieving Hellenists prevailed on certain individuals to circulate reports that they had heard Stephen "speak words of blasphemy against Moses and

[8]Joachim Jeremias, *Jerusalem in the Time of Jesus,* 66.

[9]A. N. Sherwin-White, *Roman Society and Roman Law in the New Testament,* 152.

against God." The language is vague, but the charges were sufficiently inflammatory to excite "the people" as well as their leaders, both "the elders and the teachers of the law."

The people have already been mentioned as those among whom Stephen had been doing mighty works (v. 8). Up to this time the population of the city, generally speaking, had been favorable to the followers of Jesus, and this had deterred the authorities from taking harsh measures against those who were preaching Christ publicly. But now the ominous rumor that Stephen was disloyal to what Jews held most dear was bringing a swift reversal of popular sentiment.

The Hellenists took note of this shift and turned it to their advantage by making bold to seize Stephen and bring him before the Council. Their "false witnesses" were on hand to state their allegations. Now the charges became more specific. The claim that Stephen had spoken against God became the assertion that he had been speaking against the "holy place," namely, the temple. The charge that Stephen had spoken blasphemy against Moses was now formulated as having been spoken against "the law." Finally the accusations became still more explicit. The witnesses were prepared to assert that they had heard Stephen make the claim that Jesus of Nazareth would destroy the temple.

Here one detects an echo of the Master's trial, when other false witnesses asserted that they had heard Him say, "I will destroy this man-made temple and in three days will build another, not made by man" (Mark 14:58). This was a distortion of what Jesus had declared on this subject (John 2:19). Never had He predicted that He would destroy the temple in Jerusalem, though He had predicted its destruction (Mark 13:2), which came to pass in the war with Rome. Likely Stephen had declared the truth of the new creation based on the resurrection of the Lord Jesus. In the new order the physical temple had no function to fulfill (John 4:21).

The other great bulwark of Judaism, the Mosaic Law, was likewise affected by the work of Jesus Christ. Stephen seems to have perceived what Paul later emphatically declared, that no one could be justified by the Law. Although Jesus lived under the Law and denied that He had come to destroy it, He saw that His own mission would fulfill the Law (Matt. 5:17–18), and He Himself would become the law of His people, living and not static. Any change in the "customs" (the totality of the Mosaic legislation) that Moses had delivered, the prophets had applied, and tradition had amplified, was regarded as the rankest heresy by those who had not learned to look beyond Moses to Christ.

When the false witnesses had finished their tirade, all eyes gravitated to Stephen to see what his reaction would be. What they saw was a man with face aglow, for the false testimony had brought to Stephen the realization that he was following in the succession of His Lord, being tried before the same tribunal, his words twisted as were those of Jesus, and with the multitude crying out for his blood. The Spirit of glory was indeed resting on him, betokening the presence of God. Criticism and opposition could not destroy his composure any more than it did that of Jesus. His face was radiant, like that of an angel (cf. Judg. 13:6; Luke 9:26).

Chapter 7, verses 1-8. Some introductory observations should be made before examining Stephen's address to the Council. For one thing, this is the longest of the speeches given in Acts, filling most of this chapter. The fact that Luke includes it shows that he attached considerable importance to its content and to the whole situation in which Stephen was involved. The address differs from those that have been included so far in that Christ is not prominent, being introduced only at the end (v. 52) and then not by name (cf. a somewhat similar situation in chap. 17). Furthermore, His resurrection, which had been the burden of Peter's sermons, is not mentioned at all.

Luke's interest in Stephen was probably due to his grasp of the strategic fact that this man emerged just as the church was being called on to undertake a new stage of its mission to the world, the advance to Samaria—an intermediate step between Jewish and Gentile Christianity. Stephen was hardly removed from the scene by death when Philip carried the gospel to Samaria (8:1-5). The address preserved for us contains certain evidences of Samaritan influence, particularly with reference to the temple, making probable the conclusion that Stephen was fully aware that if the young church did not assume a different stance toward the temple than that which current Judaism had, it could not hope to succeed in winning the Samaritans to Christ.[10]

It is significant that Stephen did not attempt to meet the

[10] Martin H. Scharlemann, *Stephen: a Singular Saint,* 91.

charges raised against him by direct and detailed refutation. In fact, he did not mount a defense in the technical sense, for he was less interested in clearing himself than in declaring the truth so as to reach the consciences of his hearers. He had almost nothing to say about the Law; and with respect to the temple, to which he devoted more attention, he did not discuss the allegation stated by the false witnesses (6:14).

His methodology was to sketch the history of his people from Abraham down to the days of David and Solomon, noting that divine revelation was not restricted to the land of Israel (it came in Mesopotamia, Egypt, and the wilderness) or to the temple. Interwoven with these motifs was the failure of Israel to respond to God in faith and obedience (somewhat after the pattern of Ps. 78). The address came to a sudden climax in the assertion that this rebelliousness had manifested itself most fatally in the rejection of God's supreme disclosure in the Righteous One. Yet the way had been prepared for this final accusation by the allusions to the rejection of Joseph by his brothers (v. 9) and of Moses by Israel (vv. 23–29, 39).

The first eight verses are devoted to Abraham. Stephen launched into this discourse immediately after the opening question from the high priest, who presumably was Caiaphas, the man who had presided over the Sanhedrin's trial of Jesus. The chief items stressed were that God's dealings with Abraham had started not in Canaan but in Mesopotamia and that even in Canaan he had lived as a pilgrim, yet had enjoyed a covenant relationship with the Almighty.

7:2. "Brothers and fathers" was the same form of address used by Paul in speaking to the throng in the temple (22:1). Stephen shared the legacy of Israel's history with his audience. He was no Samaritan, as some have thought.[11] His opening thrust was the reminder that God had begun His dealings with the father of the Hebrew people when he had lived in a foreign land, thus making the point that the divine presence was not restricted to the land of Israel.

A reader of Genesis 12 would naturally assume that God's command to depart came to Abram in Haran, Abram's departure being mentioned at the close of chapter 11. Note the tense of the verb, *had said,* in Genesis 12:1. In stating that the

[11] See Johannes Munck, *The Acts of the Apostles,* 285.

divine revelation came "before he lived in Haran," Stephen was following Jewish tradition.[12] Even before touching on the place of revelation, Stephen noted the quality of it by observing that the *shekinah* that appeared on Mount Sinai and later engulfed the shrine of the tabernacle was already anticipated in God's disclosure to the patriarch Abraham, and this outside the land, apart from the tabernacle, long before the Law was given.

7:3–5. Following the will of God may involve great sacrifices. In this case it meant separation from land and kindred. The life of faith is a pilgrim life (cf. Heb. 11:13–16). Close at hand was the moment when believers in Jerusalem would be leaving land and kindred because of the gospel (Acts 8:1; 11:19).

Stephen did not attempt to account for the period of residence in Haran before the journey to Canaan was resumed. The mention of the death of Abraham's father, Terah, at this point has led some interpreters to conclude that Terah had been opposed to going any farther than Haran, and that Abram had waited until his father died. Some of his relatives remained in Haran (Gen 24).

Abraham's adopted country is curiously described as "this land where you are now living." Why did Stephen say "you" rather than "we"? This is too slender a basis on which to claim that by dissociating himself from his hearers Stephen was admitting he was not a Jew. Probably all that was intended was a pointed reminder to his audience that if they wished to boast about being Abraham's descendants, they should be grateful for their forefather's faith and not settle down too securely in their land, as though it were their fixed inheritance. Special emphasis was put on the fact that Abraham was not permitted to own "even a foot of ground," though he walked up and down in it. Stephen was speaking of the early years of nomadic wandering rather than of the more settled period when Abraham purchased a burying place from the Hittites (Gen. 23). Passing notice was taken of the twofold promise to the patriarch regarding the land and offspring. His posterity would inherit the land in which he lived as a pilgrim. Abraham had had to believe God for both provisions, for in those early years he had no son.

7:6–8. Prior to the enjoyment of the land as their home,

---

[12] Cf. Philo, *On Abraham* 70–72; Josephus, *Antiquities* I.7.1.

Abraham's descendants would have to be tested in the furnace of affliction in a foreign country. This experience was often referred to by Moses and the prophets, along with the deliverance wrought by God, as the background for the emergence of Israel as a nation and as the chosen people. Even so, some preferred Egypt with its bondage to the prospect of Canaan with the difficulties of arrival and acquisition (vv. 39–40). "Four hundred years," being a round number, agrees with the time notice in Genesis 15:13. More precise is the figure of four hundred and thirty years given in Exodus 12:40. Paul used the latter reckoning (Gal. 3:17) but spreads out the interval to make it commence with God's promise of offspring to Abraham.

In quoting from Genesis 15 the promise of God to restore Abraham's posterity to their "place" in Canaan, Stephen added an item apparently taken from Exodus 3:12 (it is not in Genesis 15), that there Israel would "serve" God.

"The covenant of circumcision" was given to Abraham (Gen. 17), the man of faith (note how Paul handled this in Rom. 4:11), a point that needed emphasizing because the Jews had come to associate circumcision more with Moses and the Law than with Abraham (John 7:22–23).

Verses 9–16. Having mentioned "the twelve patriarchs," Stephen now singled out one of these sons of Jacob for detailed comment, and this for several reasons. As with Abraham, so with Joseph, God manifested His presence outside the land of Canaan. The bad treatment he received from his brothers served to foreshadow the rejection of the Lord Jesus by His own people, even as his forgiveness of his brothers was a foretaste of the readiness of the Savior to forgive the imposition of death on the cross (Luke 23:34).

7:9–10. Joseph's early days at home are passed by with only a brief notice. Because his brothers were "jealous" of him (Gen 37:11), they sold him into Egypt. The same chapter emphasizes that the jealousy deepened into hatred. But "God was with him." This was evident in Joseph's prospering as Potiphar's right-hand man and in his successful resistance of temptation in the household of his master. The "troubles" that he suffered in prison (cf. Ps. 105:18) were not an indication that God had deserted him, for they befell him because of his righteous stand and were followed by a display of God's favor when He rescued His servant from these distresses and gave

123

him favor and good will in the eyes of Pharaoh. His wisdom enabled him to interpret the sovereign's dreams and later to set forth a plan for sustaining life during the seven years of famine that he predicted. This brought him into acceptance and led to his exaltation next to Pharaoh (Gen. 41:39–40).

7:11–113. The famine that Joseph had predicted came in due course and was felt not only in Egypt but also in Canaan. It proved to be a providential means of bringing Joseph's brothers to Egypt in search of grain and in this way into his presence. On their second visit Joseph made himself known to them in a highly emotional scene (Gen 45:1–4). This reconciliation was followed by a favorable reaction on the part of Pharaoh, paving the way for the settlement of the whole clan in Egypt.

7:14–16. In his latter years in Egypt Joseph was surrounded by all his kindred, whom he had sheltered and cared for, "seventy-five in all." Stephen was using the LXX text, as he did throughout and as a Hellenist would be expected to do. The LXX differs at this point (Gen. 46:27) from the Hebrew, which reads "seventy." The LXX figure was apparently calculated by including Joseph's posterity (cf. Gen. 50:23).

In what follows, Stephen was concerned with the death of the patriarchs. Curiously, he made Shechem the burial place, although it was well known that Jacob was buried with Abraham at Machpelah near Hebron (see the fairly lengthy account in Gen. 50:4–13). Further, it was Jacob, not Abraham, who purchase land from the sons of Hamor in Shechem (Gen. 33:19). Possibly, in the rapidity of his summary of the patriarchs' demise, Stephen ran together two events that were separated in time and place—the burial of Jacob in the Hebron area and that of Joseph at Shechem. That no alteration was made by Luke or anyone else to bring the statements into conformity with Genesis speaks well for the accuracy with which the speech of Stephen was transmitted and later recorded by Luke. Bearing in mind that the section before us concerns Joseph primarily, it is natural to suppose that this burial, which occurred at Shechem, was chiefly in the mind of the speaker.

Stephen's mention of Shechem was probably not casual but deliberate. This was the great center of Samaritan life, and nearby stood the Samaritan temple on Mount Gerizim, a rival of the temple at Jerusalem, which was destroyed by the Hasmonean John Hyracanus approximately a century and a half before Stephen's time. This event deepened the hostility that had existed since the days of the restoration from Babylonian captivity, when the Samaritans were refused any participation in the rebuilding of the temple at Jerusalem, and soon thereafter built their own. Added to this was the reproach presented by the mixed origin of the Samaritans to a Jewish generation sensitive to this matter (Ezra 9:10).

The rift had existed in Jesus' day (Luke 9:52–53; John 4:9–20), and He had done much to heal it by mingling with Samaritans and ministering to their needs (Luke 17:15–16), and by including a Samaritan in His teaching (Luke 10:29–37). It seems that He paid a price for this (John 8:48).

Luke himself doubtless had an interest in these neglected people. He had already reported the inclusion of Samaria in Jesus' commission (Acts 1:8), and now, with the evangelization of Samaria near at hand, he was careful to include this note about Shechem in Stephen's speech. A rigid Jew might want to forget the patriarchal contacts with Shechem, but Stephen would not permit that. To mention Shechem was almost the equivalent of calling attention to Samaria.

Verses 17–22. Here begins the great central section of the address, the portion that is concerned with Moses (vv. 17–43). The first three verses are transitional, and the remainder of the paragraph deals with his birth and early years.

7:17–19. The descendants of Abraham enjoyed a prosperous period during which their numbers increased greatly, an increase that finally troubled the Egyptians. An alien people within the land could join forces with an invader and turn on their benefactors. By playing up this fear, Egypt's king was able to make slaves of the Hebrews (Exod. 1:8–11). Even so, their numbers continued to grow (Exod. 1:12); so inhumanity was added to oppression by compelling the Hebrews to "throw out their newborn babies" (confined to the male children, according to Exodus 1:15–16).

Infanticide was a common method of limiting population growth even at the beginning of the Christian era.[13] Probably the memory of this enforced limitation during the days in Egypt helped to create a distinct hatred for this practice among the Israelites, and this, together with the biblical teaching on the sacredness of human life, caused the astounding growth of the

---

[13] W. Tarn, *Hellenistic Civilization*, 3d rev. ed. (London: Arnold, 1953), 102; Tacitus, *Histories* 5.5.

nation from what some estimate to have been a few hundred thousand at the time of the Babylonian captivity[14] to perhaps some seven million in and out of Palestine in the days of the early church. The one man Abraham ("father of a multitude") had indeed become a host.

7:20–22. What an unfavorable time in which to be born! Yet such was God's plan for Moses. The child was lovely, and therefore to abandon him was all the more painful for the loving parents, though they did so in faith (Heb. 11:23). Moses was "no ordinary child." "Extraordinary" literally meant "pertaining to the city," and since the city was, at least ideally, a place of beauty where man's skill in design and craftsmanship could be displayed to best advantage, the term took on this additional meaning. In somewhat the same way, the word *urban* provided the foundation for *urbane,* the former relating to the environment and the latter emphasizing the personal qualities suitable to such an environment.

Whereas Hebrews 11:23 accents parental feeling for the baby, Stephen's address had in view the divine estimation— lovely before God. This knowledge of the divine attitude derives from what happened when the child became a man who had an important niche in God's plan. The sparing of the little life was in keeping with His purpose.

Not only did Pharaoh's daughter save the infant, she adopted him. Her identity remains obscure. Josephus called her Thermuthis, but other ancient writers gave different names. The account of Josephus runs as follows:

> Such was the child whom Thermuthis adopted as her son, being blessed with no offspring of her own. Now one day she brought Moses to her father and showed him to him, and told him how she had been mindful for the succession, were it God's will to grant her no child of her own, by bringing up a boy of divine beauty and generous spirit, and by what a miracle she had received him of the river's bounty, 'and methought,' she said, 'to make him my child and heir to thy kingdom.' With these words she laid the babe in her father's arms; and he took and clasped him affectionately to his breast and, to please his daughter, placed his diadem upon his head. But Moses tore it off and

[14] See J. Juster, *Les Juifs* (Paris: Librairie Paul Geuthner, 1914), 209–10.

flung it to the ground, in mere childishness, and trampled it under foot; and this was taken as an omen of evil import to the kingdom.[15]

No figure in the history of Israel has been given the attention that has been given to Moses. The seven-volume work by Louis Ginzberg, *The Legends of the Jews,* supplies an abundance of legendary material for various phases of his life. Due to his place in the royal family, Moses as a lad was provided with the best education Egypt could offer. His curriculum was "all the wisdom of the Egyptians." Exodus omits this phase of Moses' preparation, but Jewish tradition magnified it. Philo declared that teachers were summoned from far and near, including Greece and Assyria.[16] In much the same way as the apocryphal Gospels make the boy Jesus uniquely precocious, Philo pictured Moses as propounding problems that his teachers could not readily solve.

The description of him as "powerful in speech and action" carries us into Moses' young manhood and may reflect Jewish tradition. His own self-estimate was somewhat different after his initial failure and flight from Egypt, compounded by isolation in Midian (Exod. 4:10). Stephen's description bears a marked resemblance to what is said of Jesus in Luke 24:19.

Verses 23–29. Here we are taken from Moses' youth to his mature years. Stephen divided the life into three segments of forty years each, so these are the middle years of Moses. It was in this period that he made an abortive attempt to identify with his people and become their deliverer. As a result of his rashness he ended up a lonely figure in Midian.

7:23–29. The statement "he decided to visit his fellow Israelites" is put in stronger language in the parallel passage in Hebrews 11:24–25, where it is recorded that Moses had come to a decision to cast his lot with Israel, though they were slaves. This meant renunciation of his claim to the throne and the whole prospect of a comfortable life in Egypt. He was prepared to suffer with his people. As the saying goes, "Blood is thicker than water."

Seizing an opportunity to intervene on behalf of a Hebrew who was being mistreated by a taskmaster, he thought that this would be a kind of signal for an uprising, which he would be

[15]Josephus, *Antiquities* II.9.7.
[16]Philo, *Moses* 1.21–24.

happy to lead. But it was an unrealistic dream, and it became a near disaster for himself when he ended up by killing the Egyptian. He had not learned to match bravery with self-control. God was unwilling to entrust the leadership of His people to one who was not yet fit to lead. The evidence for his unfitness lies in the fact that he was not penitent over the murder he had committed but was back the next day trying to persuade the Hebrews that he was their captain by posing as intermediary between two of their number who were quarreling.

The rebuff he received, plus the awareness that the killing was now public knowledge, determined his next step. He became an exile, a "foreigner" in the land of Midian, unwanted, it seems, by Egyptians and Hebrews alike. But God still had plans for his life. Meanwhile he married in the land of Midian and had two sons, Gershom and Eliezer, who were numbered among the Levites (1 Chron. 23:14–15).

Verses 30–34. These verses constitute an account of God's revelation to Moses at the burning bush.

7:30–34. What Moses had sought and failed to achieve on his own became his by divine appointment at the burning bush (Exod. 3). Meanwhile, forty years had passed, during which time he kept the sheep of his father-in-law (Exod. 3:1). Suddenly the monotony of his pastoral life was shattered by the appearance of "an angel." He became aware that he was in contact with the heavenly world. This prepared the way for "the Lord's voice," announcing that He was the God of the fathers of Moses, hinting that the present revelation was bound up with the covenant promises made to these patriarchs.

The command to remove his shoes because he was standing on "holy ground" was significant for Stephen's purpose, because it underscored the truth that God is free to reveal Himself wherever He is pleased to do so; and this place was well outside the so-called Holy Land (cf. Acts 7:2). God's time had come to deliver His people from affliction (cf. Gen. 15:13–16), and He proposed to make Moses His instrument in restoring them to the Promised Land. This servant of God, chastened by his failure and the price he had paid for it for forty years, was now almost as reluctant to lead as he had formerly been rash (Exod. 4:1–17).

Verses 35–43. Two main thoughts dominate this passage. One is the success of Moses, under God, in effecting the deliverance of Israel from Egypt and transmitting to them the Law (vv. 35–38). The other is the failure of the people to respond to Moses and their disregard of the Law he brought to them, thus meriting their ultimate removal from the land that the Lord had promised to them (vv. 39–43).

7:35–38. The very man whom Israel had refused became God's chosen instrument. Implicit here is the contrast drawn on a higher level with reference to Jesus of Nazareth at the close of the address (v. 52). Whereas Israel would not have Moses at the beginning as "ruler" and "judge" (cf. v. 27), God not only made him such but also set him apart as the "deliverer" of Israel from bondage (v. 35). Here again, one with discernment could be expected to draw the parallel with the two separate missions of Jesus, one as Savior, the other as Ruler and Judge. As deliverer, Moses performed his work in three places and over a span of forty years (v. 36).

Turning from what Moses had accomplished, Stephen spoke of what he had received from God—approbation for his exercise of the office of "prophet," to such an extent that the prophet who was to come (Deut. 18:15, 18; cf. John 1:21, 25; Acts 3:22–23) was foretold as being like him, having a unique relationship to God not enjoyed by the prophets as a whole. The Lord God was accustomed to speak to Moses face to face, as a man speaks to his friend (Exod. 33:11).

This promise of a Prophet to come was the only messianic prediction acknowledged by the Samaritans (they accepted only the Pentateuch as Scripture, and even this they altered here and there to give warrant for their position and beliefs). Gradually the Samaritans came to think of the passage as teaching that Moses would reappear and act as the Taheb (restorer) who would restore the theocracy and the worship of God in its purity. A curious circumstance is that the Samaritan Pentateuch has the passage about the prophet to come not only in Deuteronomy 18 but also inserted into the text of Exodus 20 in connection with the giving of the Law.[17] Scharlemann concludes, "There can be little doubt, therefore, that Stephen is here echoing a Samaritan context dealing with the revelation on Mount Sinai."[18]

Continuing the description of Moses and his work,

[17] Scharlemann, *Stephen*, 44–47.
[18] Ibid., 46.

Stephen noted that he was "in the assembly in the desert." The rendering "church" in the KJV is unfortunate, in view of the proper reservation of the word for the New Testament body of God's people (Matt. 16:18) and the fact that in no instance does the KJV render *ekklēsia* in this manner in the Old Testament, where it occurs dozens of times in the LXX as the translation of several Hebrew terms.

It is not said that Moses was over the assembly (cf. Heb. 3:5–6), for these were the days of the theocracy. In line with this, Moses was kept in touch with God through "the angel" of the Lord, who gave assurance of the divine presence and enablement. Perhaps a hint was intended also of the participation of angels in the giving of the Law (cf. v. 53).

It is to this subject that Stephen referred next, describing the Law as "living words" (v. 38). By the word "words" the divine origin of the Law is affirmed. But how are we to understand "living"? If the purpose was to emphasize that the Law should engage the life of God's people (Deut. 32:47), the Jews—especially the Pharisees—could affirm that they had made the Law exactly that. More likely, however, is the thought that obedience to the Law was the way to life, whereas disobedience brought death (Deut. 30:19). Paul was prepared to acknowledge that the Law, ideally considered, pointed to life, though in actuality it brought death (Rom. 7:10). Similarly Stephen held that the Law had been divinely given and had supernatural authority. He differed from his audience regarding the tenure of the Law and its power to save.

7:39–43. Having touched on the benevolent purpose of the Law, Stephen elaborated the failure of the nation Israel under it, both at the time it was given and in later days. He returned to this theme at the very close of his speech (v. 53).

Israel's rejection of Moses and of the Law are intimately connected (vv. 39–41). When "in their hearts" the people "turned back" to Egypt, they showed a hankering after the idol worship of that land and a repudiation of Moses' leadership. They rejected his espousal of a God who could not be seen and who warned them not to approach the mount where the Law was delivered. Moses had made himself invisible to the people by his trek up into Mount Sinai, and the people concluded that he was probably gone for good. Their request of Aaron, second in command, was not that he should lead them in the place of Moses, but that he should made gods to go before them. This was blatant idolatry, and it reared its ugly head again in the days of the divided kingdom (1 Kings 12:28). The godly remnant, however, never ceased to look on it as a reproach (Neh. 9:18; Ps. 106:19–22).

The lure of idolatry lies in the fact that an object is provided that appeals to the senses and removes the seeming unreality of a purely spiritual approach to the Deity. But however high the motive, the tendency is to make the physical object the recipient of worship rather than merely a means to the end of honoring the invisible God. In the light of the express prohibition of the Law, it is clearly contrary to the divine will. The deleterious effect on character and life is only too apparent in the subsequent history of Israel. "Such as thou makest thy God, such wilt thou make thyself."[19]

Part of the gratification of idolatry is the feeling of having contributed something to the worship rather than being utterly dependent on God. This is brought out in the observation that the people were rejoicing in "what their hands had made." They had contributed the gold, and the calf had been shaped by human skill (Exod. 32:2–4). That which God ordains is often described as made without hands (Mark 14:58; 2 Cor. 5:1; Col. 2:11).

The transgression proved costly to Israel (vv. 42–43), for it increased the desire for false worship, on account of which God allowed the captivity many years later. He "gave them over" to forms of worship they preferred. This is judicial language such as that used by Paul in Romans 1:24, 26, 28, where the theme is basically the same as here.

Israel was particularly attracted to the adoration of "the heavenly bodies" (astral deities). To support this statement, Stephen quoted from Amos 5:25–27. The opening question seems at first glance to suggest that Israel did not offer sacrifices to God during the wilderness wanderings. Such offerings are mentioned in the Pentateuch (Exod. 24:4–5; Num. 7), and without any suggestion that they were unacceptable. But the references are scanty, hinting that possibly the people as a whole neglected them, as they did circumcision (Josh. 5:5). Another possibility is that they went through the motions of sacrifice, much as their descendants did (Isa. 1:11–13), which was only a

---

[19]F. Godet, *Commentary on St. Paul's Epistle to the Romans* (Edinburgh: T. & T. Clark, 1883), 1:181.

formal obedience lacking true purpose and desire to honor God. As time went on, the people became more addicted to an alien worship, that of the host of heaven. The two deities mentioned here were astral—Molech, the god of the Ammonites, was also known as the Venus Star;[20] Rompha (or Rephan) is the Babylonian name for Saturn. In the Hebrew and LXX texts of Amos we read "Damascus" rather than "Babylon," for Amos was referring to the exile of the northern kingdom. But because Stephen was talking to men of Judah, he took the liberty of substituting "Babylon," the place of captivity for the southern kingdom. Judah's offense in the matter of astral worship is noted more frequently than Israel's (2 Kings 21:3, 5; 23:5; Jer. 8:2; 19:13; Zeph. 1:5).

Verses 44–50. This passage describes the transition from the tabernacle to the temple of Solomon.

7:44–50. Instead of recounting the history of Judah following the captivity, Stephen drew a contrast between the tabernacle and the temple, and to this extent gave some attention to the charge that he had spoken against the holy place (6:13). The tabernacle had the distinction of being constructed in accordance with a divinely given pattern (v. 44; Exod. 25:40; Heb. 8:5). It was eminently suitable to the period spent "in the desert," since its various parts could be detached and carried to the next encampment and there assembled. During the conquest of Canaan it symbolized the presence and conquering might of Israel's God.

A change came with David, who felt grieved that whereas he lived in a house of cedar, the Ark of the Lord continued to be under a tent (2 Sam. 7:2). David's desire to build a house for the Lord was not granted, but the privilege was given to his son Solomon (2 Sam. 7:12–13).

It is true that the initiative for the erection of the temple came not from a divine directive but from David's desire. God did not require it (2 Sam. 7:5–7), yet He permitted it to be erected and gave it His blessing by filling it with the *shekinah* of His presence (1 Kings 8:10–11). Solomon, indeed, indicated that the Lord had commended David for the desire to build a house for His worship (1 Kings 8:18). Stephen seemed intent on emphasizing that God cannot be confined to a house "made

[20] *IDB*, 3:422b.

by men," the work of their hands, a truth that Solomon recognized when he dedicated the temple (1 Kings 8:27).

To reinforce his point, Stephen quoted Scripture again, this time Isaiah 66:1–2. In view of the fact that heaven is God's throne and earth His footstool, the Almighty can ask the question, "What . . . house will you build for me?" The words apparently refer to the erection of a temple after the Exile. "He is the Being who filleth all, the Creator, and therefore the possessor, of the universe; and if men think to do Him a service by building Him a temple, and forget His infinite majesty in their concern for their own contemptible fabric, He wants no temple at all."[21]

One can see something of a parallel between the problem presented by sacrifices (v. 42) and that which the temple posed. Both could be abused by serving to exalt human beings rather than the Lord.

Was Stephen maintaining that the erection of the temple was wrong, an act of rebellion and pride, and that only the tabernacle represented the will of God? Or was he intent on pointing out that by magnifying the temple and its cultus, the Jewish nation in his time had made the temple almost an end in itself and were glorying in it rather than in the God for whose sake it was constructed?

The answer is not easy. If we had a digest of Stephen's discussions in the synagogue, light would be thrown on this question. To appeal to the Qumran community and its opposition to the temple is not particularly helpful, since the opposition was not to the temple per se but to the corruption of the priesthood that controlled it. If Stephen was influenced by the attitude and teaching of Jesus (something that can be neither affirmed nor denied) it is difficult to see how he could reject the temple entirely, seeing that Jesus regarded it as His Father's house and a place of prayer, not only for the Jews but for all nations (Mark 11:17). Our Lord's attitude was reflected in the cleansing of the temple at the beginning of Holy Week. If He repudiated the temple, why had He bothered to cleanse it? It is rather hard to accept the idea that Stephen rejected the temple and did so on the authority of Jesus, when the apostles, who were under the teaching of our Lord, continued to make use of the temple and to regard it as the house of God.

[21]Franz Delitzsch, *Commentary on Isaiah* (Edinburgh: T. & T. Clark, 1873).

Of some relevance, perhaps, is the fact that the writer of the Epistle to the Hebrews made frequent reference to the tabernacle but did not mention the temple. The motive for this choice may well have been that the tabernacle suggested movement, going along with God under His direction, whereas the temple was static and served to symbolize a certain satisfaction in the status quo that made the nation unresponsive to further revelation, especially that which came in the person of God's Son. He was the new Temple made without hands (John 2:19, 21), into which believers are incorporated as living stones (1 Cor. 3:16; 1 Peter 2:4–5). So the Jerusalem temple was not intended to be permanent. Such concepts may well have been shared by Stephen.

Verses 51–53. The speaker turned from his résumé of Israel's history to a charge that his audience and the nation were perpetuating the sins and failures of their ancestors.

7:51–53. Coming to the close of his address (he may have planned to say more but was interrupted) Stephen was prophet-like in the directness and severity of his accusations. He described his hearers as "stiff-necked" people, as God had done in the case of Israel at Mount Sinai (Exod. 33:3, 5). This national characteristic had been present all along ("you always resist the Holy Spirit"). The proneness to rebel against God manifested itself in the persecution of the prophets, as Jesus had charged (Matt. 23:37; Luke 11:47–48). He Himself had experienced the enmity of the Jewish leaders, meeting death at their hands (cf. 1 Thess. 2:15).

Stephen did not shrink from accusing the Sanhedrin of direct responsibility for handing over Jesus to death and thereby becoming His murderers. He used even stronger language than Peter had used (Acts 3:13–15). He, like Peter, called Jesus "the Righteous One." This act of rejection was the crowning offense, and it was in line with the failure to keep "the law" that came from God rather than from human wisdom and authority, as attested by the mediation of "angels" in connection with its delivery to Israel (cf. Heb. 2:2). That very Law had prohibited murder in general. How much more heinous was the crime of murdering the Son of God!

Possibly Stephen intended to mention the Resurrection as the divine reversal of the human action, as Peter was accustomed to do, but his strong language so inflamed his hearers that further discourse was rendered impossible.

Verses 54–60. The martyrdom of Stephen is reported as coming immediately after his address before the Council.

7:54. The words of Stephen, especially at the close, filled his hearers with rage. There was no atmosphere of calm in which his statements could be discussed. This man had been ostensibly put on the stand to defend himself, and he had chosen not to do this but rather to turn the tables by bringing charges against the leaders of Israel. It was intolerable to them, and they beset him on every side to silence him once and for all.

7:55–56. "Full of the Holy Spirit" (cf. 6:5), his source of wisdom and strength, Stephen was caught up in the ecstasy of the privilege of bearing witness to his Lord. Enraptured, he gazed into heaven and saw "the glory of God," the glory that had ceased to fill the earthly sanctuary (Ezek. 11:22–23) but did not fail to betoken the presence of God in the heavenly sanctuary (Rev. 21:22–23).

The vision of glory included "Jesus standing at the right hand of God." This implies the resurrection and ascension. Usually Jesus is represented as seated there (Luke 22:69; Acts 2:33–34; Heb. 1:3, 13). Stephen commented on the standing posture as he went on to identify Jesus as "the Son of Man." A twofold problem presents itself here: the posture of Jesus and the use of the title *Son of Man*. In the Gospels that title is used only by Jesus for Himself (it does not occur in the Epistles). These two items can be considered together.

The standing posture is hardly to be explained as indicating that the Son of Man was on the point of returning to earth as Judge, for that did not happen. Quite naturally the standing can be looked on as the welcome of Jesus for the spirit of the martyr. Yet this will not explain the extraordinary use of the title "Son of Man." A variation of this is the idea that the universal aspect of the last day when the Son of Man comes is here individualized to express the hope of the believer. "Only dying Stephen was in position to see the coming of the Son of man. It was at the 'last day,' in the hour of death, that the Son of man would be seen. . . . Only Stephen qualifies, as a dying Christian, for an individual *parousia* of the Son of man."[22]

A possible objection to this viewpoint of Barrett is that the typical way of describing Christian death is to make it a

---

[22] C. K. Barrett, "Stephen and the Son of Man," in *Apophorēta*, 36.

departure to be with Christ (e.g., Phil. 1:23) rather than as an advancing of the Lord to meet His own (the typical way of setting forth the eschatological appearing). It would be hard to find a passage to support Barrett's formulation. Some have taken John 14:3 in this sense, but the interpretation is doubtful. A different solution to the problem presented by the text is to see in the combination of standing and the use of the title "Son of Man" an indication that the Lord was here taking the position of witness and vindicator on behalf of His servant.

> In short, this is a double trial scene, exactly as in the scene in which Jesus witnessed a good confession before Pontius Pilate (I Tim. 6:13) or before the Sanhedrin: just as there Christ is condemned by the human court but declares that the Son of Man will thenceforth be exalted with the clouds and vindicated, so here Stephen is condemned and put to death, but in the heavenly court, where the books have been opened, this member of the Son of Man community is already being vindicated by the head of that community—*the* Son of Man *par excellence*; and as Stephen's witness confessed Christ before men, so Christ is standing to confess him before the angels of God. It is the more significant, if so, that the martyr with his dying words begs the heavenly court for mercy towards those against whom he is vindicated.[23]

7:57-58. Despite the judicial setting, a tumult broke out as men rushed toward the prisoner, screaming at him and holding their ears so as to hear no more from his lips, that he might know they regarded his words as blasphemy. In the eyes of the Jews, Stephen's closing words about Jesus as the Son of Man involved a claim that Jesus supported him in his stand. Very well, they would see to it that Stephen should have the same fate as the Nazarene. Both of them were iconoclasts meriting death. The probable explanation for this unseemly conduct is that others were present besides the Sanhedrin, according to the custom that permitted outsiders, especially students, to stand at the rear of the room.[24] Punishment followed the pattern laid

---

[23] C. F. D. Moule, "From Defendant to Judge—and Deliverer: An Enquiry into the Use and Limitations of the Theme of Vindication in the New Testament," *Studiorum Novi Testamenti Societas*, 3:47.

[24] Bo Reicke, *The New Testament Era,* 145.

down in Leviticus 24:11, 14. That the stoning was a matter of official decision and not simply mob action seems indicated by the prominence of "witnesses" in the actual stoning.

There may be a certain awkwardness in holding that the Sanhedrin acted on its own initiative in this instance, when our sources indicate that it was not free to do so in the case of Jesus, for whose condemnation Pilate's consent was required (John 18:31). But the situation had probably changed by Stephen's time, if his death can be put in the year 36 or later. Reicke notes that Vitellius, the imperial legate from 35 to 37, had a lenient attitude toward the Jews. To gain their good will he deposed Pilate, whom they detested, and replaced Caiaphas with a strong high priest named Jonathan. At the same time Vitellius restored the high priestly vestments to the custody of the high priest (they had been kept in Roman hands). "The high priest did not bother to have his decision ratified by the procurator, but rather let the stoning and persecution go ahead without consulting the Roman authorities."[25]

On the other hand, if it could be demonstrated that the stoning occurred prior to A.D. 36, this solution can no longer be relied on. But even so, as Sherwin-White observes, "It is possible that the Sanhedrin, which before the Herodian period had been the sovereign court of Judaea, tried to exercise its full power whenever there was a chance of doing so unchecked."[26]

The witnesses, in order to be able the better to cast the first stones, as the Law prescribed (Lev. 24:14; Deut. 13:9–10), removed their outer garments and placed them "at the feet of a young man named Saul." This was a convenient way for Luke to call attention to a figure who would dominate much of the remaining narrative of the book.

Was more intended? Was Luke saying that in the providence of God the mantle of Stephen was falling on Saul? Those who think so are prone to go further and suggest that Stephen's Hellenistic outlook must have made him eager to take the gospel to the Gentiles, and though prevented by death from doing so, his desire was destined to be realized through Saul after the latter's conversion.

But one looks in vain for evidence that Stephen had the vision of reaching out to the Gentile world. As far as the

[25] Ibid., 91.
[26] Sherwin-White, *Roman Society*, 40.

evidence goes, he was concerned for the mission of the church to his own people and also to the Samaritans, but nothing more. True enough, it was a group of Hellenists who began the Gentile work in Antioch (Acts 11:19–20), but any connection with Stephen has to be read into the text. The mention of Saul at this point in the narrative is mainly to prepare the reader for his prominence in the persecution that broke out after Stephen's death.

7:59–60. Two things are noted about the manner of the death of the first martyr, and both of them link him with the Master. "Lord Jesus, receive my spirit" recalls the prayer of Jesus to the Father, "Into your hands I commit my spirit" (Luke 23:46). Also, in asking the Lord not to hold this sin of murder against those who put him to death, Stephen seems to echo the request of Jesus that the Father would forgive those who had a part in bringing about His crucifixion (Luke 23:34). The similarity does not stop with these two items, for there are more. Stephen wrought wonders and signs, his words could not be refuted, he was filled with the Spirit, and he died under a charge of blasphemy.

His last thought and his last plea were for others, and then without a word he "fell asleep," the term for Christian death (1 Thess. 4:15), an expression that should not be understood as suggesting soul sleep (cf. 2 Cor. 5:8; Phil. 1:23).

PERSECUTION OF THE CHURCH (8:1–3)

Previous efforts to suppress the followers of Jesus had been confined to the beating and imprisonment of apostles. Now for the first time the rank and file began to pay the price of discipleship.

8:1. The mention of Saul as "giving approval" to the action taken against Stephen (7:59) helps to interpret the item about him in 7:58, which otherwise might be taken as mere happenstance. This second statement is the bridge between 7:58 and 8:3. Saul was in complete accord with those who put Stephen to death, as he later acknowledged (22:20). It was not simply passive consent, but rather active approval (cf. the use of the word in Rom. 1:32). Doubtless Saul swung into action without delay, heading up the persecution.

The KJV rendering, "at that time," is too general. Rather, it was "on that day" that the campaign was launched against the

Jerusalem church. Luke seems to say that *all* believers were scattered abroad with the exception of the apostles. But this can hardly be taken strictly, since many were detained and imprisoned. This is an example of hyperbole that is not uncommon in Scripture when emphasis is desired (e.g., Mark 1:5). It is probable that the brunt of persecution was borne by the Hellenists, those who were closely attached to Stephen. Their use of the Greek language would help to identify them.

Those who escaped are described as scattered throughout the regions of "Judea and Samaria." Luke could have used a general term for scattering but chose instead to use a word that means to scatter as seed is scattered on the ground. This suggests that as the episode was viewed in retrospect by the church, it was seen as a providential event to facilitate the mission set before His followers by the risen Lord (1:8). The people went as missionaries more than as refugees.

Why, then, did the apostles not take the lead in this exodus? Why did they remain in the city? The very fact that they were able to do so without being arrested indicates that the fury of the persecution was not directed primarily toward the Hebrews (6:1) who (in contrast to Stephen) had continued to make use of the temple and maintain the customs of the Law. No doubt these leaders felt that for the time being they should stay in the city to shepherd those who escaped detention and to provide a center of control for the now-enlarging sphere of the church (Judea and Samaria). It would be a mistake to conclude that the persecution meant a permanent wiping out or withdrawal of the entire Hellenist segment of the Jerusalem church. A sufficient refutation is the fact that this church sent Barnabas, a Hellenist, to assist the Antioch church (11:22).

8:2–3. The decision of the Sanhedrin was not universally popular, as evidenced by the fact that "godly men" came forward to bury Stephen and to make lamentation over him. While it is not impossible that some of these were believers, the previous use of the word *godly,* for those who had listened to Peter's Pentecost sermon and were therefore not at that time believers, suggests that these men did not belong to the church. There is a certain parallel with the situation of Jesus, when He was lamented by women of the city as He was led out to be crucified (Luke 23:27).

But Saul was not inclined to any such show of regret. His whole energy was thrown into the task of destroying the church if he could. This word for "destroy" occurs only here in the New Testament, though much the same idea is conveyed in Galatians 1:13, 23 by a different verb. In view of the use of the imperfect tense in all these passages, it is probable that the so-called conative force of the tense is called for here. In other words, Saul kept trying to destroy the church but was unsuccessful. It proved indestructible (Matt. 16:18). The persecutor's activity is more fully described in his speech before Agrippa (26:9–11), where he stated that his authority was given to him by the chief priests and that when some of his victims were put to death his vote helped to condemn them.

Notable is the fact that up until the Stephen episode, the opposition had come to the apostles from the Sadducees, who resented the preaching of the Resurrection. But now that Stephen had spoken out on the temple and the Law, the Pharisees had been enlisted as persecutors. Such was Saul of Tarsus (Phil. 3:5–6). The counsel of Gamaliel (Acts 5:38–39) was regarded as no longer relevant, since the issue had been shifted by Stephen's speech.

Part II

THE CHURCH IN JUDEA, SAMARIA, AND SYRIA
8:4–12:25

Up to this point in the narrative the proclamation of the gospel has been largely confined to Jerusalem. We have seen people from the surrounding territory come to the city, especially to bring their sick for healing (5:16), but no information has been given about any effort to reach out into Judea. The risen Lord's final command called for a witness to Him in all Judea and Samaria (1:8). Having noted summarily the general dispersion of believers throughout these districts due to persecution (8:1), Luke now concentrates on the Samaritan mission (8:5–25), then returns to describe further ministry through Peter in Judea (9:32–11:18).

But he also has in mind the forward thrust of the church, for which this intermediate stage was a preparation. This is reflected in the account of Philip's meeting with the Ethiopian eunuch, possibly the first missionary encounter with.an African national (8:26–40). It is apparent also in the report of the activity of certain Hellenists who ministered along the Phoenician coast and then began to preach to Gentiles in Syrian Antioch, which became the major missionary base for outreach to Gentiles farther removed (11:19–26). An even more evident token that Luke is looking ahead to the second half of his account is his description of the conversion and early labors of Saul, the man who was destined above all others to be God's instrument in penetrating to the regions beyond (9:1–30).

5

PHILIP AT SAMARIA
8:4–25

At once the narrative becomes more detailed, suggesting that Luke was concerned to describe the witness of the church rather than to go into particulars of its trials and tribulations.

8:4–8. At this point the historian repeats the fact of the dispersion of believers from Jerusalem before concentrating on one area, Samaria. Possibly there was a conscious comparison with the well-known Jewish Dispersion, when people of Israel penetrated many lands where they lived and worked, retaining their religion and customs in the midst of a pagan population. Now another dispersion was developing, having much in common with its Jewish counterpart, yet distinguished by faith in Jesus of Nazareth as Savior and Lord (cf. 1 Peter 1:1). While the Jewish Dispersion was to a limited extent missionary in character, the Christian dispersion was much more so. The prime objective was preaching the word. This activity is strongly emphasized throughout the chapter (8:4, 12, 25, 35, 40). Though preaching doubtless continued in Jerusalem, little is said about it (9:28–29). While the city remained the home of the mother church, the theater of action that Luke was concerned to report lay beyond its limits.

With Stephen gone, Philip came to the fore as the leader in carrying the gospel to Samaria. He has been noted as a member of the seven (6:5). Eventually he became known as Philip the evangelist (21:8). Jesus had included Samaria in His commission (1:8) and had prepared the way by His own ministry in this area (John 4).

The exact location of Philip's labors is not certain, for the manuscript testimony is divided, some having the reading "the city," others "a city" (of Samaria). The former reading, despite having witnesses of good quality, is probably to be rejected here, since the old capital no longer existed. Herod the Great had rebuilt the city, calling it Sebaste in honor of Augustus (the new name is the Greek equivalent of the Latin Augustus). It is unlikely that Luke would go back to the old term if he meant to designate the district's leading city. Gitta is a possibility, since this was the birthplace of Simon Magus, who is mentioned later in the chapter.

Philip's message centered in "Christ" (literally, "the Messiah"). This means he identified Jesus of Nazareth as fulfilling the promises of the coming of God's Anointed One for whom the Samaritans were looking (John 4:25, 29).

Philip's impact was twofold, through the spoken word and through the signs wrought before the people. As a result, they gave "attention" to him when he preached, the very thing they had been doing in the case of Simon (v. 11). That charlatan was now faced with a serious rival. If no miracles had been performed by Philip, the superstitious Samaritans could easily have concluded that he represented something inferior to Simon. The signs were those that were characteristic of Jesus' ministry and reproduced in the experience of the early church's witness (3:1–10; 5:16; 9:33–34). Little is recorded of mighty works wrought by Jesus among the Samaritans (Luke 17:11–19 is an exception). But now these neglected people were given an opportunity equal to that which the Jews had enjoyed. The mission produced "great joy."

8:9–13. The section describes Simon's first contact with the Christian message and his reaction to it. Early Christian literature has considerable to relate about a man of this name who was alleged to have opposed Peter in the city of Rome, seeking to lead people astray by his diabolically inspired deeds.[1] Simon practiced "magic," the most degraded form of religion in the Hellenistic age. (We encounter it again in 13:6 and 19:19.) The Samaritans were open to such influence because of their background, for they were a mixed people both racially and

---

[1] See "The Acts of Peter" in Edgar Hennecke and Wilhelm Schneemelcher, eds., *New Testament Apocrypha*, E.T. trans. and ed. R. McL. Wilson (Philadelphia: Westminster, 1964), 2:282–86. Reports of encounters in other places are found in "The Pseudo-Clementines," 2:549–52.

religiously. It is recorded of them that "they worshiped the LORD but they also served their own gods in accordance with the customs of the nations from which they had been brought" (2 Kings 17:33).

The people were amazed at Simon's pretensions, for he announced himself as "someone great" and backed it up by a display of magic. In the original there is a possible play on words between "practicing sorcery" and the word "great." The wise men of the nativity story (Matt. 2) are called magi, but there is no basis for concluding that they resorted to magic. Their skills were of a higher order and not intended to deceive. To the Samaritans, Simon appeared as one deserving of reverence for his supernatural demonstrations. So they called him "the Great Power." The word *power* was much used in antiquity, sometimes as a synonym for Deity (Mark 14:62). Philo used the term in the plural to denote the intermediaries through whom God worked in creating and sustaining the world.

Simon had had things going his way until the preaching of Philip introduced a power more potent and blessed than any he could muster (cf. the magicians of Egypt in relation to Moses, Exod. 8:18–19). Philip's preaching centered not only on the person of Christ but also on the Good News of the kingdom of God (cf. 1:3). He was concerned to set forth God's sovereign plan, which included the universal emphasis of salvation as opposed to an exclusively Jewish message (cf. John 4:42).

Among those who responded was Simon. He both "believed" and was "baptized." After having amazed others, he himself could not help being amazed at the miracles he saw being performed before his eyes. The question as to whether or not he was a genuine believer must await the further developments in the story, but it is well to reflect that Scripture sometimes cites as belief that which the context deplores as quite inadequate (e.g., John 2:23–25). What is emphasized is the open-eyed wonder of one who was intent on studying Philip and his work, willing to be an apprentice in the hope of ultimately being a master.

8:14–25. The church at Jerusalem learned of the success of the Samaritan mission before long and moved to welcome the new believers into the fellowship. It is doubtless significant that "the apostles" as a body (cf. 8:1) sent the two men of their number who had been most prominent in the work of the Lord since Pentecost (3:1; 4:13, 19). This is the last appearance of John in Acts, but Peter continues to be prominent in chapters 9–12 and 15. The fact that he was sent to Samaria suggests that he had no preeminence of position, despite his leadership in the church.

The mission had the blessing of God, as evidenced by the giving of the Holy Spirit, after the apostles' prayer, to the converts at Samaria. In the case of these new believers, the rite of baptism had been performed, but the Spirit had not been bestowed (contrast 2:38; 10:44).

So far as the Book of Acts is concerned, no inflexible pattern for the reception of the Spirit is discernible, though usually the experience of the saints must have been that the Spirit came as the seal of faith (19:2; Eph. 1:13). That the Samaritans received the Spirit was clear evidence that God had accepted them as well as Jewish believers. This was calculated to remove any sense of inferiority and to encourage them to feel their oneness with others in the body of Christ. The delay in granting the Spirit as well as the conveyance of the Spirit through apostles from the Jerusalem church was a warning that there must be no thought of perpetuating the old antagonism between Jews and Samaritans within the church (cf. John 4:22). There was not to be a separate Samaritan church.

Regarding the Samaritan situation, G. W. H. Lampe writes:

> We must bear in mind, once again, that for St. Luke the Spirit's primary work is the furtherance of the church's world-wide mission. . . . It may not be too much to assert that this event is meant to demonstrate that a new nucleus of the missionary church has been established, and to suggest that Luke's readers are intended to infer that the Gospel proceeded to radiate outwards from this new center of the Spirit's mission.[2]

Simon was an attentive observer of what happened when the apostles prayed and laid their hands on believers. Evidently there were some outward tokens that accompanied the gift of the Spirit, perhaps such as are noted in 19:6. Simon was intrigued. Here was a power he longed to possess for himself,

[2]G. W. H. Lampe, *The Seal of the Spirit,* 72.

thinking it would add to his stock in trade and increase his prestige. He was quite prepared to pay for it. The term *simony,* which describes an activity that was common in the medieval church—the purchase of ecclesiastical offices—stems from this incident.

Peter was so shocked that he reacted with severity. Was he thinking of Judas when he said, "May your money perish with you" (v. 20; cf. 1:18)? Money has no more to do with the gift of the Spirit than with the gift of eternal life. Peter's remarks to Simon may not be sufficiently clear to determine whether the apostle held him to be a child of God who sadly needed correction and illumination or considered him unregenerate. "Perish" is a strong word, as is the statement, "For I see that you are full of bitterness and captive to sin" (v. 23). On the other hand, the admonition that Simon had "no part or share" in this matter bears a striking resemblance to what the Lord said when Peter resisted Jesus' attempt to wash his feet (John 13:8). On that occasion Peter was sorely mistaken but did not lack faith.

Peter's reference to forgiveness as the pressing need for Simon can be taken either way, as something every sinner needs in coming to God or as a fresh experience of divine grace for an erring believer. This much is clear: throughout the report of this incident there is a complete lack of spiritual perception on Simon's part, and little if any recognition of wrongdoing against the Lord. The fear of punishment is very much like the attitude of Cain, essentially self-centered.

Their mission ended, Peter and John made their way unhurriedly back to Jerusalem (v. 25). Their recent experience encouraged them to minister in other Samaritan communities. What a change from the day when John had been prepared to call down fire from heaven on a Samaritan village that had refused hospitality to Jesus (Luke 9:51–55)!

6

PHILIP AND THE ETHIOPIAN
8:26–40

Hardly had the gospel reached Samaria, when by a great leap it jumped to the uttermost part, in this instance to the continent of Africa. For all we know, there may have been other contacts with travelers from afar that resulted in the spread of the faith to remote places. Luke was content to relate this one example.

8:26. Guidance came to the early church at times through "an angel of the Lord" (cf. 5:19–20). The message was clear, and the command uncontested. Philip must leave Samaria, but he was leaving behind him men and women who now had the Spirit to enable them to grow and be strong in the Lord. They could take up the task of witnessing where Philip laid it down. Human wisdom might reason that it was a mistake to leave a thriving work, especially since no intimation was given as to the scope of the new theater of action (contrast 23:11). As it turned out, the witness was given to one man, yet he was a potential witness to many in his own land. God's thoughts and ways are often not ours, but they are always vindicated.

The direction given by the Lord pointed Philip to the south, to the road from Jerusalem to Gaza. Judging from verse 40, it is probable that God's servant made his journey to a point somewhere near Gaza rather than in the Jerusalem area. Some have called into question the description of this line of travel as a desert road. It certainly is less true of the area between Jerusalem and Gaza than between Gaza and Egypt. But often, especially in the Gospels, the word *desert* does not mean wasteland or a sandy area but rather a place without human habitation. Philip was to meet this man in a lonely spot where nothing would distract from the communication of the message.

Another solution to the problem has been proposed, namely, that in this instance "desert" has the force of "deserted" and refers to the old Gaza that had lain in ruins since it was destroyed by Alexander the Great. The new Gaza was on the coast, some two miles away. The Greek clause "this is desert" could refer to Gaza as well as to "road," and since the directions given to Philip would then be quite explicit, this interpretation should not be lightly dismissed, though verse 36, which mentions the road, may favor the former view.

8:27–28. In spite of being uninformed as to the reason for the journey, Philip "started out." This implicit obedience recalls that of Abraham when he was given a most difficult command (Gen. 22:3). It is in contrast with Peter's attitude toward an unwelcome order from the Lord (10:14). Faith in God calls for a readiness to trust in His wisdom and does not demand an explanation.

Attention shifts to the man whom Philip was about to meet, a stranger from Ethiopia. In ancient times, this term indicated a large territory lying directly south of Egypt, hence to be distinguished from modern Ethiopia located to the southeast. This man was an "official" of the court of Candace,[1] the queen (more accurately, the queen mother) of the land, and was her leading financial officer. Incidentally, there is a play on words here, as "treasury" in the original closely resembles the name "Gaza."

Another item of information is provided—this individual was a "eunuch." It is well-known that in the Orient eunuchs were placed in charge of the harems (Esth. 2:3). They also sometimes rose to positions of prominence in the government, as in this case. His rank may have given him a certain amount of freedom of movement, accounting for his visit to Jerusalem.

He had come to "worship," which raises a question as to his status. That he was a convert to Judaism (a proselyte) is unlikely, since the Law excluded eunuchs from the congregation of Israel (Deut. 23:1). But if he was a God-fearer, he could take his place with other Gentiles in the court reserved for them (1 Kings 8:41–43; Mark 11:17). We read of Greeks coming to Jerusalem to worship during our Lord's ministry (John 12:20).

---

[1] *Candace* is a title (cf. *Pharaoh*) rather than a personal name.

Worth observing is the timing of the encounter with Philip—he was "returning" from his visit to the Holy City. When he was on his way to Jerusalem, he would likely have been annoyed at any interruption, since he was bent on fulfilling a sacred pilgrimage. But now that his mission was over and his heart was as needy as ever, conditions were ripe for the introduction of the gospel (cf. the strategy of Jesus recorded in John 7:37).

The visitor was taking home with him as a memento a scroll of the prophet Isaiah in the LXX, as indicated by the fact that the words quoted correspond with this version more closely than with the Hebrew text. The eunuch was probably reading aloud, since he did not reread the passage before asking for an explanation of it from Philip. The matter is made certain in verse 30.

8:29–31. With the Spirit prompting him, Philip mustered sufficient boldness to intercept the chariot and engage the occupant in conversation. Apparently the eunuch was quite preoccupied with his reading, not noticing the stranger until he was questioned as to what he was reading, or more exactly, as to his understanding of it. The interruption was received kindly, and the response was a veiled invitation to Philip to serve as interpreter of the Scripture involved. At last the reason for Philip's long trip to the south was beginning to unfold. The meeting, the reading, the precise passage being read—all this was clearly providential. The pounding of Philip's heart was not due entirely to running as he mounted the chariot and took his seat beside the eunuch.

8:32–35. In his reading the Ethiopian had come to the high point of Isaiah (chap. 53), with its mysterious words about the Servant of the Lord and what was to happen to Him. He was puzzled about the identification of this figure. This is not surprising in view of the variety of interpretations that have been put forward: Israel the nation, Israel the remnant, and the personal Servant of the Lord. The eunuch felt sure that the prophecy concerned an individual but was unable to fix his identity.

What an embarrassment it would have been for Philip to admit that he shared the eunuch's perplexity. That he was able to proclaim Christ from this passage shows that already within the church there was an understanding of its interpretation. All that is necessary is to move back through our Lord's teaching about Himself from the prophets after the Resurrection (Luke 24:25–27, 44) to His earlier predictions concerning His death, couched in the language of this chapter from Isaiah (Mark 10:45; Luke 22:37). Unquestionably Jesus had identified Himself and His mission with the unnamed Servant of Isaiah 53 and other passages. That Philip "preached Jesus" makes it certain that the person of our Lord was included along with His work.

What is not clear is the phrase "began with that very passage." Are we to understand that Philip used other portions of the chapter and perhaps other prophets in addition to Isaiah, or that he proceeded immediately to a recital of fulfillment in terms of the ministry of Jesus culminating in His death and resurrection? In this story we find a classic illustration of the truth affirmed in 1 Peter 1:10–12, that the same Spirit who provided the message to the prophets concerning the sufferings of the Christ and the glories to follow, guides and illumines those who make use of the prophecies in preaching the gospel. It is not at all unlikely that Philip went on down the chapter to include the truths that the Servant bore the sins of many and was rewarded (a hint of the Resurrection).

8:36–40. Although no statement is recorded to the effect that Philip went on to state that faith in God's Servant was essential for salvation, the narrative implies this. The eunuch's request for baptism rested on his understanding that in this act he would be confessing his faith as well as repenting for his sins (cf. 2:38; 8:12).

Quite early in the transmission of the text an effort was made to clarify this matter, with the result that manuscripts of the Western text add verse 37, a statement making faith requisite. This verse lacks sufficient authority to include it in the text. We may assume that when this scribal addition originated, sometime fairly early in the second century, this sort of a response was commonly made by the candidate for baptism.

During the conversation the chariot had been rolling along on its way toward Africa, but now the eunuch ordered a halt, that he might be baptized in the water he had glimpsed near the road. Philip was pleased to comply with the request, evidently satisfied as to the genuineness of the eunuch's faith.

The association of the two was abruptly terminated as they emerged from the water, for the Spirit removed Philip from the scene (cf. 1 Kings 18:12). "Took away" is from the same Greek word that Paul used to explain that the saints will be "caught up" when the Lord comes again (1 Thess. 4:17). Apparently the disappearance of the messenger of Christ did not disconcert the new convert or make him doubt the reality of the experience that had come to him, for he "went on his way rejoicing" (cf. 8:8).

We can only speculate about Philip's reaction to the mission that had taken him from crowded Samaria to a lonely road in the south. Perhaps he thought in terms of fulfillment of the psalmist's word, "Ethiopia will quickly stretch out her hands to God" (Ps 68:31 NASB).

Commentators have noted a certain similarity between the experience of Philip and that of Elijah, especially in respect to sudden appearance and disappearance and the fact that such removal is attributed to the Spirit of the Lord (cf. 1 Kings 18:12; 2 Kings 2:16). As for Philip, he ended up at Azotus, the Ashdod of the Old Testament, a city on the coastal plain some twenty miles north of Gaza. He seems to have interpreted his arrival there as an indication that he was not to return to Samaria, but should bear witness in that area. So he pursued a northerly course, preaching "in all the towns" as he went. This would include Joppa, farther up the coast, and possibly Lydda also, which was somewhat inland. It is conceivable, therefore, that Philip laid the foundation for Peter's ministry in these places (9:32–43). When he reached Caesarea, his travels ended but his preaching did not. Here he settled and raised a family, who shared in ministry along with him (21:8–9).

7

SAUL'S CONVERSION
AND EARLY LABORS
9:1–31

Three accounts of Saul's conversion are recorded by Luke. The one immediately before us is the historian's own narrative, no doubt based on information supplied by Paul himself. It emphasizes the role of Ananias. In the second account (chap. 22) Paul addressed hostile Jews and sought to present his experience as above all a divine intervention in his life, declaring that to the divine Intervener he bowed in obedience. The third account is also Paul's, but this time spoken in the presence of Festus and Agrippa (chap. 26), omitting all reference to Ananias and majoring instead on Paul's commission to go to the Gentiles.

At the very least one must say that the inclusion of three accounts of Saul's conversion is an indication of the importance Luke attached to this event. The one who was turned to Christ on the Damascus road was destined to be the leading instrument of the risen Lord in extending the gospel beyond the bounds of Palestine to remote places and to Gentiles as well as Jews. Paul is the key figure in most of the remaining narrative of Acts.

Verses 1–2. This transitional section deals with Saul's persecuting activity and is a continuation of what has been related in 8:1–3.

9:1 Not satisfied with what he had done to terrorize the church in Jerusalem, Saul began to look farther afield, with his ferocity unabated. We are to understand "murderous threats," not as stating Saul's intent to kill personally, but in the sense of 26:10. Luke might well have hesitated to use such strong language of one who had become his friend and companion, had not Paul pictured himself in the same light: ". . . how intensely I persecuted the church of God and tried to destroy it" (Gal. 1:13; cf. Acts 26:11).

How is this to be explained, especially in one who was a Pharisee schooled in the necessity of caution in executing punishment (see comments on 5:33–39)? The pupil (22:3) had parted company with his teacher. Whatever difference in temperament may have existed between the two will not suffice to explain the devastating rampage of this wolf of Benjamin (Gen. 49:27). Some scholars are content to hold that Saul was bitter because in his eyes Jesus of Nazareth was a pretender, an imposter who thought of Himself as the Messiah and made dupes out of His followers. But this is not sufficient to explain the vehemence of the persecutor.

Saul was deeply devoted to Judaism, a fact that he mentioned in conjunction with his attacks on the church (Gal. 1:14). At the heart of Judaism stood the Torah, which Saul sensed was in jeopardy since the time Stephen launched his campaign against the Law (6:13). This ardent Jew had organized his life around the Torah and felt he was blameless respecting its demands (Phil. 3:6). His zeal for the Law explains his zeal in persecuting the church. The one had to go if the other was to stand.[1] So he was willing to put to death as well as to prosecute the followers of Jesus.

He could point to precedents for this. Others had been zealous for the Law and willing to resort to violence, sometimes with divine approval. When Antiochus Epiphanes was bent on destroying the religious life of the Jews, Mattathias and his sons took up the sword to defend their Jewish heritage after Mattathias had slain a fellow Jew who was prepared to lead in a pagan sacrifice (1 Macc. 2:23–28). Significant is the language Mattathias used in urging others to take the same stand: "Whosoever is zealous for the law . . . let him come forth after me." This recalls Galatians 1:14 and Philippians 3:6. Mattathias was able to defend his conduct on the basis of Old Testament examples, including Phinehas, who had won the commendation of the Lord for smiting the errant Israelite and his Midianite consort (Num. 25:6–13), and Elijah, who slew the prophets of Baal for leading Israel astray (1 Kings 18:40). The zeal for the Lord and His Law on the part of these worthies is underscored by Mattathias (1 Macc. 2:50–58).

[1] For a fuller discussion of this matter, see Jacques Dupont, "The Conversion of Paul," in *Apostolic History and the Gospel*, 176–94.

Closer to Saul's time, some Pharisees had taken up arms to get rid of Herod the Great for what they regarded as impious acts.[2] Saul had ample precedent.

9:2. The persecutor was aware that if he hoped to stamp out the church, he had to follow believers wherever they went, including those who had fled Jerusalem in recent days. So he secured letters from the high priest to the synagogues at Damascus stating his identity and giving him authority to deal with the disciples.[3] This ancient city had several synagogues, and Saul was reasonably certain that they harbored some followers of Jesus. His procedure would be to apprehend all whom he could lay hands on and return them to Jerusalem for action by the Sanhedrin.

There is no clear basis here for insisting that Saul, highly trained in Judaism and zealous for its traditions, must have been a member of the nation's supreme Council. As Bruce points out, Saul's youth (Acts 7:58) would likely exclude him from such a body of elders[4] (for further discussion see under 26:10). What is clearly implied here is the recognition of the Sanhedrin's authority by Jews even outside the bounds of Palestine (cf. 1 Macc. 15:15–21). Evident also is the fact that believers in Jesus still frequented the synagogues—much as early disciples in Jerusalem, the apostles included, had felt free to make use of the temple.

That they had their own gatherings in addition may be regarded as certain. But from the standpoint of the Jewish authorities, they were still within the fold of Judaism and known as the sect of the Nazarenes (24:5). As such, they were subject to correction and discipline in the hope of changing their thinking. They needed to be brought into line and made "regular" again. It is instructive to note that Paul himself, as a Christian, was disciplined by the synagogue on several occa-

---

[2] Josephus, *Antiquities* XV.8.2.

[3] A problem presents itself here. Would Rome permit such a persecution as Saul conducted? Rome gave the church protection from the Jews on various occasions, as Luke relates later on. It is possible that at the time when Saul went to Damascus the city was under the control of Aretas IV, ruler of the Nabatean empire (Arabian in constituency). This kingdom had not been subdued by Rome. To gain favor with the Jews, who were also anti-Roman in their feelings, Aretas may have permitted the Sanhedrin to exercise authority in this distant city. See W. L. Knox, *St. Paul and the Church of Jerusalem*, 53 n.20, 59 n.47.

[4] F. F. Bruce, *New Testament History*, 238 n.14.

sions (2 Cor. 11:24), implying that he was regarded as still within the ranks of the chosen people. And Paul was not averse to being considered so, since it kept open for him the door of access to his nation as a witness for Christ. He could be driven out of a synagogue or out of a town, but there is no indication of excommunication or any attempt at excommunication (cf. 28:17–20).

The term *Nazarene* is not used in the present passage. Instead, believers are described as belonging to "the Way," which was an early designation they gave to their own group. It was devoid of the derogation attached to "the Nazarene sect" (24:5; cf. v. 14). Whether or not it owed its origin to the claim of Jesus to be "the way" (John 14:6) cannot be determined. What is clear is that this group was asserting that it possessed the secret of salvation and life in an absolute sense. Christianity was not regarded as being merely one way among many possible choices.

Verses 3–9. Here the conversion of Saul is recounted objectively, with no attempt to diagnose the thoughts that coursed through the persecutors's mind.

9:3–6. This great event of conversion, or better, of being laid hold of by the Lord (Phil. 3:12), occurred when Saul's journey was almost completed. It is vain to conjecture, as some have done, that on the way he had been thinking seriously about his own spiritual state in the light of what he knew about Jesus and His claims, with a growing uneasiness and lack of self-confidence, until finally he capitulated and looked away to Jesus, thus effecting an inner change or conversion. From all we know of this man, he was likely anticipating, with pent-up feeling, purging from the synagogues of Damascus those who confessed their faith in Jesus of Nazareth. Paul's own writings give no justification for imagining a psychological build-up of self-distrust combined with misgivings about the rightfulness of his course as a persecutor. The change that occurred that day was initiated not from within but from without.

"Suddenly a light from heaven flashed around him." To a Jew, the combination of a "light" of great intensity with a "voice" was calculated to bring awareness that a divine revelation was taking place (Exod. 3:2, 4–5; Matt. 17:2, 5). The message was for him: "Saul, Saul, why do you persecute me?" The Lord deliberately identified Himself with His church, a truth that became deeply ingrained in Paul as he grew in understanding of its meaning (e.g., 1 Cor. 12:12).

For the moment he was nonplussed, because he had thought of his persecuting activity as directed simply against men and women. This fact, however, does not warrant rendering his response, as Goodspeed does, "Who are you, sir?" Granted, *kyrios* is capable of this pedestrian meaning of "sir," especially as people meet for the first time (John 4:11); but in this case, in view of the light and the voice, the word had a numinous significance. Saul knew he was in the presence of a supernatural manifestation, but he could not yet cope with it, and his question reflects his bewilderment. That very bewilderment underscores the likelihood that he had not been thinking about the Lord Jesus along the way. Suddenly he had to think about Him and communicate with Him.

Enlightenment about the source of the heavenly voice came quickly: "I am Jesus, whom you are persecuting." The use of the human name rather than a divine title put everything into focus for Saul. Jesus of Nazareth was alive. His disciples had been right after all in proclaiming His resurrection from the dead. What the arguments of Stephen and others could not do, this Christophany, graciously given to the persecutor, accomplished without deliberation or debate. Everything was suddenly in right perspective. The one whom he had called Lord out of deference, lest he offend the Deity or His messenger, was now seen to be Lord indeed (cf. 2:36).

It was His prerogative to command, and He did so at once, telling Saul to rise and go into the city, promising that there the next step would be made known to him. The city, of course, was Damascus. In writing to the Galatians Paul incidentally confirmed the location of his conversion experience (Gal. 1:17). All the New Testament references to Damascus have to do with his conversion or early activity at this spot.

"And you will be told what you must do" might seem to suggest that Saul would have the gospel explained to him by someone and on this basis would be able to make his decision. If this were so, it would contradict Paul's own statement that the gospel he preached did not come to him from man or by human instruction, but rather through a revelation of Jesus Christ (Gal. 1:12). But in neither Acts 9, 22, nor 26 is there anything to indicate that men imparted the knowledge of the gospel to him. He was helped by Ananias—greeted, delivered from his blindness, baptized, and received into the fellowship of believers—but by his own statement, it was God who had been pleased to reveal His Son in him (Gal. 1:15–16).

9:7–9. Set forth here are the effects of the confrontation on Saul and the involvement of his companions. Of the men who journeyed with him, it is said that they "heard the sound but did not see anyone." A problem is created by the fact that in 22:9, in some versions (e.g., KJV, RSV), it is stated that those who were with Saul did not hear the voice of the one who spoke to him. At least two attempts have been made to resolve the difficulty. One is to note that although the verb "hear" is the same in the two passages, it is followed by the genitive case in 9:7 and by the accusative case in 22:9. Some Greek scholars take the position that the genitive denotes merely the physical sensation (sound), whereas the accusative conveys the idea of hearing with comprehension. This distinction is based on classical Greek usage. However, a study of the data in Epictetus and in the LXX, both of which fall in the period of Hellenistic Greek as does the New Testament, has called in question this distinction for New Testament times.[5]

A different tack is taken by F. F. Bruce, who writes regarding 9:7: "Luke may very well mean here that it was Paul's voice that his companions heard, although they could neither see nor hear the person whom he appeared to be addressing."[6] This is ingenious, but it is hardly natural to refer "the voice" (used without any qualification) to Saul in a situation dominated by the communication of the Lord to him. In the parallel passage (22:9) the voice clearly belongs to the Lord Jesus.

The former solution is still the more likely. An echo of 9:7, it may be, occurs in connection with the death of Polycarp in the second century. "Now when Polycarp entered into the arena there came a voice from heaven: 'Be strong, Polycarp, and play the man.' And no one saw the speaker, but our friends who were there heard the voice."[7]

By saying that the men saw no one (22:9 simply notes that they saw the light) Luke seems to imply by contrast that Saul did see someone. Other passages state with sufficient clarity that he saw the Lord (9:17, 22:14; 26:16). Paul based his apostleship on this fact (1 Cor. 9:1; 15:8–9). Both items—the hearing of

---

[5] Horst R. Moehring, "The verb *akouein* in Acts 9:7 and 22:9," *Nov Test*, 3 (1959): 80–99. C. F. D. Moule takes the same position in his *Idiom Book of New Testament Greek* (New York: Cambridge University Press, 1959), 36. But see Nigel Turner, *Grammatical Insights into the New Testament*, 86–90.

[6] F. F. Bruce, *Commentary on the Book of the Acts*, 197.

[7] *Martyrdom of Polycarp* 9.1.

the voice by others and the seeing of the Lord by Paul—help to establish the fact that the conversion was effected by something objective rather than by an internal process in the persecutor. The blindness he suffered points to the same conclusion (cf. Acts 22:11).

Helpless because of his blindness and humbled by the realization that in his misguided zeal he had been guilty of attacking the very congregation of God, the true Israel (Gal. 1:13; 6:16), and of wounding the exalted Lord (Acts 9:4), Paul was assisted to quarters in the city. There he remained quiet, spending three days in fasting, pondering recent events, and praying (cf. v. 11). His life had reached a crisis point. What lay before him? He had no means of knowing.

Verses 10–19a. The significance of this section, so far as Saul and Christ are concerned, is well expressed by R. B. Rackham: "He is crucified with Christ, and the three days of darkness are like the three days in the tomb. But on the third day with Christ he rises from the dead in baptism; after that he is filled with the Holy Ghost—his Pentecost."[8]

9:10–12. Though the words of the risen Lord to Saul about what would happen to him in Damascus (v. 6) were vague enough to keep him in suspense, they contained a promise. To fulfill it, the Lord selected a messenger among the believers in Damascus, appearing to Ananias in a vision. Judging from what is said about him in 22:12, namely, his devotion to the Law and his good standing with the Jewish community, he was not a Hellenist who had fled from Jerusalem but one who had been settled in Damascus for some time. He was of a different stamp from the individual of the same name who had disturbed the church at Jerusalem (chap. 5)—even as Judas, the man to whose home he was sent, was of higher caliber than the betrayer of Jesus; and Saul, to whom Ananias was called to minister, was vastly superior to Saul the king of Israel.

The Lord directed Ananias to go to "Straight Street." H. V. Morton noting that this street was a mile long, observes, "It was so named because, like the main streets of nearly all the great Hellenistic cities, it ran straight as an arrow from one end of the city to the other."[9]

Saul is designated as "a man from Tarsus." This is the first

---

[8]R. B. Rackham, *The Acts of the Apostles,* 133.
[9]H. V. Morton, *In the Steps of St. Paul,* 44.

of five references in Acts to the city, all of them relating to Saul. Perhaps as old as Damascus, it was the capital of the province of Cilicia. On the basis of Galatians 1:15, Sir William Ramsay contended that the divine preparation of the human vessel must have included the environment, and that on the basis of available knowledge of this place there was no other spot in the ancient world that could have prepared Saul equally well.[10] It was here that he had spent his early years before going to Jerusalem for training in Judaism (22:3).

By granting a "vision" to Saul, in which he perceived Ananias coming in to lay hands on him for the recovery of his sight, and then by informing Ananias of this fact, the Lord made it difficult for the latter to refuse the commission of being His messenger. To be sure, there was a measure of protest, but it was quickly overcome.

9:13–16. The protest was natural, in view of all that Ananias knew of Saul and in view of his lack of information about his conversion. "Many" people had told him of the terrible inroads Saul had made on the church at Jerusalem. Some had doubtless been eyewitnesses of his ruthlessness before fleeing to Damascus. Ananias was well informed about Saul, knowing even of his mission to Damascus. How he had received this information is uncertain. Possibly he had received letters from people in Jerusalem, or first-hand reports from some who had left the city just ahead of Saul and now felt free to divulge the purpose of the trip in view of what had happened to their leader. It is a testimony to the courage of Ananias that despite the threat of persecution he did not panic and resort to flight. His objections were not answered directly but were silenced by a word of command—"Go!"

To leave the matter there would have meant sending Ananias on his way still filled with misgiving, so the Lord shared with His servant the importance of Saul in His plans for the future progress of the gospel: "This man is my chosen instrument." The word translated "instrument" more often occurs in the sense of "vessel," especially when it refers to a material receptacle. In the Old Testament it was sometimes used, in a metaphorical sense, of Israel (Hosea 8:8; cf. Jer. 18:1–11) or of an individual (Ps. 31:12). This meaning is strong

---

[10] William M. Ramsay, *The Cities of St. Paul*, 88.

in Paul's writings. The idea of inherent weakness that must be transcended by divine power is prominent in 2 Corinthians 4:7 and may be latent in the passage before us. Saul, despite his apparent unsuitability due to his past conduct, would prove to be a potent instrument for the Lord as he submitted his life to be used by Him.

The figure of the vessel is carried forward in the statement of the Lord's purpose, "to carry my name." Saul would be His personal representative wherever he went. The "Gentiles" are named first as a special sphere of ministry. No conflict with Romans 1:16 is involved, for there the apostle was speaking in general terms of the historic fact that the gospel had been given first to the covenant people (cf. Acts 3:26). But as the rest of Acts shows, the Gentiles were to be the main object of Paul's labors. "Kings," including Agrippa and Caesar, come into prominence after his arrest. Other rulers were the Roman governors Felix and Festus. "The people of Israel" were not forgotten, and they remained close to the apostle's heart throughout his ministry (Rom. 9:1–3; 10:1). Through his use of the synagogue for testimony, Paul was able to reach both Jew and Gentile at the same time on numerous occasions.

The privilege of being Christ's representative was balanced by the announcement that Saul must "suffer" much for the Lord's sake. There is no hint here or elsewhere that the former persecutor must now endure suffering because he had inflicted so much of it on the saints. It was not because of them, but for the Lord's sake (Acts 9:16; cf. Phil. 1:12–14). Saul would enter into fellowship with the sufferings of Christ (Phil. 3:10). This became a distinguishing mark of his service and of his apostleship, one that would-be apostles were unable to match (2 Cor. 11:22–27). However, it should not be thought that Saul was to be in this respect unique among the Lord's true servants (Matt. 10:16–25; John 15:20–21).

9:17–19a. The first act of Ananias on entering Judas's house was to lay his hands on Saul. In the initial sense, this pertained to the healing of the blindness (cf. Acts 28:8), but it had relevance also to the filling with the Spirit that is noted here (cf. 8:17). The commission of verse 15 would have had little meaning apart from the divine enablement to fulfill it.

Since Ananias was not an official of the church, Saul was not put in the position of being subordinated to a "higher-up." No doubt the hands were gently applied, but what reassured

Saul more than this was the opening word in his greeting: "Brother Saul." To be counted as a brother in Christ after his attempts to ruin the church must have suffused his soul with astonishment and joy. What a blessed introduction to Christian fellowship! There was no word of reproach for his persecuting activities, only a hearty welcome into the fold.

Saul responded by being baptized and then eating a meal, which broke his fast. The spiritual took precedence over the physical. Whether he was filled with the Spirit in connection with his baptism or prior to it is of little moment, since Acts provides examples of both sequences (2:38; 10:44). A sidelight here is the observation that baptism was administered by a layman, without any question as to its validity.

A comparison of the words of Ananias to Saul with what the Lord had disclosed to him concerning Saul's future is instructive. Ananias had nothing to say about the suffering in store for him. After all, the Lord Jesus had indicated that He would unfold this to Saul (v. 16).

Verses 19b–25. The compact narrative is about evenly divided between a recital of Saul's mission in Damascus and the story of his escape from those who sought his life.

9:19b–22. Almost overnight the persecutor became the preacher, building up the faith that formerly he had sought to destroy (cf. Gal. 1:23). One receives the impression that for "several days" Saul was content to bask in the delight of the new fellowship "with the disciples," in which case "at once" (v. 20), in connection with the commencement of preaching, involves something of an interval, in contrast to the "immediately" of verse 18. But by temperament as well as by reason of his dedication to the Lord, he was eager to confess his newly found faith, and the synagogues of the city provided the platform he needed. What he had expected to make the scene of interrogation and possibly the application of third degree tactics (v. 2) was now a forum for his proclamation of the gospel. No wonder those who heard him were "astonished."

The Christian Jews must have shared this amazement. God had done a marvelous thing. Not only had He demonstrated care for His own by halting the persecution on their very doorstep, but in the process He had gained for Himself a herald of the message of grace. Men would have counted it a great thing if the hand of God had rewarded the persecutor by striking him dead (cf. 12:1, 23). But to salvage the opponent and enlist him on behalf of the cause was a far greater victory.

Saul's message is gathered up in two statements, both centered on the Lord Jesus. One is the declaration that He is the Son of God (v. 20), the other that He is the Christ, the Messiah (v. 22). The same combination is found in Peter's confession (Matt. 16:16) and in the statement of purpose behind the writing of John's Gospel (John 20:31). The concept of the Lord Jesus as the Son of God continued to be central to Paul's Christology, as can be ascertained from Romans 1:3–4 (cf. Acts 13:33). It had been prominent in the teaching of Jesus Himself (Matt. 11:27) and basic to Mark's presentation of His person (Mark 1:1). What had been true before the Resurrection was more evident after the Resurrection, and Saul had very recently been in touch with the Risen One. The title "Son of God" must have been highly meaningful to him and also intelligible to his audiences (cf. Ps. 2:7; Luke 3:22; Acts 13:33).

Saul's immense learning in the fields of Scripture and Jewish tradition, now set on fire by his conversion, proved too much for any who ventured to contend with him. He made a convincing presentation by yoking prediction to fulfillment in reference to the messiahship of Jesus. This continued to be his approach in the synagogues (17:3; 18:5), and it was shared by Apollos (18:28). Peter used the method also (2:36), taking it over from the Master (Luke 24:44–46).

Luke says nothing in this account about Saul's departure from Damascus for Arabia and his return to the city (cf. Gal. 1:17). From his omission of this journey one may perhaps conclude that the major purpose of this trip (which need not have taken him far, since the kingdom of Aretas was directly east of the city) was not to evangelize but to meditate on what had been revealed to him. This is agreeable to the Galatian context. At the same time, it is hard to picture this man refraining from preaching for any great length of time. Other factors may have operated, such as the desire to spare the saints in Damascus from persecution that was being stirred up against him in the city because of his outspoken testimony.

9:23–25. The final stage of Saul's stay in Damascus is pictured here. The persecutor became the persecuted; the hunter became the hunted. A ministry of "many days" was now coming to a head, with the opposition becoming organized and determined. In writing to the Galatians, Paul indicated a three-year period between his conversion and his first journey to Jerusalem (Gal. 1:15–18), but there is no indication as to how much of this period was spent in Damascus and how much was spent in Arabia. The sojourn in the latter place may well have been brief.

At any rate, the Jews in Damascus made their plans to get rid of Saul. This was the first of many attempts on his life after he became a believer. Another was made in Jerusalem shortly after this (Acts 9:29). Others occurred at Corinth (20:3), at Ephesus (20:19; cf. Rom. 16:4), at Jerusalem in connection with his final visit (23:21), and when he was at Caesarea (25:3). No wonder he could write of "dangers from [his] countrymen" (2 Cor. 11:26). That he was able to travel and preach with this kind of pressure on him much of the time is an indication that he had committed his life completely to the Lord and was trusting Him for safekeeping.

This protection was worked out in various ways—by the help that his Roman citizenship provided (e.g., Acts 25:11), by division among his adversaries (23:6–10), but mainly by the assistance of fellow believers. On this occasion, "his followers" managed under cover of darkness to lower him through an opening in a Christian's house abutting the city wall, or more properly, built into the wall (cf. Josh. 2:15).

Paul referred to this incident later on (2 Cor. 11:32–33), adding the information that the ethnarch under Aretas the king was involved in the effort to seize him. This may indicate that he had offended the Arabs during his stay in their territory, perhaps by his witness for Christ. Or it may be that the Arabs felt it was to their advantage to cooperate with the Jews who were trying to apprehend him. There is even a possibility that the Romans, in a gesture of good will toward the Nabataeans, had restored Arabian control over Damascus, the emperor Gaius being eager to placate Aretas, who had been the target of a military campaign planned by Emperor Tiberius, Gaius's predecessor.[11] Saul had a capacity for making bitter enemies as well as firm friends.

It should not escape our notice that those who helped him are called "his followers" (literally "learners" or "disciples"). The word *disciple* is prominent in the Gospels and Acts, but fails to appear at all in the remainder of the New Testament, being replaced by such terms as *saints, believers,* and *brethren.*

[11]Josephus, *Antiquities* XVIII.5.1–3.

Verses 26–31. The scene changes to Jerusalem and Saul's first contact with the church there. After only a few days it proved expedient to depart, as strong opposition developed. With the departure, an era of peace came for the church in Palestine.

9:26–28. Quite naturally, no indication is given of any contact between Saul and the Sanhedrin after his arrival in Jerusalem. His life was in a different orbit now. The members of the Council knew what had happened, and they would have liked to forget all about Saul if they could.

Even on the part of the disciples there was a measure of hostility, or at least of suspicion (cf. the reaction of Ananias, v. 13). Doubtless there had been some reports from Damascus about the conversion of Saul, but it was felt that this might be a trick, that the archpersecutor had decided that he could do more damage by becoming a wolf in sheep's clothing. The very fact that he seemed to be trying so hard to be accepted at Jerusalem could have confirmed their suspicions. Apparently he had come without any written commendation from the brethren in Dasmascus.

Hungering for Christian fellowship, Saul must have been on the brink of despair. Then he found in the church one man of influence who recognized his sincerity and accepted at face value his account of his experience with the risen Lord and his testimony at Damascus. Barnabas was never more truly "a son of encouragement" (4:36) than on this occasion. By taking Saul first to the apostles and persuading them, he was able to break down the suspicion of the church as a whole. Apparently the new arrival made himself at home with the leaders of the church and joined them in public testimony.

From Galatians 1:18 it is evident that Saul had a special purpose in going to Jerusalem at this time. He wanted to become acquainted with Peter, and was able to spend fifteen days in his company as his guest. At that time he also had contact with James the Lord's brother (Gal. 1:19). Consequently Luke's statement about the apostles (Acts 9:27) should not be thought of as meaning that the entire group was on hand. Doubtless most of them were out shepherding the churches of Judea, for these churches had recently felt the bruising effect of persecution. Paul's statement that he remained unknown by sight to the Judean churches (Gal. 1:22) confirms that he remained in Jerusalem.[12]

Little imagination is required to appreciate what this visit meant to Saul. From James he was able to learn much about the early life of Jesus at Nazareth. The two could rejoice together over what the Resurrection had made possible in the life of each of them. From Peter must have come many a helpful account of how the Lord had ministered to the multitude and how He had taught His disciples. This fortnight left him rich with memories he would treasure in days to come.

9:29–30. Saul was not content to remain only in the company of believers. Drawn irresistibly to the synagogue where he had heard Stephen declare his faith, he now picked up the torch and entered into dialogue with the Hellenistic Jews. He had no greater success, apparently, than Stephen had enjoyed. Probably the pattern was repeated—inability to answer the messenger of Christ brought a determination to silence him by death (cf. 6:9–12). This happened within a few days' time (Gal. 1:18).

Word of the contemplated attempts on his life came to the attention of the leaders of the church, who acted swiftly to get Saul out of the city. The Lord's warning to him at this time (22:17–18) must have gone far to make him willing to leave. Furthermore, he did not care to be responsible for a fresh wave of persecution for the church such as he himself had instigated (8:3). His stay in Jerusalem ended on the same note as his sojourn in Damascus. Boldness in witness had nearly cost him his life a second time.

Friends accompanied him as far as Caesarea (was there contact with Philip there?), then he proceeded on his own to Tarsus, his boyhood home. It is possible that he had not been back home for a good many years, in view of his time of study in Jerusalem, where he had a sister (23:16). For ten years or so, a veil of silence descended over Saul's career, to be lifted when he reappeared as a leader in the church at Antioch (11:25–26). However, his own statement suggests that he did not confine his residence wholly to Tarsus, but was active in Christian work throughout Syria and Cilicia (Gal. 1:21).

---

[12]The expression "moved about freely" is literally "going in and out." But this need not have involved leaving the city. The idiom simply expresses movement. Luke distinctly states that this activity took place in Jerusalem. For another example of this idiom, see 1:21.

9:31. In this summary Luke notes the peace then pervading the church in Palestine. The point of "then" is to remind the reader of the great contrast between this state of quiet and the turmoil caused by persecution.

Saul's conversion was the primary factor in the change. Another was the shift in the political situation. Vitellius, the imperial legate in Syria from A.D. 35 to 37, had installed a certain Jonathan as high priest in Jerusalem. He became so independent and aggressive that Vitellius, when visiting Jerusalem in 37, removed him from office and appointed his brother Theophilus in his place. At the same time, word came of the death of Tiberius and the succession of Gaius (Caligula) as emperor. "The new emperor was as famous for his adherence to Hellenism as his predecessor was for his opposition to it, and so a reverse was to be expected for the recently rekindled flame of Judaism."[13] The restricting of official Jewish influence would naturally be felt by the church in terms of greater security and freedom to expand.

This summary verse is of interest also because of its use of the word *ekklēsia* (church). Although the plural form is found here in many manuscripts, the manuscripts of superior quality have the singular, suggesting the concept of the church universal as contrasted with the local sense of the word (e.g., 8:1). That is, the church in Palestine is viewed as a whole rather than as separate congregations. The three districts named— Judea, Galilee, and Samaria—comprised the whole country west of the Jordan.

Two general observations are made about the state of the church. First, it was being "strengthened," with this edification being recognized in the lives of God-fearing believers. This was a time of spiritual growth. Second, under the comfort and encouragement of the Holy Spirit there was a reaching out to minister the gospel to others, so that the church "grew in numbers."

The mention of Galilee is a reminder that Luke has not narrated the circumstances under which the witness to Jesus reached the Savior's native territory after Pentecost. The Eleven, being Galilean themselves, could not have been expected to rest easily as long as this area remained unevangelized.

---

[13] Bo Reicke, *The New Testament Era,* 193.

Probably the five hundred people to whom the Lord appeared after His resurrection (1 Cor. 15:6), presumably in Galilee (cf. Matt. 28:16–17), took an active part in witnessing to the people in this area.

8

PETER'S MINISTRY
9:32–11:18

That an intimate connection exists between this section and
the foregoing is evident. Saul's conversion has been recounted,
including his commission to go to the Gentiles, but the story of
that task has not yet been taken up. The telling of it must wait
until the narration of Peter's mission to Cornelius, which
provided the opening wedge of the campaign to reach the
Gentiles, a campaign that Saul was to prosecute with vigor and
magnificent leadership.

AT LYDDA AND JOPPA (9:32–43)

Much of Peter's itinerating activity in Judea is passed by
with merely a hint as to how extensive it was—"about the
country"—in order to describe the portion that led him to
Joppa and ultimately to Caesarea.

9:32–35. Lydda, the Lod of the Old Testament (1 Chron.
8:12), stood at the crossroads of two important travel routes,
one between Egypt and Babylon, the other between Joppa and
Jerusalem. By the time Peter visited the place, a church had
already been established, probably the work of Hellenists who
had been obliged to leave Jerusalem when persecution broke out
there (8:1). A visit by Philip (8:40) is a possibility.

It can be assumed that Peter preached the Word on this
occasion, but Luke made no reference to it, concentrating rather
on a miracle of healing. Aeneas had been paralyzed for eight
years. There is no indication in the Gospels that Jesus had
visited this area, otherwise Aeneas might have been relieved of

his distress long before Peter's coming. But now Jesus was there, working through His servant to bring healing.[1] The effect was similar to the healing of the lame man (chap. 3) in that both were well-known, so that the healing of the lame man created a sensation. A general turning to the Lord resulted, both at Lydda and Sharon. The linking of the two places gives the impression that Sharon was a town, but none is known, so the reference is probably to the maritime plain, especially the southern portion.[2]

9:36–37. Joppa, now known as Jaffa, was located on the seacoast, about twelve miles from Lydda. It was here that Hiram, king of Tyre, brought timber from Lebanon to be carried up to Jerusalem for the building of the temple in Solomon's time (2 Chron. 2:11–16). It was here that Jonah took ship to avoid going to Nineveh as the Lord's messenger.

Tabitha ("gazelle"), or Dorcas (the Greek equivalent), was a "disciple," indicating that the gospel had reached this spot as well as Lydda (cf. 8:40). Like Martha, she found that her gift lay in the area of physical ministry (cf. "helps" in 1 Cor. 12:28). Perhaps her sacrificial labors had contributed to a sickness that proved fatal. The body was prepared for burial, but no interment was held, as the sequel explains.

9:38–42. The known presence of Peter a few miles away spurred hope in the minds of the believers, which suggests that news of the healing of Aeneas had reached their city. We may take for granted that they believed in the resurrection of Jesus. Reports had come of mighty miracles at Jerusalem, Samaria, and other places. We cannot be sure that there was a report of a raising from the dead (none has been recounted thus far in Acts), but after all, Jesus had raised the dead and had promised that the works that He had done would be carried on by His disciples. So hope burned brightly. As it turned out, Dorcas's situation was like that of Lazarus, who had sickened and died— it was all for the glory of God, leading up to resurrection.

The urgent message that was sent to Peter, "Please come at once!" (v. 38), did not have in view that he would be asked to

---

[1] "Jesus Christ *heals* you" does not have the force of "heals at any time" (present habitual tense) but is an example of a relatively infrequent use of the present tense, meaning, in this instance, "here and now heals you."

[2] The fact that "Sharon" has the definite article, whereas "Lydda" does not, may have been sufficient to convey the idea of a district (cf. *the Sahara, the Sudan*).

conduct a funeral service. Peter obliged, putting aside all else to go with the two messengers. One can detect here a certain preparation for a like response to another urgent appeal soon to come (10:23).

As Peter arrived at the upper room he was quickly made aware of how great a loss the Christian community had suffered. The widows were there in force, exhibiting the garments that Dorcas had made for them. Similarly, a congregation is apt to remember a man's pastoral ministry, lovingly given in times of need, even more than the sermons he labored to prepare.

But it was not the past that concerned Peter. The lamentation was genuine, and it grieved him to see their great sorrow; so he "sent them all out" (v. 40). Was he recalling what the Lord had done when He raised the daughter of Jairus (Mark 5:40)? Sensing his need of divine power, he prayed. Had not Jesus, in promising that great works would be done through His disciples, reminded them that whatever they would ask He would perform in answer to prayer (John 14:12–14)?

It took faith to turn again to the lifeless body and say, "Tabitha, get up." Peter found it natural to use her Aramaic name rather than Dorcas, and the fact that it is so recorded favors the idea that Luke followed an early source preserved in the Jewish wing of the church. Awakened from the sleep of death, Tabitha sat up. To help her rise from the couch, Peter extended his hand. As Rackham notes, "To have done so before would have made him unclean"[3] (see Num. 19:11).

Now the people who had been barred from the room were invited in to see and greet their friend, alive again by the power of God. News of the miracle soon spread through the city, with the result that "many people believed in the Lord." Nothing is said about the prestige of Peter. He was no Simon Magus (8:9–11).

9:43. Attention is directed to Peter's residing for a time in Joppa. Probably he did not anticipate what his next move was to be. It was a time of waiting for guidance, which came in due course.

Meanwhile his host was another Simon. Being a tanner,

---

[3]R. B. Rackham, *The Acts of the Apostles*, 145.

Simon had likely been shunned by the Jewish community because of his distasteful occupation. Living close by the sea (10:6) served two purposes: plenty of water was available for washing the hides, and the unpleasant odors were not likely to reach people in the city to any great extent.

Simon had already found a welcome among believers, and this welcome must have been enhanced by Peter's willingness to stay with him. One may even see in this liberal attitude of readiness to reside with a man who handled unclean animals a preparation in Peter himself for the much larger step he was about to take at Caesarea (10:28).

THE WITNESS TO CORNELIUS (10:1–48)

Since Luke was not greatly concerned with chronology, we do not have the information necessary to date this incident with any precision. What the writer desired to emphasize is the beginning of testimony to the Gentiles. He had already given considerable attention to the ministry of Philip to an individual of this status, which is a pointer toward the present narrative. But now it was time to set forth the evangelizing of Gentiles in a Palestinian setting. The very fact that Luke narrated the story at some length and then in effect repeated it in Peter's report to the Jerusalem church (chap. 11) clearly indicates its importance in the overall plan of the book.

In view of the large place given to Paul in Acts, and especially to his work among the Gentiles, grounded in a divine commission (9:15), the placing of Peter in the forefront of this new development demonstrates that the historian was being true to the source material available to him. Luke granted that Peter took the lead at the beginning (cf. 15:7, 14). He had no associate on whom to rely for counsel, so was wholly dependent on the leading of the Spirit. "Peter's position throughout 1–8 is as a spokesman and representative of the Twelve, and is quite different in 9–15 where he acts in a personal capacity."[4]

Verses 1–8. Since the Gentiles did not know the Good News, and since the apostle Peter, steeped in Jewish Christianity, was not yet prepared to minister Christ to such people, God

---

[4]M. D. Goulder, *Type and History in Acts,* 18.

had to take the initiative. He had to deal with Peter, but first of all He moved to make Cornelius aware of divine concern for his spiritual state.

10:1. Caesarea is the setting (cf. 8:40). This city on the coast was one of the monuments of the building activity of Herod the Great, who revamped the former community known as Strato's Tower and renamed it Caesarea in honor of Augustus. The construction went on for more than a decade and included many magnificent buildings and a harbor that Josephus states was larger than the Piraeus that served as the port of Athens. Later on it became the headquarters of Roman procurators who ruled the land in the name of Rome (cf. 23:23–24). Quite naturally Gentiles predominated over Jews in this location. It was here that friction between the two groups sparked the outbreak of the war between the Jews and the Romans that flared in A.D. 66.

Stationed here at the time of this narrative was a "centurion" named Cornelius. A centurion, as the word indicates, was in charge of a hundred men. In this instance they belonged to the Italian Regiment. "His troop . . . belonged to a special group recruited originally in Italy, though it is true that auxiliary units were kept up to strength after their formation by local recruitment."[5]

10:2. Having dealt with the secular status of Cornelius, Luke went on to describe his spiritual condition—" devout and God-fearing." At first glance these two statements seem to say about the same thing; but Luke used the Greek word for "devout" only here and in verse 7, and one form of the verb in Paul's Athenian address (17:23). The term as used by Luke may well be intended to indicate, then, a reverent attitude toward God and the supernatural on the part of one who needs further information to bring him to biblical faith.

The second phrase is more precise in its reference, being a technical term for a Gentile who attended the synagogue and to some degree honored Jewish law and custom, but who had not yet been incorporated into the congregation of Israel because he had not accepted circumcision. In the synagogues of the Dispersion this group made up a fairly substantial part of the attendants, sufficient to be recognized by a speaker (cf. 13:16).

[5] A. N. Sherwin-White, *Roman Society and Roman Law in the New Testament*, 160.

The God-fearer, then, must be distinguished from the Gentile who was thoroughly absorbed into Judaism and was known as a proselyte (2:10; 6:5; 13:43). The latter were usually harder to reach with the gospel than God-fearers, for they had committed themselves fully to Judaism, while the God-fearers had not.

Cornelius had the strength of character to influence his entire household, which may have included a family and certainly included servants and some soldiers in attendance on him (cf. v. 7). This broad significance of household is familiar from Philippians 4:22.

The piety of Cornelius extended not only Godward but toward the people around him, apparently the Jewish people (cf. 26:17). In helping them with his gifts he was expressing his thanks for what he had received in the synagogue. The centurion whom Jesus had encountered, whose servant He healed, had been similarly generous toward the Jewish people, even to the extent of building a synagogue for them (Luke 7:5).

It was during the intertestamental period that almsgiving began to be associated with the idea of merit, regarded as able to secure forgiveness of sins for the giver (Tobit 12:9; Ecclus 3:30). It is impossible to say whether Cornelius shared this notion, but the fact that his activity in this realm is favorably noted (v. 4) inclines one to think that he did not consider it meritorious, but as something his heart inclined him to do. Neither his alms nor his prayers had availed to bring him salvation (11:14)—a reminder that religion, no matter how honestly motivated and how sacrificially carried on, whether by cultus or benevolence, is not able to achieve salvation, which comes only through Christ (4:12). Nevertheless, Cornelius's devotion had great value because it made him a candidate for salvation (v. 4), prompting guidance from heaven to give him the knowledge whereby he could be saved, in line with the truth expressed in Romans 2:6–7.

10:3–6. God's response was not to save Cornelius by fiat, but to show him how he could learn of the appointed way. Three o'clock in the afternoon was one of the stated times observed by the Jews (cf. 3:1) to which Cornelius had conformed his practice. Absorbed in his devotions, he found himself experiencing a vision that included an angel speaking his name. As with Saul on the Damascus road (9:5), he responded by using the term "Lord," knowing that he must be in divine presence. It was a circumstance that alarmed him, for it might betoken God's displeasure. But his fears were immediately allayed through the message that his devotions and acts of kindness had been noted in heaven.

The vision was tantalizing because it contained directions to send to Joppa for Simon (his surname Peter distinguishes him from the other Simon who was his host) but said nothing about what would be accomplished by such a mission. But Cornelius showed that he was not far from the kingdom by having a readiness to act without doubting or arguing. The least he could do was to obey the heavenly command.

10:7–8. The response of the centurion was immediate. He did not make the mistake of Naaman and request that some extraordinary thing be done for him (see 2 Kings 5:11). but was content to send as directed. For this purpose he selected two household slaves and a soldier, all of whom presumably shared the pious stance of their leader and lord. Cornelius did not want unsympathetic men for this task, but men akin to him in spirit. To them he imparted a knowledge of the vision he had received and the commission they were to fulfill. Joppa by the sea, some thirty miles to the south, was their destination.

Verses 9–16. The scene shifts to Joppa, where Peter had already spent many days (9:43), apparently not sure what God had in store for him. Now he was to learn afresh that God "acts on behalf of those who wait for him" (Isa. 64:4, RSV). His waiting on God in prayer (matching Cornelius) was not in vain but opened up one of the most thrilling chapters of his life.

10:9–10. It was on the second day of their journey that the servants of Cornelius found themselves nearing Joppa. And it was just at this time, in this dramatically told narrative, that God gave Peter a vision to prepare him for their coming.

In Palestine, the housetop was flat and approached by a flight of steps on the outside of the house. Since it was a good spot for reflection or prayer, Peter made his way there to pray at the noon. There is some evidence that godly Israelites had observed this period as well as the morning and evening for prayer (Ps. 55:17; Dan. 6:10). Peter was hungry, and God used his hunger to make the forthcoming vision relevant to him. "He fell into a trance" (not the same words as "vision" in v. 3 but occurring again in the case of Paul in 22:17), or an ecstatic state, which God induced for His own purposes of revelation and instruction. Consciousness was at least partially suspended (cf. Gen. 2:21 LXX).

10:11–12. First of all Peter saw something being let down from the opened sky before his uplifted eyes. It appeared to resemble a "large sheet," held by its four corners so as not to lose what was contained in it. The sheet descended to a point where Peter could readily see the contents. In it were all kinds of animals, including walking, crawling, and flying varieties. For the sequel to have meaning, it is necessary to understand that both clean and unclean animals, in terms of the Levitical code, were present for Peter's inspection.

10:13–16. Unexpectedly, the Lord proceeded to instruct Peter by bidding him, "Kill and eat," thereby to satisfy his hunger. Peter replied without hesitation. He must have felt that he was being tested, and it was his nature under such conditions to want to show his loyalty (cf. Matt. 26:33). So he protested that nothing unclean had ever entered his mouth. He had been a practicing Jew all his life.

Probably it did not occur to him that he was actually disobeying the Lord, who had just given him a command. At Caesarea Philippi he had disputed with Jesus the necessity for the Lord's going to the cross. Here the issue concerned his own conduct, and he was just as vigorous in his protestation as on the former occasion (Matt. 16:22). Probably he had forgotten that Jesus had taught the disciples, "Nothing that enters a man from the outside can make him 'unclean'" (Mark 7:18). According to Matthew's account it was Peter himself who had inquired about the meaning of those words (Matt. 15:15). Quite likely the editorial note in the parallel passage, Mark 7:19 ("In saying this, Jesus declared all foods 'clean'"), owes its origin to Peter's experience on the housetop after its significance had dawned on him. (According to several early Fathers, Mark wrote his Gospel as the interpreter of Peter.)

The voice came "a second time" with a final word to settle Peter's complaint. "Do not call anything impure that God has made clean." Altogether the vision of the sheet was given three times, to impress it on Peter's mind, and then was withdrawn.

Verses 17–23a. Peter's perplexity over what he had seen is understandable in a practicing Jew. He did not yet perceive that the restrictions of the Mosaic Law had been valid while the Law was in force but were not binding when Christ, the end of the Law, had brought that dispensation to a close. As far as foods were concerned, the edict at creation had declared that everything God had made was good (Gen. 1:31). This principle was now reestablished.

The termination of the Law was not recognized by unbelieving Jews and was only gradually perceived by Jews who trusted in Christ. It required a period of education to free them from the outlook of years of living under the Levitical code. Even in the period after the Cross a Christian Jew such as Peter, now aware of the situation, could be expected to avoid giving offense to a fellow Jew who was not a Christian by refusing to eat "unclean" food when in his company. But the principle of freedom in this area was clearly established (cf. 1 Tim. 4:1–5).

10:17–23a. Peter's reflections on this matter were interrupted by the arrival of the men from Cornelius. The timing was perfect. Their mission would enable Peter to solve his perplexity by substituting unclean men for unclean food in his thinking. The Spirit did not provide the solution by direct revelation, but prompted Peter to go with the men without misgivings, thus assuring him of God's blessing on the venture (cf. 8:29; John 16:13).

Three men had come, according to the almost unanimous testimony of the manuscripts. One important witness, Codex Vaticanus, has *two* at this point, possibly due to the reference to two servants in verse 7. But *three* is undoubtedly the correct number, harmonizing with the total of three mentioned in verse 7.

When Peter greeted the men and asked about the reason for their visit, they responded with restrained pride as they told of their master, Cornelius. One item emerges here that is not openly stated in verses 1 and 2, namely, the high esteem in which Cornelius was held by "all the Jewish people." This exaggeration is pardonable. The statement was indeed true of the Jews in the Caesarea area, as a natural result of his almsgiving to the Jewish nation (v. 2).

Cornelius had been divinely "told" to send for Peter. Every time this verb appears in the New Testament in the passive voice it refers to supernatural guidance (cf. Luke 2:26). This was enough to satisfy Peter. In showing hospitality to the new arrivals he was already manifesting a willingness to have contact with Gentiles, a kind of firstfruits of his full illumination about his forthcoming mission to the house of Cornelius.

Verses 23b–29. This section deals with the arrival at Caesarea and provides the setting for the explanation given by Cornelius.

179

10:23b–29. Peter had been told by the Spirit to go without misgivings, but this did not mean that he should go without foresight. He showed foresight by taking some brethren from Joppa with him, six in number (11:12). The reason for his precaution is fairly evident. As witnesses to what was to transpire at Caesarea, they would be able to corroborate Peter's testimony when he was called on to explain the incident to the leaders at Jerusalem (11:1–18). Clearly Peter was aware that his mission at Caesarea might well be a turning point for the church.

He (some manuscripts say "they") arrived at the destination and found Cornelius expecting them. No doubt he had carefully calculated the time required to make the trip from Joppa and had summoned his relatives and friends accordingly. This man did not question in the least the reality of the vision, nor did he question the certainty that Peter would come. His faith resembled that of the centurion at Capernaum (Matt. 8:10).

So great was his gratitude on seeing Peter that he prostrated himself before him. The word "worshiped" (NASB) is probably too strong a term here, for Cornelius, as a faithful attendant at the synagogue, must have known that God alone is worthy of worship. But even the physical prostration was altogether unnecessary, since he was dealing with a man. Even an angel is not entitled to receive worship (Rev. 22:8–9).

On entering the house Peter discovered an assembled company waiting for his arrival. The same unselfishness that characterized Cornelius in his giving of alms had motivated him to share the anticipated blessing of Peter's visit with others.

It was natural that Peter's opening words should set forth the awkwardness of his position and the daring required to set foot in this house filled with Gentiles. Even though his hearers were aware of the exclusivism of the Jews and their avoidance of Gentiles lest defilement should result, Peter felt the need of reminding them of the unusual nature of what was transpiring. Ordinarily a Jew would neither "associate" with a Gentile nor "visit" him. He would have as little to do with him as possible.

This may sound unreasonable, since the Jews welcomed Gentiles into the synagogue. But fraternizing with them was a different matter. The explanation takes us back to the return from Babylonian captivity, when the Jews, realizing that too close contact with the nations surrounding Israel had brought their fathers into idolatry and other sins, determined to remain separate from the people of the land (Neh. 13:3, 23–27). Business relations with Gentiles were sometimes necessary, but social contacts were frowned on. The Jews felt that they must do everything necessary to retain their own religion and culture apart from Gentile contamination.

However, God had been dealing with Peter. Either before leaving Joppa or on the way, his eyes had been opened to see the meaning of the vision on the housetop; namely, that he should not call any person unholy or unclean. The lesson had sunk in. Peter had a freedom he had never known before (cf. 15:7–9). He succumbed on a later occasion to the pressure of Jewish-Christian strictness (Gal. 2:11–12), but in principle he recognized that the middle wall of partition between Jew and Gentile had been broken down in Christ (cf. Eph. 2:14).

All this time Peter was without clear indication as to what was expected of him at Caesarea. Apparently the conversation with Cornelius at the entrance of the dwelling had not disclosed anything more than what the messengers had told him—that he was to give a message in the centurion's house. By asking why he had been sent for, Peter opened the way for Cornelius to inform the entire group of the background for this gathering.

Verses 30–33. The explanation of Cornelius gives the essentials of God's dealing with him, as recounted at the beginning of the chapter.

10:30–33. Cornelius had a word of commendation for Peter: "It was good of you [literally, "you have done well"] to come." He realized that this represented a new departure for the apostle. Also he encouraged Peter by indicating the mood of expectancy that filled all hearts as they awaited the message. God had been moving both in his life and in Peter's, and it was in keeping with this that he expected Peter to pass on only what he had been "commanded" rather than his own ideas.

Verses 34–43. It was Peter's turn to speak. He must have been overwhelmed as he looked at his hearers, so attentive and expectant, realizing that God was breaking through Jewish prejudice by using him, a Christian Jew, to communicate the gospel to Gentiles. His message was thoroughly in accord with his own position as one who had known and followed the Lord from earliest days.

10:34–35. Peter began by commenting on the revolution in his own thinking. He was now in a position to understand the character and purpose of God in a way he had not perceived before. The uniqueness of the covenant people had blinded him to the breadth of God's operations. Not only had the Abrahamic covenant mentioned all the families of the earth (Gen. 12:3), but other passages too had cited a gracious purpose toward the nations. But the Jews were so impressed with their distinctiveness as the chosen people that they had relegated others to a subordinate position. So it was a great insight that led Peter to remark that God is without "favoritism" (cf. Rom. 2:11; 1 Peter 1:17).

The historical priority of the Jew (Acts 3:26; Rom. 1:16) does not detract from this great truth. God is prepared to receive those in "every nation" who fear Him and work righteousness, the very things that are noted about Cornelius (10:2; cf. Matt. 6:1–2). The meaning is not that such persons are thereby saved (cf. Acts 11:14) but rather that they are suitable candidates for salvation. Such preparation betokens a spiritual earnestness that will result in faith as the gospel is heard and received.

10:36–37. Jesus proclaimed this good news during His earthly ministry. "Peace" was a keynote of the angelic proclamation at His birth (Luke 2:14) and served to summarize the good news of His mission by which the estrangement between unholy sinners and a righteous God could be reconciled (*peace* is virtually a synonym for *salvation* in Isaiah 52:7). Probably the Lord Jesus had this in mind as well as physical preservation when He made Himself the key to Jerusalem's peace (Luke 19:42).

Peter had indicated that this message was heralded to "the people of Israel" (v. 36). Now, as though to anticipate the emphasis of verse 43 with its inclusion of Gentiles, he added almost as an afterthought: "who is Lord of all." Gentiles as well as Jews have a stake in Him and both alike are brought under His sway when they receive the gospel.

In saying, "You know what has happened," Peter was unquestionably referring to the Christ event, the breaking in of the Son of God on human life and history. He was able to assume that the story of our Lord's life and work in broad outline did not have to be recounted as something new; for the life, ministry, and death of the Prophet of Nazareth were public knowledge, seeing that these things had not been done in a corner (26:26; cf. 2:22). This helps to account for the summary character of the description of the ministry.[6]

In speaking of all Judea, Peter was using the term in its broadest sense as covering the homeland of the Jews (cf. Luke 23:5). "Beginning in Galilee" confirms the representation of the synoptic Gospels that Galilee was the place where the ministry began. The time, "after the baptism that John preached," is also in harmony with what the Gospels report (Mark 1:1–14).

10:38–41. Making a fresh start, as it were, Peter emphasized that the Good News revolves around "Jesus of Nazareth"; then he highlighted the leading features of the ministry, including the baptism, where God anointed Him "with the Holy Spirit and power" (Luke 3:22; 4:14; Acts 4:27). Jesus Himself affirmed this anointing (Luke 4:18). It signified that He was the Christ (which means "the Anointed One").

Jesus' ministry proper is compressed into the two items of "doing good" and delivering people from Satan's power. The former is an apt description of those acts of mercy and compassion that so occupied the Savior that there was scarcely time to eat. The other aspect seems to refer to the exorcisms, though a wider range could be intended so as to include some healings (cf. Luke 13:16). Success in these activities was due to the fact that "God was with him" (cf. Acts 2:22). What was implied in the anointing was shown in the mighty works.

Nothing is said about the teaching. For the most part this seems to have been reserved for the instruction of converts (cf. 2:42).

To assure his audience that he was not relying on hearsay in these matters, Peter included the fact that he and others had been witnesses of all that Jesus did throughout the land and then in Jerusalem, concluding with His death on the cross. The value of this death was not declared immediately but was reserved for a later point (v. 43). As in earlier addresses by Peter, the human responsibility for Jesus' death was placed in the foreground.

The sequel to the Cross was the Resurrection "on the third day" (cf. 1 Cor. 15:4), followed by the appearances (cf. 1 Cor.

---

[6]In a comparative study of statements of the gospel found in Paul's Epistles, in Acts, and in the Synoptic Gospels, C. H. Dodd traces the similarity between this address by Peter and Mark's Gospel (*The Apostolic Preaching and Its Development* [London: Hodder & Stoughton, 1936]. Once more it is helpful to note the close contact between Peter and Mark as a background for this similarity.

15:5–7). No attempt was made to link the Resurrection with Old Testament prophecy, since the audience was made up of Gentiles. Peter freely acknowledged that there was no appearance of the risen Lord to the general public, but only to the chosen few who had been with Him during the course of His ministry, to whom the return from the dead was far more meaningful than it could possibly have been to others. It is here (v. 41) that the word *witnesses* is used a second time (cf. v. 39) as though to say that of all the things the disciples could attest as witnesses, this stood out as the most important (cf. 1:22).

The mention of eating and drinking with Christ after the Resurrection goes beyond what the Gospels relate (Luke 21:30, 41–43; John 21:13), yet it was a natural thing both as a token of His identity and as an expression of fellowship. There may seem to be here a contradiction with the Master's assertion at the Last Supper that He would not drink again until He drank the wine anew with His own in the kingdom; but He had been referring to drinking the wine of the Passover, not to drinking of anything else (see Matt. 26:29).

10:42–43. In the sequence of statements, the command of the risen Lord to His disciples to preach was naturally taken as a command issued between the Resurrection and the Ascension. Nothing that fits this exactly is found in the Gospels, but we do not have a complete account of what Jesus communicated to His followers during the appearances. Such a command is implied in the authority vested in Him by virtue of the Resurrection (Matt. 28:18).

"The people" were members of the Jewish nation. This observation by Peter could have served in that instance as something of a reason for the delay in reaching Caesarea, a largely Gentile community, with the gospel. The first obligation of the apostles was to proclaim the message to their own people (3:26).

For the first time in Acts we read of the judging function of the Lord Jesus Christ. Reports of early preaching do not always contain all the elements that belonged to the *kerygma,* or gospel proclamation, but this is not an isolated reference (cf. 17:31; 24:25). Mention of the dead as well as the living implies the power of the risen Lord to raise unbelievers as well as the saints (24:15). The phrase "judge of the living and the dead" is readily recognizable as the source of an article in the Apostles' Creed (the old English *quick* being the equivalent of *living*).

Considerable difficulty surrounds Peter's final Christo-logical statement, the one that claims prophetic anticipation of forgiveness of sins for all who believe in the Lord Jesus. I. Howard Marshall observes:

> At first sight this is a strange statement. Prophecies of forgiveness by the Messiah are hard to find, and the allusion to "all the prophets" seems highly exaggerated (cf. Luke 24:27). The solution to the problem lies in two statements. First, in the Old Testament forgiveness is associated with the name of Yahweh, "the Lord." It is the prerogative of God; those who seek the Lord find that he will abundantly pardon them (Isa. 55:6f.). Second, the effect of the resurrection is that Jesus is exalted and receives the title of Lord (Acts 2:36). The conclusion is obvious: by virtue of his exaltation Jesus has received the prerogative of God the Lord to dispense forgiveness of sins (cf. perhaps Stephen's prayer, Acts 7:60). What is asserted of God in "all the prophets" can now be asserted of the exalted Jesus.[7]

The statement about the prophets was not out of order in addressing these Gentiles, for at least some of them had frequented the synagogue and were familiar in a general way with the content of Old Testament revelation.

Verses 44–48. The effect of the message on Peter's audience is here spelled out.

10:44–48. The juncture at which the Holy Spirit came on the hearers is significant, for they had just received the assurance that belief in the risen Lord would bring forgiveness of sins. The descent of the Spirit on the audience was in itself proof that acceptance of the Lord had indeed taken place on the part of the people. God's answer was swift and unmistakable. It was a source of amazement to Peter's companions as they sensed that the Spirit had indeed been poured out, the "speaking in tongues" being evidence. "Praising God" is a reasonable equivalent of the activity of the apostles in Jerusalem when the Spirit had come on them (2:11).

What is so striking about the event in the house of Cornelius is that the experience of these Gentiles was recognized

---

[7]I. Howard Marshall, "The Resurrection in the Acts of the Apostles," in *Apostolic History and the Gospel,* 104.

to be the same as that of the Twelve. They were not treated as the Jewish converts on the day of Pentecost had been, for those converts had heard the message, believed, and were baptized before they received the gift of the Spirit (2:38). Nor were they dealt with in the same manner as the believers at Samaria, who had been obliged to wait some time after their baptism for the gift of the Spirit (8:12, 15). These Gentile converts were treated just as the apostles had been treated at Pentecost—the Spirit descended, and they spoke with tongues and magnified God. The granting of this gift of the Spirit to uncircumcised Gentiles who had not yet been baptized was a powerful demonstration to the church of the acceptability of Gentiles on the basis of faith alone, anticipating the decision of the Jerusalem Council (chap. 15). It amounted to a declaration of the equality of Jew and Gentile in the body of Christ, the church.

Peter could see no difference between the ministry of the Spirit on this occasion and the ministry to the apostles at the beginning (v. 47; cf. 11:15). Baptism was promptly administered, even though it might have seemed an anticlimax. It was the Lord's command, and it was a means of confessing faith to others. Peter's six companions may have performed the baptisms (cf. 1 Cor. 1:13–17).

Nothing is said about circumcision. The presumption is that the seal of God was so overwhelming and so final as to overcome doubts on this point. All barriers came down, as evidenced by Peter's acceptance of an invitation to be a house guest for a few days. This implies the eating of food that was not kosher, and in fact it led to a charge of misconduct when he returned to Jerusalem (11:3).

REPORT TO THE JERUSALEM CHURCH (11:1–18)

The shock of what had occurred at Caesarea was felt in congregations throughout the land and especially in the mother church at Jerusalem. Whatever joy there may have been over the salvation of Gentiles was overshadowed by misgiving, as evidenced by the criticism leveled at Peter when he returned to the Holy City. The apostle had anticipated objection and was prepared to meet it. After he spoke, fears were allayed for the time being.

11:1–3. When the news reached them, the apostles were likely scattered in various places, preaching and ministering to the churches of Judea. Word came to "the brothers" as well. Their reaction was probably not greatly different from that of the leaders. There was intense interest but also perplexity and anxiety. That "the Gentiles also had received the word of God" may sound commonplace to us, but it was new and strange to the Jewish church. The evangelization of Samaritans had not created a stir, nor had the winning of the Ethiopian eunuch, since he was a solitary case and was on his way out of the land when he was converted. But now a group of Gentiles had believed. What did this mean for the future of the church?

On his arrival at Jerusalem Peter was challenged by "the circumcised believers." Ordinarily this description would mean simply Jews, or Jewish Christians if the context called for this sense (cf. 10:45). This may be the meaning here, but there is a strong possibility that the phrase is a bit more precise in this instance, indicating those Christian Jews who were prepared to insist that Gentile converts to the faith must submit to circumcision, in line with the practice during Old Testament days. If Luke intended this nuance (and it seems that he did, because all believers in Jerusalem would have been circumcised, and this seems to be a reference to a certain number), the reader is being prepared for his observation in 15:5.

The charge against Peter was not that he preached to Gentiles and permitted them to be baptized, but that he had fraternized with uncircumcised men and had gone so far as to eat with them. Peter himself had voiced the Jewish attitude when he began to address the people in Caesarea, and he had only consented to come to them because God had directed him (10:28). These two issues—the reception of Gentiles into the church and having table fellowship with them—were bound up together. If Gentiles were taken into the church without circumcision and then were refused table fellowship on the very ground that they were uncircumcised, the reception would be hollow indeed. Logically it would then be impossible for Gentile believers to sit at the Lord's Table with Jewish believers. The end result would inevitably be two churches rather than one. Paul saw this clearly, and on this account he was stirred up by Peter's momentary lack of consistency in the incident at Antioch (Gal. 2:11–16).

11:4–17. Peter's answer to the charge of the circumcision group is contained here. It is an answer based not on Scripture or tradition but on recent history, on the intervention and direction of God Himself. Who could contest such evident leading? The best defense was to relate what had actually happened, and this is what Peter proceeded to do.

His account was orderly and comprehensive, omitting only details that were not essential, such as his position on the housetop and the time of day. It was important to retain the fact that he had been "praying," waiting upon God. Some details were added, such as the observation that the object being lowered came down directly to him and that he fixed his gaze on and observed it closely (RSV). Thus he had been able to see that the object contained animals of all kinds, not simply those that were clean according to the Law. So his refusal to eat had been grounded on close inspection and the realization that he would be violating the Levitical code by eating (v. 8).

Peter was careful to note that the divine correction of his refusal had occurred three times, as though to impress on him that what he had done in the past was not a guide in the present situation. The divine command had been unmistakable. To emphasize the striking way in which God had confirmed His command by circumstances, he explained that "right then" (a time notice absent from chapter 10) three men sent from Cornelius had come to the house. To seal it all, the Spirit had bidden him go with these men without misgivings, thus bolstering his confidence by putting him immediately into contact with Gentiles.

He had been given the foresight to ask certain brothers (Jewish Christians) from Joppa to go with him, so that he could now report, "We entered the man's house." Peter's testimony had the support of men who had been on the spot and had witnessed all that took place at Caesarea (cf. 10:45). They had taken the trouble to come up to Jerusalem with him to give support and corroboration. The Law required only two or three witnesses. To muster six can only mean that Peter felt the need of impressing the Jerusalem church with the realization that a new thing had happened and that the facts were beyond challenge.

Included in Peter's report was the information given by Cornelius that an angel had appeared to him and directed him to send to Joppa for Peter. From this the mother church could understand that God had been working in Cornelius's life as well as in Peter's. An important item is added here (not in chapter 10), that God's purpose in all this activity was to bring

Cornelius and his household the knowledge of salvation (v. 14).

Still holding to the bare essentials, Peter declared that his message to these Gentiles was not even completed when "the Holy Spirit came on them"—the same Spirit who had bidden him go to Caesarea—as though to emphasize the divine sovereignty at work in welcoming Gentiles into the fold. Peter saw in this bestowal a repetition of what had occurred at Pentecost. It was not necessary to mention the gift of tongues, for this would be implied in the very fact that the two incidents were of the same nature. There in the house of Cornelius the words of the risen Lord had flashed into Peter's mind (something not stated in chapter 10), predicting the impending baptism with the Holy Spirit (1:5). Surely it was of the utmost importance that what had been granted to the apostles of the Lord should now be extended to those outside the ranks of Israel. It was "the same gift." God was making no difference between the two groups—marvelous indeed.

"Who was I to think that I could oppose God?" (cf. 5:39). Peter had resisted the command to eat of animals judged by him to be unclean. To resist a second time when the higher reality was being acted out before his eyes would be unthinkable even for a man as stubborn as Peter. God had used the right man to persuade the Jerusalem church. If he was convinced, their opposition could no longer stand.

11:18. With their objections silenced, Peter's audience turned to praise. They were genuinely astonished that God would move in this unprecedented fashion among Gentiles. It was a fresh and mighty revelation of His grace. We are accustomed to think of "repentance" as a humanly inspired act that prepares the soul for faith that leads to "life." But in the last analysis both the possibility and the actuality of this turning away from sin and turning to God is His gracious work (cf. 5:31). It embraces Gentiles as well as the children of Israel (cf. 20:21; 26:20).

This joy in the enlargement of the divine operations unfortunately did not last, at least it did not become the portion of the entire Jerusalem church. Some who were absent that day remained dubious about the extension of the gospel to Gentiles apart from the demand of circumcision, and perhaps even some who heard Peter were not prepared to endorse a continuing work among Gentiles. They may have thought of the Cornelius episode as a solitary thing that should not be allowed to set a precedent. At any rate, it was from the Jerusalem church that the demand was made later that such converts be required to accept circumcision and the yoke of the Law (15:1). The maintenance of the Christian faith as a Jewish phenomenon was deemed essential, and this was being imperiled.

It may be significant also that, so far as the Book of Acts informs us, Peter did not continue to work among Gentiles. He was known as the apostle of the circumcision (Gal. 2:7–9). Primary leadership for the Gentile mission was to belong to the apostle Paul.

9

OUTREACH TO ANTIOCH
11:19-30

At this point Luke reaches back to the period of Stephen and the dispersion of the Hellenists from Jerusalem (11:19 begins with exactly the same expression as 8:4). This is to bring the reader up to date respecting the missionary activities of this group, especially those who carried the gospel northward to Phoenicia and Syria, laying the foundation for further advance into Europe. Therefore the passage before us is of crucial importance in the expansion of Christianity and in the plan of the Book of Acts.

11:19-21. Apparently it was before Peter went to Caesarea that these missionaries had passed through Phoenicia, probably visiting the major centers at Ptolemais, Tyre, and Sidon. References later on to believers at Tyre (21:3) and Ptolemais (21:7) may indicate that churches were established there in connection with this northward expansion. Cyprus, an important island off the Syrian coast, has been mentioned as the home of Barnabas (4:36) and will figure again in Luke's account of the first missionary journey of Barnabas and Saul (13:4-12). The place named last, Syrian Antioch, held such great opportunity that there was no further movement into more remote areas at this time.

In all these places the gospel proclamation was restricted to Jews; but sometime after the witness had begun at Antioch, a change of strategy took place in that some of the Hellenists began to give the word to "Greeks also."[1] The word "also" requires us to think that those who began a mission to the Greeks did not abandon the attempt to reach the Jews. In all likelihood the word "Greeks" is used as a synonym for "Gentiles" (cf. 14:1; Rom. 1:16). In this part of the world "Jew and Greek" summarized the population, for ever since the days of Alexander the Great the influence of Greek language and culture had molded the Near East, especially the cities. The Jews, even though they were affected by Hellenization, retained in large measure their own national heritage, which was a combination of religion and culture.

The men who were responsible for this new departure at Antioch had been dispersed, like the others, from Jerusalem. Their original homes had been in Cyprus and the Cyrene area of North Africa (cf. 2:10). There is a distinct possibility that they may have visited Antioch prior to their period of residence in Jerusalem and were aware of the unusual opportunity for evangelism presented by this city.

Antioch was founded by Seleucus, one of the generals of Alexander. Favored by climate and geographical position, it grew rapidly and became the capital of the Seleucid Empire. When the Romans came in shortly before the middle of the first century B.C., Pompey made it the capital of the province of Syria. Under the Romans it enjoyed the status of an autonomous city, and its fame increased as a center of commerce and of luxurious living, the third most important city in the empire. The mixed population included a large number of Jews, perhaps twenty-five thousand or more. In such a cosmopolitan atmosphere people learned to live with one another in a spirit of toleration, a fact that is borne out by the fact that Luke recorded no persecution of the church there, either by Jews or pagans.

The unprecedented move to reach the Gentiles met with divine approval, "for the Lord's hand was with them." Luke used the same expression in connection with the early life of John the Baptist (Luke 1:66). The hand of the Lord was symbolic of divine activity and intervention (4:28, 30; 13:11).

[1] Some manuscripts have "Hellenists" instead of "Greeks," but, because of what the context indicates, this reading cannot stand. A contrast is obviously intended with the proclamation to "Jews alone" (v. 19), and Hellenists were Jews.

Believers in considerable numbers were gathered into the fellowship. As though to underscore the overwhelmingly Gentile character of the church, Luke did not indicate that there was a ministry in any of the synagogues, though verse 19 implies such a ministry at the beginning. For the first time the Christian faith had established itself in one of the major centers of the Roman Empire.

To judge from the deliberate effort of Luke to tie in this mission with the associates of Stephen, as noted above, we are no doubt intended to understand that the outlook of the first martyr—an appreciation of the new revelation in Jesus Christ, transcending alike the temple and the Law—was to characterize the Antioch church. It would face forward, eager to take a leading role in Christ's victorious march through the world.

11:22–24. Before long the news of the growing work at Antioch came to the Jerusalem church, resulting in the sending of Barnabas to supervise and aid in the ministry. Similar action had been taken in the case of Samaria, except that two apostles had been sent on that occasion (8:14). A further difference emerges in that whereas Peter and John had returned to Jerusalem when their mission was completed, Barnabas stayed on, thus identifying himself permanently with the work among Gentiles. When he visited Jerusalem later (11:30; 15:2), it was not to make a report or give an accounting of his work at Antioch. In Galatians 2:1–10 he appears as the associate of Paul, not as a representative of the Jerusalem congregation. The choice of Barnabas as the one to go to Antioch was singularly fortunate. He was a native of Cyprus (4:36) and as such had much in common with the men who first sowed the gospel seed among the Gentiles at Antioch (11:20).

What he saw of the manifest operation of divine "grace" was a source of satisfaction to him. He was happy to see it, and instead of raising questions about the propriety of evangelizing Gentiles or dwelling on the Law and circumcision, he entered heartily into the work, doing all he could to encourage the new converts to continue to be faithful to the Lord. He was living up to his name, "Son of Encouragement" (4:36). It is likely that he sensed the strategic importance of a strong church at Antioch, although he may not have foreseen its full significance as a base for missionary outreach.

Luke was so impressed with the sterling quality of this man that he went out of his way to list some of his qualifications: "a good man," marked by integrity and wholesomeness, also "full of the Holy Spirit and faith," a description that tallies with that of Stephen (6:5). As though to stress the impetus that the presence of Barnabas gave to the work, Luke comments again on the addition of converts. In fact, whereas a goodly number had been brought to faith before his coming (v. 21), now the influx became a great number of people (v. 24).

11:25–26. Apparently it was this great increase that prompted Barnabas to seek help. He thought of Saul, whom he had come to know at Jerusalem several years before (9:27). At that time Saul had needed him. Now he needed Saul. Possibly he had heard from the mouth of Saul that Gentiles had been specifically included in his call (9:15; 22:21).

Leaving Antioch, he set out in person "to look for Saul." The language suggests uncertainty as to Saul's whereabouts (cf. Luke 2:44–45, the only other occurrences of the word.) He might have been in Tarsus, where he had gone from Jerusalem years before (9:30) or possibly was laboring in other parts of Cilicia or northern Syria (Gal. 1:21–23). Tarsus lay northwest of Antioch and could be reached by sea as well as by land. The latter route would require a journey of over one hundred miles and would consume several days. As he traveled, Barnabas must often have resorted to prayer that God would lead him to Saul and incline his friend to respond favorably to the request he would make.

God was pleased to give success to Barnabas. Doubtless Saul could see for himself that the work he had been doing (passed over by Luke) had prepared him for just such a ministry as Barnabas pictured to him. That Saul had been witnessing mainly to Gentiles during this period of obscurity is attested in 22:21. The rigor of his service is reflected in the variety and intensity of his sufferings (2 Cor. 11:23–27), many of which he must have experienced in those early years rather than in the period that Luke narrates from this point on.

The two men combined forces to lead the church for "a whole year" in a teaching ministry. This does not mean, of course, that evangelism ceased or even slackened, but that special emphasis was now placed on instruction and growth in the Lord, after the example of the Jerusalem church (2:42) and in obedience to the Lord's command (Matt. 28:20). A detail in the narrative at verse 26 reflects this change of emphasis. The expression denoting those who were taught ("great numbers") is identical with the description of the converts in verse 24. An earnest effort was made to mature these babes in Christ.

C. H. Dodd ventures the plausible suggestion that the catechetical materials that appear in the Pauline letters, beginning with 1 and 2 Thessalonians, derive principally from the teachings that were used in the Antioch church.[2] Converts from paganism, even more than God-fearers, would need help in understanding the nature of the new life in Christ and its implication for Christian conduct. The temptation to allow themselves to conform to the pagan environment they had known would have to be met by setting forth the obligations of discipleship and the glorious resources of the risen Lord that were available to them (cf. Phil. 4:13).

It was at Antioch that the disciples of Christ were first called "Christians" (v. 26). The contention that this name was given by God through revelation is not well founded, for cases in which the word translated "called" has this connotation (Matt. 2:12, 22; Acts 10:22) are marked by contextual features (such as dreams or instruction) clearly indicating divine activity. Such intimation is lacking here. A strictly parallel example to the one before us is provided by Romans 7:3, "She is called an adulteress." It is in usages such as this that a person (or a group, as at Antioch) is labeled.

The problem centers in finding a suitable source responsible for the naming. Who first described believers in Christ (used as a personal name rather than a title) as Christians? Jews can be ruled out, for they refused to concede that Jesus was the Christ (Messiah) whom their nation expected. Believers can be eliminated also, since they had other terms for describing themselves—mainly *disciples, believers, saints,* and *brothers.* By elimination, the responsibility is to be placed on the pagan population of Antioch.

The non-Christian origin of the name is to some extent confirmed by the fact that the two remaining occurrences of the word in the New Testament (Acts 26:28; 1 Peter 4:16) involve its use by outsiders. In line with this we have the remark of Tacitus that Nero, to counter rumors that he himself had set fire to Rome, "falsely accused culprits and subjected to most

---

[2]C. H. Dodd, *More New Testament Studies* (Grand Rapids: Eerdmans, 1968), 16.

unusual punishments those whom, hated for their shameful deeds, the populace called Christians."[3]

That the label was first affixed at Antioch makes understandable its use in several of the letters of Ignatius, bishop of Antioch, early in the second century.

A variation from the usual approach to the problem of the origin of the name is provided by H. B. Mattingly.[4] He notes that the word in the original owes its form to the Latin, where it would be written *Christiani*. Positing that it was a popular designation of pagan origin, he understands it to have been coined as a playful take-off in opposition to the coterie of *Augustiani* who surrounded the idolized Nero. The argumentation is ingenious, but the dating (59–60) makes it tenuous. Though Luke did not say that the name was given at the time he was describing (in the 40s), that is the impression left with the reader.

The place at which Luke injected his remark, following the account of evangelistic and teaching activity, makes it evident that the new faith made a strong impact on a great city in a comparatively short time. Incidentally, the new name bears testimony to the essentially Gentile complexion of the church, setting the community of believers quite apart from the Judaism with which the people had been familiar for a much longer period. The supposition that the name was given in ridicule is problematical, even though later on it was sometimes used in derision, as in the quotation from Tacitus.

11:27–30. About this time an unexpected opportunity presented itself for the Antioch congregation to express its appreciation to the Jerusalem church for those who had come with the gospel and with gifts of ministry.

The arrival of some prophets from Jerusalem manifests the continuing interest of the mother church in the Christian community at Antioch. In his account of the Jerusalem church Luke has not previously mentioned the presence of prophets, though the phenomenon was not unexpected in view of 2:17–18. Such men spoke by revelation from the Spirit (1 Cor. 14:29–30), usually in terms of edification and encouragement (1 Cor. 14:3, 31) and even of fundamental doctrine (Eph.

---

[3] Tacitus, *Annals* 15.44.

[4] H. B. Mattingly. "The Origin of the Name *Christiani*," *JTS* 9 (1958): 26–37.

3:4–5). But occasionally, as here, their ministry included prediction. Agabus appears again in such a role (21:10–11).

The Western text of verse 28 states that the prediction occurred "when we were gathered together," indicating Luke's presence. This may reflect a reliable tradition, in which case he may have been a native of Antioch. Probably he was a convert during those early days. One can imagine him sitting under the instruction of Saul and coming to share his deep devotion to Christ and the Christian gospel. This would help to account for his readiness to travel with his friend on the second missionary journey. Perhaps it was at the urging of the apostle that he was led to prepare an account of Christian beginnings that we know as Acts and to reach even further back to pen one of the synoptic Gospels.

It is not possible to substantiate from ancient historians that there was "a severe famine . . . over the entire Roman world" at this time, as Agabus predicted. However, there were serious shortages from time to time during the reign of Claudius. One of these is noted by Suetonius, who says, "There was a scarcity of grain because of long-continued droughts."[5] So it is legitimate, as F. F. Bruce observes, to think in terms of dearth at various intervals rather than of a single famine.[6] The word *oikoumenē* (also used in Luke 2:1) means the entire inhabited world, and therefore the famine was not limited to Palestine but included the Roman Empire as a whole.

The mention of Claudius, who reigned from A.D. 41–54, prepares the reader somewhat for the events recorded at the beginning of the next chapter, since Claudius was responsible for putting Herod Agrippa I on his throne in Judea.

Acting on the prophecy and without any request from the Jerusalem church, the saints at Antioch responded beautifully, each of them determining to give in proportion to his means. It was democratic, congregational action. How long the gathering of funds went on we are not told. If the plan that Paul used later (1 Cor. 16:2) was used here, believers put aside what they could on the first day of the week until such time as an adequate sum was realized. The word "help" (*diakonia*) means simply service or ministry and is the same term already used for the daily "distribution" to the needy at Jerusalem in the early days of the church (6:1).

[5] Suetonius, *The Lives of the Caesars* V.18.2.
[6] F. F. Bruce, *Commentary on the Book of Acts*, 243.

The rationale of this gesture of brotherhood could not be better stated than in the words of Paul concerning a later offering from the Gentile churches to the needy of the Jerusalem congregation: "They were pleased to do it, and indeed they owe it to them. For if the Gentiles have shared in the Jews' spiritual blessings, they owe it to the Jews to share with them their material blessings" (Rom. 15:27). It is possible that this experience at Antioch was the chief inspiration behind Paul's plan for the later collection. So important was this love gift in the eyes of the Antioch church that they asked Barnabas and Saul, their most prominent leaders, to convey it on their behalf to the elders in Jerusalem. The line between the material and the spiritual has at times to be very thinly drawn.

This is the first notice of elders in connection with the Jerusalem congregation. It may indicate two things: (1) that the seven (chap. 6) were no longer functioning because the lack of means had forced the abandonment of the common fund, and (2) that the apostles were perhaps absent from the city ministering to the churches throughout Judea as at an earlier time (cf. 9:27; Gal. 1:18–19). Just when elders were appointed in the Jerusalem church is not indicated. The more the apostles were needed in areas outside the city, the more would elders be useful to guide the congregation and provide needed administration. The prophets from Jerusalem must have brought the Antioch church up to date on conditions in the mother church.

The exact time of departure for Jerusalem cannot be fixed, but the great drought can be determined with some precision as falling in the period A.D. 46–47. Since the events of the next chapter belong to the year 44 (the date of the death of Herod), it was likely after his death that the two deputies made their trip, anticipating the worst of the famine condition by their alacrity in bringing relief.

10

PETER'S DELIVERANCE AND HEROD'S DEATH
12:1–25

At this point Luke picks up the story of Peter once more, relating his imprisonment and miraculous escape, concluding this segment with an account of what happened to his persecutor.

12:1–5. The circumstances surrounding Peter's imprisonment are sketched in simple but dramatic fashion—the power of an earthly monarch pitted against the power of prayer to the Almighty. The Herod of this story was the third ruler by that name to cross the pages of the New Testament: first Herod the Great; then Herod Antipas; and now a grandson of the first Herod, the son of Aristrobolus, known as Herod Agrippa I. His youth was spent in Rome, where he cultivated a friendship with Gaius (also known as Caligula), who later became emperor. As a result, Gaius favored him, granting him in A.D. 37 the tetrarchies of Philip, the brother of Antipas, which included districts north and east of Galilee, and of Lysanias in southern Syria (cf. Luke 3:1). In the year 39 Galilee and Perea were added to his realm, and in 41 he was made king of Judea, ruling over a territory approximating in extent that of his grandfather. He made it plain that he would do all in his power to be agreeable to the Jewish people, who responded by according him widespread popularity.

Joachim Jeremias[1] notes an item in the *Antiquities* of Josephus (XIX.7.4) about a verbal attack on Agrippa by a

---

[1] Joachim Jeremias, *Jerusalem in the Time of Jesus*, 332–33.

certain Simon when the king was absent from Jerusalem. The charge was that the king, being unclean, ought to be excluded from the temple. Jeremias, perhaps incorrectly, interprets this to mean that Agrippa was being accused of being a non-Jew (he was an Idumean, but had some Hasmonean blood) rather than of being ritually unclean. Josephus went on to praise Agrippa for summoning Simon and freely forgiving him this denigration.

As a further indication of the embarrassment felt by Agrippa because of his lineage, which he did not attempt to hide, Jeremias cites a passage in the Mishnah (*Sotah* 7.8). The custom prevailed, going back to Hasmonean days, when the kingship and the high priesthood were held by one person, that he should read from the Law at the Feast of Tabernacles, seated in the Court of Women. But Agrippa remained standing while reading the Law, out of humility. When he came to the passage that said, "Thou mayest not put a foreigner over thee which is not thy brother" (Deut. 17:15), he broke out into tears, whereupon the people cried out, "Our brother art thou! Our brother art thou! Our brother art thou!"

Because of his position as king, he felt able to do what no Roman procurator in previous years would have dared to do, namely, attack the church. Luke speaks of "some" who were his targets, but names only two, both of them apostles. James, the brother of John, and Peter may have been the only members of the twelve in Jerusalem at the time. Jesus had predicted the martyrdom of both men (Mark 10:39; John 21:18–19). But it is important to notice that with reference to Peter, Jesus explicitly stated that he would lose his life only when he was old. His time was not yet. James died by "the sword," probably beheaded like John the Baptist. This "pleased the Jews," encouraging Agrippa to "seize" Peter (the same word is used of the seizure of Jesus in the garden, Luke 22:54).

The fact that such strong and direct action against the church met with general approval (cf. v. 11) reveals "how little Judaism had become reconciled to the existence of the Congregation of Jesus in their midst."[2] Even when Stephen's preaching had brought down wrath on the church, the apostles had found it feasible to remain in Jerusalem when others had to flee (8:1).

[2]Leonhard Goppelt, *Apostolic and Post-apostolic Times*, 59.

No longer was this true. Agrippa knew what the people wanted, and he was ready to give it to them. Perhaps this outbreak is what Paul made reference to in 1 Thessalonians 2:14.

Providentially Peter's arrest came during the time when the "Feast of Unleavened Bread" was being observed. Since the intention was to execute Peter when the Passover was concluded, and since the festival of Unleavened Bread came during the week after Passover, it follows that "Passover" in this passage is used as a broad term for the whole festival season, as in Luke 22:1. Evidently scrupulous Agrippa, trying to be ceremonially correct so as to avoid criticism, would not pollute the holy season by shedding blood, so he put Peter in prison. Perhaps someone had told him about Peter's violation of Jewish exclusivism in the Cornelius episode at Caesarea. However, this is only conjectural.

The pains taken to guard Peter might give the impression that he was public enemy number one. He was chained to two soldiers, who took positions on either side of him. Two others were stationed outside the inner prison cell. Every three hours these four gave way to replacements. The explanation for such strict precautions is likely to be found in the recollection by many members of the Sanhedrin that Peter had somehow escaped from prison on a previous occasion (5:19). They did not want this to happen again. If in addition fears were expressed to Agrippa that Peter's friends might make an effort to free him, this would help to explain the tight security. It would also be a testimony to the growth of the Jerusalem church over the years. Many from other parts of the land would be in the city for the festival, so it was thought wise to prepare for any eventuality. Agrippa eagerly awaited the time when he could bring Peter out "for public trial," impressing them with his zeal for Judaism.

"So Peter was kept in the prison," and what his thoughts were we can only guess. Probably his mind turned back to the trial and death of his Lord, also at Passover time. He had failed the Master then by his denial, but by the grace of God he would not fail Him now. He knew that when one suffered as a Christian, that was the very time in which to glorify God (1 Peter 4:16).

Meanwhile, the church was bestirring itself to make urgent prayer to God on his behalf. Ordinarily the Passover season was a time of celebration, when believers recalled not only their nation's deliverance from Egypt but also their Savior's death and resurrection. But now the usual rejoicing was muted by the need for constant prayer. The church prayed "earnestly," with unusual intensity. Now was the time when the resurrection power of the Lord Jesus was desperately needed. It is to the credit of these believers that they had not fled in fear of Agrippa or sought out hiding places. One house (cf. v. 12) could not contain the whole church, so we are permitted to think of many groups, or at least of the maintenance of a "chain" of prayer, so that at no time was the voice of supplication stilled in those days of waiting.

What was the burden of the prayer? We are told only that prayer was made "for him." Petition for his release would be altogether natural in view of a previous intervention (5:19) and of Peter's usefulness to the Christian cause. Some may have been content to pray for his strengthening in the hour of trial, which accords with their surprise at seeing him alive and free (vv. 15–16).

12:6–11. The account passes to an explanation of how God answered prayer, defending His flock and showing that He is able to deliver His own when they are in peril. By waiting until the eleventh hour, so to speak, He tested the faith of the church and at the same time deepened the disappointment and chagrin of all who had waited with satisfaction for Peter's execution. On the very night preceding the day appointed for his execution, Peter was sleeping in his cell, surrounded as usual by guards. He had committed his soul to God, the righteous Judge (1 Peter 2:23), and was able to find rest in sleep, a remarkable testimony to the reality and effectiveness of his trust in the Lord. He had learned the secret that he was later to pass on to others, that one can cast all his anxious care on the Lord because the Lord has concern for His own (1 Peter 5:7).

When Jesus in Gethsemane had come to the point of resting in the will of God, an angel had appeared and strengthened Him (Luke 22:43). Now His disciple had committed his case to God, and an angel appeared to lead him out to freedom (cf. 5:19; Heb. 1:14). If angels have a strong desire to gaze into the secrets of God's salvation (1 Peter 1:12), they are all the more eager to effect deliverance for those who proclaim that salvation. Suddenly there was a light, a voice of command rousing Peter from sleep, and a loosing of his bonds. Through it all the soldiers remained in deep sleep (cf. 1 Sam. 26:12). The angel treated Peter as a parent would a child in an emergency, one crisp command following another until he was ready to exit. Although his legs moved, he was in a daze, thinking that he was seeing a vision (the same word is used for the housetop vision in Joppa, 10:17). Successfully passing the two guards who were stationed outside the cell, the pair stood presently before the iron gate that led to the outside. Although tightly closed, it "opened for them by itself."[3] With the opening of the gate and the departure of the angel, "Peter came to himself" (cf. Luke 15:17), realizing that his experience was not a dream and that he was a free man. The Lord had intervened on his behalf, leaving Herod and his followers bitterly disappointed.

It is worth observing that God ordained a different result for Peter than for James, in line with His providential ordering of events at other times (see Heb. 11:35–37). It is natural to raise questions as to why some are spared and others, as fully dedicated, are called on to yield their lives; but such questions are largely futile. One can only rest in the wisdom and goodness of God, for He does all things well.

12:12–17. Peter made his report to the faithful, who had been praying for him. It is impressive that he deemed this more important than immediately taking to flight. He owed it to his brethren to make contact before seeking his own safety.

The home of Mary was likely the principal meeting-place of believers in the city, perhaps the same dwelling utilized by the 120 disciples following the Ascension (1:13). The mention of Mary's son, John Mark, indicates that he had some prominence in the early church, and it prepares the reader for his share in later developments (13:5, 13; 15:37–39). Paul called him the cousin of Barnabas (Col. 4:10), who must have been a frequent visitor to Mary's home. Another visitor was Peter, who had a close relationship with Mark, as attested in 1 Peter 5:13, where the apostle called him "my son"—presumably an indication that Peter had had much to do with his spiritual development and possibly even with his conversion. This young man had many advantages, which ultimately showed up

---

[3] In his *Jewish War* (VI.5.3) Josephus tells of the strange phenomena occurring at Jerusalem prior to the outbreak of hostilities, which some interpreted favorably for the Jews, others as portents of doom. Included is a report that the eastern gate of the inner court of the temple opened of its own accord (*automatōs*, the same root word as in Acts 12:10).

in his character and usefulness (Col. 4:10–11; 2 Tim. 4:11). Mark's contacts with leading personalities of the Jerusalem church must have given him valuable help in the writing of the Gospel that bears his name.

The house was filled with people engaged in prayer. Although Luke does not give information about the time (the particular watch of the night) when Peter left the prison, the impression made by the narrative is that the night was perhaps half gone. The presumption is, then, that this was an all-night prayer meeting. Believers, like their Lord, learn to value long seasons of waiting on God.

When Peter arrived at the outer entrance and knocked (the gate was locked), his knock brought Rhoda out to see who it was. The fact that the family could afford a servant accords with the spaciousness of the house. In true-to-life fashion Rhoda, on recognizing Peter's voice as he called to be admitted, instead of opening the door, ran back to the company to report this exciting development. Astonished, they questioned her mental balance. Perhaps the tension of the long hours had taken its toll. "You're out of your mind!" they exclaimed. But she stood her ground. A compromise suggestion was that Peter's "angel" might have paid a visit, having so identified with him as to reflect his quality of voice.

The teaching about guardian angels is comparatively little developed in Scripture. There is no doubt about the guarding, protecting function of angels (Ps. 91:11), but in such situations angels appear as a group rather than alone (note especially Luke 16:22). Even Matthew 18:10, the passage most relied on to confirm the idea of the guardian angel, is indecisive, for again the plural is used, as in Hebrews 1:14. But at least it is possible to say this much, that the passage before us testifies to a belief in Christian circles that each saint has an angel assigned to him.

What was on the minds of those who proposed this explanation to Rhoda? Did they think it meant that there was a message from Peter? Or was it a more somber thought, as Johannes Munck surmises? He comments: "Probably an instance of the not uncommon belief that the moment a man dies his guardian angel appears. In this case, it would have been a sign that the Christians' prayer (cf. v. 5) had not been granted, but that Herod had had the apostle executed in prison."[4]

---

[4]Johannes Munck, *The Acts of the Apostles,* 114.

Whether hopeful or fearful, the saints were fully alert by this time, many moving toward the entrance to determine the true state of affairs. When they opened the gate, to their amazement, Peter stood before them.

Why were they amazed? Did they lack faith? Or had they expected God to intervene at a still later hour? The questions multiply. Sometimes Christians receive such assurance from God about the answer to their prayers that they no longer feel a burden to continue their supplications, but go their way expecting the answer to follow. Apparently there had been no such assurance in this case. Perhaps we are to learn from it the lesson that we should not become so completely absorbed in our praying that we fail to listen to the voice of God meanwhile so as to learn when prayer is no longer needed.

Precious time would be lost if everyone present were given the opportunity to greet the apostle and congratulate him on his deliverance. So he motioned for silence and tried to answer their questions by relating what had happened in the prison. Then he requested them to pass on the information he had given to "James and the brothers." This James was the brother of the Lord (Gal. 1:19). It would be unnatural to assume that "the brothers" were the Lord's other brothers (cf. Acts 1:14), for the language suggests that Peter was asking James to assume the active leadership of the Jerusalem church. Luke took for granted that his readers would know which James was intended—it was the one who soon became recognized throughout the church. The brothers could have been the elders of the church (11:30) or, more generally, the believers who were not present at the prayer meeting.

From this time on, James, rather than Peter, was the acknowledged head of the Jerusalem church. Paul confirmed this by recounting a meeting he and Barnabas had with the leaders of the church and naming James ahead of Peter and John (Gal. 2:9). His leadership was made plain again when Paul went up to Jerusalem for the last time (21:18). James was in favor with the Jews because he continued faithfully to observe the Law and the customs. As a result, when he was killed (c. A.D. 62) by the highhanded action of the incumbent high priest, there was such indignation that the high priest was dismissed from his office.[5] The appearing of the risen Lord to James

---

[5] Josephus, *Antiquities* XX.9.1.

(1 Cor. 15:7) must have been regarded by the church as in some sense prophetic of the leadership into which he was now placed.

The time had come for Peter to bid the brethren farewell. We read that he "left for another place." There is no way of knowing where he went. To have informed the group of his plan (if he had one at this time) would be to endanger his safety and theirs in case Agrippa instituted interrogation of church members. Some Roman Catholic interpreters have suggested that Peter made his way to Rome, but a visit to the imperial city at such an early date is highly improbable. That he did so later, prior to writing 1 Peter, can be reasonably established. When Agrippa was removed by death, conditions were favorable for Peter's return to the city. He was there several years later to take part in the Jerusalem Council (15:7) but after that does not appear further on the pages of Acts.

12:18–19. At the break of day Agrippa's soldiers were thrown into consternation, for they were responsible for the missing prisoner. When word of the situation reached the king, he at once ordered a thorough search, but it proved unavailing. Peter was nowhere to be found. Thinking that the circumstances pointed toward an "inside job," Agrippa grilled the guards. Although they were unable to explain Peter's escape, they were under suspicion, so the king closed the inquiry by commanding that they be executed. This was in line with rigid Roman discipline. Munck notes that similar cases are cited in Acts (16:27; 27:42) where Roman soldiers feared for their lives in case they lost custody of their prisoners.[6]

A change of scenery might help Agrippa to dismiss from his mind the unsatisfactory conclusion of his attempt to please his subjects by attacking the church, so off he went to his headquarters at Caesarea. This was the seat of government for the procurators who ruled Palestine in the name of Rome. Probably Agrippa alternated between Jerusalem and the seaside city.

12:20–23. This account of the death of the king was not strictly necessary for Luke's narrative of the history of the church (in his Gospel he did not indicate what the fate of Pilate was). But we know from his writings as a whole that he had an interest in correlating the events of redemption history with

[6]Munck, *Acts*, 114.

secular affairs (cf. Luke 3:1–2). Beyond this, however, he may have desired to instill in his readers the spirit that Paul wished to see in his friends at Philippi: not "being frightened in any way by those who oppose you. . . a sign to them that they will be destroyed, but that you will be saved—and that by God" (Phil. 1:28). It is always an encouragement to the saints to realize that they do not need to fear what man can do to them, for God still occupies the throne, and He knows how to deal with those who afflict His people (2 Thess. 1:6).

It seems that Agrippa had a quarrel with the inhabitants of Tyre and Sidon, prominent cities on the coast of Phoenicia, although the cause is unknown. Baffled by his failure to do away with Peter, his "fighting mad" mood was worse than usual. Asking for peace does not in this case imply the existence of armed conflict, but only the termination of the quarrel. It was necessary to come to terms with Agrippa, because these cities relied on northern Palestine for much of their food supplies. The suppliants made an adroit move by establishing contact with "Blastus, a trusted personal servant of the king," since he presumably had a closer relationship with Agrippa than any others of his official household. His cooperation was doubtless gained at a price.

Herod's willingness to settle differences may be explained in part as in line with his policy of cultivating leaders and governments in his general area, a policy that made Rome look askance at him as possibly seeking to get more power into his hands. It is significant that at the time of his death the Emperor Claudius did not appoint his son to succeed him as king, but restored Roman rule through procurators.

"On the appointed day," that is, the day agreed on when Herod would meet with the envoys from the Phoenician cities, the king made a state occasion by donning "royal robes" and dignifying the concord by making a "public address" to the visitors from the north. To the obsequious people of Caesarea, largely Gentiles, it presented an opportunity to hail their monarch as "a god" (the Jews, of course, would not take part in any such acclaim). Josephus, in describing this event, locates it during a festival in honor of Claudius.[7]

---

[7]Josephus, *Antiquities* XIX.8.2. His account is quite detailed: "Clad in a garment woven completely of silver so that its texture was indeed wondrous, he entered the theater at daybreak. There the silver, illumined by the touch of the

The two accounts agree that Herod did nothing to resist or refuse the plaudits of the throng and that from this very time he was smitten with an incurable illness that speedily brought death. Josephus credits the monarch with a speech in which he recognized that the sentence of death was on him, fate providing thereby an immediate refutation of the lying words of the multitude. Scripture does not use any such pagan terminology, but attributes death to angelic action (cf. 2 Sam. 24:16) because of unwillingness to "give praise to God."

Although Luke did not tie in the death of Herod with the persecution of the church, no doubt this connection was made by believers, and possibly by many of the Jews. Speculations as to the physical cause of Herod's death have been varied.[8] It is enough to be reminded that God knows how to bring low the proud.

12:24. In a summary statement that surveys the situation of the church following the incidents reported in the chapter, Luke succinctly notes that the progress of the gospel was not really impeded by what had happened but rather was set forward (cf. 6:7; 19:20).

12:25 The casual reader might suppose that Barnabas and Saul had been in Jerusalem during the persecution outlined at the beginning of the chapter, but actually a period of about two years intervened between the death of Herod and the famine conditions noted in 11:28. This item about the return of the two men could have been put at the end of chapter 11, but Luke inserted it here as a transition to the events of chapter 13, which it suitably introduces.[9] The trip to Jerusalem was probably not

first rays of the sun, was wondrously radiant and by its glitter inspired fear and awe in those who gazed intently upon it. Straightway his flatterers raised their voices from various directions—though hardly for good—addressing him as a god." (*Antiquities* XIX.8.2).

[8] Bruce, *New Testament History,* 263.

[9] The difficult textual situation in this closing verse of the chapter should be noted. The manuscripts that ordinarily are the most reliable read "returned to Jerusalem," but this does not make sense in view of the fact that the two men went from Antioch and are said to have fulfilled this mission. Many manuscripts have a smoother reading: "returned from Jerusalem"; but if such were the original wording, it is hard to account for the origin of the reading "returned to Jerusalem." One conjecture is that the original wording (including the terms that indicate the completion of the ministry) was "they returned having completed the ministry to (or 'intended for') Jerusalem" (B. F. Westcott and F. J. A. Hort, *The New Testament in the Original Greek,* Amer. ed. [New York: Harper, 1882], appendix, 94).

made till after the death of Herod. No data are given as to the length of time spent in Jerusalem, but the contact could well have been longer than on Saul's first visit to the church (9:26–30), and probably much less turbulent.

The opportunity to become better acquainted with James, not to speak of others who had been in the church since Pentecost, would not be passed by. The mention of Mark indicates that the contact of Barnabas with Mary and her family had been renewed, and this prepares the reader for the observation about her son in 13:5.

Part III

THE CHURCH IN ASIA MINOR AND EUROPE
13:1–19:41

In this segment of his story Luke incorporates his report of what happened in a series of journeys undertaken by Paul and various helpers who were sent out by the church in Antioch. In this period, probably the most fruitful of the apostle's life, congregations were established in the leading cities of Galatia and in Philippi, Thessalonica, Corinth, and Ephesus (together with its hinterland in the province of Asia). It was also a period during which Paul was obliged to develop a writing ministry as a means of keeping in touch with these churches. From the letters to the Thesssalonians, Galatians, and Corinthians we can learn much that reflects and illuminates Paul's experiences in founding these congregations. These experiences were characterized by a certain sameness, in that some who heard the Word rejected it and others accepted it, but each situation had its own special features.

A crucially important event is reported in the midst of the record of these strenuous labors—namely, the apostolic council in Jerusalem (chap. 15). Here the question of Gentile converts was thrashed out, with far-reaching consequences for the more rapid spread of the gospel. Paul and Barnabas, along with Peter and James the Just, played a significant role in this gathering.

11

MISSION OF BARNABAS AND SAUL IN CYPRUS AND SOUTH GALATIA

13:1–14:28

As noted earlier, the Jewish Christians who evangelized Antioch do not seem to have gone any farther. But the work they started gathered strength quickly and became the base from which the gospel went forth to the west and north.

Much less information is given about the Antioch church than about the church in Jerusalem. What stands out is its willingness to pour its life into the task of carrying the message to the regions beyond. As the Jerusalem church had fostered practically all the evangelism attempted thus far, the Antioch church was destined to have the same role in the establishing of churches (largely Gentile) in Asia Minor, Macedonia, and Achaia. But whereas the outreach of the Jerusalem church was occasioned by persecution and the dispersal of its people, no such circumstance marked the launching of the campaign from Antioch. Ernest Best quotes approvingly the observation of Johannes Weiss: "We are here concerned with a more or less fully organized mission for which a plan was made beforehand."[1] The leading of the Spirit and the responsiveness of the entire church toward the new step also stand out as characterizing this fresh advance.

THE COMMISSIONING (13:1–3)

Having served the Antioch church as its representatives on a mission to Jerusalem, Barnabas and Saul were now designated

---

[1] Ernest Best, "Acts XIII.1–3," *JTS* n.s., 11 (1960): 346.

to lead a new departure in the history of the church at Antioch and of the church as a whole.

13:1–3. Up to this time the ministry within the Antioch church had been led by Barnabas and Saul (11:23–24, 26), but now three other men are noted as sharing this leadership. Probably all five had the double gift of prophecy and teaching (cf. the combination in 1 Cor. 12:18). Light is thrown on the distinction between the two gifts by a passage from Paul: "Now, brothers, if I come to you and speak in tongues, what good will I be to you, unless I bring you some revelation or knowledge or prophecy or word of instruction?" (1 Cor. 14:6). Since revelation is joined to prophecy in the same chapter (14:29–30), it is natural to connect the two in verse 6, which leaves knowledge to be yoked to teaching.

As a prophet, a person spoke in response to a distinct moving of the Spirit, providing edification, exhortation, and consolation (1 Cor. 14:3). As a teacher, one presumably had a more sustained ministry, making use of the Old Testament and the traditions of the life and teaching of the Lord Jesus as handed down in the church (Acts 2:42; cf. Matt. 28:20). The teacher provided the basic information for living the Christian life; the prophet furnished special guidance from the Lord as needed. G. B. Caird notes that the Book of Revelation, written by one who calls himself a prophet, contains many hymnic passages, and there are traces of this kind of writing in Paul. He suggests, therefore, that perhaps "we owe to the inspired words of Christian prophets the beginnings of our hymnody."[2]

Of the five men, the first and last are familiar from previous chapters. Possibly during the time Barnabas and Saul were absent on their mission to Jerusalem, the other men began to take a more prominent place in the life of the church and to manifest more and more their Spirit-given gifts.

Simeon is a Semitic name for which Simon is the Greek equivalent.[3] It has been conjectured that this is the Simon who bore the cross for Jesus (Mark 15:21). If this be so, it is strange that he is not indicated as coming from Cyrene, in line with the Markan passage, especially since Lucius, who is named next, is so designated. Further, Simon was a common name, often

---

[2]G. B. Caird, *The Apostolic Age,* 64.

[3]In regard to Simon Peter, the manuscripts at 2 Peter 1:1 are divided, some having Simeon," others, "Simon."

appearing in Scripture. This Simon was known also as Niger, a Latin term meaning "black-skinned."

Lucius is not to be identified with Luke (see comments on Acts 11:28).[4] He may have been one of the company of men who first brought the gospel to Antioch (11:20).

Manaen, which means "comforter," is of special interest because of his background, "brought up with Herod the tetrarch."[5] He may have been the source of information about Herod that Luke utilizes in his Gospel (e.g., Luke 8:3; 13:31–33; 23:6–12). Luke records more about the tetrarch than the other Synoptists (cf. Acts 4:27 also).

Saul is placed last in the list, but presumably not because he was the least conspicuous in his service (cf. 11:25–26, 30).[6] If the intent is to indicate that he was the youngest in the faith, it follows that the three who are listed between Barnabas and Saul must have been believers for several years and must have come to Antioch to aid in the work.

Some interpreters are inclined to think that Luke intended to designate the first three of the five as prophets and the last two as teachers. The Greek construction makes this possible but not certain, since the particles involved are used so freely in Acts as to indicate a stylistic feature sometimes employed for the sake of variety.[7]

What persons are being indicated by the phrase "While they were worshiping the Lord"—the prophets and teachers or the church? Since the praying and sending forth of two from this group was almost certainly undertaken by the church as a whole (v. 3) and no change of subject is indicated from verse 2, it is probable that the ministering (or worshiping) applies to the congregation. If the ministering were intended to refer to the

---

[4]One should consult, however, William M. Ramsay, *The Bearing of Recent Discovery on the Trustworthiness of the New Testament* (Grand Rapids: Baker, 1953), 370–84; H. J. Cadbury, "Lucius of Cyrene," in *BC*, 5:489–95.

[5]"Foster-brother [of]" is also a possible translation of *syntrophos*, here translated "brought up [with]."

[6]Noting that Barnabas is listed first and Saul last, Haenchen suggests that the separation of the names is deliberate: "in order that their future association may appear founded solely on the direction of the Spirit" (*The Acts of the Apostles*, 395).

[7]Kirsopp Lake and H. J. Cadbury, eds., *BC*, 4:141; Robert W. Funk, ed., *A Greek Grammar of the New Testament* (Chicago: University of Chicago Press, 1961), 230b.

gifted men only, it would be natural to say that they were ministering to the church rather than to the Lord. Furthermore, it is questionable that the Holy Spirit would reveal His will for the church to the leaders only rather than to the entire congregation assembled for worship.

The word "fasting" hints at an awareness of a definite need for guidance. Was the church, perchance, beginning to sense its responsibility for a missionary advance beyond Antioch? In this atmosphere of urgent desire, the Holy Spirit responded, designating Barnabas and Saul for a specific work to which He was calling them. How the Spirit conveyed this message is not stated, but it is reasonable to suppose that the human instrument was one of the other men mentioned in verse 1, a man with the gift of prophecy. The Antioch church, no less than the Jerusalem congregation, knew what it was to experience the reality of the Spirit presiding over the life and work of the body of Christ. Both of these chosen servants of God were gifted as preachers and teachers of the Word. The missionary task required people of the highest caliber, those who were already proven in Christian work.

There is no reason to feel that the local congregation suffered from the departure of the two brethren. Gifted men remained to provide strong leadership.

"So" (v. 3) introduces the response of the congregation, made without doubt or question, but with complete and cheerful compliance. They proceeded to set apart Barnabas and Saul. It was done with fasting, prayer, and the laying on of hands. The first two items appear again in connection with the designation of elders for newly created congregations (14:23). Since both men had been laboring for years in the Lord's work, the laying on of hands was not for the purpose of ordination, much less to bestow the Spirit, but rather to identify the congregation with its representatives and to signify that the whole group was going with them in spirit, committed to faithful prayer on their behalf.

Nothing is said about financial support. The church was certainly able to provide it (cf. 11:29–30), but both men seemed committed to self-support (1 Cor. 9:6). Barnabas had disposed of his property for the benefit of the Jerusalem saints (4:36–37), and probably from that time on worked to support himself, a plan in which Paul was pleased to share.[8]

Apparently Saul sensed no conflict between his own call from the risen Lord to missionary service and his being set apart by the church for a specific mission. Similarly, he saw no contradiction between insisting that the gospel he preached was revealed to him by the risen Lord (Gal. 1:11–12) and referring to the gospel as something passed on to him by the Jerusalem church (1 Cor. 15:1–11). The gospel was the same.

CYPRUS (13:4–12)

Here Luke describes the first stage of the journey, the ministry on the island of Cyprus, the original home of Barnabas. This makes all the more striking the rapid emergence of Saul as the leading figure of the missionary team.

13:4–5. Notable is the change in terminology denoting the relation of the missionaries to the Holy Spirit. Whereas the church had "sent them off" (v. 3), or "let them go" (indicating that the parting was not altogether easy), the two men were "sent on their way by the Holy Spirit." It was by His authority and designation that they went forth.

After reaching Seleucia, the seaport of Antioch, they took ship for the trip to Salamis, over one hundred miles away to the southwest, the leading city of Cyprus. Barnabas's acquaintance with the island made this a natural beginning point. Furthermore, the area had already received some Christian testimony (11:19), though nothing is indicated about its effect. Salamis offered more than one synagogue as an opening for their ministry, and in availing themselves of these opportunities Barnabas and Saul were following the plan of proclaiming the message to the Jew first (Rom. 1:16). Nothing is said here about Gentiles. Probably they were not frequenting the synagogues as much as those in the large cities on the mainland. Luke does not include any account of the results achieved at Salamis.

A third member of the party is introduced here: John Mark (cf. 12:12), a cousin of Barnabas (Col. 4:10). He went along as a helper. The nature of his assistance is not indicated. It may have gone beyond ministering to the comfort and convenience of his

---

[8] A. Schlatter, *The Church in the New Testament Period*, 113.

companions, since the word for "helper" may mean also a minister in connection with Christian testimony (Luke 1:2; Acts 26:16; 1 Cor. 4:1). In Luke 4:20 it designates a functionary of the synagogue, and this has led to the speculation that John Mark could have included catechizing of converts among his duties. Rackham suggests that he may have baptized converts (cf. 1 Cor. 1:13–17).

13:6–8. The journey westward to the other major center, Paphos, is noted without comment. However, "traveled through" may hint at more than travel. The verb occurs twenty times in Acts and nearly always connotes travel in which testimony is borne to the unsaved or believers are edified.

In this second principal city, the missionaries experienced both testing and triumph. The opposition came from a Jew, Bar-Jesus by name, who was a "sorcerer" and a "false prophet." Some similarity is discernible between this man and Simon Magus (chap. 8). Delving into the realm of the occult and trading on popular superstition, such characters abounded in the Hellenistic period. If religion was involved, it was with the hope of finding in it a way of gain (cf. 1 Tim. 6:5).

Posing as a prophet, Bar-Jesus had gained the confidence of the proconsul (the title of a ruler of a senatorial province). Quickly he perceived that the new arrivals menaced any hold he might have on the Roman official, for if Sergius Paulus began to incline toward their teaching, he could hardly do otherwise than abandon all contact with Bar-Jesus. So when the proconsul expressed a desire to hear the visitors, Bar-Jesus summoned all his powers of persuasion to keep the official from becoming involved in the Christian faith. If his superior became a believer, he himself could expect to be ejected from the court circle of the proconsul.

Apparently this prophet was known also by the name of Elymas, but in what way this name relates to Bar-Jesus is difficult to determine. At any rate, the double name anticipates a similar situation in the case of Saul (v. 9).

13:9–12. At this point Saul took the initiative and became the actual leader of the party (vv. 13, 16, 42, 50). It is tempting to suggest that a change of name from Saul to Paul accompanied this new prominence, but Luke does not say this. He does not say that henceforth Saul was known as Paul, but that he was also known as Paul, implying that he had both names before this time. It was natural for Paul to be known as Saul in a Jewish setting, but now that he was moving out into an essentially Gentile mission, the suitability of the Roman name was obvious.

This is the last time the Jewish name is used in Acts, and it does not appear in any of Paul's letters. There is no proof that the assumption of the name Paul had any connection with Sergius Paulus. At this point the proconsul had not yet become a believer (cf. v. 12). Sherwin-White observes, "Perhaps the author was only trying to distinguish *his* Paul, the apostle, from the proconsul Sergius Paulus in the same passage."[9]

In the boldness that the Holy Spirit imparted, Paul faced Elymas and with the utmost solemnity rebuked and unmasked him. It was a crucial moment in the history of missions.

> It was the first presentation of *the word of God* to the Roman world: and naturally it was not easy for Sergius Paulus to detect the vital distinction between the true prophets and the false. Once and for all that distinction and the separation of Christianity from all trafficking in spiritualism must be demonstrated.[10]

The indictment was severe: he was allied with the devil rather than with God, and for that reason an enemy of righteousness, making use of deceit and fraud to gain control over the minds of men. As God's representative, Paul pronounced a punishment that was sufficiently drastic and obvious to make clear that his rebuke was not a matter of prejudiced opinion. The physical blindness imposed for a time would serve to symbolize the spiritual darkness in which the false prophet lived and moved (cf. John 3:19–20; 9:39). His helplessness was pitiable, a sharp change from his self-confidence and arrogance. God knows how to bring the wicked low before Him. When the blindness descended on the victim, Paul stood vindicated as a prophet of the Lord (cf. 2 Kings 5:27).

"When the proconsul saw, . . . he believed." The miracle was a strong confirmation of the teaching, as in the ministry of our Lord (cf. Mark 1:27). Nothing is said about baptism, but this in itself is hardly sufficient ground for doubting the genuineness of the conversion, especially in such a condensed

---

[9] A. N. Sherwin-White, *Roman Society and Roman Law in the New Testament,* 153.

[10] R. B. Rackham, *The Acts of the Apostles,* 201.

narrative. Though Paul did not revisit the area, Barnabas did (15:39), probably with a view to evangelizing further and helping the church to be established in the truth.

PISIDIAN ANTIOCH (13:13–52)

For the first time the reader is given a sample of Paul's synagogue preaching. The fullness of the narrative from this point on during the first journey is in contrast to the sketchy character of Luke's report of the Cyprus mission.

Verses 13–16. Here, however, the narrative becomes exceedingly compact, as details of travel are passed over in silence in order to bring the reader to the scene of Paul's synagogue address, which is reported with considerable fullness.

13:13–16. The Elymas incident had given Paul a certain prominence that is reflected in Luke's terminology, as he states that "Paul and his companions" sailed away from Paphos and landed at Perga in Pamphylia. This small and somewhat backward province faced the sea and was almost sealed off from the regions to the north by the Taurus mountains. It was not a promising area for evangelizing, since Greek and Roman influences had not been strong in this region and the inhabitants were not very receptive to new ideas. Some who had heard Peter preach on the Day of Pentecost were from Pamphylia (2:10). Luke does not record any ministry in connection with this visit. A suggestion has been made by Richard N. Longenecker "that the ignoring of Perga at this time was largely because of uncertainty within the missionary party itself regarding the validity of a direct approach to Gentiles."[11] Later, on the way back to Antioch, a witness was made to Perga (14:25).

An upsetting incident occurred when the trio reached this town on their way inland. John Mark decided to turn back. Significantly, he did not journey to Antioch to report to the church, but he went to his home in Jerusalem. No reason is given for the departure. In view of his later rehabilitation, Luke probably wished to spare him embarrassment. It is possible that Mark was not entirely in sympathy with the outlook of the

---

[11]Richard N. Longenecker, *The Ministry and Message of Paul,* 43.

older men about carrying the gospel to the Gentiles. Mingled with this may have been a degree of displeasure over the ascendancy of Paul as the real leader of the group. Other less likely possibilities are homesickness and apprehension of dangers to be faced in penetrating the inland areas. Fortunately, Mark's withdrawal did not terminate his ministry (see comments on 12:12), but it led to a regrettable break between Paul and Barnabas at a later time (15:37–39).

The missionaries headed next for Pisidian Antioch. Sir William Ramsay, making use of Galatians 4:13, where Paul states that it was a bodily illness that led him to preach the gospel at first to the Galatian churches, conjectured that the apostle contracted malarial fever in the lowlands of Pamphylia and sought relief in the higher altitudes of southern Galatia, where he was able to preach while recovering. He identified this ailment with Paul's thorn in the flesh (2 Cor. 12:7).[12] However, Paul's vision experience probably befell him prior to his association with the church in Syrian Antioch (2 Cor. 12:2). If the apostle contracted some illness at this time, he must have had great courage and physical strength to make the rugged overland journey under such conditions. Luke was content to give the external facts of the journey, and in the briefest way possible.

Pisidian Antioch was part of the Roman province of Galatia. Ever since 25 B.C. it had been a Roman colony, the most important city in the southern part of the province. Its Jewish inhabitants were numerous, their settlement there going back to Seleucid days.

Paul and Barnabas made their way on the Sabbath to the synagogue, perhaps going early to meet the rulers of the synagogue and identify themselves. Paul's credentials as a former student of Gamaliel (22:3) would be sufficient to prompt an invitation to speak during the service. The invitation was tendered following "the reading from the Law and the Prophets" (cf. Luke 4:16–21). That such a homily customarily came after the reading is certified from Jewish sources.[13]

The word of exhortation could be based on the Scripture reading, but this was not a requirement. Although the invita-

[12] William M. Ramsay, St. Paul the Traveler and the Roman Citizen, 92–97.
[13] Israel Abrahams, "Rabbinic Aids to Exegesis," in Cambridge Biblical Essays, 166.

tion was addressed to both men, Paul was the one who responded (cf. Acts 14:12). His discourse may be taken as fairly representative of what he must have spoken on other occasions in the synagogues of the Dispersion. It resembled Stephen's (chap. 7) in that it contained something of a résumé of Israel's history, and also had some affinity to Peter's Pentecost sermon in its references to David and to the resurrection of Jesus. Paul's quotations from the Old Testament were less extensive than Peter's. His coverage of the life and ministry of the Lord Jesus was confined to the work of John the Baptist and to the Savior's trial, death, and resurrection. Unlike Peter's sermon at Caesarea, Paul's included nothing about the baptism of Jesus and His deeds of mercy in Galilee.

Here and there the speaker interrupted the narration of historical events by indicating to his audience the relevance of these things to their lives (vv. 26, 32, 38, 40). He recognized that his audience was composed of two groups: "men of Israel" and "Gentiles who worship God." Paul's inclusion of the second group was not done out of mere courtesy, as is indicated by a repetition of the twofold address in verse 26.

Verses 17–21. At the beginning of his message Paul noted in passing the period of the patriarchs and then reviewed with great economy of language the Egyptian sojourn, the Exodus and the wilderness wanderings, the conquest of Canaan, the period of the judges, and the beginning of the monarchy with Saul.

13:17–21. Important stages is Israel's history are gathered up in a very few words: "chose" refers to God's sovereign dealings with Abraham, carried forward by means of promises to Isaac and Jacob; "made . . . prosper" covers the period of Joseph in Egypt; "led . . . out" focuses on the Exodus; and "endured" stresses the forbearance of God despite Israel's shortcomings in the wilderness (cf. 7:39–41). The giving of the Law is omitted (in v. 39 its inadequacy is noted). Paul did not pause to name the "seven nations" whose territory was given to Israel. They were too well-known to need repetition (cf. Deut. 7:1). Roughly four hundred and fifty years were required for the events listed so far (from the sojourn in Egypt to the distribution of the land to the twelve tribes under Joshua's direction). The period of the "judges" is noted, coming to a close with Samuel, a key figure in that he marked the transition to the era of the kingdom by anointing Saul as king and endeavoring to help him.

Verses 22–25. Paul completed his review of the Old Testament by moving directly from David and God's covenant with him to the inauguration of the new age, with the transitional ministry of John, the forerunner of Jesus.

13:22–25. In moving on to David and his pivotal importance in redemption history, Paul dismissed Saul's failure with the simple observation that God removed him to make way for a man after his own heart. And now it was unnecessary to trace Old Testament developments further, for God's dealings with David pointed on to the coming of David's greater Son, even Jesus (Ps. 132:11; Isa. 11:1–2; Rom. 1:3).

Except for Peter's reference (5:31), this is the only mention in Acts of Jesus as Savior. By referring to the Lord Jesus in this way, rather than as Messiah, Paul avoided an emphasis that might have been taken in a political sense. He was concentrating on the theme of salvation. The last and greatest of the prophets, John, by means of his baptism of repentance, his refusal to identify himself as the coming One, and his confession of unworthiness to serve Him, sought to turn the eyes of Israel to God's Anointed. The ministry of John was doubtless known in most places (Acts 10:36–37; 19:1–3).

Verses 26–41. The remainder of the sermon differs from the early portion in that the recital of Old Testament history was abandoned in favor of quoting Scripture relevant to the person and work of Christ. Along with this there was repeated reference to Paul's audience; they were reminded of their heritage and warned not to sacrifice it by rejecting the Savior.

13:26–41. Two principal lines of thought are observable here: the issue of Jesus' death and resurrection, both events fulfilling Scripture; and an appeal to accept forgiveness of sins made possible through Him. To fail to make such a response is to perish. Both Jew and Gentile are privileged to have the opportunity of responding to the message of salvation (v. 26). Both were included in Paul's commission (9:15).

The Jews of Jerusalem had had their opportunity to know and receive the Savior, but they had not recognized Him (John 1:11; 8:19), nor had they seen the fulfillment of Scripture in Him (John 5:39). Unwittingly they had fulfilled Scripture by condemning Him to death (cf. Acts 3:17–18; Isa. 53:3). There was no "proper ground" for putting Him to death, since the charge of blasphemy wrongly presupposed that He was not what He claimed to be. Pilate, faced with the request that Jesus be executed, repeatedly announced that he could find no basis for such a verdict (Luke 23:4, 14, 15, 22).

After Jesus' death on the cross came His entombment (Acts 13:29), to which Paul referred also in his statement of the gospel in 1 Corinthians 15:4. The reversal of the human verdict came dramatically in God's action of raising His Son from the dead. Witnesses encountered the Lord in the days that followed. Paul was content to limit the witnesses to those who had followed Jesus from Galilee to Jerusalem. His own experience of the risen Lord came later and under wholly different conditions, so he omitted mention of it rather than going into a detailed explanation of his early opposition and the circumstances of his conversion (a line of thought quite appropriate when defending himself, chap. 26).

"We tell you the good news," Paul continued (v. 32). Not only the early disciples but "we," Barnabas and Paul, proclaimed this message. It was especially important to Jews to know that the Good News concerned "what God promised [their] fathers." This was hardly the promise of the Spirit, for that promise was made by the Father to the Son and was passed on to the disciples in anticipation of Pentecost (Luke 24:49), whereas this promise was made to the fathers of Israel and surely centered in the sending of the Messiah. The promise of the Spirit, so far as this appears in the Old Testament (e.g., Joel 2) is ancillary to the more central promise of the Redeemer. God has fulfilled this fundamental pledge in the person of Jesus (Luke 2:29–32).

But to whom has He fulfilled it? The manuscripts are divided between four readings: "to us the children," "to our children," "to their children," and "to us their children." The second has the best manuscript support, though it is a somewhat unexpected statement. With this difficulty in mind, the NIV has "for us, their children," which is the fourth reading.

The promise was fulfilled "by raising up Jesus." To apply this to the Resurrection is dubious, for several reasons. For one thing, there are two references to the Resurrection in the immediate context (vv. 30, 34), and both are explicit as pointing to resurrection from the dead. There is no mention of the dead in the passage before us. Again, it is unlikely that the promise of the Messiah would be regarded as fulfilled in the resurrection— to the exclusion of the birth, life, and ministry—of God's

Anointed. Finally, the word "raised," though it can be used for resurrection, can also mean "raised up" in the sense of providing, bringing into the arena of history. It is used in this way by Peter in 3:22, 26 (cf. 7:37). In line with these considerations, the support given by quoting Psalm 2:7, "You are my Son; today I have become your Father," was for the purpose of referring not to the incarnation (it is not so used in the nativity accounts in the Gospels) but "to the whole saving act of God through Christ."[14]

A second quotation follows immediately (v. 34), closely related to the first (v. 33) and the third (v. 35). If the first refers to the Christ-event, the second goes on to affirm that the end in view is the confirmation of the covenant made with David: "Your house and your kingdom will endure forever before me; your throne will be established forever" (2 Sam. 7:16). It is to this promise that the "sure blessings promised to David" (Isa. 55:3) applies. The only way this promise could be realized was through the enduring, death-defying life of the Son, who is also the Messiah. Consequently the truth enunciated in Psalm 16:10—"Nor will you let your Holy One see decay"—is necessary to complete the circle of thought. His life is indestructible (Heb. 7:16). Elsewhere Paul mentions together the same three ingredients, those of sonship, relation to David, and resurrection (Rom. 1:3–4).

Judging from Peter's use of Psalm 16 in Acts 2:25–28, this must have been a leading proof text for the Resurrection, doubtless stemming from Jesus' inclusion of the Psalms in His teaching about Messianic prophecy after He rose from the dead (Luke 24:44). Paul took pains, as Peter had done, to point out that Psalm 16:10 was not fulfilled in the David of history, for he died and was buried and his body suffered decay (v. 36; cf. 2:29). But this was not true of Jesus of Nazareth (v. 37).

Having touched on the kingly aspect of Christ's work by mentioning the Davidic covenant, Paul turned in conclusion to that aspect that is of more immediate concern, the procuring of "forgiveness of sins" (v. 38). This is offered to "everyone who believes." Christ's saving efficacy is put over against the inability of the Law to free (literally, "justify") from sin. This

---

[14] C. S. C. Williams, *A Commentary on the Acts of the Apostles,* 164. He notes the varied application of this text elsewhere—to the baptism of Jesus in the Western text of Luke 3:22 and to the ascension in Hebrews 1:5; 5:5.

line of thought anticipates that more fully developed in the apostle's teaching on justification in Galatians and Romans. To say, as some do, that Paul meant to teach that the Law can free from some things, but Christ goes beyond this by freeing from all that remains, is quite foreign to the apostle's teaching. For him the Law did not justify anything, but condemned (2 Cor. 3:9).

There is a point of difficulty, however, in the language used here by NIV—to be "freed from"—since in his letters Paul does not state justification in this way. In one passage, however, he uses the word as he did here—"Anyone who has died has been freed from sin" (Rom. 6:7)—so there need be no misgivings about the passage before us. To render the verb as "free" rather than "justify" in these two passages is warranted, since in the more highly theological treatment in his letters the apostle does not identify forgiveness with justification, seeing that the latter term refers strictly to the bestowal of a righteous standing before God, for which forgiveness is a necessary preparation. Forgiveness may be granted over and over, but justification is a once-for-all pronouncement on behalf of the sinner.

The final note sounded in the sermon was a warning of judgment should God's salvation in Christ be repudiated or neglected. Such warnings are common in "the prophets," but Paul cited Habakkuk 1:5 as representative. Most of his listeners would recognize the passage and realize that it had been fulfilled in the Chaldean invasion of Judah and the ultimate destruction both of the city Jerusalem and of the temple. The close of the Areopagus address furnishes a rough parallel in that a warning of judgment to come concluded that message (17:31) as well.

Verses 42–43. Having reported the sermon, Luke sketches briefly the effect of the message on those who attended the service.

13:42–43. As the two missionaries were leaving the synagogue at the conclusion of Paul's remarks, some of the audience crowded around them with the request that a similar message be brought to them the following Sabbath. Their hungry hearts had been captivated by the realization that God had fulfilled His promises. And when the service was dismissed, many of the people, evidently greatly affected by what they had heard, rushed out of the building to overtake Paul and Barnabas. Some of these were Jews; others were "devout converts to Judaism."

It is tempting to identify these two groups in terms of the twofold description of the attendants given in verses 16 and 26, but this would require the assumption that the devout converts were proselytes, that is, Gentiles already converted to Judaism, and would destroy the clear distinction preserved elsewhere between devout converts and proselytes. In view of this difficulty, it is likely that in this instance "devout" is to be understood simply as "worshiping," with the result that the proselytes are noted merely as having been engaged in worship during the service. This still leaves a rather awkward situation, namely, that the devout converts who had been so clearly noted and addressed by Paul not once but twice were not represented in the group that followed the missionaries. It is possible, of course, that they were reticent about speaking to the visitors.

The very interest being shown was indicative to the missionaries that "the grace of God" was working in many hearts. They urged them to foster it by continued inquiry and obedience to the truth as it was received.

Verses 44–52. The happenings on the following Sabbath are recounted, as well as the ultimate effects of the mission in terms of reception and rejection of the message of salvation.

13:44–47. No information is given about the activities of the missionaries during the following week, but the great concourse of people on the next Sabbath may indicate contact with the community. Since the number of Jews in attendance at the synagogue would be approximately the same from week to week, the great increase must be credited to Gentile interest. The influence of the service held on the preceding Sabbath is evident in that the people came "to hear the word of the Lord" (cf. v. 42). Although the Western text does state that they came to hear Paul, it is careful to indicate that he spoke about the Lord.

That Paul was indeed the spokesman also on this occasion is clear from verse 45. It was his presentation that drew opposition from some of the Jews and turned the service into something of a debate. Luke indicates that "jealousy" was a factor, prompted by the sight of the large turnout to hear the visitors. But judging from Paul's experience in synagogues elsewhere, the opposition had other grounds as well. The Jews were not prepared en masse to receive Jesus as their Messiah, when their leaders in Jerusalem had rejected Him. What Paul had said about the Law (v. 39) would not have been to their liking either. Further, since the apostle had addressed his remarks to converts as well as to Jews and had said nothing about the necessity of circumcision for such Gentiles when he offered forgiveness of sins through Jesus Christ (v. 38), it was fairly clear that he was opening the door of faith to these people. This would have been totally unacceptable to Jews, as it was to many converts from Judaism (15:1).

"Blaspheming" (NASB) in this context probably indicates the derisive and reviling manner in which Paul's opponents contended with him, though the name of Jesus may have been included (cf. 1 Cor. 12:3).

Before long the point was reached when Paul, joined by Barnabas, had to tell the unbelieving Jews forthrightly that their attitude of rejection meant they had forfeited the right to hear the word of the gospel. It was their privilege to hear it "first" (cf. Rom. 1:16), but their refusal of it opened the way for the missionaries to turn to the Gentiles (cf. Rom. 11:11). This is the pattern that Paul's evangelism followed in city after city, even in Rome (28:25–28). Just as he had been able to support his gospel preaching by citations from the Old Testament (vv. 33–35), so he and Barnabas could justify their intention to turn to the Gentiles by the Word of God. In Isaiah 49:6 the mission of the Servant-Messiah is seen to be larger in its scope than the confines of Israel, bringing salvation "to the ends of the earth." Echoes of the same passage are discernible in the words of Simeon (Luke 2:30–32) and in the commission of the risen Lord to His disciples (Acts 1:8).

Turning to the Gentiles did not imply abandonment of ministry in synagogues as a policy for the future, but it implied a readiness to reach Gentiles, if need be, apart from any synagogue context. Indeed, this had already occurred in the case of Sergius Paulus (13:7–12) and was to be repeated in the mission to the community of Lystra (chap. 14). Such a procedure was bound to create antagonism among unbelieving Jews and to deepen their hostility toward the church not only in the Dispersion but also in Palestine.

13:48–52. The Gentiles may not have been able to follow the synagogue discussion in all its ramifications, but they had no trouble grasping the significance of the opportunity to share in the blessings of Christ's redemption along with believing Jews. It seems that a considerable number put their faith in Christ then and there and joyfully extolled the goodness of God in sending them His word. In the expression "all who were appointed for eternal life" we are intended to sense not a restrictive emphasis but a wide one. These people were "Gentiles," yet they were included, whereas members of the chosen nation of Israel were excluding themselves by their unbelief (v. 46).

No doubt it was these new converts who made themselves responsible to spread the Good News throughout the surrounding area. Ramsay notes the suitability of Luke's observation here, since "Antioch was the governing center of a wide region that looked to it for administration."[15] Bringing the gospel to the major cities usually resulted in a broad extension of the church to rural sections, a deliberate element in Paul's missionary strategy (cf. 19:10; 1 Thess. 1:8).

Meanwhile the unbelieving Jews were busy adding to their already heavy burden of guilt by stirring up opposition to Paul and Barnabas in the city. They persuaded certain women of prominence that the missionaries were undesirables, and these in turn seem to have influenced the "leading men" of the community (who might not have given heed if the Jews had approached them directly), so that the missionaries were forced to leave the region (cf. 1 Thess. 2:15–16).

They responded by doing what the Lord had commanded His disciples to do under these circumstances (Matt. 10:14). Shaking off the dust of one's feet was an act that symbolized repudiation. The townspeople were making themselves responsible for denying to the community further light on salvation and the opportunity to receive it from those who were capable of making the way plain.

Still, the new converts remained, and they could bear their testimony. To strengthen them for this very task, the missionaries dared to return later (14:21–23). After noting that Paul and Barnabas went on to Iconium, Luke gives a felicitous description of the believers whom they left behind: "filled with joy and with the Holy Spirit." With such equipment they could be counted on to stand fast in case persecution should be directed at them also.

---

[15] Ramsay, *St. Paul the Traveler*, 109.

ICONIUM (14:1–7)

This city, situated about sixty miles east and somewhat south of Pisidian Antioch, belonged to the district known as Phrygia, but lay close to the border of Lycaonia. In New Testament times the area was part of the Roman province of Galatia. Iconium is today the Turkish city of Konya. The fertility of the surrounding region made it a populous place at the time the missionaries visited there.

14:1–2. In several respects the campaign here resembled that in Pisidian Antioch: the preaching was carried on in the synagogue, where both Jews and Gentiles were present; converts were made from both groups; and opposition developed quickly, initiated by unbelieving Jews. Probably the presentation of the gospel followed the same lines as in the sermon reported in Acts 13, which Luke seems to have intended to serve as an example of Paul's preaching in the synagogue as he went from place to place.

In reporting the Iconium ministry the historian is content to emphasize the effectiveness of the preaching: the two men spoke "so effectively that a great number . . . believed." This translation might mislead one into thinking that the secret of success was winsomeness or the use of fine rhetoric. Any such conclusion is ruled out by Paul's own description of his spoken word (1 Cor. 1:17; 2:4), which doubtless characterized his proclamation from the beginning. It was powerful preaching, indeed, but the power lay in the truth of the message and in the work of the Holy Spirit as He attested that truth to the hearers. The missionaries preached for a decision, not simply to impart information.

A unique feature of this passage is that here alone among the accounts of the Galatian cities visited on this journey, the Gentiles are called Greeks. "It is . . . one of the many slight and almost accidental examples of accuracy in details, which abound in the book of the Acts, that Luke gives the name Hellenes to the population of Iconium, alone among the Galatian cities."[16] The Greek character of the community is amply attested by coins and inscriptions. Roman influence did not eradicate it but rather conserved and built on it.

---

[16] W. M. Ramsay, *The Cities of St. Paul* (New York: Armstrong, 1908), 359.

Instead of attempting a confrontation with Paul and Barnabas in open debate, the unbelieving Jews stirred up trouble by poisoning the minds of the populace against them. The tactics were similar to those used at Antioch (13:50), except that here the opposition worked on the masses rather than on the influential people of the community.

14:3–4. "So" seems to indicate that it was the persecution that caused the missionaries to stay in the city for a long time. Opposition can indeed be a challenge to God's servants to stand their ground, for this is evidence that the gospel is making an impact (cf. 1 Cor. 16:8–9). But here one must reckon also with the probability that the process of sowing seeds of mistrust and hatred among the people took a long time, so that there was a period during which public ministry went on unhindered.

With the Lord's help the missionaries spoke out boldly. As they were faithful in sharing "the message of his grace" (cf. 20:32), He showed His approval by working "miraculous signs and wonders" through them. Later on, when writing to the Galatian churches, Paul recalled to the minds of his readers these miraculous manifestations (Gal. 3:5). They are mentioned in Acts only in connection with the mission at Iconium and Lystra, but they must have occurred in the other two cities also. Luke majors on the preaching at Antioch; his account of the stay at Derbe gives no details about the ministry.

At Iconium matters eventually came to a head, with the people of the city sharply divided in their attitude toward the visitors. The issue was no longer confined to the synagogue. It was the talk of the town, and some of the people were on the side of the Jews, and some on the side of the apostles. In producing division by their work, Paul and Barnabas were reproducing an important aspect of the ministry of Jesus (Luke 12:51–53).

Luke uses the word "apostles" for the missionaries only here and in verse 14. Probably it was intended to remind the reader that these men had been sent forth by the Holy Spirit (13:4).

14:5–7. Finally we learn the source of the agitation against the missionaries. The leaders of the Jews—the primary source of the opposition—and the leaders of the Gentile community joined forces. They were ready to resort to violence, planning to use the Jewish method of stoning the victims. Providentially the apostles learned of the plan and were able to escape. Their departure was not a sign of cowardice, but rather an act of prudence. Moreover, it was in line with the instruction given by Jesus to His disciples (Matt. 10:23).

Lystra was the next stopping place, a smaller community about twenty miles to the south. Since Paul ordinarily kept to the cosmopolitan centers, the motive for going there, as Ramsay suggests,[17] may have been to find a place of refuge until it was safe to return to Iconium. As it turned out, hostility followed the missionaries to this sequestered spot, so that it was not a place of rest. Actually the apostles could not remain inactive and were soon involved in ministry.

Before going on to describe the work in Lystra, Luke mentions that the party, always engrossed in preaching the gospel, also touched the town of Derbe and the surrounding territory.

LYSTRA (14:8–18)

Lystra was the home of Timothy (16:1–2). In addition to native Lycaonians there were in this city Roman colonists and officials, as well as a few Jews, though perhaps not enough to warrant a synagogue. At least Luke does not mention one. Therefore the approach of the missionaries would be different from that used in Antioch and Iconium, where the Old Testament was central to the presentation.

Luke's account of the mission consists of three elements: the healing of a lame man; the resultant attempt of the inhabitants to worship the benefactors, leading in turn to a short message by the missionaries about the nature of God; and the stoning of Paul by determined Jews from the north.

14:8–10. What looms large here is not the preaching ministry of Paul so much as the miracle performed on the lame man. His helpless condition is indicated by a threefold description. "Lame from birth" is the identical wording used in the case of the man healed by Peter at the temple (3:2). Other features are the same also—the intensity with which the apostle looked at him (cf. 3:4); and the result of the miracle: leaping and walking about (cf. 3:8).

A slight variation among the manuscripts produces some

17Ibid., 408.

uncertainty as to whether the crippled man heard Paul speaking on this occasion only or whether he had been listening to him previously as well. At any rate, his bearing caught Paul's attention, who discerned in his openness and eagerness the faith necessary to be healed.[18]

14:11–13. The healing produced an immediate and profound effect on those who witnessed it. (Presumably they had been listening to Paul speak.) In the excitement of the moment they began talking to one another in their native Lycaonian language. In keeping with the relative unimportance of Lycaonia politically and economically, there are no literary remains of the language. This episode makes it clear that most of the inhabitants understood Greek, otherwise they would not have been listening to Paul, unless he spoke through an interpreter.

Despite their backwardness, the inhabitants knew something of the Greek pantheon. They quickly dubbed Barnabas Zeus, the father of the gods, perhaps because of his seniority and imposing appearance. Paul they identified as Hermes, because of his role as spokesman. In Greek mythology Hermes was the messenger of the gods and the patron of orators. The miracle had convinced these superstitious people that the gods had taken human form (a commonplace in the Homeric poems) and had come down to people (cf. 28:6). In accordance with this notion, the priest of Zeus came forth from the local temple devoted to the worship of the fathers of the gods and made his way into the city, prepared to sacrifice to the deities who had deigned to visit the area, an honor that was in line with the mood of the crowd.

The people's excitement is made more understandable with the help of a story narrated by the Roman poet Ovid (*Metamorphoses* 9:618ff.) relating what happened to an old couple in the Phrygian hill country. It is admirably summarized by James L. Kelso:

> Ovid tells how the Greek gods Zeus and Hermes came to this area disguised as men. They tried to find hospitality in a thousand homes, but no one offered them a place to stay except a very poor, aged couple, Philemon and Baucis, who gave them everything they had to eat. When the empty wine bowl on the table refilled itself, the peasants

[18]The word is "saved" or "made whole," as in connection with many of the miracles of Jesus (e.g., Mark 5:28, 34).

recognized that these men were gods! The couple were then taken up to the top of a nearby hill where they saw the gods inundate all the countryside which had denied them hospitality. They also saw their tiny hut transformed into a large marble temple with a gilded roof.[19]

14:14. The arrival of the sacrificial animals and the festal spirit of the throng must have brought inquiries from the missionaries. On learning what was afoot, they were appalled. They had no time to lose. Tearing their garments, they showed their horror at the contemplated worship of men as gods (cf. Matt. 26:65). Such a tear was from the neck down and usually extended about the length of one's hand. Custom dictated its appropriateness in times of distress (Josh. 7:6) and especially in a season of sorrow (2 Sam. 1:11).

To this demonstration of distress, the two men added their verbal protest. Luke provides a digest of their remarks.

14:15–18. To be made the recipient of divine honors was coveted recognition to the vain, pagan mind (e.g., Antiochus Epiphanes and Caligula) but it is farthest from the desire of godly men and of angels (Rev. 22:8–9). Barnabas and Paul were quick to affirm that they were made of the same human nature as the Lycaonians were. One is reminded of what Scripture says concerning Elijah being like his fellows—a challenge to imitate his titanic accomplishments in the realm of prayer (James 5:17).

The central purpose of the missionaries in coming to the city had been to proclaim "good news" that, if accepted, would wean people away from such superstitions as presently gripped them. "Worthless things" are false gods, or idols (1 Kings 16:13, LXX). Paul and Barnabas had not invited worship of themselves but were pointing people to God, who is a "living God," in sharp contrast to their idols. Idolatry was common in much of the religious life of Gentiles, so the gospel proclamation among such people called for a renunciation of this misplaced devotion (Acts 17:29–31; 1 Thess. 1:9). Notable is the fact that the apostles did not poke fun at the crudity of idolatry and thereby needlessly offend their audience, but were content to point out its futility and then pass at once to an exposition of the better way.

The remainder of the address advances reasons for making

---

[19]James L. Kelso, *An Archaeologist Follows the Apostle Paul,* 48.

a right-about-face. First, God is the Creator. Quite naturally the Old Testament is used here, since it has so many pronouncements on this subject. But the source is not indicated, because the Lycaonians were not familiar with the Scriptures. The quotation is from Exodus 20:11 (cf. Ps. 146:6). Second, there is a brief reference to divine providence. God had permitted the nations to go their own way, neither revealing Himself as He did to Israel nor bringing severe judgment on them for their idolatrous practices. But this time of leniency had now passed (cf. 17:30–31). And during past generations God had not really been indifferent, but had borne "testimony" to Himself as Benefactor of the race by making nature fruitful for the good of man. However, this is not the same thing as saying that the witness had been understood and received.

So strong was the impression made by the miracle that even this plain talk barely sufficed to divert the multitude from their purpose to honor the visitors as deities. What they thought they had seen was so potent that the spell could scarcely be broken by words.

DERBE AND THE RETURN TO SYRIAN ANTIOCH
(14:19–28)

This paragraph covers briefly a variety of subjects, including the stoning of Paul, the move to Derbe, the return journey through the Galatian cities to the sea by way of Pamphylia, the sea trip back to Antioch, and the report given to the church in that city. It is clearly a summary account.

14:19. Rather abruptly a new turn in the situation at Lystra is introduced. From the two cities that the apostles had already evangelized, certain Jews arrived, a testimony to their determination to oppose the gospel and equally a testimony to the impression made by the missionaries. As the saying has it, "Nobody kicks a dead horse."

The antagonism of these men was far more deep-seated than that of the Gentiles whom they succeeded in inflaming (13:50; 14:2, 5). They could have subscribed to everything Paul included in his address to the Lystran multitude (vv. 15–17), yet they stoned him; and it was because they had heard him say that Jesus of Nazareth was the promised Messiah.

To accomplish their purpose they first had to win over the people of the place, which may have taken a few days. Possibly the chagrin of the populace at being mistaken about the identity of the two men was used by the Jews to turn them against the missionaries. Although Lystra was a Roman military colony, not many Romans lived there, and the Jews' plan proceeded without official interference.

That was the only time Paul experienced stoning (2 Cor. 11:25), and it must have made him reflect on what had happened to Stephen (Acts 7:58). That he was not called on to share the fate of the first martyr was due to the mercy of God, for the assailants were confident that they had permanently silenced him. When writing later to the Galatian churches, the apostle retained a vivid collection of his suffering in their midst (Gal. 6:17, cf. 2 Tim. 3:11).

14:20. The stoning marked the end of the ministry at Lystra for the time being. Yet that ministry had not been in vain, for a band of "disciples" gathered about Paul's form, no doubt in mourning. Imagine their joyful surprise when he stirred and rose to his feet and walked back into the city with them! The same power of God that had been efficacious through Paul to heal the crippled man was potent to restore his own physical powers. God had vindicated His servant.

Yet it did not seem expedient to continue working there as long as the atmosphere was hostile, so Paul and Barnabas left for Derbe the following day. A Roman road connected the two communities. Recent surveys of the area have made more certain the belief that Derbe was about thirty miles east of the site formerly held to be the location,[20] and this raises the question whether Derbe was actually within the Roman province of Galatia. The rendering of this verse is also affected, as the journey would require more than a day. Since Luke does not say that the travelers arrived at Derbe on that same day, his wording can be understood to mean that when they left Lystra, Derbe was their destination.

14:21–23. The brief statement about the work in Derbe is significant for what it says and for what it does not say. As expected, the missionaries preached the gospel, with the result that many became "disciples" (literally, "they discipled many," i.e., won many converts [cf. Matt. 28:19]). As a church, this believing group became in time sufficiently strong to have a

---

[20]Bastian Van Elderen, "Some Archaeological Observations on Paul's First Missionary Journey," in *Apostolic History and the Gospel,* 151–61.

representative among the number who went along with Paul on his final mission to Jerusalem (20:4).

Notable is the absence of any mention of persecution in this remote city. Years later, when Paul reminded Timothy of the sufferings he had endured on this missionary journey, Derbe was the one city in the whole region that was omitted (2 Tim. 3:11). To have a peaceful mission here was a blessing after the stoning at Lystra.

It took courage to return to the very places that had resisted the gospel and mistreated its messengers, yet the decision to return was not dictated by bravado but by the practical necessity of shepherding the converts. Doubtless many of them were encountering opposition among kinfolk and neighbors because of their commitment to Jesus Christ. They were reminded that the path they had chosen involved many hardships. But it led to "the kingdom of God," with its future glory and peace. The "must" of suffering that governed the Savior's mission (Luke 9:22) applied in principle to His followers, who were taught the privilege of knowing the fellowship of His sufferings (Acts 5:41; Phil. 3:8, 10). The missionaries themselves had provided an example.

Edification was not the only purpose of this return journey. Organization was needed and was effected through the selection of "elders" in each church. The apostles "appointed" them. While it is true that the word used here could indicate congregational choice (see 2 Cor. 8:19), such is not the case in this context.[21] Conversations with the church about the qualifications of its members for such an important post, though, are certainly not to be excluded. The solemn responsibility attached to such a function of leadership is underscored by the reference to prayer and fasting (cf. 13:3). It would fall to the lot of these men to teach the congregation and exercise authority, especially in matters of discipline (1 Tim. 5:17).

It seems strange that in writing to the various churches he had founded, Paul did not refer to officers of the group (Phil. 1:1 is the exception). This need not imply a conflict with Luke's account, since Paul was accustomed to use more general terms that could well be intended to denote elders (see Rom. 12:8; 1 Cor. 12:28; 16:16; 1 Thess. 5:12). This is also true in

---

[21] See the discussion in W. Telfer, *The Office of a Bishop*, 192.

Hebrews 13:17, 24. Luke is careful to indicate that the large church at Ephesus was governed by elders who were responsible for overseeing and shepherding the flock of God committed to their charge (Acts 20:28).

However capable and godly were the newly appointed presbyters in the Galatian congregations, they needed divine wisdom and grace, so undoubtedly they were included in the parting prayer for the congregation, a prayer that committed all the believers to the loving care and faithful protection of the Lord. What He had done for Paul and Barnabas was an indication that the churches could face the future unafraid even though the apostles were no longer available in person.

14:24–26. Reversing the route they had followed on their way to Galatia from the south, Paul and Barnabas found themselves once more in Perga of Pamphylia. Their previous visit had been marred by the defection of Mark, which may have been so upsetting as to keep them from public ministry (cf. 13:13–14). If so, this circumstance must have made them the more eager to bear their testimony here before going on. It was a wise decision, for there is no indication that either of them ever returned to this area. In later times Perga became a Christian center with several churches.

Apparently the sea journey from Attalia to Seleucia was uneventful. The missionaries returned to Antioch with a sense of satisfaction that they had completed their mission. But this was no ground for boasting, for apart from "the grace of God" it would have proved fruitless (cf. 1 Cor. 15:10). Actually, the word translated "completed" means "fulfilled, carried out to the full limits of possibility" (cf. the use of the word in Rom. 15:19; Col. 4:17).

14:27–28. To judge from Luke's account, there was no appreciable interval between the arrival of Paul and Barnabas at Antioch and their report to the congregation. The people were as eager to hear it as the missionaries were to give it. In contrast to the sending out, when the church had taken the initiative (Acts 13:3), the missionaries now took charge, for it was they who "gathered the church together."

There may have been many church-in-the-house groups scattered throughout the city, but this did not demand separate congregations. The same was true of the large church at Jerusalem, with its thousands of people. They were not organized into separate entities; always they are described as constituting one church.

Another item of interest here is the tense of the verb "reported," which contains a hint that more than one service was needed for the full account that the apostles were prepared to give. This impression is strengthened by Luke's term "all." Nothing of importance was omitted. This was a great occasion for the congregation and they wanted a full report. Special emphasis was laid on the fact that God had opened a door of faith to the Gentiles, something that would strike a responsive chord among saints who were themselves mostly Gentiles (cf. comments on 11:26).

No doubt the apostles continued to minister to the people during the "long time" they were able to remain among them. There was no divine leading to direct them to embark at this juncture on a new missionary expedition. As the following chapter discloses, their presence was needed at a crucial meeting in Jerusalem.

12

INTERLUDE OF THE JERUSALEM COUNCIL
15:1–35

Further missionary work had to be postponed until a vital question affecting the whole church had been faced and settled. For background, one needs to recall that the Jerusalem church was composed of believing Jews. Some astonishment was created there by Peter's ministry to Gentiles at Caesarea, but the situation was so surrounded by divine guidance and blessing that it was allowed to pass (11:18). It was probably viewed as exceptional rather than as normative.

The growth of the Gentile church at Antioch must have raised questions, but apparently it was the establishment of Gentile churches in Asia Minor (chaps. 13–14) that stirred into action a certain segment of the Jerusalem church. The leadership of that church throughout the world seemed threatened, and the leaders began to doubt whether they could successfully appeal to Jews with the gospel much longer if the Christian community was about to be dominated by Gentiles. So the meeting in the Holy City was a momentous gathering for the future of the Christian cause.

Verses 1–5. Here the immediate occasion for calling the Council is set forth, together with a brief account of the journey to Jerusalem by the representatives of the Antioch church and their initial encounter with those who were to oppose them at the conference. (For a brief assessment of the problem of harmonizing this visit with that reported by Paul in Galatians, see "Historical Worth" in Introductory Matters.)

15:1. Those who arrived at Antioch from Judea are indefinitely described as "some men." Several witnesses of the

Western text identify them explicitly by adding the first part of verse 5 at this point, no doubt on the ground that the platform of both groups was the same. The remarkable thing is that instead of objecting to the reception of the converts made by Paul and Barnabas on their recent trip, the new arrivals dared to direct their propaganda at the Gentile members of the Antioch church. This is evidence that the growth of this congregation during the past two or three years, unchallenged by any official inquiry from the mother church at Jerusalem, had rankled in the minds of some who belonged to that church. Now their concern was coming out into the open.

Objection was centered not in doubt about the genuineness of the faith in Jesus held by these brethren in Antioch but in concern about the incompleteness of their status. Historically, when Gentiles wished to identify with the congregation of Israel, they were required to be circumcised (Exod. 12:48) and to order their lives according to the Mosaic Law, after the fashion of the Jews. Circumcision had been instituted as the seal of God's covenant with Abraham (Gen. 17). Many Gentiles, however, resented this necessity as a personal indignity, so that in spite of their interest in Judaism, they refused to take this step that would have made them proselytes, preferring instead the status of devout converts (cf. 13:16).

The visitors from Jerusalem were saying that what the synagogue had done back through the years, the church must now do, namely, receive as full members only those Gentiles who met the ancient qualifications. They relegated the rest to the status of hangers-on and dared to suggest that if Gentiles chose not to submit to these requirements, they could not "be saved."

It was this contention that was carried also to the Galatian churches and led to Paul's fiery epistle of protest and his affirmation of the sufficiency of faith in Christ alone for Gentile converts. If Jewish believers wished to circumcise their children and live in terms of the demands of the Mosaic Law, that was their privilege; but even so, there was no saving power in anything but the cross of Christ.

15:2. Luke is content to note that the Antioch church, through the two men who had been preaching the gospel of the grace of God, vigorously denied the rightfulness of the Judaizers' position advocated so openly in their midst. The nature of the apostles' refutation may be gathered in a general way from the report of the Jersualem Council that follows.

According to the Western text, the men from Judea demanded that Paul, Barnabas, and others go up to Jerusalem, apparently because they were sure that their own position would prevail over that of the representatives of the Antioch church. However, the superior text makes it clear that the initiative was taken rather by the local church. Their existence as a Christian community as well as their plans for further missionary expansion turned on the decision. Of course it might be said that this church could have continued its present course even if the Council should support the agitators; but then the unity of the whole Christian community would have been sacrificed, and this would have had serious repercussions on evangelism as well as on Christian fellowship. The believers were haunted by the specter of two churches existing instead of one.

While there was concern, there was also confidence among the Antioch brethren. They must have known about Peter's experience at Caesarea, a precedent that had a bearing on the present controversy. Then too, Barnabas had come to Antioch with the blessing of the Jerusalem church, and there had been no official disapproval of his work. "Some other believers" went along with Paul and Barnabas, among whom we may count Titus, who was a test case because he was an uncircumcised Gentile (Gal. 2:1–5).

15:3. "Sent . . . on their way" is a stock expression used not only in the Bible but in other literature, denoting far more than saying good-bye. It involved provision for the journey, including arrangement for security when necessary, and sometimes arrangement in advance for overnight stops. In Christian usage it must have included a parting prayer of committal to God and a promise of faithful intercession during the period of absence.

The existence of churches along the travel route guaranteed hospitality and the opportunity to inform the brethren of the progress of the gospel, especially among Gentiles. This is the first mention of churches in Phoenicia, though witness in this area has been noted earlier (11:19). Still earlier, Samaria had received the gospel. They had already reported to the Antioch church (14:27) and would do so at Jerusalem as well (15:4, 12). More than anything else, Paul and Barnabas were desirous of giving a full report of their work that had resulted in the conversion of the Gentiles. This conversion did not involve becoming Christian Jews. Luke emphasized that the apostles were describing what had happened in detail, the Greek word for which is used only here and in 13:41. As Knox reminds us, "These communities derived their knowledge of the faith from the same movement that had led to the foundation of the church of Antioch, and naturally sympathized with its teaching."[1] The reports were received with great joy in these Jewish and Samaritan churches, encouraging the apostles as to their possible effect on the church in Jerusalem.

15:4–5. At length the party reached its destination, and any misgivings about the reception it would have proved needless, for the apostles and elders and the church as a whole were cordial. The two men had not been to Jerusalem since the famine visit (11:30). Opportunity was given them to relate all that God had done through them. Necessarily this included a report of their work in bringing many Gentiles into the fold.

Believers who had belonged to "the party of the Pharisees" felt constrained to stand up and object, interposing the same contention that had been voiced at Antioch about the necessity for Gentile believers to be circumcised and to keep the Law of Moses. A legalistic bent was natural for those who had belonged to the Pharisees, but it was not inevitable—Saul himself was a Pharisee. This group in the church could not be satisfied merely to impose circumcision on Gentile converts. They also demanded full adherence to the Law, which they regarded as necessary to the promotion of morality among those who had known little of high standards of conduct in the lax environment of the Greco-Roman world.

In this initial stage the issue to be debated was made clear. Quite likely at this juncture the apostles felt the need of conferring privately with Paul and Barnabas before the matter was debated in the presence of the congregation. Such a conference is reported by Paul in Galatians 2:1–10. It established unity between the leaders involved and may also have set the agenda for the open meeting that followed.

Verses 6–11. This section is devoted to Peter's testimony before the Council. It was appropriate that the one who had opened the door of faith to Gentiles at Caesarea (chap. 10) should declare the bearing of that experience on the present discussion.

---

[1] W. L. Knox, *St. Paul and the Church of Jerusalem*, 223–24.

15:6. First of all we must face the question of the composition of the meeting. Luke mentions only the apostles and elders. Nothing at this stage is said about Barnabas or the Judaizing group whose position is described in the previous verse, but the very fact that there was debate (v. 7) implies their presence.

Some scholars incline to identify this meeting with the one described in Galatians 2:1–10, where there is evidence of pressure put on Paul from some quarter to have Titus circumcised. Although elders are not mentioned in Galatians, it is conceivable that some of them could have been present. The apostles, on the identification in this passage, must have been James the Lord's brother, Peter, and John. One can grant the possibility of this interpretation, but it seems more natural to insert the meeting of Galatians 2 between verses 5 and 6 as a phase that Luke does not record. A reason for concluding this is the fact that the "whole assembly" is mentioned in such a way as to indicate that a large body of people was present during Peter's address (Acts 15:12).

Luke does not say that all the apostles were on hand. Some may have been occupied elsewhere, for it is unlikely that at this period of the development of the church the whole group would remain in the city. On the other hand, they could have been summoned for this important gathering. As for the elders, they have been noted at an earlier point (11:30) and should be thought of as assisting James in the affairs of the Jerusalem congregation (cf. James 5:14).

15:7–9. Wisely, Peter did not take the floor at once, a move that could have given the impression of railroading. What actually occurred was "much discussion." Only when thoughts and emotions had been expressed and energies had spent themselves did Peter come forward. Without calling attention to his rank as apostle, his leadership of the apostles during the Lord's earthly ministry, or his great service in the early days of the Jerusalem church, and without suggesting that his testimony would settle everything, he launched out on a recital of what God had taught him on this issue. It was not something new ("you know that . . ."), and it was not something recent, but had occurred "some time ago." The church ought to have grasped the lesson long before; for Peter himself the matter had been settled quickly.

The incident at Caesarea would not have been definitive for

the church if Peter had acted on his own initiative and depended on his own wisdom. But it was God who had chosen to use him as His mouthpiece. And it was God, the One who reads human hearts like an open book, who had discerned the genuineness of the faith of Peter's Gentile audience and had attested to this reality by granting them the Holy Spirit even before they had made any open confession (cf. 10:44). God had given these believers the same purifying of heart given to the apostles and those who had responded at Pentecost. Water baptism gave outward recognition to a work of grace already done. God's recognition of faith by granting the Spirit implied that nothing more—such as circumcision and shouldering the yoke of the Law—was needed for divine acceptance.

15:10–11. To impose such things as these on Gentile believers in the present situation would be to test God. It would be to question His right to receive the Caesarean Gentiles as He had done. It would be to sit in judgment on the Almighty. It would be to provoke His displeasure and even invite His chastisement (cf. 5:9). It would also have the effect of imposing a heavy and unnecessary burden on Gentile believers, a burden that Peter characterized as a "yoke," something galling and unbearable. The word "yoke" has about the same force as burden or load (cf. Matt. 23:4). Quite different is the yoke of Christ (Matt. 11:30).

Was Peter talking about the Law as a way of life for the redeemed, or as a condition for salvation? He answered this question in verse 11 (cf. vv. 1, 5). One who took the Law seriously, especially as interpreted by Jesus in the Sermon on the Mount, was bound to discover how sinful he was, how greatly in need of a salvation he could not help to provide. Peter emphasized this by noting that the Law was a yoke "that neither we nor our fathers have been able to bear." Paul made a similar observation when he accused the circumcision party of failure to live up to the Law even while they were seeking to impose circumcision on Gentile converts (Gal. 6:13). Salvation, said Peter, comes not by the Law at all, but by an entirely different means—"the grace of our Lord Jesus."

Quite remarkable is the way he stated the matter, indicating that the Jew has no advantage over the Gentile, for "we" (Jews) are saved in the same way (by grace) as "they" (Gentile believers). The thrust of the apostle's remarks is strikingly similar to the language of Paul in Galatians 2:16. That the two men were in accord on the nature of the gospel is clearly indicated in Galatians 2:7–9. Peter was not contending, nor was Paul, that Christian Jews should abandon observance of the Law; this group of believers was not in view here. Even so, it is clear that such observance by believing Jews had nothing to do with their obtaining salvation. It could be helpful, however, in winning other Jews to Christ by disarming their prejudice (cf. 1 Cor. 9:19–20). If objection were raised that freedom from the Law was dangerous, even disastrous, from the standpoint of maintaining right conduct, the answer of Paul, and no doubt of Peter also, would resemble what is recorded in Romans 8:4.

A most important aspect of Peter's testimony was its effective refutation of the Judaizers' contention that the apostles of the Jerusalem church were favorable to their point of view in the controversy. On the contrary, Peter's position was the same as that of Barnabas and Paul.

Verses 12–21. After Peter's words, Barnabas and Paul had an opportunity to speak, giving way to James, who sought to show that the Old Testament prophetically included the salvation of Gentiles in the divine plan. With this background, the leader of the Jerusalem church was able to proceed with counsel about appropriate action to be taken in the present crisis.

15:12. The company, after lively debate, was quieted by Peter's words, for no one had the temerity to challenge his experience at Caesarea or the conclusion he drew from it. This improved atmosphere was to the advantage of Barnabas and Paul as they took the floor. Luke shows sensitivity to the local situation by listing Barnabas ahead of Paul, in contrast to the order in verse 2 (cf. 4:36–37; 11:22). He does not quote from their remarks, since a report of their activities had already been given to the church (v. 4). It was important at this juncture, however, to emphasize how God had endorsed their work among the Gentiles by "miraculous signs and wonders," showing that He approved of their ministry as well as of Peter's at Caesarea. Circumcision had not been imposed in either case.

15:13–14. At this juncture James, exercising his authority as chairman of the gathering and head of the Jerusalem church (12:17; 21:18; cf. Gal. 2:12), took charge rather than throwing the meeting open for further discussion. He sensed that the time had come for action and prepared for it by giving the gist of Peter's remarks before making his own contribution. It was expedient at this point to capitalize on the testimony of the apostle to the circumcision rather than to refer to Barnabas and Paul. Along the same line is to be understood his use of the name *Simeon,* in preference to *Simon.* "It was fitting that Peter should be addressed by a Palestinian Jew by his Jewish name and even in its most Jewish spelling."[2]

15:15–18. James was content to make his contribution consist largely in buttressing Peter's words by showing that what was happening in the experience of the church had been anticipated in "the words of the prophets." His quotation is taken from Amos 9:11–12, as representative of other passages. There are textual problems incident to the use of the LXX rather than the Hebrew text of Amos, but these need not concern us here.[3] It is important to bear in mind that the one thing the use of Scripture was designed to support here is the fact that God was at work taking from the Gentiles a people for Himself (v. 14). James seems to have been implying that the rebuilding and restoration of the tabernacle of David had occurred in the person and mission of Jesus of Nazareth, who was of the seed of David. The result was the building of His church, a church that at the beginning had been composed of the sons of Israel, but that now was opening itself to include also many Gentiles. Wilhelm Michaelis puts it thus:

> For Luke the rise of the Christian community is the restoration of David's *skēnē,* which Amos promised and which is now being achieved. If the first part of the prophecy has been fulfilled in Jewish Christians (15:16), these should be convinced that the second part is also being fulfilled (15:17) and that the Gentile mission is thus legitimate.[4]

A different understanding of the passage is maintained by those who take "after this" (v. 16) to refer to the taking of a people from the Gentiles (v. 14) rather than to the context in the prophecy of Amos, which deals with divine judgments on Israel by which that nation is reduced to a mere remnant. Then the remainder of the quotation is taken to refer to the

---

[2] Kirsopp Lake and H. J. Cadbury, eds., *BC,* 4:175.

[3] See F. F. Bruce, *Commentary on the Book of Acts,* 310, for a discussion of the textual phenomena.

[4] *TDNT,* 7:374–75.

restoration of Israel in the future Davidic (messianic) kingdom, which will also have a place for the Gentiles who will come under the rule of the Messiah. No doubt these things are predicted in Scripture at various points, but the introduction of a whole panorama of prophecy at the Jerusalem Council goes far beyond the demands of the situation. Again it should be noted that the one item James was concerned to validate from Scripture was the inclusion of the Gentiles in the Christian fellowship (v. 14).

It may appear to be a serious limitation of James' contribution that he made no reference to the central feature of the debate, the issue of circumcision. The Judaizers were quite willing to grant that Gentiles should have a place in the church, but they were not willing to receive them apart from circumcision. While James did not tackle the circumcision issue head on, he did stress the Gentiles' acceptability to God, as will be seen by the close of verses 14 and 17. That Gentiles should be called by the name of the Lord (cf. James 2:7) meant acceptance based on divine grace. Those whom God has received need nothing additional to fit them for membership in the household of faith.

15:19–20. James followed up his use of Scripture with a "judgment," or conclusion, that had a negative and a positive aspect. He suggested that there should be an end to the troubling of the Gentiles who were turning to God. The verb "make . . . difficult," whether so intended or not, answers very closely to Peter's thought about putting a yoke on Gentile converts.[5] On the positive side, he proposed that a letter be written to the Gentile churches affected by the current dispute, asking that they abstain from certain things that were offensive to their Jewish brethren. It is clear that the items included here (v. 20) were not conceived of in legalistic fashion as conditions for salvation, since it was already the consensus of the Council that the salvation of Gentiles depended on divine grace alone, apart from human works. The purpose of the so-called decree (cf. 16:4) was to ease tension between Jews and Gentiles in the church. An additional result would be a more favorable attitude on the part of unbelieving Jews toward the Christian movement.

The decree is mentioned three times (15:20, 29; 21:25) with

---

[5] See Ernst Haenchen, *The Acts of the Apostles,* 448–49.

slight variations. "Food polluted by idols" (15:20) is changed to "food sacrificed to idols" (v. 29) and to the singular form in the final occurrence (21:25). The expression "food polluted" is rare, this being its only occurrence in the New Testament. However, the verb form is used twice in the LXX, each time of ritual defilement (Dan. 1:8; Mal. 1:7). But the term "food sacrificed to idols" appears several times in Paul's counsel to the Corinthians (1 Cor. 8:1, 4, 7, 10; 10:19), where the context makes it clear that the thing sacrificed was meat. For the Old Testament background, Exodus 34:15 is relevant.

"Sexual immorality" seems oddly inserted amid ceremonial requirements. However, Jakob Jocz may be right in his assertion, "The division between the strictly moral and the 'ceremonial' in our modern sense was entirely unknown to the Jews."[6] Some help is gleaned from the fact that among pagans the practice was rarely frowned upon and could thus be classified with ritual matters. More to the point, perhaps, is the fact that Leviticus 18:6–18 carefully excludes from lawful marriage a relationship with anyone near of kin, and strangers among the children of Israel were apparently included in this prohibition (Lev. 18:26). So it may be that unlawful marriage, rather than the usual force of the phrase "sexual immorality," is intended here in Acts 15.

"Strangled animals" have not had the blood drained from them before being used for food (Lev. 17:13). "Blood," in this context, signifies the drinking of blood, a pagan practice that is expressly forbidden to Israel (Lev. 17:10, 14). In fact this is a creation ordinance, not merely ritual, as we see in Genesis 9:4: "You must not eat meat that has its lifeblood still in it."

In addition to the Old Testament background for the decree, there was the consideration of Jewish practice. The rabbis had long insisted that Gentiles who lived among Jews should not sacrifice to strange gods, violate the laws of consanguinity when marrying, labor on the Sabbath, consume blood, or eat leavened bread during the Passover. So the apostolic decree would not come as a surprise to many Gentiles, for they would be familiar with the Mosaic requirements and also with current Jewish regulations regarding Gentiles who were in close contact with Jewish communities. Therefore they

[6]Jacob Jocz, *The Jewish People and Jesus Christ* (London: SPCK, 1954), 68.

could be expected the more cheerfully to accept the restrictions involved here.

Certain witnesses for the Western text, notably Codex Bezae, have a different rendering of verse 20 and the parallel passages, omitting any reference to things strangled. This makes possible a moral rather than a ceremonial frame of reference. On this interpretation, the decree would rule out idolatry, murder, and immorality. But this is not all, for the Western text in 15:20, 29 proceeds to add a warning not to do to others what one would not care to have done to himself (invoking the Golden Rule in negative form). The reason for the addition is fairly clear. Three sins do not include the whole gamut of the Decalogue, so the Golden Rule is inserted to cover those that are not here specified. The origin of these textual phenomena is probably to be assigned to a somewhat later period of the church, when the legalistic controversy was a thing of the past and a new moralism had crept into Christian circles.

15:21. The interpretation of James's remark is far from easy. One suggestion is that he appealed to gratitude on the part of believing Gentiles. "Since the road to the conversion of the Gentiles was by way of the Jews and their synagogues in the various cities, it was both reasonable and right to show consideration for the Jews by keeping the rules mentioned in vss 19–20—thus making co-existence possible."[7] Perhaps all James wanted to do was to underscore the fact that Gentiles who had been in the habit of attending the synagogue (available almost everywhere) were well acquainted with the Levitical regulations applicable to Gentiles (as noted above), so the request of the Council should not be regarded as arbitrary or harsh. It is just possible that he simply wanted to point out that Jews were so prevalent in the world and so attentive to what the Law required that Gentile converts to the new faith would do well to avoid antagonizing them and making more difficult their evangelization.

Verses 22–29. Two tasks remained. One was to formulate a letter to the Gentile churches setting forth the results of the

---

[7] Johannes Munck, *The Acts of the Apostles,* 140.

conference. Evidently James was responsible for its composition.[8] The other was to select two brethren to carry the communication and explain it to the various congregations in Syria and Cilicia.

15:22. Luke does not record a vote on James's proposals, but agreement is clearly implied from the wording of the letter that follows (see vv. 28–29). The agreement involved "the apostles and elders, with the whole church." From 16:4 it is apparent that the first two groups expressed their assent, followed by the congregation. If there were dissidents (15:5), they now held their peace. The decision not to require circumcision had gone against them. It was a courageous decision, for it was bound to bring the disfavor of unbelieving Jews upon the Jewish-Christian church at Jerusalem. The task of that church in bearing a faithful witness to the nation would now be more difficult than ever, but it was willing to shoulder the burden for the sake of making the evangelization of the Gentiles easier. This should not be forgotten when it is pointed out that the Jerusalem church did little actively to expedite the spread of the gospel among the Gentiles. The verdict of the Council was a tremendous contribution in itself.

Two brethren were chosen from the congregation to go to Antioch with Paul and Barnabas to provide personal assurance of the good will and spiritual unity of the saints at Jerusalem in relation to believers in Antioch, where men from Jerusalem had precipitated the controversy. Why should two be sent? Possibly they were to represent the two groups in the church, the Hebrews and the Hellenists (cf. 6:1). Judas called Barsabbas may have been a brother of the Joseph called Barsabbas (1:23). From all that is known of Silas, whether from Acts or from the writings of Paul and Peter (in 1 Peter 5:12 his name appears as Silvanus), he could very easily have been a Hellenist, able to move freely in the Greek milieu and to minister the Word of God there. These two had already achieved prominence in the Jerusalem church as "leaders among the brothers."

15:23–29. The letter was framed on behalf of the church, particularly its leaders, the apostles and the elders. A certain awkwardness surrounds the use of the word "brothers." Some

---

[8]J. B. Mayor, in *The Epistle of St. James* (New York: MacMillan, 1913), iii–iv, lists half a page of verbal coincidences between this letter and the Epistle of James.

translations limit it to the elders. Other possible renderings are "the apostles and elder brothers" or "the brothers, both the apostles and the elders."

The letter was directed primarily to the Gentile church at Antioch, where the agitation had begun (15:1), and secondarily to Gentile congregations in the surrounding areas (cf. 15:41; 16:4). The communication carefully dissociated the Jerusalem church from those of their number who had made the demand contained in 15:1, since there was no authorization (v. 24). The letter went so far as to indicate that in the course of the deliberations the participants had "all agreed." So it was a united church that sent the letter and deputed the two representatives.

The letter likewise provided opportunity to commend the dedicated labor of their "dear friends Barnabas and Paul." Their companions are named, and indication is given that these representatives of the Jerusalem church had something to say to the Antioch brethren, but nothing precise is said about what they were to share. We are free to suppose that the most important matter would have been Gentile freedom from the necessity of circumcision, but to state this openly in the letter would have diminished the impact of the announcement these brethren were to make to the gathered church.

Most important was the assertion that all the decisions of the Council, including the decree, had had their origin in the Holy Spirit.[9] The church had simply followed His leading (cf. 10:19–20; 13:2–3). A church with such an awareness had no reason to doubt the correctness of its decisions. An individual could experience a similar confidence (1 Cor. 7:40).

Noteworthy is the fact that there is no mention in the decree (v. 29) of the observance of the Sabbath. The church at Jerusalem must have found it expedient to observe the day in order not to offend the Jewish community, but it seems not to have been a great problem in the Dispersion. Where pressure was applied, Gentile Christians could stand on their freedom in Christ (Col. 2:16).

[9] W. Telfer (*The Office of a Bishop*, 12) affirms a connection between two things here: crediting to the Holy Spirit the decision regarding Gentile freedom and the formulation of the decree, and choosing prophets (men inspired by the Spirit) to communicate the decision to the Gentile churches. He suggests that prophets were active in framing the decree. See also E. G. Selwyn, *The First Epistle of St. Peter* (New York: Macmillan, 1964), 369–75.

253

To sum up the letter, it had nothing explicit to say about the Council's decision on circumcision (that being left to the spoken word of the two delegates), but it stressed the responsibility of Gentile believers to observe the rules of the decree, which were "requirements" not for salvation but for the peace and progress of the church. Incidentally, this is a feature of many of the letters of the New Testament—touching lightly or simply assuming the privileges of the saints, and stressing their responsibilities.

It would be difficult to overemphasize the importance of what was accomplished at Jerusalem:

1. The Gospel of divine grace was reaffirmed.
2. The unity of the church was safeguarded.
3. The evangelization of the Gentiles could proceed without hindrance. Most of Paul's churches were founded after the Council, and they were Gentile churches.
4. The Gentile churches that had already been established were given encouragement (cf. 16:4–5).
5. The future of the church as a whole was guaranteed. In a few years its Jewish-Christian wing was destined to fade into virtual oblivion because of persecution and the Jewish War against Rome (A.D. 66–70) or to shrivel because of heretical tendencies (Ebionitism). But before all this happened, Christianity among the Gentiles had grown strong.

One cannot fail to see the providence of God at work in the Jerusalem Council.

Verses 30–35. Attention is now directed to the reaction of the Antioch church to the decree and to the ministry of the representatives of the Jerusalem church.

15:30–35. In this glimpse of the Antioch church following the Council meeting, quite naturally Judas and Silas are given special prominence as they are pictured fulfilling their appointed mission in communicating the contents of the letter to the congregation. However, they could not stop there, but went on to minister with a lengthy exhortation (v. 32). In noting that the two men were "prophets," Luke is hardly intending to suggest that their messages were predictive. Elsewhere the ministry of prophets is described in terms of exhortation or encouragement (1 Cor. 14:3; cf. Acts 4:36; 13:1). The spoken word brought much joy to the saints. But the blessing was not one-sided, for the pleasure of fellowship with this body of

Christians was enough to make Silas ready to return to Antioch when the opportunity came (v. 40).[10]

After the departure of Judas and Silas, the Antioch church continued to thrive under the ministry of Paul and Barnabas, aided by "many others"—a reminder of the great wealth of gifted leadership enjoyed by this congregation (cf. 13:1).

---

[10] A slight difficulty arises here regarding verse 34, "but Silas decided to remain there" (NIV mg), which is absent entirely from the leading manuscripts. It is undoubtedly a scribal addition designed to explain how Silas was available for service with Paul a short time later. But Luke's statement must stand that both Judas and Silas returned to Jerusalem. So we are to conclude that after the disagreement between Paul and Barnabas, Silas was summoned by Paul to return to Antioch and be ready for missionary service.

13

MISSION OF PAUL AND SILAS IN MACEDONIA AND ACHAIA
15:36–18:17

Although the mission began largely as a visitation of churches already founded and then moved uncertainly for a time in Asia Minor, when guidance for the next development was lacking, its decisive advance came with the crossing over into Macedonia. There Paul had new companions and faced many new situations. Several churches were established, and during this time the apostle wrote his first letters to congregations he had planted.

DEPARTURE (15:36–41)

The unity of the Antioch church, so recently crowned with joy over the victory at Jerusalem, was disturbed by a disagreement between its two outstanding leaders, Barnabas and Paul.

15:36. "Some time" is too indefinite an interval to enable us to calculate the time involved. It was probably a relatively short time, for Paul was restless to experience more triumphs for the gospel, especially among the Gentiles. His proposal to Barnabas was to revisit the cities they had touched on their first journey, in order to consolidate and expand the work. But due to the rupture that developed between them, neither one followed precisely this pattern.

15:37–38. The altercation centered around John Mark, their helper on the first expedition (13:5). It is not likely that Barnabas, in his desire to include Mark, was motivated simply by the fact that the young man was his relative (Col. 4:10). In all probability Mark had had second thoughts about his abrupt abandonment of the party (13:13) and wished to redeem himself. It is possible that the decision of the Jerusalem Council respecting Gentiles gave him a different perspective than he had had before. Understandably, Barnabas was eager to aid in his reinstatement. But Paul was adamantly against it.

We have only the surface facts here; much more may lie in the background. For example, Paul could have been aware that Mark had not only "deserted" his companions and returned to Jerusalem but had also alarmed the church there by reporting that Paul and Barnabas were prepared to receive Gentiles wholly apart from synagogue influence (note that the conversion of Sergius Paulus immediately preceded Mark's decision, 13:12). If this actually occurred, it could have stirred up exactly the kind of protest that was reported by men from Jerusalem in 15:1. At any rate, Paul felt that the stakes were too high to risk giving Mark a second chance.

One may raise the question here whether Galatians 2:13 throws any light on Paul's attitude. If we are right in identifying Paul's visit to Jerusalem in Acts 15 with his own record in Galatians 2:1–10, then it follows naturally that the incident reported in Galatians 2:11–21 must have fallen in this very period after the return of Paul and Barnabas to Antioch. Peter's temporary concession to Jewish sentiment, at the expense of his fellowship with Gentile believers, drew others, including Barnabas, to join him. Thus Paul was left alone to point out the wrong that had been done. It is unlikely, however, that Paul would have allowed this circumstance to prejudice him against Barnabas. The very fact that he had invited his colaborer to go with him on the contemplated mission (v. 36) implies a good relationship at that time.

15:39. The "disagreement" between the two men grew so sharp that they separated, bringing their period of partnership in the Lord's work to a close. The word *paroxysm* is derived from the Greek word used here, giving some idea of the violence of the disagreement (cf. Deut. 29:27; Jer. 39:37 LXX).

Paul owed much to Barnabas, who had given him an entree to the apostles and the Jerusalem church early in his ministry (9:27) and had invited him to share in the ministry at Antioch (11:25–26), an invitation that opened the door for all that followed. Was Paul ungrateful? Hardly that; rather, he put principle above the closest friendship and the will of God above personal relationships, however precious (cf. Matt. 12:46–50).

The decision to part probably clouded Paul's standing with some in the Jerusalem church, where Barnabas was highly esteemed, and may have made his situation there on his last trip (chap. 21) much more precarious than it would have been with Barnabas at his side.

It is to Barnabas's credit that he refused to make an issue of the disagreement before the Antioch church or to seek their support on his behalf. He had led the church in its early days (11:22–24) and had brought Paul into the work. He had been the leader of the first missionary venture of the church (13:2) and had ably represented the church, along with Paul, at the Jerusalem Council. But he refused to use his prominence or his past services as leverage to enlist the congregation on his behalf or to seek from it a reprimand of Paul. This noble man accepted the situation with quiet dignity and went his way in the Lord's service. His choice of Cyprus was natural (cf. 4:36; 13:4) and quite in accord with Paul's suggestion regarding an itinerary (15:36).

The mere fact that Luke reported the contention is a sufficient refutation of the charge that he was intent in his work to present an idealized picture of the early church. Since his purpose in the second half of Acts was to present the growth of the church as it pertained to the work of Paul, it is not strange that at this point Barnabas's name drops out of the account. However, Luke's silence does not entitle us to think that God ceased to work through Barnabas—during this campaign Mark was being groomed for greater usefulness (2 Tim. 4:11).

15:40. "But Paul chose Silas and left." The situation was rather different from the circumstances surrounding the beginning of the first journey, when the initiative of the Holy Spirit and the prayerful, concerted action of the church were given prominence. Yet Haenchen seems to go too far when he asserts, "Paul now set out on his missionary task independent of that congregation."[1] Surely when Luke adds that Paul was "commended by the brothers to the grace of the Lord," he is indicating more than a detached and formal interest in the new undertaking. Paul made contact with the church as he passed through to begin his third journey (18:22), although no record is given of what transpired.

---

[1] Ernst Haenchen, "The Book of the Acts as Source Material for the History of Early Christianity," in *Studies in Luke-Acts,* 271.

In the divine overruling, the apparent evil of the separation of these leaders yielded this measure of good, that now there were two missionary teams at work instead of one. Silas was well fitted, apparently, to be Paul's companion. As a prophet (v. 32) he could bring instruction and encouragement to God's people as well as set forth the gospel to the unsaved. The fact that later on he was useful to Peter in the drafting of his first letter (1 Peter 5:12) demonstrates his proficiency in the Greek tongue. Like Paul, he had Roman citizenship (16:37), and he had had experience in the mother church at Jerusalem. His recent visit to Antioch naturally elicited the esteem and prayerful interest of that church on his behalf.

15:41. Yet another advantage in having Silas as a colleague appears here. The Jerusalem Council had addressed its letter not only to Antioch but also to the churches of Syria and Cilicia, with Silas as one of the men deputed to communicate the message personally. This charge he was now able to fulfill. His presence with the apostle was a visible token of the victory that Paul's position had secured at the conference.

The existence of these churches is probably to be accounted for by the labors of Paul before he was called to Antioch the first time by Barnabas (cf. Gal. 1:21). That some of them came into being as a result of the work of the Antioch church is a possibility, but Luke does not report such activity (in contrast to 19:10). It must have been a time of joyous reunion for Paul as he met with converts of his earlier labors and observed their progress in the Lord.

Even as Barnabas had taken a route that led to his native territory, Paul's would take him to his home city of Tarsus. But Luke, with his economy of language, does not go into details. He does not even say how Paul managed his traveling, but it is almost certain that he went afoot, the most healthy, safe, and sure means of travel.

EARLY STAGES (16:1–10)

Two phases of the campaign are clearly distinguishable. In the first (16:1–5), the missionaries are pictured visiting the churches of southern Galatia, to which they communicated the results of the Jerusalem conference and ministered the Word. In the second (16:6–10) we can trace the probing of new territory in the hope of finding a responsive area for testimony to the truth. The trek ended at Troas, a seaport far to the northwest, which became the point of departure for the mission in Europe.

Verses 1–5. Three things were accomplished by revisiting the churches in southern Galatia: the congregations were informed of the decision of the Jerusalem Council, believers were encouraged, and Timothy was added to the missionary team.

16:1–3. The visit to Lystra was particularly notable, for it meant augmenting the missionary party by the addition of Timothy. As God had supplied Silas to replace Barnabas, He now supplied Timothy to replace Mark. Since this is the one incident that Luke selected for mention out of this visit to the Galatian churches, he must have seen in it great significance for the Christian cause. Indeed, this young man became one of Paul's leading helpers, so in reporting Paul's labors Luke could ill afford to neglect this background material.

Timothy is called a "disciple," indicating that he was probably converted on the first journey. Paul claimed him as his child in the faith (1 Cor. 4:17; 1 Tim. 1:2), Paul's preaching and his miraculous deliverance from death must have made a deep impression on the lad (2 Tim. 3:10–11). He had been taught the Scriptures from childhood (2 Tim. 3:15) by his mother and grandmother (2 Tim. 1:5), and this instruction was providential preparation for his conversion under Paul. "The fine fruit that has for so long been slowly ripening falls at a touch into the husbandman's basket."[2]

These women were the more driven to prayer and instruction because Timothy's father was a pagan. Whatever his intentions and promises may have been, he never identified himself with the Jewish faith. Whether the mother came to Christ at the same time Timothy did or whether she was won later, perhaps by the testimony of her son, we are not informed.

The people in the church at Lystra were able to commend Timothy for his Christian life and testimony, and the same was true of brethren as far away as Iconium. Paul was encouraged, therefore, to select him for ministry. Elders from the district met in a solemn service to consecrate young Timothy, at which time he received a spiritual gift (1 Tim. 4:14), apparently that of evangelism (2 Tim. 4:5). The laying on of Paul's hands probably occurred at this time (2 Tim. 1:6).

---

[2] Alexander Whyte, *Bible Characters: Stephen to Timothy* (New York: Revell, n.d.), 289.

A problem had to be faced, for Timothy was half Jewish, a fact that was well known to the Jews in that whole region. If he were to go forth with Paul and Silas, his uncircumcised state (a testimony to his father's resistance to Judaism) would be an offense to the Jews, and this could hinder the work of the entire team. The very fact that Paul circumcised him indicates clearly that he had no thought of giving up his ministry to his own countrymen, even though he was an apostle to the Gentiles.

Haenchen claims that in this matter of circumcising Timothy, Luke was "the victim of an unreliable tradition."[3] This verdict is based on the judgment that circumcision was so theologically conditioned, carrying with it the whole philosophy of salvation by works, that Paul could not have acted in this way, for it contradicted his teaching in Galatians.

Several things should be kept in mind here. First, Paul makes clear in Galatians that *in itself* circumcision is nothing, and the same is true of uncircumcision (Gal. 5:6; 6:15; cf. 1 Cor. 7:19). Second, in keeping with these pronouncements, Paul could consider Timothy's circumcision a matter of expediency, in line with his avowed principle that in spite of being a Christian he was prepared to make himself a Jew to Jews that he might the more easily win them for Christ (1 Cor. 9:20). Third, before long Luke had joined the missionary group, of which Timothy was by then a member (Acts 16:10), and was brought into close contact with the recent recruit. It is incredible that he would be so lacking in courtesy and interest as not to inquire into Timothy's background. The present passage is evidence that he did. He was not dependent on tradition, either reliable or unreliable.

16:4. One purpose of this trip was to acquaint the churches of Galatia with the letter from the Jerusalem Council containing "the decisions" (plural, for several items were involved). The Council had had a more limited geographical area in view (15:23), but the letter could be of value in Galatia also. The controversy debated and settled at Jerusalem could easily arise in these more remote churches, as we know was true from the Galatian letter. Luke says nothing at all to indicate that the Judaizing activity had already invaded these congregations, which fits with the conclusion that the letter to the Galatian churches was penned at a somewhat later time.

[3] Ernst Haenchen, *The Acts of the Apostles*, 482.

A question arises as to which "towns" are in view here. Three have been mentioned; Pisidian Antioch has not. Judging from the information provided in verses 6–7, it was on the line of travel and probably was visited. The account is exceedingly brief here.

16:5. This is a summary such as Luke often used to close one phase of his narrative before proceeding to another. An earlier example is 9:31, but whereas there the location of a group of churches is indicated, here such information is not given. Perhaps the intention is to designate only the churches of Galatia, but since this verse rounds off the whole section dealing with the legalistic controversy and its settlement, it is more probable that the churches of Syria and Cilicia are included also. With the solution adopted by the Council, those churches, which were mainly Gentile in character, gained new confidence and new boldness in evangelism. The result was "daily" increase (cf. 2:47).

Verses 6–10. This passage is devoted entirely to travel, with no mention of ministry, for the next sphere of labor had not yet been revealed.

16:6–8. It seems that sometime before the missionaries arrived at Pisidian Antioch, which was on the border between Galatia (that part that was designated as Phrygia) and Asia, they received an intimation from the Spirit that they were not to evangelize Asia. ("Asia" denotes, not the continent, but the Roman province of that name, which occupied the western part of what we know as Asia Minor.) How this knowledge was communicated we are not told. A communication through Silas is a possibility (cf. 15:32).

Since the prohibition was confined to ministry and did not rule out travel, the party moved in a northerly direction through the eastern part of the province of Asia. Some scholars are of the opinion that their route took them back into the northern part of Galatia and that there the churches were founded that Paul addressed in his letter to the Galatians. But if that was the case, we would expect Luke to have given some account of the ministry, such as that which he provided concerning the southern Galatian churches (chaps. 13–14). The narrative simply traces the route traveled until guidance was given that would permit ministry.

The northward course fits the observation that the missionaries "tried to enter Bithynia," the province to the northeast of

Asia, bordering on the Black Sea. It appears likely that when they reached Dorylaeum, which was in Asia but fairly close to the border of Bithynia, they turned west because of a warning from the Spirit of Jesus.

It must have been frustrating to have such negative guidance. But the experience was profitable inasmuch as it reminded them that the Spirit was in charge of operations. If He said no, this simply meant that when He said yes, the plan would prove wiser than any that the missionaries were projecting. Their hope of reaching the cities of Asia (including Ephesus) had been dashed, followed by a similar rebuff in their effort to push into the important centers of population in western Bithynia, where both Jews and Gentiles could be reached. But this did not mean that these areas were to be deprived of gospel testimony. Asia had its turn (chap. 19), and so did Bithynia (1 Peter 1:1).

Meanwhile the district of Mysia also had to be left untouched, since it was part of the province of Asia. But it was here, at the coastal town of Troas, a few miles south of the ancient Troy, that positive guidance finally came. Troas was an important place, a Roman colony, whose extensive city walls are still visible in part. Paul made other visits to this center (Acts 20:6; 2 Cor. 2:12). In addition, it seems that he was there a short time prior to his final imprisonment and death (2 Tim. 4:13). The circumstances of the founding of the church there are unknown, but someone other than Paul must have started the work.

16:9–10. Here at Troas the will of God was finally made known through a "vision" that Paul had during the night. What he saw was a man of Macedonia asking for help for his country. It is unnecessary to speculate that Paul recognized him as a Macedonian by his dress or anything about his appearance. Rather, the request for Paul to come to Macedonia indicated sufficiently to what country the man belonged.

Are we to think of the Macedonian as a pagan (cf. 17:27) or as a Christian brother who had already begun a work there and was appealing for others to come to his aid? Against the latter possibility, the following points should be noted: (1) he is not called a brother but "a man"; (2) the word translated "help" is used nowhere else in Acts or in the rest of the New Testament to mean collaboration in the Lord's work; (3) it is doubtful, in view of Paul's preference for pioneer ministry (Rom. 15:20) that he would be drawn to the idea of assisting in a work already begun, though admittedly he had done this in the case of Syrian Antioch.

Probably before the night was spent, Paul excitedly shared his vision with his companions, who were ready to agree with him that the vision was a call from God to cross over to Macedonia "to preach the gospel." This fits with the conclusion already drawn that the call for help did not come from a Christian.

For the first time, the pronoun *we* slips into the narrative (v. 10). It could easily be assumed that one of Paul's companions, either Silas or Timothy, is the narrator here; but then the question must be faced as to why this construction has not been used up to this point and ceases to be used after the campaign in Philippi is described, and why it resumes when Paul and his helpers return to Philippi for the last time on the journey to Jerusalem (20:5–6). It is fairly evident that the writer joined the party at Troas for the trip to Philippi and remained there to direct the work when Paul and the others went on to Thessalonica. He chose not to disclose how he came to join the others at Troas. Possibly he felt that Paul needed him because of his medical skill (cf. 2 Cor. 12:1–10), but since he included himself as one who was to preach the gospel to the Macedonians (Acts 16:10), it is obvious that he was more than an attending physician.

Ordinarily, a move from one continent to another involves a considerable change in culture and civilization, but in the case before us this was not so. Asia and Europe, at this location, were in close proximity and were bound together by influences that went back to the days before Alexander the Great. Rome had continued to honor Alexander's aim of marrying the East to the West through Hellenization.

Alexander had moved from west to east to conquer brilliantly and infuse the Levant with everything Greek. Now a converted Jew was moving in the opposite direction, from Asia to Europe, to conquer for Christ.

PHILIPPI (16:11–40)

The story of the founding of one of Paul's most trouble-free churches is told mainly in terms of two notable conversions, together with a report of his first encounter as a missionary with Roman governmental authorities (his experience with Sergius Paulus had hardly been an encounter).

Verses 11–15. The sea journey from Troas is described, followed by information about Philippi and the first witness in this area.

16:11–12. It is possible to gather from Luke's journals made on shipboard that he was quite at home on the sea. The first leg of the journey was from Troas to Samothrace, an island south of the coast of Thrace, which was a large territory to the east of Macedonia. The island was slightly more than halfway to Neapolis, the port of debarkation. To save time the passengers probably stayed on board overnight. The next day's run brought them to Neapolis, about 125 miles from Troas. This journey of two days is quite in contrast to a later one, which reversed this route and required five days (20:6). The missionaries must have felt that such a propitious journey was a confirmation of the vision and a token of divine prospering in the work that lay ahead of them.

Almost ten miles beyond Neapolis was the city of Philippi, which derived its name from Philip of Macedon, the father of Alexander. It had the status of a Roman colony, many of its residents being retired army veterans. The famous Egnatian Way ran right through the center of the city, furnishing access to the Adriatic Sea on the west and thence to Rome. It is tempting to suppose that Paul's thought of going to Rome, which became a fixed objective at Ephesus (19:21), had its incubation in the days at Philippi.

In one respect the wording of verse 12 is uncertain. We have a choice between rendering it "the leading city of that district of Macedonia" (as in NIV) or "a city of the first district of Macedonia." As to the former, it is awkward to have Macedonia spoken of as a district, for it was a province. The latter fits well with the historic fact that the Romans had divided Macedonia into four districts, and Philippi was in the first district, though not the capital, a distinction that belonged to Amphipolis.

16:13–15. With the coming of the Sabbath, the visitors began to search for a place of worship. No synagogue was available in this Roman colony. Jews seem to have been few, anyway.

Since synagogues were often constructed near water to facilitate the ritual ablutions, the missionaries judged that they might find a place of worship near the Gangites River, somewhat over a mile west of the city. The word *proseuchē* can denote the place of prayer as well as the activity of prayer. Philo used it consistently in preference to the word *synagōgē*. Since Luke uses the word synagogue regularly, he may be indicating here that the spot they found was merely an open place or some sort of shelter less elaborate than a synagogue building. When Luke says, "We sat down," he may be indicating that some sort of seats were available. The fact that this meeting consisted of women may be adduced as an added reason for concluding that the place fell short of being a regular synagogue—Jewish law required ten men in order to warrant the building of such an edifice.

Paul and his companions did not disdain to speak to the group of women. In this informal atmosphere it was no doubt easier to get directly to the theme of the gospel than it would have been in a characteristic synagogue service. Luke's report suggests that all four men may have spoken on this occasion, though Paul was evidently the chief speaker (v. 14). As for the listeners, he indicates the effect on Lydia only, presumably because she was outstanding by reason of both her position and her eventual leadership in the church formed at Philippi.

Lydia was a native of Thyatira, a prosperous city of Lydia, the section of Asia Minor to the south of Mysia. Several hundred years before, in the days of Croesus, the region had gained prominence and considerable power, only to be conquered by Cyrus and the Persians. Thyatira was famous for its industry and its trade guilds. One source of income was the making of purple dye from the secretions of the mollusk or from the root of the madder plant. The woman Lydia owned a business in Philippi as "a dealer in purple cloth," which was highly prized in those days.

Since there was no synagogue at Philippi, Lydia's status as "a worshiper of God" is best explained as a carry-over from her days in Thyatira, a center that must have had a considerable settlement of Jews on account of its commercial importance. But Lydia had not become a proselyte to the Jewish faith, so she was the more open to the gospel that the Old Testament anticipated. In addition, "the Lord opened her heart" (cf. Luke 24:45) so that she responded favorably to what she heard.

Luke does not say when Lydia and her household were baptized. It may have occurred somewhat later, when she was

267

able to persuade the rest to share her faith (contrast vv. 31–32). The term "household" could indicate other members of the family (if there were any), business helpers, and servants. When Paul referred to those of Caesar's household (Phil. 4:22), he was evidently designating believers drawn from the ranks of several thousand employees and slaves of the emperor rather than the emperor himself or his immediate family.

Conversions of groups were quite common in the early days of the church, and the church in the house had a cohesive strength because it was not merely an aggregation of individuals who happened to gather periodically in a certain house; rather, it involved many who had already been associated but now found that association deepened by the transforming power of the gospel.

The immediate result of Lydia's conversion was the lodging of the missionary party at her house in response to her insistent invitation. She had the means and the space to match her hospitable spirit. Becuase of her generosity, Paul found it unnecessary to pursue his trade while in Philippi. Lydia's example seems to have made the church there especially solicitous for Paul's needs, as he himself testified (Phil. 4:16). He consented to set aside his rule of not taking anything from his converts, feeling that he would not be misunderstood by this congregation if he did (contrast 2 Cor. 11:7–9; 1 Thess. 2:9).

Verses 16–18. These verses provide the background for an incident that was to affect greatly the remainder of Paul's stay in the city and was to terminate his ministry so far as this visit was concerned.

16:16. On the way to the place of prayer, the missionaries were intercepted by a demon-possessed slave girl, whose condition gave her ability at fortune-telling. "A spirit by which she predicted the future" (*pneuma pythōna*) is possibly intended to relate the girl to Pythian Apollo, the Greek god so called because of the tale of his having killed a serpent (*pythōn*). The priestess of the Delphic oracle, connected with the temple of Apollo, northwest of Corinth, was often resorted to in antiquity by those who sought guidance. The Greek term for predicting the future is found only here in the New Testament. Its use in the LXX, where it occurs several times, is significant in that the practice is always disapproved (see Deut. 18:10 and context). In form, the term is related to the word *mantic,* and it suggests a certain abnormality in the state during which the divination takes place.

This girl was a source of profit to those who owned her. Those who commit fraud prey on others for gain; believers are eager to expose fraud and destroy its effects.

When did the initial confrontation occur? Some think it happened on the very Sabbath that the visitors had gone out looking for the place of prayer. But Luke seems to introduce it as something that developed afterward. It is hardly convincing to say that after Lydia's conversion Paul and his companions would no longer have frequented the spot outside the city, since there is no proof that others were saved on that day. The missionaries probably returned to continue their discussion with the women who habitually gathered there, in the hope of winning them to Christ.

16:17. In spite of having had no apparent contact with the missionaries, the girl was able to announce loudly and publicly that these men were in the service of "the Most High God" (cf. Mark 5:7). This title for the Deity has been found not only in Jewish and Christian literature but also in pagan.

Her second declaration concerned the message. She confessed that the missionaries were proclaiming "the way to be saved." In the ancient world at this period there was a considerable longing for salvation, though it was frequently a salvation from the vexations and burdens of life rather than from sin. In the Gospels, demons were aware of the identity of Jesus, but they did not speak of His saving mission.

16:18. This went on for many days, and at length Paul had had enough. Turning around, he addressed the spirit (not the girl), commanding it in the name of Jesus Christ to come out of her. That he had not done this earlier may have been because he recognized the peril into which an exorcism of this kind might bring him and his friends. Yet to fail to exorcise the spirit was to encourage the notion that Paul was himself affiliated with the spirit, who seemed to know him and his mission so well. Somewhat similarly, on many occasions Jesus had rebuked and exorcised the spirits that confessed Him as the Holy One of God (e.g., Mark 1:24–25). Testimony from such a source was not a desirable endorsement.

Verses 19–23. Paul and Silas were beaten and imprisoned as a result of the exorcism. Luke did not include himself in this section (in contrast to v. 17). He would not give the impression that he and Timothy were involved.

16:19–21. Already irritated that the girl had deviated from her normal routine by calling attention to the missionaries and their message, the owners were furious when they saw that now their "hope of making money" had vanished. The girl was now useless to them, so they turned away from her to lay hands on Paul and Silas and drag them to the local officials. In all likelihood the terms "the authorities" and "the magistrates" refer to the same individuals. The former is a general term for rulers or leaders, whereas the latter is *stratēgoi*, of which Sherwin-White notes, "The author is simply using the commonest Hellenistic title to render the untranslatable term *duoviri.*"[4]

The complainers said nothing about the exorcism, but instead charged that the visitors were disturbing the peace, adding that the instigators were Jews trying to introduce their "customs" among those who were Romans. A deliberate appeal to local prejudice is apparent in the tension between the terms "Jews" and "Romans." Cases are on record of action by Roman authorities against foreign religions that were judged a danger to public welfare and morals, but such religions were not opposed on the ground of their being foreign. Noting the peculiarity of the accusation at Philippi, with its total lack of emphasis on "the depravity of the practices introduced by Paul" and instead its underscoring of their non-Roman character, Sherwin-White suggests that the recent expulsion of Jews from Rome by the Emperor Claudius may have been relied on here to arouse feeling against these outsiders.[5]

16:22–23. The propaganda was successful in assembling a "crowd" that was visibly incensed at the alleged introduction of foreign customs, whatever that might mean. All they knew was that their detached, Roman manner of life was being threatened, and that was enough to arouse their anger.

The spirit of the mob communicated itself to the authorities, who acted on these vague charges without examining the matter for themselves. That the mood of the crowd had swayed them is evident in the strong word Luke uses to describe their rough and unseemly tactics as they grabbed at the garments of the prisoners and literally tore them off their backs the more

[4] A. N. Sherwin-White, *Roman Society and Roman Law in the New Testament,* 93.

[5] Ibid., 80–81.

quickly to expose the flesh to the rods that were used for the flogging, a peculiarly Roman ordeal. This was one of the three occasions when Paul suffered this sort of chastisement (2 Cor. 11:25).

It is a strange misunderstanding of the situation that has led some to suppose that the magistrates tore their own garments to express their horror and indignation. The custom of the Jewish high priest (Mark 14:63) should not be imputed to a Gentile ruler.

Verses 24–34. The passage presents a great contrast between the ignominious imprisonment engineered by men and the mighty deliverance of God's servants that led to some dramatic conversions.

16:24. Severely beaten, the two men were pushed into prison, where the jailer fastened their feet in the stocks. The intention was doubtless to pursue the case further before a higher Roman official, but in the providence of God, that did not happen. Months later, Paul reflected on the treatment he had received (1 Thess. 2:2).

16:25. Instead of concentrating on their suffering or suggesting that the two men spent their time commiserating with one another, the account emphasizes their good spirits, reflected in their singing. This means that Paul's emphasis on joy, in his letter to the Philippians, was not something theoretical. It had been demonstrated in their community years before, under trying conditions. To be sure, the prisoners were praying also, possibly alternating prayer with their praise. There is no indication that they waited till "midnight" to begin. Doubtless they had been so engaged for hours. These brethren could say with the psalmist, "At night his song is with me—a prayer to the God of my life" (Ps 42:8). His presence turns a prison into a place of peace and exhilarating joy.

Others besides God heard them. The other prisoners were listening and wondering, for they had seen the two, battered and bleeding, as they were hustled into the inner prison and fastened there with no one to help or comfort them.

16:26–27. It was about midnight that the answer came, in the form of an earthquake (cf. 4:31) intense enough to shake the foundations of the building, open the doors, and take off the chains of the prisoners throughout the prison. Adjacent were the quarters of the jailer, who was jarred out of bed and roused to instant anxiety about the prisoners, fearing all had escaped.

The opened doors confirmed his fears. (Note that he did not see the doors being opened, but he saw them standing open.) His charges must have fled. He was responsible, and since he must die for failure to keep them, it was better to die by his own hand than by order of his superiors.

16:28–29. Only the voice of Paul deterred him from self-destruction. "We are all here!" (not both, but "all"). The chains were loosed, but the prisoners had stayed. Was it because of fear of being recaptured and punished for attempted escape, or was it because of the magnetic leadership of Paul and Silas, who had no intention of fleeing? Paul's language suggests that the whole lot had gathered together. No longer was the inner prison allowed to separate the special prisoners from the rest.

As soon as he could get lights on the scene, the jailer rushed in, trembling with fear. The young girl had been right. These two must be representatives of God Most High, who had now intervened on their behalf. What was it she had said about their showing the way of salvation? That was on his mind supremely just now.

16:30–32. As soon as he could secure the other prisoners, he brought out the two servants of God from the prison and demanded of them what he must do to be saved. Presumably he had not heard them preach.

Paul answered in the simplest and yet the most comprehensive of terms: "Believe in the Lord Jesus." That would bring salvation. One almost senses the atmosphere of the Gospel of John here. *Believe* is pitted against *do*. Human achievement is worthless, and needless as well. The Lord Jesus has done it all. What remains is to appropriate His saving work by faith. A similar assurance was given regarding the jailer's household (cf. v. 15).

Shortly, the three of them were inside the house, facing people who were almost as fearful as the jailer had been. The opportunity was there for testimony, and they embraced it. Other things could wait. When the Spirit of God convicts, everything else pales into insignificance compared with the necessity of becoming right with God. Further teaching was given to enlarge on the summary word spoken about salvation (v. 31.)

16:33–34. Only when the spiritual task had been discharged did the missionaries consent to have their physical needs met. Their wounds, left unattended the day before, now received loving ministration. As soon as this was completed, the whole group entered into a service of baptism, by which the new converts expressed their faith (cf. v. 15). Family solidarity was such that a decision on the part of the head of the household involved the rest. This could have adverse as well as good results (cf. Titus 1:11). Chrysostom notes the element of reciprocity here, remarking about the jailer, "He washed them, and he was washed; he washed them from their stripes, he himself was washed from his sins."[6] Then, at length, the physical hunger of Paul and Silas received attention. We get the picture of the jailer insisting that he serve his benefactors himself, doing it with a grateful and rejoicing heart. He and his entire household had experienced salvation.

"Had come to believe in God" does not refer to some prior experience that prepared them for faith in Christ, but it emphasizes their previous paganism (cf. 1 Thess. 1:9). The jailer had not been, like Lydia, a God-fearer.

Verses 35–40. The final phase of the encounter with the authorities in this Roman colony reveals the two parties in roles that differed sharply from those of the previous day. Two factors likely played a part in the changed attitude of the magistrates. First, reflection on their hasty action, taken without investigation, may have decided them not to pursue the case. Further, they must have felt the earthquake, or at least learned about it, and concluded that there might be more in this situation than they had realized.[7] It would be safer to let the prisoners go before something worse happened. Romans could be highly superstitious at times.

16:35–39. The "officers" who acted as messengers for the magistrates were the same men who had inflicted the beatings the day before (the title means "those who hold the rods"). Each colony was permitted two of them.

In passing on the word that the prisoners were now free to go, the jailer must have been astonished at Paul's negative reaction. His reasoning behind refusing to leave consisted of four elements: there had been a public beating, without a trial,

---

[6] Chrysostom, *Homer* 36.2.

[7] This is broadly hinted at in the reading of the Western text of verse 35, which adds, after "When it was daylight," the following: "the praetors came together into the forum and, calling to mind the earthquake that had taken place, they were affrighted and sent the lictors."

inflicted on men who were Romans (possessing Roman citizenship), followed by imprisonment. A great injustice had been committed. The key item here is the claim of Roman citizenship. It could go hard with officials who had failed to honor this dignity, which accounts for the magistrates' fear when the officers reported back to them.

The question that naturally arises, however, is why the missionaries had waited until this moment to declare their status. It has been conjectured that amid the uproar at the time of the beating the two men had tried to explain that they were Roman citizens but had not succeeded in communicating the point.

More likely, Paul had anticipated the course of events (recall that he had waited several days before exorcising the demon) and determined to withhold the information until it would count for the most on behalf of the group of disciples he was leaving behind in Philippi. When the Roman officials realized their mistake, they would be inclined to avoid taking any illegal steps against members of the infant church. If this surmise is correct, it reveals the unselfishness of these leaders and their pastoral concern.

As for the magistrates, these men who had humiliated God's servants a few hours before were now humiliated over their own mistake and are pictured as requesting Paul and Silas to leave the city. Their continued presence would only be a thorn in the side of those who were guilty of municipal bungling. Once more the men of God responded in the right way, refusing to put on a display of stubbornness that would take the edge off their victory.

16:40. They went "out of the prison," meaning they must have gone back to the place of confinement after the events of the early morning hours. To be found fraternizing with the jailer in his living quarters would be irregular, to say the least.

Prior to the departure from the city, the two men insisted, however, on the privilege of spending a little time with the brethren who gathered at the house of Lydia for fellowship. There is no mention of any ministry to the missionaries after their ordeal, though such may well have been proffered. Rather, they were the ones who used the opportunity to encourage the new converts, preparing them for the days ahead when they must carry on without apostolic leadership.

Luke modestly kept out of the record the fact that he stayed to shepherd this congregation. Doubtless he kept in touch with Paul and his companions, reporting from time to time on the progress of the believers. This church remained close to Paul's heart, and conversely he continued to be deeply appreciated and faithfully supported by this band of Christians (Phil. 1:5, 7, 19, 26; 2:17, 25, 28, 30; 4:10–19).

THESSALONICA (17:1–9)

Thessalonica, the most important center in Macedonia, was a populous commercial city at the head of the Thermaic Gulf and bore the name of the step-sister of Alexander the Great. In contrast to Philippi, which was a Roman colony, Thessalonica was a free city; that is, it was not subject to the provincial administration in local affairs and could pass its own laws and have its own institutions, such as customs duties. In addition to its rulers, who were called "politarchs," it had its own popular assembly.

Our knowledge of the mission in this place that is provided by Luke can be supplemented by Paul's letters to the Thessalonians, especially 1 Thessalonians 1–2.

17:1. The journey from Philippi to Thessalonica covered a hundred miles along the Egnatian Way. If there were overnight stops at Amphipolis and Apollonia, this meant a trek of thirty miles or so per day. Some have suggested that the party may have gone by horseback.

Apparently no ministry was undertaken at these intermediate points. No description is given of the journey (cf. Gen. 12:5), only of the situation at Thessalonica. Here, in contrast to Philippi, the synagogue provided a base of operations. Doubtless the missionaries were well aware in advance of the great opportunity presented here, not only by the city but also by the territory surrounding it (1 Thess. 1:8).

17:2–3. It was Paul's "custom" to go to the synagogue. Identical language is used of our Lord in Luke 4:16. The ministry lasted for three Sabbaths; this does not exclude the possibility of a further ministry concentrated on reaching Gentiles, particularly since they constituted a majority of the church (1 Thess. 1:9). The receipt of a gift from the Philippian brethren on more than one occasion at Thessalonica (Phil. 4:16) argues for a stay longer than three weeks.

In regard to this gift, a problem arises as to why Paul found it necessary to ply his trade at Thessalonica (1 Thess. 2:9; 2 Thess. 3:8). Two factors deserve consideration: the working period may have been confined to the time before the arrival of financial help; and, in addition, Paul may have felt the desirability of continuing his labors despite the aid, in order to provide an example of diligence (2 Thess. 3:9).

Paul "reasoned with them from the Scriptures." While "reasoned" could hint at discussion, this is not as likely here as the other meaning of the word—"to give an address"—which occurs several times in this chapter and the next. In fact, it is doubtful that any of the examples in Acts can mean anything else than delivering an address.[8]

Paul was intent on presenting the Scriptures, and his methodology involved "explaining" and "proving." The former expression is literally "opening," and it is used of Jesus' instruction to the Emmaus pair (Luke 24:32), and therefore need not be thought of as necessitating the literal opening of a book. The other expression means "to bring forward by way of proof." Explanation was buttressed by marshaling the data of Scripture in support of the necessity that the promised Christ "suffer and rise from the dead" (cf. Mark 8:31). The final stage in the presentation was the assertion that the Christ of prophecy was identical with the Jesus whom Paul was proclaiming. Here we must suppose that if we had a full account rather than a digest, there would be a setting forth of the death of Christ and His resurrection similar to what is reported in the Pisidian Antioch address (Acts 13:27–37).

Since the "I" is emphatic, it is probably intended to denote Paul in contrast to Silas and Timothy, for whereas they could expound the Scriptures respecting Christ, they could not bear witness to His resurrection as Paul could from his conversion experience (9:3–9).

17:4. The message he gave bore fruit. "Some" (Jews) were persuaded. Aristarchus was one of them (20:4; Col. 4:10–11). Jason was probably another (vv. 5, 7). The converts are said to have joined Paul and Silas. They attached themselves to the missionaries, casting their lot with them, come what may.

A second group of converts consisted of "God-fearing Greeks," and they were far more numerous than the Jewish

[8]G. Schrenk, *TDNT*, 2:94.

brethren. This presents a difficulty, in that in his correspond- ence with this church Paul said that his readers had turned to God from idols (1 Thess. 1:9), as though they had been untouched pagans before their conversion. It does not help too much to adopt an alternate translation, "worshiping Greeks," because even that rendering implies a certain devotion to the God of Israel. Perhaps we are left to the conclusion that despite the conversion of many God-fearing Gentiles during the synagogue ministry, the number was small as compared to the vastly greater number who became believers during Paul's ministry apart from the synagogue.

Several of the leading women (cf. v. 12) constituted a third group.

17:5. The greater the response, the greater the opposition from unbelieving Jews. Jealousy is noted as the motive for stirring up trouble (cf. 13:45).

Being a minority in the city, the Jews could not mount a successful persecution without help. But it was easy to induce the rabble in the marketplace (the public square) to join them. It gave them something to do, something a bit novel. The resulting "mob" churned the city into a tumult. It was a demonstration against unwelcome outsiders, and it gained momentum as it moved toward the house of Jason, where Paul and Silas were known to be guests (Timothy had not been in the public eye sufficiently to attract attention). "The rabble is apparently summoned to make the attacks upon the Christians appear like a popular movement."[9] It is difficult to be certain whether "the crowd" was the popular assembly or the unruly mob itself.

7:6–7. Foiled in their attempt to locate the missionaries, who were not there at the time, the crowd decided to vent its displeasure on Jason and a few brethren who were with him, dragging them before the city authorities, the politarchs (cf. 16:19). Luke's accuracy in using this term has been vindicated by the discovery of several inscriptions bearing this technical word, including one on the excavated Vardar gate of the city.

It was scarcely an orderly scene, as charges were shouted before these dignitaries. "These men," by the position in the sentence, would seem at first to refer to Jason and the others,

[9]Haenchen, *Acts of the Apostles.*

but the identity is clarified by what follows—Paul and Silas were meant.

Since the allegations are not likely to have been invented by the mob, we must suppose that the real initiators of the charges were the unbelieving Jews. The charge of causing "trouble all over the world" is a hyperbole, but it reflects the closeness of communication between Jewish communities in the Dispersion. The first missionary journey had left a deep impression on Asia Minor Jews. This first allegation is somewhat vague, and the second is scarcely more precise, since "Caesar's decrees" are not spelled out. But the third was obviously intended to be climactic, since it posed a rivalry between Jesus and Caesar. "King" is used here in a universal rather than a local sense. The unbelieving Jews would have liked nothing better than to make trouble for the Nazarenes with the Roman authorities. Despite their hatred for Rome in general and of certain worship-hungry emperors in particular, the Jews could point to the fact that sacrifices on behalf of Caesar were regularly offered in the temple at Jerusalem. The politarchs were bound to be concerned with an accusation such as this, just as Pilate had been concerned when a similar charge was raised against Jesus Himself by the Jews (Luke 23:2).

Since it is clear from the Thessalonian letters that during this visit Paul had preached the return of Christ, the passage before us can be said to reflect that preaching, however slanted was the report of it by his adversaries.

17:8–9. The crowd mentioned here is apparently to be distinguished from the crowd that went to the house of Jason. It must refer to those who were in the marketplace in the vicinity of the politarchs when the mob arrived in that area of the city. The mood of alarm was being spread throughout the community.

Since Paul and Silas were not available as suspects, the only ones who could be immediately dealt with were Jason and his friends. The authorities required them to "post bond." This is hardly to be thought of as a bail pending a formal trial, for there was no real basis for a trial of the men who were present. More likely the "bond" was assurance exacted from Jason and the others that the missionaries would leave town and would not return. That was the easiest way to dispose of the problem.

The limitation thus imposed on the apostle and his companions may be reflected in his complaint that he tried more than once to return to encourage the believers, but found no way to do it. Satan had gained an advantage in this situation (1 Thess. 2:18). In the same passage Paul makes the charge that the Jews had persecuted him (1 Thess. 2:15). He seems also to indicate that the church did not cease to be persecuted even after he and his colaborers had left the city (1 Thess. 2:14). Slanders on his ministry continued to be made by the Jews (1 Thess. 2:13–16).

BEREA (17:10–15)

This city lay some fifty miles to the southwest of Thessalonica, on the road that led to Achaia, the province south of Macedonia. The ministry there was promising but brief, terminated by Jews who came from Thessalonica to stir up trouble (cf. 14:19).

17:10–12. The Thessalonian brethren located Paul and Silas, advised them of the new situation, and kept them under cover till nightfall, when they sent them on their way to Berea. Paul may have been reluctant to go, not happy at being compelled to slip out of town, but he was helpless to do anything about it, since Jason and the others had given their pledge. Timothy may have made his way to Berea independently.

The synagogue presented a fresh opportunity for testimony, especially since the Berean Jews were "of more noble character" than those who resisted the truth in Thessalonica. The description indicates a quality somewhat different from high-minded, referring to a generous spirit free from prejudice. The nobility consisted in this, that instead of having a suspicious attitude that was ready to reject out of hand what was set before them, they actually "received the message with great eagerness." By "message" we are not to understand "the Scriptures," but the spoken word of the missionaries (cf. 1 Thess. 2:13). The point is that these people, for all their eagerness, were not gullible; they insisted on comparing what they heard with what they had—the Scriptures—considering them the final court of appeal.

Some Jews could search the Scriptures and fail to find the way of life (John 5:39). Paul knew from personal experience in dealing with his countrymen that their minds were veiled from an understanding of the oracles of God until they turned to the

Lord Jesus Christ, who alone gives clarity of meaning to the Old Covenant (2 Cor. 3:14–16).

Undoubtedly the message given to these Jews in Berea was identical with that which Luke summarized in connection with his report of the mission to Thessalonica (Acts 17:2–3). "Every day" suggests that contact was maintained with Paul and the others during the week, each message calling for fresh examination of the Scriptures to confirm what had been heard.

Luke notes that there was a close connection between searching the Scriptures with open mind and attaining the result, namely, that many believed. God honors honest inquiry into His truth.

These were Jews, but there was other fruit during this mission. The synagogue here, as elsewhere, was attended by some Gentiles. Luke notes that not a few of these, both men and women, put their faith in Christ. He mentions the prominent "women" before the "men." In the accounts of all three of the Macedonian centers where the missionaries worked, women converts are given separate mention (16:14; 17:4, 12). This accords with our knowledge of Macedonian women from secular sources. "The extant Macedonian inscriptions seem to assign to the sex a higher social influence than is common among the civilized nations of antiquity."[10]

17:13–15. Information about the campaign in Berea found its way back to the Jews of Thessalonica, suggesting that in Berea there was some opposition to the missionaries, however subdued it was. This was the signal for a determined effort to repeat in Berea what had been done in Thessalonica. Volunteers were ready to make the trip and do their utmost to stir up trouble, using the same basic method they had employed in their own city, "agitating the crowds." Note that this was popular rather than official action. The city government of Thessalonica had not dispatched representatives to apprehend Paul. "There is no evidence that the police forces of different cities ever acted in concert."[11]

Anxious to avoid the reputation of being disturbers of the peace, the local brethren acted promptly, sending Paul alone out of town with an escort. This testifies to the position of

[10]J. B. Lightfoot, *Saint Paul's Epistle to the Philippians* (London: Macmillan, 1910), 56.

[11]Sherwin-White, *Roman Society*, 98.

leadership the apostle enjoyed and also to the animosity he engendered by his forthright presentation of the gospel to his countrymen (cf. 18:12; 21:28).

Some uncertainty about the movements of Paul results from a comparison of statements in verses 14 and 15. On the one hand he was sent away to go down "to the coast," yet we read that those who escorted him "brought him to Athens," a distance greater than the total he had traveled in all of Macedonia. Rackham gives a plausible account of what happened:

> A large party of Beroean Christians accompanied the apostle as far as the coast; then instead of taking ship, as might have been expected by his adversaries, he turned to the right into Thessaly with a smaller escort, while the rest of the brethren returned to Beroea.[12]

This conjecture is favored by the fact that Luke mentioned no port of embarkation, as he usually did.

For the third time Paul had been forced out of a Macedonian city. Should he give up and return to Syria? That would be unthinkable. His spirit was akin to that of Livingstone, who said, "I am prepared to go anywhere, as long as it is forward." Luke does not tell us whether the apostle had planned a campaign in Achaia, the province south of Macedonia, but that is where he was being led by circumstances.

He wrote no letter to the church at Berea as far as is known, yet there is evidence that the group continued to thrive, for they took an active part in raising funds for needy believers in Jerusalem, sending a representative with Paul (20:4). As for Paul's companions in the work, it seems they rejoined him in Athens, but Timothy was sent back to Thessalonica on a mission (1 Thess. 3:2), whereas Silas perhaps went to Philippi. They both rejoined Paul in Corinth (Acts 18:5).

ATHENS (17:16-34)

A situation quite different from any he had faced before confronted the apostle here. The city had been the intellectual center of Greece, especially in the sixth and fifth centuries B.C.

---

[12]R. B. Rackham, *The Acts of the Apostles.*

Something of its past glory lingered on, represented in its university and its various philosophical schools, but it was living largely in the past, preferring reputation to the reality of culture.

17:16. It seems almost as though the apostle had no plans for a campaign here but was marking time until Silas and Timothy caught up with him. If this is a correct estimate of the situation, then the quality of his presentation before the Areopagus looms as all the more amazing, since it was not the result of long reflection and studied preparation.

But Paul was not a man to take it easy; this was not a vacation. In fact, his spirit could find no rest, distressed as it was by what he saw around him, a city filled with idols (in 15:39 the noun form of this verb "distressed" is translated "disagreement"). Paul could not come to terms with the idea that idols had any place in genuine culture. Any appreciation that might have been extended to these objects as works of art was precluded by the use to which they were put. He could not be a bystander much longer. Every day he came closer to entering the arena of conflict.

17:17–18. The conclusion just stated is verified by the "so" with which verse 17 begins. For some days Paul carried on a dual ministry, presenting the gospel in the synagogue to the Jews and God-fearing Gentiles, and carrying on daily discussion in the *agora,* or public square. Here people of all types mingled, especially those who were eager to converse.

Rather than indulge in small talk with those who had little to offer, the apostle gravitated to the "Epicurean and Stoic philosophers." The former school of thought was named after its founder, Epicurus. Deistic in point of view, the Epicurean emphasized pleasure (in the sense of tranquility and freedom from pain) as the chief end of human existence—an idea that suited the Greek temperament rather well. The Stoic system of thought, founded by Zeno of Cyprus, derived its name from the Stoa, or portico in Athens, where Zeno first taught. It was pantheistic in its outlook and emphasized duty and self-discipline, proving especially congenial to the Roman temperament. Henley's poem "Invictus" contains ingredients that are basically Stoic.

It is not at all certain that the slighting comments made about Paul and recorded here came from the philosophers themselves. More likely they came from their hangers-on who thought to show their loyalty to their teachers by heaping ridicule on the unprepossessing Jew who dared to debate with them. The term translated "babbler" is picturesque, filled with local color. As the birds fluttered here and there in the square, eager to pounce on any stray scrap of food, so with this stranger. He was out to snatch up any bits of knowledge he could find, a mere seedpicker (the literal meaning) rather than a man of genuine knowledge and well-digested thought.

Others had a less depreciatory estimate, emphasizing that he was a religious protagonist rather than a would-be philosopher. Yet this evaluation, for all its intended mildness, was actually far more menacing than the other, for to allege that Paul was an exponent of "foreign gods" made him undesirable, a danger to the entire Athenian community. Recall that Socrates lost his life on the ground that he was guilty of introducing such deities into Athens. Each city was jealous of its gods, especially those that were regarded as its patrons. To explain to his readers how such a comment could be made about Paul, Luke added that it was made because he was preaching "Jesus and the resurrection." As some have noted, in the original the two words could have been understood respectively as "healing" and "restoration." How ironic that Paul should be thought of as a polytheist!

17:19–21. A decisive moment had come. The verbs in the preceding sentences are in the imperfect tense, picturing what went on for a period of time, day after day. Now a crisis was reached—"they took him and brought him." Paul was not a prisoner, but he was under suspicion and had to be interrogated before the Areopagus. "Areopagus" could mean the hill of Ares, the god of war ("Mars," in Latin), but since the word is used also in verse 22, it doubtless has the same meaning here as there. It is very awkward to say that a person stood in the midst of a hill (cf. v. 33). The attempt to make "areopagus" mean "an informal crowd on Mars Hill"[13] does not meet the problem. It must mean either the hill, or the court that in early times held its session there but later met in a location adjoining the agora.[14]

Once again the apostle found himself on the spot; but this time instead of being harried by his countrymen (there is no

---

[13] W. G. Morrice, "Where Did Paul Speak in Athens—on Mars' Hill or Before the Court of the Areopagus?" in *ExpT* 83 (1971–72): 378.

[14] Jack Finegan, "Areopagus," in *IDB,* 1:217.

intimation of any involvement by the local synagogue), he was being pressed by intellectual dilettantes. But there was at least the appearance of courtesy, as they expressed the desire that he make clear "this new teaching." This probably had special reference to Jesus and the resurrection (v. 18) Actually in his address, most of what the apostle said was not new but could have been learned in the synagogue at Athens.

The Court of Areopagus was a council that had oversight of the educational, moral, and religious welfare of the community. Bertil Gärtner is of the opinion that Paul did not meet with the entire Areopagus but only with its education commission.[15] But that this should be considered a trial is doubtful. Luke's account seems to favor the idea that a hearing of an exploratory nature was held, since no accusers were called and no verdict pronounced at the close of the session. Paul was free to go his way (v. 33).

Significant is the repetition of the word "know" in successive verses (19–20). Hereby a mild tension is established with the term "unknown," used two times in verse 23. The supposed leaders in the realm of knowledge were sadly in need of being informed. In Athens, as Luke tells us parenthetically (v. 21), the solid quest for truth that was the glory of the ancient philosophers had largely given way to a passion for novelty, at least on the part of the population as a whole. Paul must have entered on his assignment realizing the difficulty of handling spiritual and eternal things in such a situation, yet determining to give his best to the effort.[16]

A crucial moment in world history had come, as a Jew faced a cultivated Greek audience and discoursed on that which could bring them together. Basic to true religion is a right understanding of God, an issue that Greek philosophy had wrestled with but had failed to resolve, because it lacked specific, divine revelation. Paul's line of thought moved majestically from God to man and then to the God-man who must become the focal point of faith if a right relationship to God is to be achieved.

17:22–23. Here we have the setting for the speech proper. Paul began by noting that the Athenians were "very religious."

---

[15] Bertil Gärtner, *The Areopagus Speech and Natural Revelation,* 58–59.

[16] For a brief account of current approaches to Paul's speech, see the Introduction under "Theology."

This much-debated term could be either a criticism (cf. "unknown" in v. 23), in which case "very superstitious" would be the preferred rendering, or it could be a compliment. The latter is more probable if Paul wished to create a friendly atmosphere for his remarks. But it is not to be construed as flattery, for this was forbidden at hearings conducted by this body,[17] and it was alien to Paul's character. Presumably the apostle was aware of the ambiguity of his language, which allowed his hearers to make their own decision on the meaning. They would then be aware from the start that they were listening to a man skillful in the handling of words and ideas.

Passing to the basis for his statement, Paul mentioned his encounter with an altar in the city that bore the inscription, "TO AN UNKNOWN GOD." Several ancient authors mention altars to unknown gods at Athens, but so far none has been noted as dedicated to a single deity. Such altars were erected "either because an unknown god was considered the author of tribulations or good fortune, or because men feared to pass over some deity, and therefore prayed and made sacrifices to an unknown god."[18] Paul was eager to grasp the opportunity to write on that anonymous altar the name of the God he knew. This was the burden of his message.

17:24–26. God was set forth as the Creator of all things. The Christian has no difficulty in viewing the world as the handiwork of God, for he has learned to do this from the Old Testament (Ps. 19; Isa. 40); but with the Greeks that was not the case. They regarded the physical universe as eternal, so that even if a Demiurge had shaped the things that are seen, he had done so out of preexistent materials. So the teaching about God as Creator was directly opposed to Greek ideas.[19]

The Hebrew way of designating the world was usually "heaven and earth" (Gen. 1:1). Enthroned above His creation as Lord, God does not make His abode in humanly constructed temples (cf. 1 Kings 8:27). As Creator of all, God is self-sufficient. He does not need the ministrations of human hands (cf. Rom. 11:35). He is able to care for the world He has brought into being, continuing to impart Himself by giving to

---

[17] F. Field, *Notes on the Translation of the New Testament*, 127.

[18] Gärtner, *Areopagus Speech*, 245.

[19] H. P. Owen, "The Scope of Natural Revelation in Romans 1 and Acts 17," in *NTS* 5 (1958–59): 138.

all "life and breath and everything else." This cancels out any thought of an absentee God.

He relates Himself not merely to individuals but to nations. "From one man" came in due course "every nation of men." This struck a blow at the Athenian pride of native origin. With increase of numbers came the need of regulation. God provided for this. The nations have their set "times" (not the same as the "seasons" of 14:17) for emergence and development (cf. Dan. 2:36–45). Likewise the "exact places where they should live," the areas they are to occupy, have been determined by a wise Providence.

17:27–28. All that had been said was now focused on the purpose it is intended to serve, namely, that people may seek God. Those who lack special revelation (Scripture) may have to grope for Him (suggesting that the light of nature is but semidarkness compared to the revelatory power of the Word of God). Yet the divine intent is not to tantalize those who seek, but to enable them to "find" God.

Paul did not discuss here the reason for human failure in this matter. This is developed in Romans 1:18–21. Because of sin people suppress the truth that, if followed out, would furnish just the preparation that is needed for reception of the gospel message.

Human failure to find God cannot, as an explanation or excuse, argue for the unavailability of God, for He is "not far from each one of us." To explain and buttress this observation, Paul made another, his famous declaration, "For in Him we live and move and have our being." (Compare the triadic structure with the closing statement of verse 25.) Any attempt to find here a concession to Stoic doctrine is misguided, for while that system held that the divine was immanent in the human, since the human was a part of the cosmos, it did not affirm that man resided in the deity.

It is clear that Paul was speaking here of man's life as a creature, so one cannot cite as a parallel construction the Pauline teaching about the believer being in Christ. Gärtner is probably right in holding that the meaning to be conveyed by the entire expression is "man's absolute dependence on God for his existence."[20] Agreeable to this is the quotation, derived from

---

[20] Gärtner, *Areopagus Speech*, 188.

Aratus's *Phainomena*, "We are his offspring." Man derives his life from God. The word "offspring" refers to creation and is no basis for the notion that all men are children of God in a spiritual sense. Such an interpretation would make the cross of Christ unnecessary and would contradict the biblical teaching that faith in Christ is needed before one can enter the family of God (John 1:12; Gal. 3:26).

17:29. If the connection between man and God is the life derived from the Almighty, then it is folly to represent the divine by an image that originates in the thought of the creature and is bodied forth by his skill in shaping an object of "gold or silver or stone." It is an offense against the dignity of man as well as a travesty of the Deity.

Twice in the address Paul used the neuter gender in speaking of Deity—here ("divine being") and in verse 23 ("what you worship"). This is understandable as an effort to find common ground with his audience, and it does not represent a lowering of his own view of God.

The apostle is probably not to be understood as charging his hearers with blatant idolatry, for these sophisticated people would doubtless have asserted that the idol had significance for them merely as a tangible aid in thinking of and worshiping the deity (cf. the Israelites' statement about the golden calf, Exod. 32:4). But the commandment against making any representation of God is well founded, for such a practice only clouds the unique and spiritual nature of God. If men are God's offspring, they should come to Him directly rather than by means of material objects.

17:30–31. Then the preacher moved to his conclusion by drawing a contrast between God's treatment of people in general during past ages and what He now requires of them. He "overlooked" the ignorance, not in the sense of condoning it or the conduct that resulted from it, but in the sense that He did not upbraid the nations as He had the covenant nation, Israel, when idolatry marred her relationship with Him. The thought is strictly parallel to Paul's statement in 14:16 (cf. Rom. 3:25).

Because of the demand that God now makes, that His creatures repent, it is clear that the ignorance referred to must be regarded as culpable. People have been guilty of wrong, and they are responsible for it. However, this aspect is not pressed in the passage before us as it is in Romans 1:18–23, where essentially the same theme is under discussion. The linking of divine forbearance with the need for repentance is clearly stated in Romans 2:4.

In the passage we are considering, the translation "commands" is preferable to other readings, in view of the association with repentance. God does not merely announce repentance, He demands it. The scope of the demand is universal, reaching to "all people everywhere."

The explanation for the "now" in verse 30 follows immediately. A new age had come. Paul touched first on its conclusion, which will be marked by judgment, the time for giving account, when repentance in this life will be richly rewarded, and failure to have repented will prove catastrophic.

But is this time of reckoning merely an empty threat to persuade people to straighten up their lives? By no means, for God has given "proof" (or pledge) of His firm intentions by raising the "man" of His choice from the dead. This use of *Man* is comparable to *Son of Man* (cf. John 5:27). Those who have repented—and this is repentance in faith unto life—can face that judgment unafraid; for the risen Lord, the One through whom God will judge the world in righteousness, will be their Deliverer from that coming wrath (1 Thess. 1:10). The resurrection of Jesus Christ, which points to His future function as Judge, also points backward to confirm the efficacy of His death on the cross for the sins of humanity. One should compare the import of "justice" here with "righteousness" in John 16:8 (the Greek word for both is *dikaiosynē*). The resurrection vindicated the claims of Jesus, including His fitness to be Judge as well as Savior.

Paul could have furnished evidence of Christ's resurrection (cf. 1 Cor. 15), but his audience was in no mood to hear him out. His allusion to resurrection was too much for their prejudiced minds to receive (cf. Acts 22:21–22).

The speech is concluded. What shall we say about it? Some have questioned whether Paul could have uttered these words. Granted that much of what he says here does not appear elsewhere as credited to him, yet the address bears marked affinity to his words spoken at Lystra (chap. 14). The Areopagus address is of course longer and more philosophical in tone, but the latter feature is readily explained by the intellectual cast of his audience, whereas the Lystra message was for simpleminded folk. Those who have to defend and expound the Christian faith in a highly sophisticated atmosphere can take courage and guidance from the notable achievement of the apostle on this historic occasion.

17:32–34. The courtesy that had given Paul a hearing up to this point was wearing thin. Interruption came with the mention of resurrection, an idea repudiated by all schools of Greek thought. Two reactions are recorded. Some began to sneer, unable to hide their disdain. Others, desiring to maintain at least the appearance of courtesy, talked about giving the apostle further opportunity to speak at another time. But he discerned their real sentiments; they were brushing him off. Had he felt that there was a genuine desire to hear more, he would doubtless have stayed longer in the city.

The session was over, so Paul left the gathering and went his way. But he was no longer a solitary figure, the one over against the many, for there were some who believed. They were at least four in number, probably more. Two are identified, one of them being an Areopagite, that is, a member of the council of the Areopagus. The other was a woman named Damaris. Her presence indicates that others besides council members had been present (cf. comment on 7:57). One may note a contrast with Luke's description of women in Pisidian Antioch, Thessalonica, and Berea, where their noble birth is emphasized. This woman is not given any such distinction.

No mention is made of the formation of a church in Athens, nor is there any record of a later visit by Paul to shepherd this small flock. Yet there was a church, and it is noted by patristic writers of a later time, especially by Origen.[21]

Two questions call for brief consideration. Did Paul really preach the gospel at Athens? Those who question that he did can point to the fact that no mention was made of the death of Christ, an integral part of the *kerygma* (1 Cor. 15:3). Yet the very fact that Luke went on record as saying that some believed surely presupposes the presentation of the death of our Lord. Possibly Paul had been on the verge of developing this aspect of the truth when he was interrupted, and did so privately to those who gathered around him at the conclusion of the hearing. The apostle had most certainly proclaimed the death of the Savior in his synagogue appearances in the city prior to this day.

The other question is closely related to the first. Was Paul

---

[21] Adolph Harnack, *The Expansion of Christianity in the First Three Centuries,* 1:333–34.

conscious of failure at Athens, and did he attribute that failure to the philosophical orientation of the address as opposed to his usual straightforward presentation? Some have appealed to 1 Corinthians 2:2 in support of this viewpoint, as well as to his general mood of weakness and discouragement as he went on to Corinth. But the conclusion is dubious. In 1 Corinthians 2:2 there is no emphasis on the words "with you," which one would expect if the apostle were contrasting the presentation in Corinth with that in Athens. Any time four or more people respond to a message delivered to the intelligentsia, the speaker need not feel that he has failed.

What Paul learned above all at Athens is that "the world through its wisdom did not know" God (1 Cor. 1:21). The great center of learning had demonstrated its ignorance of Him. What did Corinth hold in store?

CORINTH (18:1–17)

This city, some fifty miles almost due west of Athens, presented a challenge entirely different from the one Paul had just encountered. It was noted for its commerce rather than its culture. The church that resulted from the apostle's fairly long residence reflected the fact that the character of the city had been a factor in shaping the pre-Christian lives of its members (1 Cor. 1:26; 6:9–11). This congregation gave Paul more anxiety than any other. It seems that he visited it three times (2 Cor. 13:1) and wrote to it no fewer than four times, with the two letters found in the New Testament and two others (1 Cor. 5:9; 2 Cor. 2:3, 9).

It is possible to discern several stages in the work of the apostle at Corinth: (1) a period when he spoke in the synagogue on the Sabbath and labored at his trade during the week (vv. 3–4); (2) a full-time synagogue ministry dating from the arrival of Silas and Timothy (v. 5); (3) increasing opposition, resulting in a separation from the synagogue and a greatly enlarged work among the Gentiles (vv. 7–8); (4) the attempt of the Jews to have him condemned by Gallio (vv. 12–17); and (5) a further ministry, about which no specific information is given (v. 18).

Verses 1–4. Luke gives prominence to Aquila and Priscilla in connection with Paul's settling in Corinth—not only because they were of great help to him there, but because they continued to aid him (18:18–19, 26; Rom. 16:3; 1 Cor. 16:19).

18:1. Once again Luke has nothing to say about the circumstances of the next journey, but simply records the change of location from Athens to Corinth. The very fact that Paul made the move in this direction shows that he was not hindered by doubts that this was a proper mission field for him. True, his original summons to Europe was to Macedonia (16:9); but there was evidently no sense of divine hindrance in moving on to Achaia such as he had experienced before going to Troas (16:6–7). If there was a shadow of a doubt, this was removed by the vision from the Lord at Corinth (18:9).

The location of the city was strategic, right on the narrow Isthmus of Corinth, which connected northern Greece with the Peloponnesus. To the west, less than two miles away, was the seaport Lechaeum, on the Gulf of Corinth, which opened out onto the Ionian Sea, permitting ready shipping to Italy. To the southeast of the city, several miles away, was the port of Cenchrea, on the Saronic Gulf, which handled trade on the Aegean Sea and Asia Minor coast as well as with points farther east. Goods were transshipped across the isthmus to avoid risking the storms that frequently battered the southern tip of the peninsula.

Provoked by the recalcitrance of the leaders of the city, the Romans destroyed Corinth in 146 B.C. For a century it was allowed to lie in ruins, until Julius Caesar rebuilt it.

> The primary motive of the colonial movement was in fact to provide land for certain classes of Roman citizens, and any services which the settlements might perform in the districts where they were planted were a secondary consideration. Caesar was chiefly interested in the urban proletariat of Rome, and his eastern colonies were probably peopled from this class—Corinth, about which alone we have definite information, certainly was so.[22]

Under Nero an attempt was made to construct a canal across the isthmus, but it was abandoned, and the task remained uncompleted until late in the nineteenth century. The growth of the new Corinth was rapid. Although it was a Roman colony, its population was much larger and far more diversified than that of Philippi. But along with prosperity and luxury came an

[22] A. H. M. Jones, *The Greek City*, 62–63.

abandonment to licentious living that was notorious throughout the entire Mediterranean area. Politically it was the capital of Achaia. Religiously it was a center for the worship of Aphrodite, the goddess of love, a worship that encouraged immorality in the service of religion.

The combination of only limited success at Athens, loneliness, and the prospect of facing this city, with its commerce and vice, accounts for the weakness and fear that gripped the apostle as he arrived to begin his work (1 Cor. 2:3).

18:2–3. The initial problem facing him was to find living quarters and remunerative work. He was in financial need when he came to Corinth (2 Cor. 11:9). Happily, his contact with Aquila and Priscilla met both requirements, for he was able to live with them and work alongside them at their common trade. They were "tentmakers," a word that was taken by some patristic writers to mean leatherworkers. Possibly the tents they made were sometimes of leather and sometimes of cloth made of goats' hair, for which Paul's own province of Cilicia was noted.

Aquila (meaning "eagle") is called a Jew; the status of his wife Priscilla (the diminutive form of *Prisca*, "old or venerable woman") is not indicated. Opinions differ as to whether these people were already believers when Paul met them. That Aquila is called a Jew no more excludes him from being a Christian than does the same designation in the case of Apollos (vv. 24–25). It is doubtful that Paul would have taken up residence with them if they had not been believers.

If this conclusion be accepted, it follows that there were believing Jews in Rome by the middle of the first century, for Luke tells us here that this couple had been obliged to leave Rome because of the edict of Claudius banishing Jews from the city. From Suetonius we learn that the occasion for this order was a tumult among the Jews instigated by a certain Chrestus.[23] A probable conclusion, though not accepted by all, is that the Jews had become restless and agitated at the preaching of those who proclaimed Jesus as the promised Messiah (*Christus* and *Chrestus* were readily confused). The edict does not seem to have been totally or permanently effective, for the Jews were too numerous and too essential to the life of the capital to be

---

[23] Suetonius, *Claudius* 25.4.

banished for long. Certainly during Nero's reign they were back in force. Paul found many of them when he came as a prisoner to the imperial city (chap. 28).

18:4. Having sketched Paul's activity during the week, Luke now summarizes his work on the Sabbath, a ministry in the synagogue to both Jews and Greeks (for this combination see 14:1; 19:10; 20:21; cf. Rom. 1:16). He was "trying to persuade" them, a statement that suggests resistance but does not rule out some success. Doubtless Stephanas and his household became believers at this time (1 Cor. 1:16; 16:15).

The Western text at this point provides an interesting sidelight on the apostle's method of presentation in his synagogue preaching by adding the note that he inserted the name of the Lord Jesus. In other words, in dealing with the prophetic passages of the Old Testament that were messianic in character, he identified the Lord Jesus as the One who fulfilled them.

Verses 5–11. The acceleration of the mission, aided by the arrival of his helpers from the north and his ability to devote full time to the work, is pictured as resulting in an increase in converts and in intensified opposition.

18:5–6. The arrival of Silas and Timothy seems to be associated with a new impetus to the testimony of the apostle. Apparently these brethren had been sent back to Macedonia by Paul when he was at Athens. Now they rejoined him and became active in preaching (2 Cor. 1:19).

The remainder of the verse is not wholly clear. One possibility is that these fellow workers found the apostle engrossed in the proclamation of the gospel. But this is strange, for the preceding account indicates that up to this time he had had only a limited ministry, confined to the Sabbath. Since the imperfect tense of the verb can serve to emphasize the inception of an action, the wording of the NASB is quite feasible: "Paul began devoting himself completely to the word."

The good news about the steadfastness of the Thessalonian believers acted like a tonic, providing relief for Paul's anxiety. Perhaps an even more important factor in enabling him to give himself wholly to evangelism was the financial assistance sent by the Macedonian churches (2 Cor. 11:9).

The thrust of Paul's message to the Jews was, "Jesus is the Christ." A reversal of order is possible—the Christ is Jesus. In the former wording the starting point is proclamation about Jesus leading to His identification with the Messiah of prophecy. In the latter, the starting point is the Jewish expectation based on the Old Testament, concluding with a demonstration from evidence about the historical Jesus that the two are identical. This is the more natural procedure in gaining a hearing from a Jewish audience.

Resistance to the message was so strong that Paul felt it necessary to terminate his appeal to the Jews. His shaking out his garments is probably to be associated with his parting word to his countrymen: "Your blood be on your own heads, I am clear of my responsibility." Paul's charge to reach his own people in Corinth with the gospel had been fulfilled. Those who had resisted had to bear the guilt of closing the door of faith for those who might otherwise have come to know the Savior. "From now on" should not be read as committing the apostle to a lifetime of shunning the Jews. His turning to the Gentiles pertained only to the Corinthian situation. There is abundant evidence that he continued to observe the rule "first for the Jew" (Rom. 1:16).

18:7-8. Paul's verbal outburst was followed by his abandonment of the synagogue. The Western text's interpretation of "from there" as a reference to his leaving Aquila's home is a misunderstanding of the situation. True, Paul went to a "house"; however, the house was not a place of residence, but a place for meeting with those interested in hearing the word of the Lord. The house belonged to Titius Justus, who, judging from his name, was a Roman. He had been a God-fearer for some time. Now, under Paul's preaching, he had become a believer.[24]

Some scholars have advanced the suggestion, probably sound, that the full name of this man was Gaius Titius Justus,[25] since Paul referred to a certain Gaius as host to the whole church at Corinth (Rom. 16:23), which fits the data in the passage before us. The incompleteness of the name in verse 7 is not fatal to this identification, since in no case does the New Testament list all three names when referring to a Roman.

The new location adjacent to the synagogue was convenient, so that people who had an interest in hearing Paul further

---

[24] Some manuscripts read "Titus" instead of "Titius," but the chance that this is the Titus referred to in Paul's letters is remote.

[25] On the subject of Roman names, see H. J. Cadbury, *The Book of Acts in History,* 69–71.

had only a slight adjustment to make. Even some Jews, it seems, risked the disfavor of their fellows by identifying with Paul. One, Crispus by name, the leader of the synagogue, is singled out as a convert. Did this synagogue have only one ruler, in contrast to the situation at Pisidian Antioch (13:15), or is the definite article to be explained as indicating the prominence of this man? The latter view is perhaps preferable. This notable conversion, along with that of Gaius, led Paul to break his own rule against baptizing his converts personally (1 Cor. 1:14). The coming of these influential men to the Lord seems to have led "many of the Corinthians" to a similar decision.

18:9–11. The reason for the vision of the Lord granted to Paul is explained by the recent turn of events. Fed by resentment about the move next door, the defection of Crispus, and the increase in conversions among the people (many of whom had been adherents of the synagogue), Jewish antagonism seemed ready to break the bonds of restraint. Paul's apprehension is understandable. We know that he hoped to be able to return to Thessalonica to minister to his converts there (1 Thess. 2:17–18) and could therefore have readily interpreted increased opposition at Corinth as a signal that he should leave the work. But the vision brought not only assurance that he would be unharmed but also a command to continue his labor in the city. There were still "many people" to be won to the faith. The Lord already claimed them as His own (cf. John 10:16).

As a result of the vision, Paul settled down to a rather extended ministry lasting for a year and a half, second only in duration to his stay at Ephesus. He was obedient to this vision as he had been to the first (Acts 26:19).

Verses 12–17. In this transitional section Luke describes the incident that brought Paul's ministry at Corinth to a close, or nearly so. The reader is prepared for the next stage of activity, which involved a return to the mainland of Asia.

18:12–13. The Jews, vexed by the inroads that Paul's mission had made in their former sphere of operation, determined a united action against him, choosing to appear before Gallio, who had recently become proconsul of Achaia. He was a brother of Seneca the philosopher, who praised him for his many fine traits of character. Possibly the Jews were expecting him to be a "soft touch." His handling of the case now submitted to him reveals his penetration of insight and his practical wisdom.

Archaeologists have uncovered what is almost certainly the judgment-seat to which Paul was brought. Finegan writes, "Built of white and blue marble, the bema must have presented an impressive appearance, and it served very well for the function of a public-speaking platform with the possibility of a large crowd assembled in front of it."[26]

The Jews' complaint was phrased somewhat vaguely: "This man is persuading the people to worship God in ways contrary to the law." It is not clear whether Jewish or Roman law was meant. Perhaps the statement was designedly ambiguous. Roman law forbade the proselytizing of Roman citizens, and there were some people with Roman names, as noted above, who had become believers under Paul's ministry at Corinth; but there is no certainty that they were Roman citizens. Judaism was a permitted religion, sanctioned since the days of Julius Caesar, and so far the Romans had not differentiated Christianity from Judaism. This is understandable in view of the fact that the church began at Jerusalem and its missionary activity had thus far been carried on almost entirely by Christian Jews who worked through the synagogues wherever possible. It may be that the Jews of Corinth were hinting to Gallio that it was high time Rome distinguished between Christians and Jews and bore down on the former as operating outside Roman law.

18:14–15. At any rate, Gallio detected that he was dealing with a prejudiced group that had no case. He indicated that he was prepared to deal with a situation involving a "misdemeanor" or "crime" but refused to concern himself with Jewish religious matters, jargon, or peculiar practices. "Your own law" may have been used in deliberate contrast to the general force of *law* in verse 13. This whole sphere lay outside Gallio's proper jurisdiction.

Paul stood exonerated. Surely this deliverance must have brought to his mind the Lord's promise that no man would be able to harm him (v. 10). More important than his personal safety was the vindication of the Christian cause in the eyes of Roman authorities. The decision of Gallio was bound to be normative in similar situations elsewhere.

18:16–17. The Jews were further humiliated when they

---

[26] Finegan, "Areopagus," in *IDB*, 1:684a.

were ordered away from the judgment seat. Nor was this the end of the matter. The onlookers, for the most part Greeks, sensing Gallio's disdain for the Jewish action, saw a chance to vent their displeasure on the complainants by manhandling their spokesman, a man named Sosthenes, who had succeeded Crispus as a leader in the synagogue. It is tempting to see in this man the same individual mentioned by Paul in writing to the Corinthian church (1 Cor. 1:1). Although this cannot be demonstrated, it is possible that Sosthenes was led to consider the gospel more seriously as time went on and ultimately followed the course taken by Crispus. If so, the cause of Christ in Corinth must have received a fresh impetus.

"Gallio showed no concern whatever." Many a sermon has depicted him as indifferent to religion, but this is not the meaning. Rather, he refused to be involved in a case over which he had no rightful jurisdiction. Another rendering of the statement is possible—"but Gallio paid no attention to this" (RSV)—in which case the reference is confined to the incident of the beating: Gallio did not interfere.

14

MISSION OF PAUL IN EPHESUS
18:18–19:41

PRELIMINARY VISIT (18:18–23)

The apostle had not lost sight of his objective to evangelize the Roman province of Asia. Providentially prevented from entering the area formerly (16:6), he sensed that now the time was ripe for shifting to this field of labor. But he had been away for a considerable time from Jerusalem and Antioch, the two churches that were his major contacts with the Jewish and Gentile wings of the Christian movement; so he felt it was time to return to these places. Therefore the initial visit to Ephesus was brief, but it laid the foundation for a lengthy and fruitful ministry that touched the entire province.

18:18. Because of his vindication before Gallio, Paul's position in Corinth was secure, and he took advantage of it by remaining "for some time"; but his eager spirit was leading him to consider his responsibility to other areas (cf. 2 Cor. 10:16). He had already tarried longer here than in any other spot since the inception of his missionary travels.

Luke's account raises some problems. One is the mention of Syria as the destination of the trip now being undertaken by Paul, and this seems to suggest Antioch as the place of intended debarkation, whereas it turned out that he landed at Caesarea, which is in Palestine (v. 22). It is possible that in the course of the journey Paul determined that he ought to visit Jerusalem before going to Antioch. Or he may have changed ships at Ephesus, finding one that would take him to Palestine.

The other problem pertains to the vow Paul had made. He was not a lifelong Nazirite, as were Samson and John the

Baptist, but he was free to assume a vow for a limited period. Why the vow was taken we do not know. It may have concerned in some way his work at Corinth. Later he made another vow at Jerusalem (21:23, 26).

The shaving of the head normally came at the termination of the period of the vow (21:24), but here it seems to have taken place at the beginning. A passage in Josephus throws light on this. Describing the rites of purification undertaken by Queen Bernice, rites that occurred about a decade later than the present incident, the historian says, "She was visiting Jerusalem to discharge a vow to God; for it is customary for those suffering from illness or other affliction to make a vow to abstain from wine and to shave their heads during the thirty days preceding that on which they must offer sacrifices."[1]

Cenchrea is of interest because a church was established there, perhaps during the time of Paul's labors at Corinth (Rom. 16:1). Several such churches developed in the area and were noted by Paul a short time later (2 Cor. 1:1).

Only Priscilla and Aquila are mentioned as Paul's traveling companions. Behind their move to Ephesus at this time was the purpose of assisting the apostle there as they had done at Corinth. Presumably Silas and Timothy remained behind to superintend the work Paul was leaving (2 Cor. 1:19 may apply here as well as to the period following their arrival from Macedonia).

18:19–21. The ship may have carried Jewish pilgrims bound for the Passover celebration at Jerusalem. As a glance at the map will show, Ephesus was not out of the way for a ship headed for Syria or Palestine.

After seeing his associates established at Ephesus, the apostle paid a visit to the synagogue and took part in the service, meeting with an unusually cordial response. Unable to stay over, Paul did the next best thing, promising to return for further ministry if God permitted. At this point the Western text injects a comment attributed to Paul to the effect that he must observe the coming festival at Jerusalem. This sufficiently explains his inability to stay longer (cf. 20:16).

18:22–23. These verses are a prime example of Luke's compressed style of narrative, either because of a lack of

---

[1]Josephus, *Jewish War* II.15.1.

detailed information or as a deliberate intent to save space for the ministry proper. Such a passage shows that Luke was not intent on glorifying Paul by recording or inventing data for effect.

At first reading it might appear that Paul greeted the church at Caesarea, but this is ruled out by two considerations. "Went up" is technical terminology for a trip to Jerusalem, which was on high ground (Luke 2:42; Acts 21:15). Also "went down to Antioch" is strange language if Paul went from Caesarea to Antioch, since both are practically at sea level, whereas the terminology is fitting for one making a journey from Jerusalem to Antioch.

The visit to Jerusalem served in a general way to maintain the ties Paul had with the leaders of the church. It may also have helped to crystallize his purpose to aid the Jewish Christian community there through donations from the Gentile churches, a plan that was consummated by a subsequent journey (24:17).

Luke says nothing about the purpose of the visit to Antioch and makes only a general statement as to the time spent there. But there must have been opportunity for reporting on the mission in Greece as well as for a renewal of fellowship with a highly motivated missionary church. As it turned out, this was Paul's final visit to this place, at least so far as the record goes.

His departure is commonly represented as the beginning of the third missionary journey, but this is somewhat artificial in view of the lack of resemblance between this event and the commencement of the earlier journeys.[2] To begin with, the trip involved a revisiting of the churches in southern Galatia (cf. 15:36), but the very brevity of the account, in contrast to the fullness of the description in the following chapter, makes it clear that a return to Ephesus was the main objective.

EMERGENCE OF APOLLOS (18:24–28)

Before narrating the Ephesian ministry, Luke inserts information about what happened there during Paul's absence. His source for this account may well have been the apostle himself, who must have learned from Priscilla and Aquila about the visit of Apollos to Ephesus. In the composition of his work,

[2]D. T. Rowlingson, "The Geographical Orientation of Paul's Missionary Interests," *JBL* 69 (1950): 341–44.

Luke probably felt the desirability of including something on the ministry of Apollos as a background for the right understanding of the incident, reported at the beginning of the next chapter, involving the disciples who knew only the baptism of John.

18:24–25. The description of Apollos is unexpectedly full, indicating the importance to be attached to him and his work, and demonstrating that Luke was not so taken up with Paul as to ignore other men who made a contribution to the spread of the gospel. This Jew was a native of Alexandria, the great Egyptian metropolis, which had a large segment of Jews in its population. It is tempting to conjure up a picture of Apollos as being acquainted with Philo, the famous contemporary philosopher and prolific author of Hellenistic Judaism, and as having familiarity with Greek as well as Hebrew learning. The word "learned" indicates that Apollos was a cultured man.

"With a thorough knowledge of the Scriptures" refers to his adeptness in handling the Old Testament, of which he had been a keen student from his early days. This is a generous appraisal in view of the deficiency that Aquila and Priscilla detected (v. 26). But considering his limited opportunities, he had attained to a notable grasp of the Word. More than this, he had been "instructed in the way of the Lord." This seems to be parallel to "the way of God" (v. 26) and denotes God's way of salvation, His plan as set forth in the Scriptures. Apollos understood this from the prophetic standpoint but was not yet informed as to the richness of its fulfillment in Jesus of Nazareth.

What he did know about Jesus he was proclaiming "accurately" as he discoursed in the synagogue. Presumably what he taught about Jesus included the high points of His life and work as well as something about His teachings. It is well to note that this confirms the existence of a reliable tradition concerning Jesus and His work. If the Western text as attested by Codex Bezae is trustworthy here, Apollos received this instruction in his native place, i.e., Alexandria.

But now, after this recital of assets, comes the liability. For all his knowledge, and despite his great fervor of spirit (cf. Rom. 12:11), he was acquainted only with "the baptism of John." His gospel, then, was one of anticipation and preparation rather than of absolute fulfillment. He knew nothing of the baptism with the Holy Spirit based on the finished work of Jesus Christ.

To explain the status of Apollos is indeed difficult. How could a man be so limited in his understanding of Christianity after more than two decades had passed since the death and resurrection of Christ and the outpouring of the Spirit? Nothing is known of the earliest Christianity in Egypt. Some of John the Baptist's followers may have left Palestine for Egypt while the ministry of Jesus was still in progress, when they had no knowledge of Pentecost. This much is clear, that Apollos had not been instructed by those who still followed John in preference to Jesus. What he knew and proclaimed was the prophetic ministry of our Lord. What he lacked was information on His messiahship as demonstrated by His exaltation and the pouring out of the Spirit. John the Baptist had not proclaimed publicly that Jesus was the Messiah.

18:26. The boldness displayed in the preaching of Apollos is to be traced to his knowledge of the way of the Lord, his assurance that God's plan would be consummated for the welfare of mankind, and his own fervency of spirit. But these admirable features could not hide from two of his hearers the glaring omission in his preaching. Aquila and Priscilla ventured on the delicate and difficult task of instructing the preacher. "They invited him to their home." They indulged in no open criticism of this man, for indeed it was not what he said but what he left unsaid that troubled them. They were able to point out that John himself had predicted the baptism with the Holy Spirit through the coming One (Mark 1:8).

No statement is given about the reaction of Apollos, but the sequel supplies all that is needed. Evidently he received with humility and gratitude the help extended to him, leading to a greatly enlarged understanding and ministry.

Students of early Christianity are intrigued as they reflect on the implications of such a conference. Here were representatives of Roman Christianity meeting with a representative of Alexandrian Christianity. True to the situation here, Rome had something to teach Alexandria, though later Alexandrian Christianity made a larger contribution along doctrinal and philosophical lines than Rome could offer.

Did Apollos receive Christian baptism? Nothing is said about it (in contrast to the men described in 19:5). Perhaps it was judged unnecessary in view of the fact that the disciples of Jesus, having received John's baptism, were not rebaptized as believers in Jesus. G. W. H. Lampe ventures this opinion:

"Possibly a direct commission from the Lord was deemed to have conferred upon him the Spirit, for he ranked very high among the apostles, being regarded by the Corinthians as standing approximately upon the same level as St. Peter or St. Paul."[3]

18:27–28. In the course of their conversations Aquila and Priscilla must have mentioned the work of Paul at Corinth. When Apollos expressed a desire to visit the church there, the believers at Ephesus smoothed the way for him by writing to the church at Corinth, urging them to receive the brother. The identity of the "brothers" who performed this service is not stated. Possibly Aquila and Priscilla had won certain persons to the faith prior to the arrival of Apollos.,

Luke is content to summarize the ministry of this man in Achaia by noting that he was a great help to the saints in that area. For more complete information we need to consult 1 Corinthians 1–4. Not only did he help the saints by his teaching, but he brought pagans into the fold (1 Cor. 3:5). Luke emphasizes his ministry to the Jews, in which he confronted them with the teaching of their Scriptures that led irresistibly to the conclusion that Jesus is the Christ (or, the Christ is Jesus). No mention is made of a ministry in the synagogue, which had been closed to Christian testimony (Acts 18:6).

Through Aquila and Priscilla, Paul made a distinct contribution to the growth and usefulness of Apollos that greatly affected the Corinthian congregation. Understandably the Alexandrian, trained in rhetoric and captivating in speech, appealed to many of the Corinthians, some of whom developed such an adulation for him that they tended to depreciate Paul (1 Cor. 1:12; 4:6). Yet Apollos cannot be held responsible for this factionalism and seems to have refused to return to Corinth lest he strengthen this tendency (1 Cor. 16:12).

A good case can be made for the position that he is the one who wrote the Epistle to the Hebrews, while Pauline elements in that book can be readily accounted for by the contact that he had with Paul both directly and indirectly (through Aquila and Priscilla as well as through the apostle's converts in Corinth).

[3]G. W. H. Lampe, *The Seal of the Spirit,* 66.

TRIUMPHS OF THE GOSPEL (19:1–20)

The setting for Paul's next campaign was the city of Ephesus, which he had long desired to evangelize, because he recognized its strategic position for reaching all the province of Asia with the gospel (19:10).

Several distinctives characterize the time spent in this city:

1. It was more prolonged than any other, extending to approximately three years (vv. 8, 10, 22; cf. 20:31).
2. It included a ministry to certain men who were imperfect in their knowledge of the faith and therefore in their personal experience (vv. 1–7).
3. Much of the time Paul's public ministry was conducted in the hall of Tyrannus rather than in the synagogue (v. 9).
4. Some unusual miracles were done by Paul, confirming the truth of the message he preached (vv. 11–12).
5. The power of occultism, which lingered even among some who had become believers, was broken (v. 19).
6. In the midst of success, Paul envisioned an enlarged ministry that would take him to the West (v. 21).
7. The mission in Ephesus was broken off, as far as Paul was concerned, by a mammoth riot staged on behalf of the goddess Artemis and her worship (vv. 23–41).
8. Additional information supplied by Paul himself pictures vividly his pastoral care of the converts (20:20, 31) and the extreme danger to which he was exposed in connection with his labors in the city (1 Cor. 15:32; 2 Cor. 1:8–10).

Verses 1–7. This paragraph deals with Paul's arrival at Ephesus and his encounter with a group of men who had an incomplete faith.

Luke has nothing to say about the city as such, but considerable information is available from ancient historians and geographers and augmented by the work of modern archaeologists. Today its great port is silted in and the site is virtually uninhabited, but in Paul's time the place was approaching the zenith of its glory. It was the leading city of the province of Asia, enriched by the extensive commerce from both east and west. The population of the city approached a third of a million. In view of all this, it is not at all surprising that of the seven churches of Asia addressed in Revelation 2 and 3, the church at Ephesus should be mentioned first. Writing to the Ephesian church a few years after Revelation was written, Ignatius of Antioch called it "famous to eternity."

The two edifices mentioned in Acts 19, the temple of Artemis and the theater, have been unearthed. The temple was found some twenty feet below the surface of the ground. It was one of the seven wonders of the ancient world and certainly one of the largest buildings of antiquity, while the theater was discovered to have been large enough to seat around twenty-five thousand people.

The opening section of this chapter is clearly intended to be viewed in connection with the close of chapter 18, not only because Apollos is mentioned in both portions but because there is a reference to the baptism of John in both. Still, the connection should not be pressed to the point of insisting that the men Paul dealt with were converts of Apollos before he had been enlightened by Aquila and Priscilla. If Apollos knew these men, it is unthinkable that he would have gone off to Corinth without sharing with them his new understanding of the faith. We do well to assume that this group was independent of Apollos and probably detached from the brethren mentioned in 18:27.

19:1. In describing Paul's arrival at Ephesus, Luke is content to picture him as having traveled "through the interior." This must be the territory lying between Pisidian Antioch and Ephesus (cf. 18:23). It could suggest traversing the Lycus valley or a route somewhat to the north, on a more direct line between Antioch and Ephesus.[4] There is no solid basis for assuming, as Deissmann did, that the apostle visited the towns in northern Galatia on this occasion.

Rather strangely, Luke has nothing to say here about Paul's reunion with Aquila and Priscilla or his fellowship with the brethren mentioned in 18:27. Instead, he abruptly introduces an encounter between the apostle and a group of disciples. In what sense they warranted the term *disciples* is much debated. One needs the remainder of the narrative to make the picture at all clear.[5]

19:2–7. Something about these disciples moved Paul to

[4] See George E. Wright and Floyd V. Filson, eds., *The Westminster Historical Atlas to the Bible,* rev. ed. (Philadelphia: Westminster, 1956), 91.

[5] For a statement of the difficulties in the passage, see Ernst Käsemann, *Essays on New Testament Themes* (Naperville, Ill.: Allenson, 1964), 136–39.

inquire about their spiritual history. They may have appeared to lack the fruit of the Spirit, such as joy and peace, or they may have failed to manifest the gifts of the Spirit, or both. Such a lack would have aroused his suspicions—hence the question, "Did you receive the Holy Spirit when you believed?" The question serves as a reminder that faith in the Lord Jesus and the reception of the Holy Spirit go hand in hand; the one leads to the other. Paul was probing to find out if they really believed, in the evangelical sense.

Quite astonishing is the answer, "No, we have not even heard that there is a Holy Spirit." The problem here is to understand how anyone connected either with John the Baptist or with Jesus in the days of His flesh could be entirely ignorant of the Holy Spirit. If these men were Jews, which is probable, they should have known of the Spirit from the Old Testament. Perhaps the language is intended to be construed somewhat as in John 7:39, "Up to that time the Spirit had not been given."

These men must have understood that John's baptism signified repentance when they submitted to be baptized with that baptism. Now Paul indicated to them that John's ministry, including his baptizing activity, had pointed to One who was coming after him, namely Jesus. From the Christian standpoint, John's baptism is incomplete because it is only preparatory.

This handful of disciples, now better informed, confessed their readiness to put faith in the Lord Jesus and accept baptism in His name. This willingness to accept baptism "in the name of the Lord Jesus" is clear evidence that they were not adherents of a Baptist sect arrayed against the Christian movement. That such competition existed is well attested. In fact there are several hints of it in the Gospel of John (1:6–9, 20; 3:30; 10:41).

Notable is the way Paul handled the deficiency about the Holy Spirit. Instead of offering instruction on this subject, he referred the needy ones to Jesus Christ. F. D. Bruner puts it well by saying:

> The remedy for those who know little or nothing of the Holy Spirit is not special instruction or knowledge on access to the Spirit, or a new set of conditions, a new regimen of emptying, added obediences, deeper commitment, or ardent prayer, but instead simply the great fact:

the gospel of faith in the Lord Jesus Christ and baptism in his name.[6]

The problem confronting the Ephesian "disciples" was not ignorance of how to experience baptism with the Spirit, as some have surmised, but failure to have put their faith in Jesus Christ for salvation and receive baptism in His name. When this was done, the Holy Spirit was granted to them. The fact that they were able to speak with tongues (presumably ecstatic utterance, as in 1 Cor. 12–14) and to prophesy (the manward aspect of their testimony) left no doubt about the presence of the Holy Spirit in their lives (cf. Acts 10:46). If the original followers of the Lord needed the outward tokens of the Spirit's coming at Pentecost to assure them of the reality of His presence and power and of the unique character of the period thus introduced, how much more did these men, with less preparation, need such tokens!

The laying-on of hands by Paul was not an indispensable condition for the reception of the Spirit (recall the case of the company in the house of Cornelius, 10:44). The situation resembled that of the believers in Samaria (8:17) and of Paul himself (9:17). Imposition of hands was apparently a regular feature of Christian baptism, and baptism marked the occasion for receiving the Spirit (2:38). This in itself was sufficient reason for the practice of the early church not to defer baptism in favor of a long period of prerequisite instruction and probation.

In regard to the development of Christianity in these early days, the overall importance of the passage should be sought in the uniting of those who were still closely attached in some sense to John the Baptist with the mainstream of the church's faith and life, thus making the formula "One Lord, one faith, one baptism" (Eph. 4:5) a reality.

It is doubtful that any special significance is to be attached to the figure "twelve" in this passage, since it is only an approximation rather than a precise number. As Meyer notes, we have here "a simple historical statement, not in order to represent the men '*as a new Israel*'"[7] (Meyer's italics).

Verses 8–10. Here Luke describes the second phase of Paul's ministry, or more accurately, the next two, since the

---

[6]Frederick Dale Bruner, *A Theology of the Holy Spirit*, 209.

[7]H. A. W. Meyer, *A Critical and Exegetical Handbook to the Acts of the Apostles*, 368.

initial period of activity in the synagogue was followed by a longer period of testimony elsewhere. A. Schlatter remarks, regarding the remaining narratives of the chapter, that they "are all intended to show the shattering effect Paul had on the whole religious life of Ephesus."[8]

19:8–9. In view of the difficulties Paul had encountered on his missionary travels in staying very long each time in the synagogue, "three months" seems an extended time indeed. It can be explained by two factors: (1) the initial cordial reception given him on his arrival from Corinth (18:19–20) and (2) the cosmopolitan character of Ephesus that promoted toleration and made it rather difficult for the Jews to display their feelings too violently. The situation was much the same as that in Syrian Antioch.

Paul's message is summarized as "the kingdom of God." While the eschatological aspect of the kingdom may have been included, the phrase "arguing persuasively" favors the interpretation that the gospel, centering in Jesus Christ as the fulfillment of Old Testament hopes, was the main thrust.

A great number of Jews remained unconvinced. With the passage of time they grew more restless and more combative under such preaching. The increasing hostility was a testimony to the impact Paul was making. Ultimately, rather than face a barrage of criticism and debate from week to week (not very fertile ground for the Spirit's work), the apostle withdrew, taking with him those who had received the Lord Jesus.

In this passage "the multitude" (NASB) refers to the congregation of the synagogue. Earlier, Luke used it of the assembled church (6:2; 15:12).

Paul's new location was "the lecture hall of Tyrannus." The Greek word is *scholē,* which denotes first of all leisure; then discussion, or lecture (a favorite way to employ leisure among the Greeks); then a group attending such lectures; and finally, the place in which such instruction was given (cf. our use of the word *church* for both congregation and building).

An illuminating addition in the Western text at this point states that Paul's daily activity in this place went on from the fifth to the tenth hour—i.e., from 11:00 A.M. to 4:00 P.M. This was siesta time for the inhabitants. It has been conjectured that

[8] A. Schlatter, *The Church in the New Testament Period,* 163.

Paul was able to rent the hall at a nominal figure because it was not used at this time of day. To draw people, the apostle had to give them something sufficiently attractive and potent to cause them to pass up their rest period.

By combining various Scripture references it is possible to piece together in a rough way a picture of Paul's schedule in those days. It seems that he worked at his trade during the early morning hours to support himself (20:34), then gave public instruction in the middle of the day at the lecture hall of Tyrannus, and during the remainder of the day visited Christians in their homes (20:20) and individually (20:31). It is possible that toward the end of the day he sometimes had to return to his trade in order to make enough to sustain himself and those dependent on him. It was a busy life, indeed.

19:10. This heavy schedule was maintained for "two years," with the result that not only the city but also the province became familiar with Paul's teaching. One would tell another, whose curiosity was piqued to attend, and so the outreach of the gospel was great. Luke's wording here—"all . . . who lived in the province of Asia"—may sound highly exaggerated, yet it is corroborated by the admission of a detractor (v. 26). There is other testimony along the same line, such as the winning to Christ of Epaphras, Philemon, and Archippus—all of them from Colosse—during this time. Through the witness of these and others, churches sprang up through Asia, not only at Colosse but also at Hierapolis and Laodicea (Col. 4:13), in addition to the other locations mentioned in Revelation 2 and 3. Paul's own testimony is to the same effect (1 Cor. 16:19). His strategy was to evangelize the hinterland through people he had brought to Christ and trained for service. This latter activity must have included instruction on how to reach both Jews and Greeks. It is clear that Paul did not go out into the province, but remained in the city.

Verses 11–20. A specific instance of divine intervention on behalf of Paul and his work came in connection with the attempt of Jewish exorcists to imitate the apostle. Their attempt is pictured against the background of some unusual manifestations of divine healing.

19:11–12. The ministry in word was accompanied by a ministry of miraculous works. Such things may have occurred in other places (Rom. 15:18–19), but Luke has noted them only occasionally (13:11; 14:3; 14:10; 16:18). No miracles are reported in Thessalonica, Berea, Athens, or Corinth (though Paul himself cited them in connection with the latter city, 2 Cor. 12:12). The miracles of Ephesus were indeed "extraordinary," recalling the healing of the woman who touched the hem of Jesus' robe (Matt. 9:20–22) and the cure provided for those on whom the shadow of Peter fell (Acts 5:15). In addition, there were exorcisms. The extraordinary miracles were so unusual as to appear incredible to some moderns. Yet Luke, a man with medical training and experience, does not discount them. In the wisdom of God they may have been deemed necessary to appeal to such a superstitious city as Ephesus (cf. 19:18–19).

19:13–16. Certain wandering Jewish exorcists, noting the power seemingly possessed by Paul, determined to capitalize on his success by using his formula for casting out demons: "the name of the Lord Jesus."

That there were Jewish exorcists in the time of our Lord is demonstrated by Matthew 12:27 (cf. Tobit 8:1–3 for an earlier period). "Magic and exorcism, and that above all for curative purposes, were commonly popular and prevalent throughout the entire Roman Empire. Nor did the Jewish people form an exception."[9] Bruce M. Metzger notes, "Of all ancient Graeco-Roman cities, Ephesus, the third largest city in the Empire, was by far the most hospitable to magicians, sorcerers, and charlatans of all sorts."[10]

In this superstitious sphere, syncretism was common. The magical papyri of Egypt reveal the use of the names of Israel's God—*Yahweh, Sabaoth,* and others—along with those of other deities. It is startling to read in the Paris Magical Papyrus the following: "I adjure thee by the god of the Hebrews Jesus." Commenting on the use of the name *Jesus* in this setting, Deissmann observes, "It was probably inserted by some pagan: no Christian, still less a Jew, would have called Jesus 'the god of the Hebrews.'"[11]

Behind the use of magic was the idea that if one possessed the proper formula he could compel the unseen powers to do his bidding. Sceva had not actually been a high priest in Israel, but he claimed to belong to a high priestly family. F. F. Bruce remarks,

[9] E. Schürer, *The Jewish People in the Time of Jesus Christ,* 2.3.152.

[10] B. M. Metzger, "St. Paul and the Magicians," *Princeton Seminary Bulletin* 38 (June 1944): 27.

[11] Adolf Deissmann, *Light from the Ancient East,* 4th ed., 260.

It was well known throughout the Near East that Jewish high priests had access to the secret name of the God of Israel and its true pronunciation, and by all magical canons the command of such a secret carried with it enormous power over the spirit-world.[12]

These exorcists looked on Paul as a competitor whom they expected to outflank by their maneuver. They were in this business for profit, whereas Paul was performing a service.

Their plans were ruined when an evil spirit refused to recognize them as having any control over him. Their use of the name Jesus was second-hand and therefore spurious. The reward for their misdeed was a severe trouncing, as the man they were dealing with, galvanized by the superhuman strength of the demon that possessed him, stripped and wounded them. This recalls the case of the Gerasene demoniac (Mark 5:2–4).

It is awkward to read that "both of them" (NASB, following Greek *amphoterōn*) were overcome, since seven individuals were involved. There is evidence that the Greek word translated "both" can mean "all" in certain cases,[13] and it should be so translated here.

19:17–20. The effect of this incident on the general populace is indicated first—"they were all seized with fear" (cf. 5:5). No longer could the name of the Lord be taken lightly. Men stood in awe of the power He had exhibited in their midst.

The effect on the Ephesian church was even greater, in that it stirred the saints to confess the hold that the occult had retained on them even after they became believers. They gathered up the "scrolls" of magic lore and put them to the torch in a great public display of housecleaning. The work of grace, despite the strong preaching of Paul, had been incomplete, for the hold of former practices had not been broken. Now they freely disclosed their "evil deeds."

It is not entirely clear whether the "number" of verse 19 were Christians also, or whether they were pagans who were shaken by what had transpired and were so gripped by fear that they joined others who were ridding themselves of the paraphernalia of magic. The latter seems probable.

The value of what was consumed was reckoned at "fifty

---

[12]F. F. Bruce, *New Testament History,* 328.

[13]James Hope Moulton and George Milligan, *The Vocabulary of the Greek Testament* (London: Hodder & Stoughton, 1930), s.v., *amphoteroi.*

thousand drachmas." Since no specific coin is mentioned in Greek, which literally has "silvers," it is impossible to estimate the amount involved. The intention is to give the impression of a very large figure.

Luke concludes his account of the episode with a summary statement about the growth of "the word of the Lord." Although the wording is the same as in verse 10, the sense is somewhat different; there the message of the gospel is in view, whereas here the Christian faith, or cause, better conveys the meaning. A cleansed and revived church was the key to continuing increase. By this time the foundation had been laid for a large and strong church on which others could build (cf. John 4:38), especially the apostle John toward the end of the century.

With the growth of the church in Ephesus, a practical problem must have arisen. Could all these believers have met together in one place? We know there was a church in the house of Aquila and Priscilla (1 Cor. 16:19), suggesting that the lecture hall of Tyrannus was not used for fellowship purposes but for evangelism and instruction. It is possible that several house churches came into being, as in the city of Rome (Rom. 16:5, 14).

PLANS FOR FUTURE WORK (19:21–22)

In this passage Luke shows that far from making the apostle complacent, the success enjoyed at Ephesus spurred him to seek new areas of ministry.

19:21–22. The ministry at Ephesus proved to be a watershed for Paul's career. He felt that from the standpoint of a pioneer missionary, sufficient groundwork had been laid for the future expansion of the gospel in the eastern Mediterranean area. The Jerusalem church had taken over responsibility for the evangelization of Palestine. He himself had worked for years in Syria and Cilicia, where the Antioch church could be counted on to do its part in the future. More recently he and his helpers had laid the foundations for the church in Asia Minor and Greece. It was time to look elsewhere.

The choice was between Egypt and the West, notably Rome. Possibly his contact with Apollos at Ephesus had something to do with the decision not to go to Egypt (1 Cor. 16:12). For all we know, Paul may have been aware that others had gone or were going to Egypt, in which case his principles would take him elsewhere (2 Cor. 10:15–16).

But if he avoided Egypt because it already had Christian testimony, ought not the same consideration have applied to Rome? Two things need to be said on this. As W. L. Knox notes, Rome was so large that Paul could find many to whom the gospel had not yet been made known.[14] Even more relevant is the apostle's intention to make Rome a springboard for sending the message of Christ out into the whole western Mediterranean area. He had no idea of settling down in Rome (Rom. 15:24).

The fact that Paul was seriously considering a change of field for his work shows that in his own estimation, his success at Ephesus had reached a high plateau. Others could carry on. The apostle's pioneer spirit was eager to push forward to other frontiers of testimony. Therefore we can understand that in the providence of God, it was just at this juncture, rather than at some earlier time, that the disturbance led by Demetrius occurred, thrusting Paul out.

Although he had twice returned to Antioch after missionary travels, his present plan to visit Jerusalem and then go to Rome shows that Paul did not regard Antioch as a permanent home base. His plan and his corresponding movement was directed inward to Jerusalem and outward into the Roman world.[15] There is evidence that the decision had been gradually forming over a long period of time (Rom. 1:13; 15:23) and actually envisioned a penetration of the West that would take Paul beyond Rome to Spain (Rom. 15:24).

But why should he begin the realization of this plan by going in another direction—to Jerusalem? The basic reason was to consummate an important aspect of his work, the taking of a fund to Jerusalem that would help to meet the need of the poor saints there and hopefully would cement good relations between the church in Judea and the congregations (largely Gentile) that Paul had founded in Asia Minor and Greece (Rom. 15:25–26).

---

[14] W. L. Knox, *St. Paul and the Church of Jerusalem,* 345.

[15] W. L. Knox, in *The Acts of the Apostles,* 54ff. has pointed out that Luke adopted the travel story as the framework for his writing. In his Gospel he pictured Jesus moving toward Jerusalem, His goal, to accomplish redemption in fulfillment of Scripture. In the Acts he pictured Paul "beginning from Jerusalem" and leading a campaign of evangelization with Rome as his objective. This is the overall pattern of Luke's dual composition, Luke-Acts.

Some attention should be given to the words "Paul decided" (lit., "purposed in the spirit"). Was this his own spirit or the Holy Spirit? In favor of the former alternative is the verb "purposed" (rather than "was moved" or "was led") and the prominence given to his own person in the statement, "I must visit Rome also." It is often difficult to distinguish between the Holy Spirit and the human spirit where a believer is concerned, because of the close relation between the two (cf. Rom. 8:16; 9:1).

With his future movements in mind, Paul dispatched two of his trusted helpers to prepare the way, no doubt to advise the churches of Macedonia and Achaia of his forthcoming pastoral visit en route to Jerusalem. As it turned out, he stayed in Corinth for three months, then returned via Macedonia to Jerusalem (Acts 20:3).

Apparently Timothy did not accompany Paul from Corinth to Ephesus (18:18) but must have come later, perhaps with Apollos. He then fulfilled a mission to Corinth on Paul's behalf (1 Cor. 4:17), not to be confused with the visit now being considered.

The name of Erastus occurs in three references. The other two are Romans 16:23, where he is described as being the city treasurer of Corinth, and 2 Timothy 4:20, where Paul seems to say that when he himself was made a prisoner for the second time and was taken to Rome, Erastus stayed in Corinth rather than accompanying him. The reference in Romans has taken on added interest since the excavations at Corinth a few years ago. "A re-used paving block preserves an inscription, stating that the pavement was laid at the expense of Erastus, who was aedile (Commissioner of Public Works). He was probably the same Erastus who became a co-worker of St. Paul."[16] Looking further at the references to Erastus, 2 Timothy almost certainly refers to the same individual as Acts 19:22, since Timothy was involved in both instances. But uncertainty clouds the reference in Romans 16:23, since it is difficult to suppose that a city official would have the leisure to be in Paul's company at Ephesus. But the possibility should be granted.

Paul himself remained in Asia for a time (Acts 19:22). It was during this period that an event occurred that confirmed

[16] Oscar Broneer, "Corinth," *BA* 14 (1951): 94.

him in the realization that there were many adversaries (1 Cor. 16:9) and that persuaded him to expedite his plan to leave the city and begin to take the steps that would facilitate his move to the West. To this event we turn.

ARTEMIS EPISODE (19:23–41)

The incident of the silversmiths has been called "the most instructive picture of society in an Asian city at this period that has come down to us."[17] Ramsay also concludes from the numerous accurate details that the author must have based his account on eyewitness reports.[18] The fact that the account is narrated at some length seems to indicate that it had special relevance for the overall purpose of the book.

The effort to bring Paul into disrepute and to curtail or arrest his work is shown to have failed, for neither the civil nor the religious authorities were influenced by it. When the apostle left Ephesus he did so voluntarily.

19:23 Luke begins by noting the magnitude of the incident—"a great disturbance" (cf. 12:18 for the identical expression). It concerned "the Way." While from the Christian standpoint "the Way" suggests the absoluteness of the claim of Jesus Christ (John 14:6) and the efficacy of the salvation He achieved, in this context, as in verse 9, we are intended to see "the Way" through the eyes of those who opposed it. This is especially characteristic of the references in the book of Acts (9:2; 22:4; 24:14).

19:24. The ringleader of the disturbance was Demetrius, who apparently was an artisan who had advanced to the point where he headed a business making "silver shrines of Artemis." He was able to furnish employment for many "craftsmen" and can be thought of as the head of their guild of silversmiths. Business had been good—until recently. The word rendered "business" can also mean "gain," or "profit," and this sense is appropriate here; but the fact that the same word means "business" in the following verse has no doubt influenced the translators.

---

[17] William Ramsay, *St. Paul the Traveler and the Roman Citizen*, 277.
[18] William Ramsay, *The Church in the Roman Empire*, 114ff.

The shrines were probably not statuettes of the goddess but small representations of her seated in her temple.[19] Devotees purchased these and presented them at the temple as an act of worship.

Although shrines of terra cotta or marble have been found, none made of silver have been located, most likely because they were too valuable to keep and so were melted down by the priests.[20]

Artemis is translated "Diana" in the KJV, because of the influence of the Latin Vulgate at the time the KJV was written (cf. the comment on 17:19). Diana was indeed the Latin equivalent of the Greek Artemis, the virgin goddess of the hunt. But Artemis of Ephesus, while retaining association with wild animals, had really become the embodiment of the fertility of nature, and in keeping with this her representation was multibreasted.

19:25-27. Demetrius's speech to the men of his own and related crafts consisted first of all in an appeal to their self-interest. The prosperity of all of them was being endangered by Paul's success in turning people away from the worship of gods made with hands (see comment on v. 35). Demetrius gave grudging acknowledgment of the success of the apostle's preaching.

Something of the same sort occurred a few decades later in Bithynia, for according to the letter of Governor Pliny to Emperor Trajan, the temples until recently had become almost deserted, with little demand for sacrificial victims.

Warming to his subject, Demetrius cleverly moved from the economic to the religious sphere, from the appeal to the pocketbook to an appeal to local pride in Artemis, the great goddess whose worship was in danger of being neglected. For effect, he permitted himself the exaggeration that not only all of Asia but also "the world" worshiped her. It is tempting to give "Asia" the wider meaning of the continent rather than the province in this case, on the ground that it fits well with the larger category of "the world." But against this is the word's uniform use in the New Testament, plus the fact that "world" must not be confused with "the globe," for it refers simply to the inhabited earth known to the ancients.

[19] Ibid., 124-26.
[20] Ibid., 134.

It would have been unseemly to press the issue of economic loss before the public, and little sympathy could be expected, but to stress the blot on the good name of the goddess was strategic. Intelligent people might say, "Let Artemis defend herself" (cf. Judg 6:28–32), but not the masses. Demetrius had planned his approach carefully, expecting the complaint against Paul to catch on with the populace.

19:28–29. His expectation was realized, for the enraged craftsmen concertedly began to chant, "Great is Artemis of the Ephesians!" Ramsay is probably right in contending that no verb should be introduced here (there is none in the original). He understands the expression not as a statement of fact but as an apostrophe, a cry of adoration—"Great Artemis of the Ephesians!"[21] The Williams translation adopts this suggestion.

The noise attracted attention throughout much of the city, and people were drawn almost involuntarily to the theater, the only place where a large crowd could assemble. It was also the place where questions of public interest were discussed. Word must have spread quickly that the demonstration was against Paul and not simply in behalf of Artemis, a fact that would account for the seizure of Paul's associates, Gaius and Aristarchus.[22]

19:30–31. Believers as well as others were drawn to the general area of the the theater, and when they learned that the agitation had Paul as its primary target, they were insistent that he should not go into the crowd (not the technical word for assembly as in v. 41, but rather a term for the crowd, as in 12:21, where it is translated "people"). Paul was brave, but there was no reason to risk his life at the hands of men who had been turned into fanatics.

It has been suggested that this was the occasion when Priscilla and Aquila endangered their own lives to save Paul (Rom. 16:3–4). This is possible, but there may have been other situations involving greater peril for Paul (20:19; 2 Cor. 1:8–9).

The present crisis was unquestionably perilous, causing "some of the officials of the province" (RSV "Asiarchs") to exert

[21] Ibid., 135–39.

[22] For the possibility that only Aristarchus was originally designated as a Macedonian in the text, leaving Gaius to be identified with the Gaius of Derbe (20:4), see BC on this passage. Yet Gaius was a common name, so a Macedonian Gaius cannot be ruled out.

pressure on Paul to stay away from the scene. The word "Asiarchs" means literally, "rulers of Asia," a term too general to give much help in identifying them.

> The title either designates the annual presidents, and perhaps the ex-presidents, of the provincial council of Asia, or it also covers the administrators of the various temples of the imperial cult, which were under the charge of high-priests appointed by the provincial council, or it may merely designate the city deputies to that council.[23]

Such men, by virtue of their office, had to be concerned with the political and religious welfare of the community. The very fact that such men of prominence and wealth were Paul's friends reveals with utmost clearness that they did not regard him as dangerous or as carrying on an unlawful activity. Here is positive proof that the imperial cult (the worship of the Roman emperor) had not yet come to the point of opposing the Christian cause. The action of Gallio (18:14–15) may have been influential in making the officials of the province[24] favorable to Paul.

19:32–33. Meanwhile the situation in the theater continued to be one of "confusion" (cf. v. 29 and 2:6), with no one taking charge and with widespread uncertainty as to what the tumult was all about.

The opening statement of verse 33 is quite obscure. One possible clarification is the wording of the NASB: "And some of the crowd concluded it was Alexander." This seems to mean that when the Jews put him forward, some of the people were disposed to think that he was the central figure around whom the disturbance had taken rise. Or, the subject of the verb may be thought of as an indefinite "they," yielding the following: "And they brought Alexander out of the multitude," followed by an explanation, as the NIV specifies, that the Jews were the ones who called on him to step out and make clear to the throng that they, in contrast to Paul and his Christian friends, were not the occasion for the trouble.

---

[23] A. N. Sherwin-White, *Roman Society and Roman Law in the New Testament,* 90.

[24] Sherwin-White noted Luke's accuracy in using the plural. "If the author of Acts had not known the peculiarities of the organization of Asia, he might well have made an error. In some other eastern provinces the corresponding title went only with the office of President of the Council. There was only one Lyciarch, and only one Pontarch or Bithyniarch" (ibid., 90).

19:34. This move failed to quiet the multitude. Alexander was not given a chance to speak. In their state of mind the crowd would be scarcely less upset at the appearance of a non-Christian Jew than at the appearance of Paul himself, for both were monotheists unsympathetic to their pagan cult. Granted, however, is the certainty that Paul would have been in the more precarious position as a possible victim of violence.

The only effect of this move by the Jews was to set off a fresh wave of chanting, lasting for two hours, in honor of Artemis. Something of a parallel is the Muslim frenzy sometimes seen after the Ramadan fasting, when celebrants become like men intoxicated as they repeat, "There is no God but Allah, and Muhammad is his prophet."

19:35–41. At this point a new figure appeared, and his role was decisive in restoring order. He is called the "city clerk," a title that hardly suggests the importance of his office. A. H. M. Jones provides some historical perspective on this:

> The post was not . . . one of great political importance during the Hellenistic age. But as the vitality of politics ebbed and the magistrates tended to become lay figures, the clerk of the city, who was bound from the nature of his office to know the ropes of the ship of state, became a more and more dominant figure, and in the Roman period he, either alone or supported by the principal magistrates, very frequently moves decrees and takes the lead in council and assembly.[25]

F. D. Gealy observes that *chancellor* or *secretary of state,* although not ideal translations, would better convey a proper appreciation of his function.[26] His duties were many, in connection with both the senate and the assembly. He was the chief executive officer of the municipality and acted as liaison between the city government and the Roman authorities. The Greek word is *grammateus,* which in a Jewish context would mean "teacher of the law," as in "chief priests and teachers of the law," but here has a totally different connotation.

This officer showed his wisdom by letting the demonstration spend its energies before intervening. To be booed by the crowd would tarnish his standing.

---

[25] A. H. M. Jones, *The Greek City,* 238–39.
[26] F. D. Gealy, "Town Clerk," in *IDB,* 4:676.

He began his speech by voicing matters of common knowledge concerning the city's relation to the goddess Artemis and her worship, emphasizing her greatness (and thus expressing his agreement with the crowd before going on to find fault with their conduct) and two other items that have not come to the fore previously in the narrative. One was the fact that Ephesus was "guardian" of the temple of the goddess. This honor and responsibility did not exclude a similar relationship to the imperial cult. Ramsay pictures an Ephesian coin, from a somewhat later period, exhibiting the goddess and three emperors to whom temples had been built in the city.[27] The other item was the observation that the image of the goddess had fallen from heaven (a meteorite?). This was the tradition that helped to give sanctity to her worship. The *grammateus* showed himself more astute than Demetrius, who had failed to introduce this point as a counterpoise in his remarks about Paul and his doctrine (v. 26).

Shifting to a consideration of the men who had been dragged into the theater (and by inference including Paul), the official exonerated them of misconduct since they had not robbed temples (no doubt used here in the general sense of those who commit sacrilege in any form) nor had they blasphemed goddess. This may be taken as evidence that Paul and his helpers had been circumspect in their approach to the question of idolatry at Ephesus. Presumably they had avoided poking fun at the tradition about the image that had fallen from heaven. Now their restraint was standing them in good stead. In this there is a lesson in missionary strategy: to attack idolatry among people who cherish their gods and know nothing better, since they had not yet received the gospel, is to leave them in a vacuum.

The town clerk could not fault Paul and his friends, but suggested that if there were a grievance, Demetrius and the craftsmen must use legal means rather than mob action (v. 38). The text can mean either that the courts were in session at the time or that they were held from time to time as needed. The proconsuls or governors presided at such sessions.

In connection with his final word to the instigators of the riot, the official referred to "anything further," a term that sounds quite vague. Sherwin-White's interpretation is helpful:

[27] W. M. Ramsay, *The Letters to the Seven Churches of Asia* (Grand Rapids: Baker, 1963), 232.

According to the clerk, no specific charges of impiety had been made, but Demetrius was alleging that in some way the prestige of the city was being attacked. This is the "further matter" which might be brought up at what the clerk calls a "regular assembly."[28]

It is clear that this official did not take lightly the commotion of the day (v. 40). He was in touch with the Roman authorities and knew their attitudes.

> The reference to the "regular assembly" . . . is valuable. The city assemblies were on their way out. Roman policy aimed over a long period at the elimination of the democratic element. . . . No such fate has yet overtaken the civic assembly at Ephesus, but the town clerk has his fears.[29]

The clerk's words about the city's inability to give a legitimate explanation for the commotion sent the crowd away in a mood of solemnity that contrasted sharply with the mad uproar that had prevailed. No one challenged his order to disperse.

Luke makes his point without calling attention to it, namely, that Paul had been cleared of the charge of responsibility for economic depression among the silversmiths and (what was more important) of crime against the religious establishment.

[28] Sherwin-White, *Roman Society*, 83.
[29] Ibid., 84–85.

Part IV

THE WITNESS OF PAUL THE PRISONER
20:1–28:31

In this entire section the central human figure continues to be Paul, but the account shows that his situation became radically altered. No longer was he establishing churches or even visiting them, except as they were located on his line of travel to Jerusalem. A journey that was designed to improve relations between his congregations and the mother church, therefore by freeing him to go on his way to Rome, created new problems for the Jerusalem church and left him a prisoner in the hands of the Roman authorities. Yet, in the providence of God, this detention gave the apostle opportunities for witness he could not otherwise have had, including the appeal before Caesar at Rome.

The apostle's speeches are given prominence, with three features predominating: considerable autobiography, with the risen Lord's intervention in his life marking the critical turning point; witness to the resurrection of Jesus, a major issue separating believing and unbelieving Jews; and Paul's mission to the Gentiles, portrayed as not demanding a forsaking of his Jewish heritage or a sacrificing of his concern for the salvation of his people Israel.

In this portion of the book we see that Paul's contact with Rome finally became personal and direct. It was a contact destined to be meaningful for the future of Christianity and the history of the world.

15

JOURNEY TO JERUSALEM AND CONFERENCE WITH CHURCH LEADERS
20:1–21:26

This section follows naturally and logically from the intimation of Paul's plans sketched in 19:21. It was advisable to revisit the churches of Macedonia and Achaia before making what might be a final departure from this region. Paul's main objectives were to confirm believers in their faith, to supervise the concluding phases of the gathering of the fund for the poor in the Jerusalem church (1 Cor. 16:1–5), and to mend relations with the Corinthian congregation. As it turned out, the apostle may also have undertaken some further evangelization in new territory.

Verses 1–6. Here we follow Paul as he journeyed from Ephesus to Corinth and back again as far as Philippi. It is likely that the time required was the greater part of a year.

20:1–3. Farewells were said shortly after the uproar in the theater. To continue longer might have been harmful to the church's relationship to the community. Aquila and Priscilla may have left with the apostle or about the same time. They were headed for Rome, it seems (Rom. 16:3), to prepare the way for Paul's forthcoming visit to that city (Acts 19:21), with which they were so familiar (18:2).

Luke's account of Paul's movements can be supplemented by a comparison with 2 Corinthians 1–2, where we learn that although a door of testimony was open for him at Troas, where he would board ship for Macedonia, he did not remain there to minister because of anxiety over the situation at Corinth and particularly over the failure to make contact with Titus at this point (2 Cor. 2:12–13). It is likely that the meeting between the two occurred at Philippi. Having received Titus's report, Paul remained there long enough to write 2 Corinthians, with its recital of his trials in Asia and his exposition of the ministry; his counsel on the completion of the fund for Jerusalem; and his warnings in view of lingering opposition to him in the Corinthian church, formented largely by outsiders. Titus was sent once more to Corinth, this time to try to complete the fund already referred to (2 Cor. 8:6, 17).

Some think Paul wrote from Thessalonica rather than from Philippi, because Timothy was with him when he wrote (2 Cor. 1:1), and this young man had especially close ties with the Thessalonian congregation (1 Thess. 3:2–6). Luke is content to say that Paul passed through the districts of Macedonia.

He would naturally visit the churches already established there. Moreover, it is probable that this was the time when he preached the gospel in western Macedonia, going as far as the border of Illyricum. This trip was fresh in his mind as he wrote about it a short time later from Corinth (Rom. 15:19). On this journey he would have been able to take the Egnatian Way, which terminated at Dyrrhachium on the Adriatic Sea. It is possible that on the way to Corinth from this northwest area he ministered at Nicopolis on the west coast of Achaia. At a later time he planned to winter there (Titus 3:12). On this entire journey Paul was making good his announced purpose to preach the gospel in the regions beyond, as he had so recently declared (2 Cor. 10:16). The trip was possible only because of the easing of the Corinthian situation as reported by Titus. Paul did not have to hurry to Corinth.

His stay in Corinth lasted three months (cf. 1 Cor. 16:6). Plans were well under way to take ship for the Holy Land as soon as navigation was safe after the winter storms. Hostile Jews learned of this and plotted to murder him, no doubt after he was on board. Jostled by his countrymen on a crowded ship filled with people headed for the Passover celebration, he would be an easy mark for an assassin's knife.

Learning of the plot, the apostle quickly changed his plan, deciding to go overland through Macedonia, where he could book passage for the journey. This delay forced him to abandon the hope of reaching Jerusalem by Passover. The best he could do was to aim for Pentecost (v. 16). Discovery of the plot was a reminder to Paul of what the Lord had promised him in Corinth several years before (18:10). Not only was his life spared, but also the contribution of the churches remained intact.

20:4–5. Troas was the point of rendezvous with his traveling companions. The list includes men from churches that were planted on all three of Paul's journeys. Their function was to carry the gifts of their people to the needy at Jerusalem.

Notable is the lack of representatives from Philippi and Corinth. However, in view of the inclusive "us" (v. 5), it is likely that Luke took that role for the Philippian church and that he made the journey to Troas with Paul and went on to Jerusalem with him. With respect to Corinth, there are two possibilities. Bruce suggests that the absence of a Corinthian representative could hint at trouble there, presumably the church's stubborn refusal, out of a spirit of defiance toward the apostle, to complete its share.[1] But the fact that Paul had spent the whole winter in Corinth, plus the fact that the Letter to the Romans, written in this period, does not reveal any rift in his relationship with the Corinthian church, makes this improbable. One would think that pride alone would have been sufficient to move the congregation to take its place alongside the others. The alternate solution is the more credible, namely, that the breach with the church was so fully healed that they celebrated it by asking the apostle to be their representative. This would mean a shift from Paul's earlier recommendation (1 Cor. 16:3), but the following verse shows that he was prepared to go. The church may have acted on this basis.

20:6. By the time Paul and Luke left Philippi, Passover had already come and gone. Now less than seven weeks remained till Pentecost.

The journey to Troas was made in the face of adverse winds and required five days (contrast 16:11). Why Paul stayed seven days at Troas is not stated, but a ship for the journey southward may not have been available any sooner. The interval gave opportunity for a ministry that the apostle had not been able to offer at other times (16:8–11; 2 Cor. 2:12–13). From the latter passage it is evident that some believers were there on Paul's second visit. Meanwhile the church had doubtless grown in size.

Verses 7–12. Luke describes the apostle's activity on the final day of his stay in Troas, giving special prominence to these elements: the breaking of bread by the congregation, Paul's

[1] F. F. Bruce, *New Testament History,* 354.

discourse, and the Eutychus incident. The course of events seems to have been as follows: believers came together for a meeting, which was to include the observance of the Lord's Supper. Paul prepared the way for this by extended teaching, which was interrupted by the fall of Eutychus. After this the apostle led the congregation in table fellowship that included the Lord's Supper, and then he talked further before parting from these friends.

20:7. From this passage it may be assumed that Christians gathered together "on the first day of the week," the Lord's Day, our Sunday (cf. 1 Cor. 16:2). The influence of the Savior's resurrection on the observance of that day is clear, as well as the effect of His example in breaking bread with His followers on the evening of that day (Luke 24:29–30). If Luke were following the Jewish reckoning of time here, the Supper would have actually been eaten in the early morning of the following day. But it is clear that the day is being reckoned from sunrise to the following sunrise, not from sunset to sunset, for the meeting was at night, preparatory to Paul's departure "the next day," a journey made in daylight.[2] Bruce points out that many of the believers were employed by pagans, and this would make assembling during the day difficult, if not impossible; hence the night meeting.[3]

From a comparison of verses 7 and 11 it is evident that the observance of the Lord's Supper was deferred until Paul had spoken at some length—in fact, until midnight. They were aware that it might be his last opportunity to minister the Word to them.

20:8–10. Mention of the lamps (torches) is probably intended to have a bearing on what befell Eutychus. The air was oppressive (it was springtime), and the room full of people (Eutychus was sitting on the window sill) added to the stuffiness. After several hours the combination of weariness after a day's work, the bad air, and the rhythm of Paul's voice took its toll. Unable to stay awake, the lad slipped from his place and fell through the window to the ground. Luke says that he was picked up "dead." The physician does not say that he was mistakenly thought to be dead. Paul's falling upon the lad and embracing him should be understood in the light of an Old

---

[2]Kirsopp Lake and H. J. Cadbury, eds. *BC*, 4:255 n.

[3]F. F. Bruce, *Commentary on the Book of Acts*, 408.

Testament incident (2 Kings 3:32–35). While it might seem that the words of the apostle, "He's alive," were intended to indicate that he had not expired, the probable meaning is that (now) the life that had ceased was present as a result of the ministration given. The lad was indeed "fortunate," in line with the meaning of his name.

20:11–12. The meeting was resumed, and at this juncture the company observed the Lord's Supper (broke bread) and then enjoyed a fellowship meal. The procedure here was the reverse of what is indicated in 1 Corinthians 11:20–21. Afterward Paul talked with them until daybreak. The word "talking" is not the same as the one used in verse 7; it points to more informal conversation. After all, the Lord's Supper was the climax of the gathering. What followed until daybreak was a time of sharing the precious reality of knowing Him.

Lest readers wonder still about Eutychus, Luke concludes this section by noting that the people took the boy away (presumably to his home) "alive." In his restoration they were comforted. They had been remembering the Lord's death. They had also been reminded through Eutychus of His return to life through resurrection. The daybreak that morning must have cheered them with its promise of eternal day in the presence of the living Lord, when there would be no more parting such as their necessary parting from Paul.

Verses 13–16. These verses describe the journey from Troas to Miletus. The presence of several place-names in the narrative, as well as observations about Paul's method of travel, indicates that Luke kept notes on this trip to Jerusalem.

20:13–16. Paul chose to go on foot from Troas to Assos, about twenty miles away, a much shorter route than the ship had to take. He even delayed his departure after the vessel had cleared the port of Troas. Possibly he made a pastoral call at the home of Eutychus before leaving. He would have felt somewhat responsible for the lad's fall and the anxiety created among family and friends. The overland trek allowed the apostle to be alone with his thoughts. What were his thoughts? Musings on what lay before him (v. 23; cf. v. 3)? Or reflections on what God had wrought in Macedonia and Achaia, where Paul had recently been?

Making connection with the ship as previously arranged, he sailed with his companions to Mitylene on the island of Lesbos, the ship taking the inland passage between the island

and the mainland. After overnight stops at Kios and Samos, cities bearing the same names as the islands on which they were situated, the party had only one more day aboard ship until they were able to go ashore at Miletus. Luke gives the reason for bypassing Ephesus. Much as Paul would have welcomed the opportunity to renew fellowship with the church there, he felt it was necessary to safeguard his time so as to arrive in Jerusalem by Pentecost.

Verses 17–35. Here Luke (who was present, v. 15) sets down Paul's message to the Ephesian elders, after noting that the apostle summoned them to meet him. Even this arrangement meant an outlay of several days (Miletus was some thirty miles from Ephesus), which, in view of Paul's eagerness to arrive at Jerusalem, shows the strategic importance that he attached to the Ephesian church and the desirability of encouraging its leaders.

Some introductory observations about the address may be useful:

1. It belongs to a type known as the farewell discourse, which is fairly common both in the Bible and in related literature.[4] Examples from the Old Testament are the speeches of Jacob (Gen. 49) and of Moses (various parts of Deuteronomy), and from the New Testament the discourse of Jesus in the Upper Room (John 13–16).
2. The parallels between the farewell address of Paul and the Upper Room discourse of Jesus are especially close: (a) separation was imminent (v. 25; John 13:33; 16:28), producing sorrow in those who would be left behind (vv. 37–38; John 16:6, 22); (b) those who were addressed had to carry on, and they had the benefit of the speaker's example (vv. 18–21, 27, 31, 33–35; John 13:34; 15:12, 18, 20, 24); (c) they also had the help of God's Word (v. 32; John 15:7) and the Spirit (v. 28; John 14:16, 26; 15:26–27); (d) they would need these encouragements—the example and the supernatural enablement—because of problems and dangers that would face them both from without (v. 29; John 16:2, 33) and from within (v. 30; John 13:18, 21); (e) a word of blessing was

---

[4]Johannes Munck, "Discours d'adieu dans le Nouveau Testament et dans la littérature biblique," in *Aux sources de la tradition chrétienne*; Jacques Dupont, *Le discours de Milet*. The latter volume is especially concerned with the pastoral values of the discourse.

pronounced upon them (v. 32; John 14:27). Along with these resemblances there is a striking element of difference. The elders listened to Paul without breaking in, whereas the disciples interrupted the Master repeatedly during His discourse.

3. It was the privilege of an apostle to leave such a message, but others who ministered in Christ's name shrank from any such function.[5] The Miletus address is a testimony to the apostolic consciousness of Paul.

4. The impression of authenticity created by this speech is confirmed by the parallels in thought and expression between it and statements in Paul's letters. Luke did not compose it by putting down what Paul might have said on such an occasion.[6] Indeed, he had no need to do so, since he was present at the time.

20:18–21. The apostle seems to have presupposed his audience's knowledge of his work at Ephesus from the very beginning ("from the first day"). It is natural that those who were appointed elders would have been among the first converts. What they did not know firsthand they had no doubt acquired from others.

Verse 18 seems to confirm the impression given by 19:10 and the entire narrative of the Ephesian ministry that Paul had remained in the city instead of evangelizing the surrounding territory personally.

In his letter to the Ephesians, the apostle urged his readers to be humble (Eph. 4:2); this address to the elders was the only time he referred to it as an element of his own character (v. 19). As for his "tears" (cf. Phil. 3:18), these were the kind that are shed by men "who seldom if ever weep for things in the ordinary course of nature" (Bengel). His lot was made harder by "the plots of the Jews" (cf. 9:23; 20:3; 23:12; 25:3; 2 Cor. 11:26). These things were not permitted to affect his ministry of the Word. Nothing profitable was omitted. "Shrink" (NASB) is not too helpful a rendering here, though it fits well in verse 27,

---

[5] Bo Reicke calls attention to the case of Ignatius. See "A Synopsis of Early Christian Preaching," in *The Root of the Vine: Essays in Biblical Theology*, 155.

[6] Percy Gardner, "The Speeches of St. Paul in Acts," in *Cambridge Biblical Essays*, 401–3.

where the same verb occurs. The idea conveyed is to hold back, suppress, or keep silence.[7]

Matching the completeness of the message was the twofold sphere of proclamation—"publicly" (in the lecture hall of Tyrannus) and "from house to house." This may be intended to suggest contact not merely with individual families but also with groups of people (the church in the house). The same breadth of activity characterized his outreach to the unsaved, which embraced "both Jews and Greeks." Despite the great differences between these two, he treated them basically alike, for they were all sinners. They needed repentance toward God because of their sin (central to the preaching of John the Baptist and Jesus) in order to be candidates for salvation; and they needed "faith in our Lord Jesus" in order to receive forgiveness, righteousness, and life. Recall that in writing the Epistle to the Ephesians Paul underscored this same truth, that both groups needed the same message (Eph. 2:1–3) and when they received it they became one unified body rather than two in Christ (Eph. 2:12–22).

20:22–24. A major problem is encountered by the phrase "compelled by the Spirit." A reference to 19:21 is not very helpful, because of the difference in construction. Dupont argues quite convincingly in favor of "spirit" meaning the Holy Spirit,[8] making three points: the other interpretation would call for the word "spirit" to be in the accusative case rather than in the dative (cf. 21:11); Lucan usage elsewhere, involving the dative and expressing constraint or control, clearly refers to the Holy Spirit rather than to the human spirit (e.g., Luke 2:27; 4:1); and the heavy emphasis in Acts on human accommodation to the Spirit (8:29; 10:19; 11:12; 16:6–7) needs to be brought to bear on the interpretation of the verse before us. The word "compelled," then, serves the purpose of expressing Paul's sense of obligation to be obedient to the dictates of the Holy Spirit.

This compulsion did not provide any great light on what was to befall the apostle, beyond the disclosure that there would

---

[7] See Frederick Field, *Notes on the Translation of the New Testament*, 132; also Walter Bauer, *Greek-English Lexicon of the New Testament and Other Early Christian Literature*, trans. W. F. Arndt and F. Wilbur Gingrich (Chicago: University of Chicago Press, 1957), s.v. *hypostellō*.

[8] Dupont, *Le discours de Milet*, 90.

be outward imprisonments humanly imposed (note the correlation with "compelled" in v. 22) and attendant hardships or tribulations. These intimations had come to him "in every city." Luke did not mention them, but Paul threw out a hint in writing to the Romans from Corinth (Rom. 15:30–31). As we know from later developments, Paul's spirit remained unfettered, because he was obedient to the will of the Lord. He was ready and willing to lay down his life if need be.[9] But he could not come to terms with the idea that he should stop short of finishing the race and completing the task God had given him. He was able to recognize the termination when it was finally upon him (2 Tim. 4:7), but that time was not yet. The ministry he had received from the Lord Jesus was a sacred trust, so He alone must determine how it should be conducted and when it should be concluded.

In preaching the gospel entrusted to him, Paul was careful to make clear that it was a gospel of "grace" (cf. Gal. 1:6).

20:25–27. Another term containing the concept of the gospel is "the kingdom" of God (cf. 19:8; 28:31). Paul moved in the succession of Christ (Luke 8:1) and of others who were apostles before him (Luke 9:2). Grace and kingdom are not in opposition.

But there is a somber side to Christian proclamation. As Paul departed, with no expectation of seeing these people again, he could the more freely speak of the manner in which he had discharged his responsibility as a custodian of the gospel. He had resisted the temptation to withhold the reminder that rejection of the gospel of God's grace can only bring judgment. This explains his reference to being "innocent of the blood of all men" (cf. Acts 18:6; Ezek. 3:17–21). His next statement bore on the same subject. "The whole will of God" had been told forth in his preaching; he had not kept the sterner aspects of God's will secret (cf. Eph. 1:11).

20:28–31. Having reviewed his own ministry, the apostle bade the elders face their responsibility to carry on his work. They were not only elders, charged with the duty of ruling the

---

[9] A possible translation of verse 24 is, "I do not regard for myself my life as a thing even worth mentioning" (Kirsopp Lake and H. J. Cadbury, eds., *BC,* 4:260 n.; see also Walter Bauer, *Greek-English Lexicon of the New Testament and Other Early Christian Literature* [Chicago: University of Chicago Press, 1957], s.v. *logos*).

house of God, but "overseers," which from the context is not thought of so much from the standpoint of administration as of shepherd oversight and care (note the reference to the congregation as the flock of God). There was no place for tyranny or pride (cf. 1 Peter 5:2–3). Elders must stand ready not only to teach as pastors (shepherds), as in Ephesians 4:11, but also to be on guard for the flock in view of the dangers about to be noted.

But before pointing out these threats, Paul sought to impress on his hearers the preciousness of the flock in the sight of God. The church of God was purchased "with his own blood." A textual problem calls for attention here. Many manuscripts have "the church of the Lord," but the most important ones have "the church of God." The explanation for the former reading is quite simple. Some scribes revolted at the thought of the blood of God being shed for the church, so took the liberty of changing God to Lord.

Yet why would Paul say that God purchased the church "with his own blood"? An easing of the problem can be achieved by translating, "with the blood of His own," which remains true to the Greek and at the same time points to the Son as the One who shed His blood. With this change the verse includes a reference to all three persons of the Trinity in their several relationships to the church. The early chapters of Acts contain allusions to the Crucifixion, but here the Cross is not viewed as an event involving man's rebellion and guilt but rather in its theological aspect, as a divine provision for human sin, a truth hinted at in 2:23a.

The idea of God's people as a flock is familiar from the Old Testament (Ps. 95:7), and the same is true of their description as an assembly (Deut. 9:10; cf. Acts 7:38). Something of this background lingers in a passage like Galatians 1:13: "I persecuted the church of God." Paul could not get over the fact that he had been guilty of moving against the congregation of the God of his fathers, even though he had done it in blind ignorance.

He foresaw the congregation at Ephesus being in danger from two quarters. Some would arise to attack it from without. They are called wolves, a natural appellation after designating believers as the flock (cf. John 10:12). The apostle's experience in Ephesus, as related in the previous chapter, hints at what persecution may be expected when the Word is fearlessly proclaimed.[10] The danger from within, however, can best be stated in terms of schism, breaking the church apart in order to have disciples who would idolize a human leader and share his quirks of doctrine. This threat was real, as reflected in 2 John and 3 John (cf. Rev. 2:4).

Once again (v. 31) the apostle reverted to his own example, this time in terms of being alert to present and potential dangers, citing his ministry of warning believers throughout his stay in the city, which he conducted with such earnestness as to shed tears.

20:32-35. After committing the elders to the word of God's grace—a customary act of Paul when he was parting from the saints (14:23, 26; 15:40)—the apostle returned to the subject of his own example during his ministry at Ephesus (vv. 33-35).

As there is a correspondence between this address and the Upper Room discourse of Jesus, so likewise there is a certain similarity between this committal and the great prayer of our Lord, basically a prayer for the disciples after his discourse (John 17). The grace that was needed throughout the pilgrim journey and even beyond (1 Peter 1:13) was to be regarded as mediated through the Word.

Some commentators would refer the phrase, "which can build you up," to God, in which case *who* should replace "which." But the Greek construction will not permit this. To "build up" the people of God is a primary function of the Word and of the ministry of the Word. Paul is very fond of using the term *edification* (seven times in the Corinthian letters alone).

"Inheritance" is an Old Testament concept. Israel had inherited Canaan as the land promised to the fathers; but above and beyond this, the God of the fathers was Israel's inheritance (Ps. 16:5). The Christian's inheritance is a leading theme of Paul's letter to the Ephesians (1:14, 18; 5:5). Grace is the basis for it, and the Word of God communicates the promise of it to the saints who await it and have been set apart ("sanctified") for this glorious future.

The words spoken here would be entirely fitting as a close for the discourse. It is somewhat surprising to find Paul

---

[10]The figure of the wolf is sometimes used also with reference to the intrusion of heretical teaching, as in Ignatius, *Philadelphians* 2.2.

continuing, and on a more distinctly mundane level. But it is rather characteristic of him. Compare, for example, his counsel to the Corinthians about the contribution they had agreed to raise (1 Cor. 16:1–4), coming immediately after his lofty words of exhortation at the close of the Resurrection chapter (1 Cor. 15:58). Form must not stand in the way of fulfilling practical needs. So it is here. He wanted the elders to be hard-working men of integrity and could think of no better way to impress his desire on them than to cite his impartial labor among them.

His words about coveting no man's money or possessions recall the testimony of Samuel as he recounted his public service for Israel (1 Sam. 12:3). Instead of seeking or desiring the goods of another, Paul was content to work with his hands to support himself and those who labored in the gospel with him. Later, in writing to the Ephesians, he touched on this again. "He who has been stealing [and what is stealing but putting into action covetous thoughts?] must steal no longer, but must work, doing something useful with his own hands, that he may have something to share with those in need" (Eph. 4:28). B. F. Westcott comments on this passage as follows:

> Our faith constrains us to serve one another. Stealing is the typical form of using the labour of another to supply our wishes, while it is our duty to make our own labour minister to the needs of others. The inspiration of labour is not personal gain but fulness of service.[11]

In support of his teaching and his practice, the apostle proceeded to quote a saying attributed to Jesus: "It is more blessed to give than to receive." Although the saying is not found anywhere in our Gospels, it evidently came down through the medium of oral tradition. The use of it here suggests that the sayings of our Lord that do appear in our Gospels and yet fail to be expressed in Acts or the Epistles were nevertheless known before they were written by the Gospel writers, and many of them were used in the teaching of converts.[12] The saying before us gives insight into the character of God and goes far toward explaining the gospel.

[11] B. F. Westcott, *St. Paul's Epistle to the Ephesians* (Grand Rapids: Eerdmans, 1950), 73.

[12] For further discussion of this theme, see my article "The Tradition of the Sayings of Jesus," in *Toward a Theology for the Future,* ed. David F. Wells and Clark H. Pinnock, (Carol Stream, Ill.: Creation House, 1971), 41–63.

Verses 36–38. Luke describes the painful parting between Paul and the Ephesian elders, made all the more difficult by the prospect that they would probably never see each other again.

20:36–38. There is nothing like prayer to bring hearts together in the high emotion of brotherly love. The love for Paul that the elders felt deep down but was ordinarily restrained now broke all barriers. Grown men embraced and kissed him, revealing the intensity of their devotion to this stalwart servant of Christ, their gratitude for his unselfish manner of life in their midst, and their sorrow that he would so soon be whisked out of their sight, not to be seen by them again, according to his own prediction. It was a moving scene and did not terminate until Paul was once more on board his ship, ready to sail on but leaving a portion of his heart behind with these dear people. He could not tarry, for he was pastor-at-large to all the Gentile churches. Like his Lord, he must go to Jerusalem, if need be to die, that he might fulfill his course.

Chapter 21, verses 1–6. The story of Paul's trip to Jerusalem continues, concentrating on the visit to Tyre, a Phoenician city that originally was an island community famous for its commerce. David had had friendly relations with Hiram, one of its kings. Nebuchadnezzar and Alexander the Great had each had a part in its destruction, the former destroying the mainland part of Tyre and the latter destroying the island part of the city by building a causeway out from the mainland. Although its heyday was past in Paul's time, Tyre was still a prosperous place.

21:1–3. Luke provides here a brief account of the itinerary between Miletus and Tyre. The phrase "had torn . . . away" does not indicate any final farewells but rather the actual, physical separation incident to going on board (cf. Luke 22:41). Three places are mentioned in verse 1, and it is evident from the map that the distance between them was approximately the same, a normal day's run in each case. It is probable that "Cos" and "Rhodes" refer to the cities rather than to the islands on which they were situated.

Ramsay has an interesting observation regarding the daily progress of the ship.

> The ship evidently stopped every evening. The reason lies in the wind, which in the Aegean during the summer generally blows from the north, beginning at a very early hour in the morning; in the late afternoon it dies away; at

sunset there is a dead calm, and thereafter a gentle south wind arises and blows during the night. The start would be made before sunrise; and it would be necessary for all passengers to go on board soon after midnight in order to be ready to sail with the first breath from the north.[13]

Patara was on the coast of Lycia. At this seaport town the travelers found a ship that was due to sail directly to Phoenicia rather than follow the coastline. To change ships, therefore, meant saving time, even though there would be a delay of several days at Tyre for the unloading of cargo. It was evidently a considerably larger vessel than the one they had taken down the coast, and it was able to brave the open sea. Approximately four hundred miles separates Patara from Tyre.[14]

No stop was made at Cyprus, which was passed on the port side. Luke uses what may be a technical nautical term when he says that those on board "sighted" Cyprus and kept it in view for a long time, the only land to break the monotony of the open water.

There was nothing to report until the ship docked at Tyre and proceeded to discharge its cargo. Tyre was geographically in Phoenicia but administratively was part of Syria, as was Palestine.

21:4–6. Paul and his group now had "seven days" of waiting, but it was not wasted, for they made a point of locating the disciples. There is no hint here of previous acquaintance. The word here means "to look for by searching" (cf. Luke 2:16). Both fellowship and hospitality would naturally follow. Tyre had probably been evangelized some years before (Acts 11:19), when the nucleus of the church had been formed.

Luke's account concentrates on one item, the effort of the saints to dissuade Paul from going on to Jerusalem. This message came, we are told, from the Tyrian disciples "through the Spirit." Paul had already been made aware directly and repeatedly of what was in store for him (20:23). It may well be that the disciples at Tyre interpreted the information about the dangers to be faced as sufficient warrant for concluding that

---

[13] William M. Ramsay, *St. Paul the Traveler and the Roman Citizen*, 293.

[14] The Western text includes Myra, another Lycian port, after the mention of Patara, but it is questionable that so great a distance (from Rhodes to Myra) could have been covered in one day. The addition, if it is such, may have been made under the influence of Acts 27:5.

Paul should not go. The matter is discussed more fully at verse 11.

The farewell scene on the beach recalls somewhat Paul's departure from Miletus. There was prayer and kneeling down on both occasions (cf. Eph. 3:14), but no tears are recorded here. The time of association had been brief (seven days as compared with up to three years in the case of the Ephesian elders). Yet "all the disciples and their wives and children" turned out for the farewell, a tribute to the hold Paul had established on them in a brief time. The chances are that the group was small and closely knit.

Verses 7–14. With the arrival at Caesarea, Palestinian soil was now under the feet of the sojourners. The principal event at this coastal city was the coming of Agabus the prophet, with his poignant announcement of what would befall the apostle at Jerusalem.

21:7. The one stop between Tyre and Caesarea was at Ptolemais. In Crusader times it was known as Acre, and today it is called Akka. Here, too, Paul found some brethren. Luke's earlier narrative has not recounted the establishing of a church here any more than at Tyre. The voyage to this spot did not take long, and the visitors tarried for only a day. "Finished" (NASB, for NIV's "continued") is an uncertain translation in this verse. Field gives several examples of how the Greek word involved is used in a nautical context and concludes by saying, "In all these cases there is no question of *finishing* the voyage but only of *continuing* or *performing* it."[15]

21:8–9. Although Luke does not say how the party made the trip from Ptolemais to Caesarea, forty miles away, the one-day stop at the former place suggests that the ship continued to Caesarea, which had a good harbor. The overland route in this area was rugged, something to be avoided if possible.

At Caesarea Paul was destined to be detained for two years after making several appearances before Roman governors and other officials (23:33–26:32).

Lodging was available at the home of Philip "the evangelist," who is thus distinguished from Philip the apostle. Probably the primary intention is to remind the reader that this man had been active in preaching the Word following his

---

[15] Field, *Notes*, 134–35.

appointment to the seven (see chap. 8). His four daughters were also gifted by the Spirit with the gift of prophecy, though apparently they did not prophesy on this occasion, since a visitor by the name of Agabus, prominent in more than one place in the church (11:28), assumed this role. The daughters were also virgins. Two or three years before, Paul had given counsel to the Corinthians on both subjects (1 Cor. 7:25–40; 11:5). The phenomenon of women prophesying was not regarded as strange in the early church (Acts 2:17).

It may be that Agabus, more than any other, was designated to foretell events that were important for the church in general (cf. 11:27–28). He seems to have moved freely from Jerusalem (indicating the continuance of spiritual gifts in that congregation) to various places where believers congregated.

21:10–11. Agabus came down "from Judea." It is just possible that in this instance "Judea" stands for Jerusalem (cf. John 7:30), though admittedly it is often used in distinction from the city.

Dramatically the prophet reached for Paul's belt (not made of leather but of folded cloth) and proceeded to bind his own feet and hands with it. This recalls occasional symbolic acts by prophets of old (e.g., Isa. 20:24; Jer. 13:11). When Jesus announced what would befall Him at Jerusalem, He was His own prophet and did not supplement His words by anything acted out (Matt. 16:21; John 21:18).

The prophet added an interpretation of his action, indicating it pointed to what the Jews would do to Paul, binding him and turning him over to the Gentiles. A slight difficulty inheres in this statement, since the Jews did not actually bind him nor turn him over to the Romans; but Paul ended up in this condition because of the action of the Jews in seizing him (v. 27). No doubt the wording is influenced by the desire to draw a parallel between Paul and the Lord Jesus (Luke 18:32).

As indicated above, this is a convenient place to discuss the rightness or wrongness of Paul's going up to Jerusalem in the face of explicit indications from the Holy Spirit that to do so would mean a loss of freedom. Several things should be pointed out:

1. The prophecy of Agabus was not accompanied by a prohibition against going. Verse 4 contains a prohibition, without any details, and may have been due to the human transmitters rather than to the Spirit, as already noted.

2. Paul was fully aware of the sort of reception he would have (20:23; cf. Rom. 15:31) but did not understand that this information constituted an order to change his plans. To picture Paul as willfully disobedient through this drawn-out experience is a serious charge, and there is no justification for it. In fact, 20:23 must be given precedence over 21:4. "Now the Spirit could never instruct men to give advice to one which, if followed, would be an attempt to escape the very pathway of suffering that the Spirit indicated was lying ahead of him."[16] It was due to direct, divine revelation that Paul left Jerusalem at the end of his first visit (22:17–21), and it was by similar revelation that he went up from Antioch to Jerusalem to meet with the apostles in the circumcision controversy (Gal. 2:2). There is no indication of human mediation in either case. These two experiences of direct guidance would naturally make him suspicious of a claim of divine guidance by others on his behalf, as in 21:4. There are hazards in acting on secondhand guidance (see 1 Kings 13).

3. Too much hung on this visit to turn back now, with the goal almost in sight. Paul saw the tremendous possibilities in bringing to Jerusalem the fund given by the Gentile churches as a means of developing a greater sense of understanding and brotherhood between his converts and the mother church. He saw also the necessity of being there in person to answer the damaging rumors that had been floating around concerning his attitude toward the Law and the customs of the Jews. It was imperative that he remove misunderstanding. The unity of the whole church depended on it.

4. We read of no divine rebuke for Paul's going. Instead, the Lord encouraged him by a vision (after his capture), in which his testimony in Jerusalem was gratefully acknowledged and a like testimony in Rome promised (23:11).

5. We may think that Paul accomplished less as a prisoner than he would have accomplished had he refrained from going to Jerusalem. But who is in a position to assert without contradiction that this would have been so? Actually, Paul would not have been able to get the attention of a Jerusalem mob, the Sanhedrin, two Roman governors, king Agrippa, and the court of the emperor if he had remained a free man.

[16] G. Campbell Morgan, *The Acts of the Apostles,* 481.

His experience demonstrated the truth of the saying, "Man's extremity is God's opportunity."

Those who think that Paul made a mistake in going to Jerusalem despite the warnings of what would happen to him argue that the trip resulted in the assumption of a vow that required his presence and purification in the temple, and this in turn led to his being seized and later to his imprisonment. The implication is plain—all this could so easily have been avoided if Paul had only been willing to stay away from Jerusalem.

But one should realize that it was not simply Paul's going to Jerusalem that lay at the root of the problem (he had been there several times before), but his readiness to make a vow. The exegete must come to terms with this; the journey to Jerusalem is merely auxiliary to the real issue. This will require discussion at a later point in the chapter.

21:12–14. The Agabus incident created a deep impression, especially since it came on the heels of the disclosure made at Tyre (v. 4). Apparently even Luke (note the "we") joined in the effort to change the apostle's mind, together with the other traveling companions.

One can only marvel at the strength of Paul's resolve. Some may label it stubbornness; but before doing that, it is well to reflect that he was not doing it in his own strength, but was bound in the Spirit (20:22). He knew full well the love that his friends had for him and their fear of losing his valuable leadership in the church, but he knew that he must follow the course allotted to him in the plan of God. Deeply ingrained in his redeemed nature was a determination not to please men but God (Gal. 1:10). In this scene one can almost sense the influence of Another who had had to withstand the vigorous opposition of His followers on the issue of going up to Jerusalem (Matt. 16:22). Paul, like his Master, refused to be moved. He stood on the will of the Lord so doggedly that his friends came to recognize in his very determination, based on commitment, that the trip to Jerusalem was in the divine plan, unlikely as this seemed to human reason.

Verses 15–16. These verses are devoted to the trip from Caesarea to Jerusalem and the arrangements for lodging on arrival in the Holy City.

21:15–16. Luke does not give a precise indication of the length of time spent in Caesarea, but it was several days. The reader is left to wonder whether this indicates that Pentecost had already passed or whether it was still in the offing, so that no haste was required for the remainder of the journey. Luke says nothing about Pentecost in this narrative.

"We got ready" suggests substantial preparations. Since the distance to be covered was at least sixty miles and much of it uphill travel, several days would be required if the party went on foot. Ramsay, emphasizing the warmth of the season and the need of freshness on arrival, thinks that the verb used here suggests the use of horses and possibly of vehicles also.[17]

The distance to be covered required a two-day journey at least, and this is the basis for the addition in the Western text to the effect that the brethren from Caesarea who went along did so for the purpose of taking the group to Mnason, who lived in a certain village where they were to spend the night. But this is quite clearly an addition to the original text. The chances are that Mnason had a home in Jerusalem. At festival time the city would be crowded and accommodations difficult to find. Rather than put a burden on the church there, the believers at Caesarea made the arrangements involving Mnason. He was a convert to the faith from the early days of the church (a good reason in itself for holding that his home was in Jerusalem rather than thirty miles away). In view of his being from Cyprus, he may have had association with Barnabas (4:36). Luke could well have sought him out for information about the church in the days following Pentecost. That Mnason was a Hellenist is almost certain from his willingness to entertain uncircumcised brethren.

Verses 17–26 The narrative includes two facets: the meeting between the new arrivals and James, including the elders of the church, and then the incident of the vow, which took Paul into the temple and led to his being seized by the mob.

21:17–19. Their destination reached, the travelers were cordially received by "the brothers" (cf. Rom. 15:31). The official meeting with James and the elders took place on the following day. "All" the elders came, indicative of the importance of the meeting. This is the last time Luke indicates his presence ("us") until 27:1. The representatives of the Gentile churches who had come with Paul were included in the conference. Apparently there was no general convocation of the

---

[17] Ramsay, *St. Paul the Traveler,* 301–2; *HDB,* 5:398.

church such as took place when the circumcision issue was discussed (chap. 15). No mention is made of Peter.

Paul's report of his work "among the Gentiles" followed the introductions and greetings. Strangely, nothing is stated here about the fund that had been raised among these same Gentile churches on behalf of the poor at Jerusalem. Undoubtedly the church knew about it in advance because of Paul's earlier visits to the city, when the plan was being formulated. Bruce suggests the possibility that the brethren in Jerusalem may have come to look on this fund as something due them, somewhat on the analogy of the yearly temple tax brought by Dispersion Jews and paid into the treasury, in which proselytes to Judaism participated along with native sons of Israel.[18]

The difficulty may lie, however, not in the attitude of the Jerusalem church but with Luke himself, since he has avoided mentioning the reason for Paul's entourage from the time it gathered around him at the beginning of the trip to the Holy City (20:4). He does allow this aspect of the mission to appear at one point (24:17) but only as Paul's statement. It can be granted, of course, that the item Luke makes room for in the present narrative, to which he turns immediately, is of greater import than the collection.

21:20–21. The reader cannot help feeling the suddenness of the swing from Paul's emphasis on Gentiles to the elders' insistence that Jews were their major problem. This does not mean that they intended any depreciation of Paul's work. On the contrary, they were relieved and began glorifying God for what they had heard. But they could not help bringing into the open what had long bothered them, namely, the misrepresentation of his attitude toward the Mosaic Law and the customs of the nation that had been reported to the mother church from the Dispersion where Paul was laboring.

Who were "the thousands" of believing Jews who had been misinformed? Their identity is made clear from verse 22. They were members of the Jerusalem church, and they were zealots (the very same word that is used for the Zealot party) for the Law. If a general meeting had been called to present Paul to the church, one can imagine that a great deal of animosity would have been shown. We can see the wisdom of James in restricting

[18] Bruce, *Book of Acts*, 429 n.28.

the meeting to the elders. They could help to clear up the misrepresentation as they later mingled with the rank and file of the church. And one can be sure that there *were* misrepresentations.

We have no evidence whatsoever that Paul taught "all the Jews" to forsake Moses, to cease circumcising their children, and in general to abandon the customs that distinguished the Jews from other people. These were false reports, but they made the task of the Jerusalem church in reaching the Jews with the gospel very difficult, since everyone knew that Paul was a Christian Jew. His battle was for Gentile freedom from the Law and had nothing directly to do with the Jew.

While the apostle's stand may have satisfied James and the elders, they felt that actions would speak louder than words and that the fears of the Jerusalem church could be relieved once for all if Paul would be willing to demonstrate his loyalty to the law and the people's customs. This latter term refers to the cultic requirements of the Law in distinction from the moral and ethical legislation (6:14; cf. Luke 1:9).

21:22–26. A proposal was made to Paul that he identify himself with four men who were under a (Nazirite) vow, assuming the expenses incident to the fulfillment of the vow, which included the offering of sacrifices. The hair, probably intended to symbolize the life of the individual, was shaved off and burned as an offering (Num. 6:18). It is probably correct to think of the four men as poor, unable to pay their own expenses.

Josephus calls attention to the action of King Herod Agrippa I when he began his reign over Judea in A.D. 41. "On entering Jerusalem, he offered sacrifices of thanksgiving, omitting none of the ritual enjoined by our law. Accordingly he also arranged for a very considerable number of Nazirites to be shorn."[19]

Haenchen explains the situation as follows:

> At that time there were four poor Nazirites in the Jerusalem Christian community. The period of their Nazirate had already elapsed. The expense, which they could not afford, was to be assumed by Paul (the assumption of such expense counted as a pious deed); he

---

[19] Josephus, *Antiquities* XIX.6.1.

had only to report this to the priest concerned and agree upon the time of absolution. Since Paul had come from abroad, he was however considered to be levitically unclean. He had therefore first to regain levitical purity by a purification ritual. This consisted of being sprinkled with the water of atonement on the third and seventh day after reporting to the priest. Only when he was levitically clean could Paul be present at the absolution ceremony of the four, which took place in the "holy place."[20]

It was evidently on the seventh day, when Paul reported for the final ceremony, that the riot occurred (cf. v. 27).

The purpose in citing the Jerusalem Council decree (v. 25) is fairly clear. James and his friends, many of whom had taken part in that meeting, wished to assure Paul that they were not interested now, any more than when the Council met, in imposing the Law on Gentiles (did they glance in the direction of his companions as they spoke?).

Two questions emerge here. One is somewhat inconsequential: Where did the money come from to pay the expenses of the temple ceremony? It would have been questionable to deduct it from the fund for the poor saints, although the four men qualified for this description, unless the suggestion was made by the elders. Did Paul's companions come to his help? Did he have a reserve from his labors in past days? Who can tell?

The other question is far more significant: Did Paul violate his convictions in agreeing to the proposal presented to him?

1. The assumption of a Nazirite vow on his own initiative (18:18) indicates that Paul would have seen no harm or wrong in this situation. Actually there is no reference to a vow in connection with Paul in verse 24 unless it is implied in the words "join in their purification rites." Hort remarks:

> Yet the time spoken of appears too short for him to begin and complete a vow in. It is therefore more probable, though not mentioned in Acts, that he was already proposing to offer sacrifice in the Temple on his own account, possibly in connexion with a previous vow, possibly also, I cannot but suspect, in connexion with the

---

[20] Ernst Haenchen, *The Acts of the Apostles,* 612.

Gentile contribution to the Jewish Christians, not mentioned in chapter 21 but clearly mentioned in 24:17.[21]

2. Paul was ashamed to refer to this incident when defending himself before Felix (24:17–18).
3. We should not lose sight of Paul's purpose in making the trip to Jerusalem. He could not have rested content with handing over the fund that his churches had raised if the real objective of the trip—a unifying of the Jewish and Gentile wings of the church—was not achieved. Evidently he felt it could not be achieved without this demonstration of his personal loyalty to the Law and the customs.
4. Earlier the apostle had declared that he became like a Jew to the Jew (though he was no longer religiously a Jew but a Christian) in order to win Jews, and under the Law (though he was no longer under it himself) in order to win such people to Christ (1 Cor. 9:20–21). It would help the Christian Jews of Jerusalem to win non-Christian Jews if the suspicions concerning Paul could be laid to rest. This consideration alone should be sufficient to clear him of the charge of compromise.
5. There remains the problem of the animal sacrifices that the Law required in connection with the fulfillment of the Nazirite vow (Num. 6:13–17). Was Paul denying the finished work of Christ in paying for these? If so, the four Christian Jews involved were doing the same; and the elders, along with James, were likewise guilty, for they knew what the temple ceremonies required. Knowing Paul as we do from Romans and Galatians on the theological side and from Acts on the personal side, it is simply beyond credence that he would permit himself to do anything that would suggest a contradiction of the redemption for sin accomplished once and for all at the Cross. His action may raise questions for us, but apparently it did not for him. There is no suggestion of regret or any stirring of conscience over his participation.

[21] F. J. A. Hort, *Judaistic Christianity*, 109.

16

ARREST, AND DEFENSE BEFORE THE PEOPLE
21:27–22:21

It was not arrest in a legal sense, at the beginning, but seizure by a mob. What the Jews in the Dispersion had been unable to do because of the protection afforded Paul by the authorities, they were able to accomplish in Jerusalem, where they were in a majority and where the Roman presence was muted by apprehension that the populace might become offended and raise a tumult difficult to control. Tension usually characterized Jewish-Roman relations, especially in Palestine. Behind the crowd in the temple were thousands more who were like-minded about Paul, and behind them was the Sanhedrin, grieved and alienated because of his defection to Christianity years before (chap. 9). So the apostle was indeed in a perilous position.

It is significant that the Jerusalem church, despite the sympathy that James and the elders felt for Paul, made no protest either to Jewish or Roman authorities on his behalf, so far as the record indicates. Humanly speaking, he had to stand alone.

21:27–29. Certain Jews from Asia started the trouble. It is quite possible that they had been in the theater at Ephesus during the disturbance instigated against Paul (chap. 19) and had chafed over the fact that he had eluded the mischief that had been planned for him. Having come to Jerusalem, probably for the celebration of Pentecost, they saw their opportunity and seized it. No longer were they a minority. Paul was soon in their grasp.

Even so, they sought help from their fellow Jews, inciting

them on the ground that Paul had turned against his own people, the Law, and the temple (cf. 6:13). As though this were not enough, he deserved death, they said, for having "brought Greeks into the temple." Gentiles were permitted in the outer court (Mark 11:17), but a barrier separating this court from the inner temple areas bore an inscription at intervals, stating that no stranger was allowed within the limit and enclosure of the sanctuary. Any Gentile caught there would be put to death. Two museums house this inscription, excavated from the soil of Palestine by archaeologists. According to Josephus, when the Roman general Titus addressed a message to the Jewish rebels in the city during the siege, he made reference to the barrier with its inscription and added, "Did we not permit you to put to death any who passed it, even were he a Roman?"[1] As the Jews construed the matter, this warning did not necessitate a legal trial when one violated it. Such a person could be dealt with on the spot.[2] The mob intended to do just that.

Luke informs us that the assumption about violation of the temple in this case was false, based merely on observation that one of Paul's companions, whom they had seen with him in the city, was a Gentile. Evidently they recognized Trophimus (20:4) from having seen him in Ephesus. But Paul had not taken him into the temple.

Later on, in writing his Letter to the Ephesians, the apostle expressed a great truth that the unsaved Jew could not understand or accept—that in Christ the barrier between Jew and Gentile had been broken down (Eph. 2:14). Jewry was blind to this reality and persisted in maintaining the exclusivism of Israel's place in the economy of God.

The parallel between Jesus and His servant Paul is obvious when the Gospels are studied along with Acts: (1) both made a journey to Jerusalem that proved epochal in their lives; (2) both were apprehended there; (3) both were falsely accused. But whereas our Lord was soon led away to die, Paul was permitted in the providence of God to have several more years of labor, though under the restriction of imprisonment most of the time.

21:30–36. This passage describes the tumult that ensued when Paul was seized. Riot conditions developed as "the whole city was aroused" (cf. Matt. 21:10). People ran toward the

---

[1] Josephus, *Jewish War* VI.2.4.

[2] G. Dalman, *Sacred Sites and Ways* (London: Macmillan, 1935), 290.

temple from every quarter, jamming the court of the Gentiles. The mob took hold of Paul and dragged him "from the temple." This refers to the temple proper, the elevated inner portion (cf. Acts 3:2–3).

> The men who dragged Paul out of the "sanctuary" (i.e., the Court of Women) and closed the gates leading to the Court of the Gentiles (Acts 21:30), during the riot leading to his arrest, were obviously members of the Temple police, more precisely the post mounted at the "rampart" during the day-time.[3]

If the outer gates leading to the city had been closed, people would not have been able to enter the area to participate in the riot. The temple police either were unable to hold off the crowd or made no effort to do so.

The beating of Paul was of course not a judicial process. If he were a guilty man, as declared in the outcry against him, the proper method of punishment was stoning, to be administered outside the city (7:58). But so great was the hatred for Paul that the crowd sought to beat him to death on the spot, willing to violate the sanctity of the temple court by murder.

Meanwhile, a report of the violence was brought to the commander of the Roman garrison, which was stationed in the castle of Antonia immediately adjacent to the temple area at the northwest corner. Learning that the city was in "an uproar" (cf. 2:6, a nonviolent episode involving the multitudes), the commandant quickly ordered troops to charge down the steps into the court and take control of the situation. The presence of "centurions" (RSV) suggests a complement of at least two hundred men out of a garrison of one thousand. Since he was responsible for order in the city, the commander went in person at the head of the troops.

Fearing retaliation for the beating they were administering to Paul, the crowd desisted, whereupon the apostle was taken into custody and bound with chains (as predicted in v. 11) while the commander tried to learn from the crowd what he had done. But the confusion of many voices was too much, so he ordered the prisoner removed to "the barracks," where the noise of the tumult would not penetrate to disturb his

---

[3]Joachim Jeremias, *Jerusalem in the Time of Jesus*, 210.

examining Paul directly. The removal proved to be anything but easy, as the crowd, resentful at seeing their prey snatched from their grasp, surged about the soldiers, who finally lifted Paul and carried him up the stairs. Closing in behind the soldiers, the crowd pressed hard, crying all the while, "Away with him!"—the cry that the mob had voiced regarding Jesus in the presence of Pilate (Luke 23:18). It was a demand, not for removal, but for death.

21:37–40. Despite the beating, Paul was still able to speak and sought a word with the commander (Greek *chiliarch,* or military tribune). His name was Claudius Lysias (Acts 23:26). The request was spoken in Greek, and this caused the commander to realize that he did not have in custody the Egyptian who had caused the authorities trouble by leading a revolt at the head of four thousand men who took to the desert under his leadership (21:38). Ideas about the Messiah being a second Moses were current in Israel. "The Messianic pretenders mentioned by Josephus evidently saw themselves in the light of this second Moses tradition. They led their followers into the desert, or attempted to divide the waters in the manner of Moses."[4]

In identifying himself for the benefit of the Roman officer Paul was content to say that he was "a Jew of Tarsus in Cilicia, a citizen of no ordinary city."[5] He was content at this point to state his municipal citizenship.

> It is not surprising . . . that there is a certain ambiguity in Paul's references to his personal status as represented in Acts. He thinks of himself first and foremost as a citizen of Tarsus and only refers to his latent Roman status when it is expedient to do so.[6]

One cannot withhold admiration for the apostle in this situation. There he stood, in chains, bruised and exhausted, half beaten to death, yet anxious to bear a testimony to the milling crowd in the court below. When permission was given to speak, he took his place on the stairs. The whole scene,

[4] T. Francis Glasson, *Moses in the Fourth Gospel* (Naperville, Ill.: Allenson, 1963), 21.

[5] See William M. Ramsay, *The Cities of St. Paul,* 85–244.

[6] A. N. Sherwin-White, *Roman Society and Roman Law in the New Testament,* 179.

including the speech that follows, belies the accusation of his detractors at Corinth that his personal presence was unimpressive and his speech contemptible (2 Cor. 10:10). As he motioned to the crowd with his hand, the hubbub gradually died down until the mob became silent, in contrast to the uproar of a few minutes earlier.

Paul made ready to speak to them "in the Hebrew language" (RSV). It is generally assumed, and probably correctly, that this refers to Aramaic. While it is true that Hebrew had been kept alive and was used by the rabbis and by those who read the Scriptures in the Palestinian synagogues, the composition of Paul's audience was hardly such as to warrant an address in Hebrew. He spoke in the everyday language of the Palestinian Jew.

Chapter 22, verses 1–21. The continuity of these voices with Acts 21 is evident. Paul endeavored to explain to his countrymen how it was that despite his original opposition to the followers of Jesus he had become one himself. This is the second of three accounts of his conversion in Acts: Luke gives a description of it in chapter 9, which seems to depend considerably on Paul's as recorded here (Luke may have been in the crowd as he spoke); then the apostle went over the same ground but with different emphases when speaking before Agrippa (chap. 26). The presence of three accounts of the same event signals the importance we should attach to the apostle's conversion, whereas the varying emphasis in the three narratives justifies what might otherwise be regarded as unnecessary repetition.

Aside from the introductory statements (vv. 1–2) the speech falls naturally into three segments: Paul's preconversion life in Judaism (vv. 3–5); his conversion by divine intervention (vv. 6–16); and his commission to serve Christ (vv. 17–21).

Verses 1–5. In this initial phase of his defense, Paul was careful to make it clear that his Jewish background was beyond criticism—in fact, outstanding. Any shift could not be laid to defection but only to divine intervention in his life.

22:1–2. Paul prepared his hearers for the nature of his message by calling it a "defense" (*apologia*). This yields our word *apology,* which is commonly used in the sense of excuse, but is not suitable here, where the technical force of *defense* is required (cf. 25:16; 1 Cor. 9:3; Phil 1:7, 16; 2 Tim. 4:16; 1 Peter 3:15). The verb is used several times in Acts 24–26.

Paul was far from apologetic in his speech. Nor was he retaliatory, despite the roughing up he had had. By addressing his audience as "brothers and fathers," he emphasized that he had much in common with them. His choice of Aramaic underscored the desire to establish rapport. Known as a Jew of the Dispersion (v. 3), he could have been expected to speak in Greek. The crowd was immediately impressed and became very quiet, permitting him to be heard despite the tenseness of the situation.

22:3–5. Paul began by emphasizing his Jewish antecedents. He was not a proselyte to Judaism, but a Jew by birth (cf. Phil. 3:5). Although his birth had occurred in Tarsus (cf. 21:39), making him technically a Dispersion Jew, yet he was brought up in Jerusalem and was therefore at home in the life and customs and religion of his nation. Moreover, he had the advantage of education under the famous rabbi Gamaliel (cf. 5:34).

"Thoroughly" is a better translation than "strictly" (NASB), which suggests a certain severity and narrowness of viewpoint that is not necessarily conveyed by the original. As a matter of fact, Gamaliel belonged to the school of Hillel, which was the more liberal of the two predominant schools of thought (the other being that of Shammai). The idea here is rather that of care, of exactness, and of thoroughness in the training.

In describing his hearers along with himself as "zealous for God," Paul expressed a generous verdict identical to that which he had recently stated in his letter to the Romans (Rom. 10:2). His own zeal as a young man had been not only for God and for the Law but also for the traditions of the fathers (Gal. 1:14).

An important book by W. C. van Unnik[7] shows that the three verbs used in verse 3—"born," "brought up," and "trained"—are found frequently in ancient writers and in this same order. The second indicates home rearing. It appears, then, that Paul was brought to Jerusalem at an early age, years before he took his rabbinical training under Gamaliel, and this seems to be affirmed also in 26:4.

There has been considerable hesitancy on the part of some New Testament scholars to accept Luke's statement about Paul's training under Gamaliel. Among the objections brought forward, three will be noted here.

---

[7] W. C. van Unnik, *Tarsus or Jerusalem, the City of Paul's Youth*, 17–45.

First, if Paul had studied under Gamaliel, is it not strange that he should turn out to be such a violent persecutor of the church, when Gamaliel was so mild in his attitude? However, experience shows that pupils do not always agree with their teachers. Paul saw more clearly than Gamaliel the danger to Judaism presented by the Christian faith (Phil. 3:6).

Second, some have expressed doubt that Paul could have written so negatively about the Law if he had studied under this man. But what the apostle was concerned to correct was the misunderstanding that the Law was intended to be a means of justification of the sinner. That he had a high regard for the Law is apparent (Rom. 7:12; 8:4; Gal. 3:24).

Third, it has been objected that Paul's use of the Old Testament shows he was at home in the narrative and edificatory tradition of Judaism but not in the legislative tradition, which is the heart of the Talmud. Yet this allegation seems to be contradicted by Paul's evident awareness and use of Hillel's principle of analogy, as in Romans 4:1–8.[8] It is significant that Joseph Klausner, with his unquestioned knowledge of Jewish tradition and scholarship, did not question Paul's study under Gamaliel.[9] For Luke to report Paul's saying in public, in the city of Jerusalem, that this was his training without being sure of the fact would indeed be a blunder that would put his credibility in serious jeopardy with his readers.

The speaker insisted that he showed his zeal for God by persecuting the church, but because he was speaking to unbelievers he was careful to refer to it as "this Way" (cf. 9:2), a designation that would sufficiently identify the movement and at the same time indicate his former abhorrence of it. His relentlessness was revealed by including "women" in his persecution, with "death" as the penalty for conviction of belonging to this heresy and refusing to give it up. Regarding the ability of the "high priest" and the "Council" to substantiate all this, Rackham is probably correct in supposing that, in view of the more than two decades that had elapsed since that period in Paul's life, he "is really appealing to their records."[10] They were bound to have had familiarity with his activities,

[8] Otto Michel, *Der Brief an die Römer* (Göttingen: Vandenhoeck & Ruprecht, 1955); C. K. Barrett, *The Epistle to the Romans* (New York: Harper, 1958).

[9] Joseph Klausner, *From Jesus to Paul* (New York: Macmillan, 1943), 309–11.

[10] R. B. Rackham, *The Acts of the Apostles,* 423.

since from them he received letters of introduction and authorization to brethren in the Damascus area as he started out on this crusade to foreign cities. The purpose of alluding to the persecuting zeal was to demonstrate that in those early days he had had no personal interest in the Way, much less identification with it.

It may not be out of order to raise a question here. Why was it necessary to indulge in so many autobiographical details if Paul was such a well-known figure in Palestinian Judaism? It was because more than twenty years had gone by since he had waged war against the church. A new generation had arisen that knew not Saul of Tarsus. Besides, many in the audience were from areas in the Dispersion and would not have been likely to know of his background. Certainly the Sanhedrin would have been anxious to do all in their power to efface this man's memory.

Verses 6–16. This passage describes Saul's confrontation with the heavenly Lord resulting in a complete revolution in his life and activity.

22:6–16. By delving into his background in Judaism, Paul laid the groundwork to show that it was only supernatural intrusion into his life that had effected his change of attitude and set him on an entirely different course. The intervention came when he had almost reached his destination, each mile firing his zeal as he pictured to himself how he would go about stamping out the new faith in this Syrian community. The hour was important too, for at noon the sun is blazing in its intensity. It was just then that the brilliant light flashed "from heaven" (cf. 26:13). It was more than an atmospheric phenomenon, for it recalled the various self-disclosures of God in Old Testament days through the *shekinah* light (e.g., Ezek. 1:4, 28).

For verses 8–9, see the discussion on 9:4–5. It should be noted in passing that Paul called Jesus "the Nazarene" (NASB, after the Greek), another touch designed to establish rapport with the audience, since this was the usual Jewish way of identifying Jesus (John 18:5; Acts 6:14). Jewish believers in Jesus were known as the sect of the Nazarenes (24:5).

A casual reading of verse 10 might easily suggest to the reader that Paul's question and the risen Lord's answer had to do with the events of the next few days, but this is almost certainly wrong. The information Paul sought and that the Lord promised to provide had to do with his future work[11] (cf. v. 15).

Blinded by the light, Paul had to be led into the city, where he was sought out and ministered to by a certain Ananias. The description of this man as "devout" in terms of "the law" and as enjoying a good reputation in the eyes of the Jews is another deliberate attempt to underscore the entire incident as "kosher." The blindness testified to the reality of the confrontation with the Lord whom he had been unconsciously persecuting. The sending of Ananias testified to the divine purpose that Paul, now humbled by his experience, was to have the privilege of being a witness of what he had "seen and heard" during his confrontation. This put Paul on a par with the original apostles and actually gave him an experience they had not enjoyed (except by anticipation at the Transfiguration), namely, seeing the Lord in His resplendent glory. Note that Paul avoided describing the sphere of his witnessing as twofold, to Jews and Gentiles, deferring reference to Gentiles as long as possible lest he be interrupted before completing his story (cf. v. 21).

With sight restored, Paul was able to see Ananias, the first follower of the Nazarene he viewed with respect and admiration. He was now a changed man.

The message through Ananias was phrased in such a way as to underscore the fact that the Damascus-road experience had been regular, in the sense that "the God of our fathers" had intervened that Paul might "know" the divine will (he thought he had been doing God service all the time he had been persecuting). It was a part of God's purpose that Paul should see the "Righteous One," an evident reference to Jesus the Christ (cf. 3:14; 7:52).

It is possible that verse 14 should not be ended with a period, since the first word of verse 15 can be rendered "that" or "for," and in this instance may be intended to introduce the content of the "words from his mouth," namely, that Paul should be a witness for Him to all people.

As the servant of the Lord (Rom. 1:1), Paul had to learn to obey the Lord's will, which called for his baptism as an initial step. Although most of the Jewish leaders spurned the baptism

[11] François Amiot, *The Key Concepts of St. Paul*, 22.

that John had preached because it demanded repentance and confession of sins, the masses flocked to his baptism. It is possible that some in Paul's audience had submitted to John's rite. But Paul's baptism was not identical, for he was to call on the name of the Lord Jesus. Yet even this did not cause his audience to break its silence, though tension must have been mounting in some of his hearers.

Verses 17–21. This statement of Paul's commission has a somewhat later context than the conversion, placed in the setting of Jerusalem and the temple, the very area where the speech was being given.

22:17–21. The apostle needed a little more time, for he had another point to establish. He wanted to make clear that his distinctive work among the Gentiles was definitely in the plan of God and had been authorized by Him. After his conversion he came back to Jerusalem, the holy city of his people, and entered the temple, the place where Israel's God was worshiped (cf. 3:1), the place that Paul had wrongfully been accused of defiling. He had not broken with his nation. There in the temple he had fallen into a trance and in that state realized that the risen Lord was communicating a command that he leave Jerusalem at once because of the unwillingness of the people to accept his "testimony" about Him (cf. 9:28–29). The Savior had come to His own and had been rejected (Matt. 23:37; John 1:11). His servant should not expect any better treatment (John 15:20).

Yet Paul would have his hearers realize that even then, despite the command to leave, he was reluctant to go, so confident was he that his own people would be impressed by the fact that the leading persecutor had become an advocate for the cause he had once opposed so bitterly. He had approved the death of Stephen and had vowed inwardly to bring about the death of many more followers of Christ. But even as he spoke these words to the throng he had to face the reality that Jerusalem had not changed. His former zeal for Judaism against the followers of Jesus was no asset to him now, for his countrymen regarded him as a renegade.

Paul hoped to make it clear that his life's work among the Gentiles was not of his choosing. He had returned to Jerusalem after his conversion intent on remaining there, only to hear the Lord commanding him to go where he was being sent—"to the Gentiles." It is likely that Paul intended to go on and show that in responding to this command he was not obliged to spend all his energies on the Gentile mission, and in fact had used every opportunity to witness first to his own people. However, the word "Gentiles" was the last he could utter, for it was the signal for an outbreak of protest from hundreds and thousands of throats. Here ended a brave witness given under most difficult circumstances.

Why was the word *Gentiles* so offensive to the crowd? Was it an expression of their disdain for those they regarded as their inferiors? Hardly, for the synagogues throughout the Dispersion were doing their best to make converts to Judaism among these very people. No, they were protesting against Paul, and in some measure against the Jerusalem church for supporting him in his stand, as he sought to convert Gentiles to the Lord Jesus without imposing circumcision and the keeping of the Law. This was regarded as treason against the faith of the fathers. The unique position of the Jew was being undermined. Of course, the word *Gentiles* had been a key to the disturbance that had occasioned the speech, and it now brought to the minds of his hearers the assertion that he had brought Gentiles into the temple. This was sufficient cue to stir up the crowd all over again.

17

THE COMMANDER AND THE SANHEDRIN

22:22–23:11

The apostle had not sought to clear himself from charges. Like Stephen he had used his defense as an opportunity for witness. The result was a renewal of the demand for his life and a renewed intervention of the Romans to save it. Yet the Romans were prepared to use torture to extract the truth from the prisoner, an ordeal from which Paul was spared by declaring his Roman citizenship.

22:22–23. The word *Gentiles,* as we have seen, was all that was needed to spark another outbreak of rioting, with insistent demands that Paul's life be forfeited. The crowd showed its contempt by referring to him as "this fellow" (NASB; cf. Matt. 26:61 RSV). It was a scene of Eastern excitement marked by outcries, the throwing off of garments, and the casting of dust into the air. Instead of being palliated by the address, the people were outraged.

22:24. This was enough to alarm the commander of the Roman garrison, who must have been standing nearby (cf. 21:39-40). The Romans had learned by experience how volatile a Jewish crowd could be, and the commander knew he would be held responsible if trouble on a large scale developed from this incident. Unable to understand Aramaic, he was no further along in getting at the reason for the uproar than he had been before Paul's speech, so he decided to resort to flogging the prisoner as soon as they had him safely inside the barracks again. He hoped that this procedure would compel Paul to reveal the whole story that so far was an enigma.

22:25–26. A "centurion" was in charge of the flogging,

which was to be carried out by a band of soldiers. They had taken Paul and had "stretched him out" before he objected. Thongs were used to tie the prisoner in a fixed position (presumably to a post that was somewhat inclined) so that the back, stripped of all clothing, would be in position to receive the lash. This was administered not by a long whip, such as a slave driver might use, but by a fairly short but deadly instrument consisting of a stout handle to which was attached a leather thong or several of them, knotted or weighted with bits of bone or metal that could cut deeply into the flesh. Paul was faced with a frightful ordeal that might incapacitate him for a long time. It was far worse than the Jewish floggings in the synagogue that he had endured and worse than the beating with wooden rods at the hands of the Roman lictors in Philippi. This flogging was the same kind of punishment Jesus had received at the close of His trial (Matt. 27:26), rendering Him unable to carry the cross all the way to Golgotha.

Paul had a recourse unavailable to his Master, for he was a Roman citizen and knew that such scourging was illegal for a person who had this standing. So he simply raised the question as to whether the proceedings were legal in the case of one who was a Roman and had not been found guilty. He had not objected when he was bound, for this had been predicted (Acts 20:23; 21:11). But there had been nothing to indicate that he must submit to this further indignity. His question effectively halted preparations for the scourging while the centurion made haste to report to his superior. It was a serious offense to treat a Roman citizen in this fashion.

22:27–28. The commander came in person to investigate this new turn of events, quizzing the prisoner to get at the truth regarding his status. When Paul affirmed his Roman citizenship, the commander volunteered the information that in his own case it had cost him a large sum of money to acquire it. To this Paul rejoined that he had this rank by reason of birth, indicating by this that his parents had been citizens before him.

It is apparent that Paul had a double citizenship, for he had already told the commander that he had citizenship with reference to Tarsus (21:39), so the question now raised must apply simply to Roman citizenship. Such double citizenship was not possible at every period. Sherwin-White comments, "Not until the imperial period did it become normal for a man of peregrine [alien] origin to make a real use of his citizen status without surrendering his connexion with his original home."[1]

On the great sum paid by Claudius Lysias the same writer notes, "It was the bribe given to the intermediaries in the imperial secretariat or the provincial administration who put his name on the list of candidates for enfranchisement."[2] How Paul's parents had gained this coveted rank is not known. It may have been on the basis of some service rendered to the state.

In passing, one should observe in this connection the name of the commander. As Sherwin-White notes, "It is not in dispute that this man secured the citizenship from the emperor Claudius."[3] Since Claudius had reigned only a few years before, this fits in well with the Lucan narrative (Nero, the Caesar to whom Paul appealed, succeeded Claudius).

Notable is the fact that Paul's statement about his Roman citizenship went unchallenged. The reason is simple. It would cost a man his life if he advanced the claim without having the rank. If the census archives failed him, one who claimed Roman citizenship by birth "could produce a copy of the original *professio* or registration of his birth recording his Roman status and made before a magistrate."[4] Some scholars have conjectured that Paul, because of being away from home most of the time, may have carried a certificate with him for just such emergencies as he had now encountered. At Jerusalem he had relatives who could vouch for him on the citizenship issue (23:16).

Worth observing is the readiness of the commander to chat with Paul about this matter of citizenship, hardly concealing a bit of envy for the man who had come into this high standing by birth. The sharp eye of Sherwin-White has discerned how neatly this sort of a situation fit the era of Claudius, when a man might come up through the ranks and acquire citizenship at quite a price. It was not long until this status could be secured

---

[1] A. N. Sherwin-White, *The Roman Citizenship*, 2nd. ed. (New York: Oxford University Press, 1980), 189.

[2] A. N. Sherwin-White, *Roman Society and Roman Law in the New Testament*, 154–55.

[3] Ibid., 154.

[4] Ibid., 148.

with much less difficulty. "The historical atmosphere of the Lysias incident is exactly right for the time of Claudius."[5]

22:29. Without further questioning Paul was untied and removed from the place of torture. The fear of the centurion and the commander is understandable (cf. 16:38). A man could lose his position and be severely punished for subjecting a Roman citizen to flogging. Paul was detained, but not again was he made to suffer indignities. "Luke shows triumphantly how much better it is for Paul to be a Roman among the heathen than to be a Jew among his fellow-countrymen."[6]

22:30. Still baffled by the incident in the temple court, the commander determined to bring Paul before the Sanhedrin the following day, issuing orders for it to convene, a highly unusual procedure on his part. In his frustration he could think of no better way to solve this puzzling case. The apostle was "released" from confinement for this occasion but remained a prisoner.

It seems that the commander made no further effort to extract information from Paul directly, unless there is a hint in the words "wanted to find out exactly" that Paul had told him some things that he hoped would now be confirmed or denied by means of the Council session. Although the members of the Sanhedrin had not been in the mob, they were presumably better informed about the church and about Paul's activities than the people in general.

A difficulty naturally arises here, already alluded to. Was the commander in a position to order the Council to meet? Probably not under normal circumstances; but if Paul was suspected of conduct that threatened the security of the country, the Roman official presumably would not hesitate to act. Also, as Hanson points out, this was not a regular meeting of the Council, so protocol was not binding.[7]

Chapter 23, verses 1–11. One can only speculate whether Luke was present on the occasion of Paul's defense before the Sanhedrin. The likelihood of such a thing is admittedly remote, but with the discovery that the prisoner was a Roman, the commander may have been ready, even eager, to grant Paul the

---

[5] Ibid., 156.

[6] J. M. Stifler, *An Introduction to a Study of the Acts of the Apostles* (New York: Revell, 1892), 222–23.

[7] R. P. C. Hanson, *The Acts,* 220.

privilege of an attending physician, especially after the mauling in the temple court. The scene at the Council meeting was of such a nature that one could not expect Luke's presence to be indicated.

No one can read this section without being impressed with Paul's resourcefulness in a tight situation. Some scholars find here a resort to such outright expediency as to reflect on the apostle's character. But they must concede that this very reflection, if allowed, means that the narrator has not held back something uncomplimentary, and this would support his credibility as a historian. We may rest assured that Luke did not include this passage merely to underscore the cleverness of the man whose career he had dedicated himself to delineate. Rather, he was concerned to show how much Pharisaism at its best had in common with Christian faith and how readily it could be a stepping-stone to that faith, or at the very least that "the bridges between Jews and Christians have not been broken."[8]

23:1–5. A major difficulty must be faced here. Why is there no reference to the alleged offense of the prisoner that led to the uproar in the temple area (21:38), especially since the purpose of this session was to supply information on this very point for the commander (22:30)?

In all probability Paul was leading up to the temple incident by his opening remarks, but was interrupted by the summary order of the high priest (v. 2). What favors this interpretation is the apostle's claim of a "good conscience." He was not aware of wrongdoing in this matter any more than in others. C. A. Pierce suggests that the word "good" in this passage means "free from the guilt of profanation of the Jewish Religion."[9] So when Paul consented to take part in the purification rites, he saw no conflict with his Christian convictions; otherwise he could not claim a good conscience. It is one of the most remarkable things about this man that he could on various occasions affirm in the most positive way his sense of freedom from conscious transgression (1 Cor. 4:4; Phil. 3:6; 2 Tim. 1:3). The Philippian passage would seem to cover his part in the death of Stephen; this is confirmed by 1 Timothy 1:13.

Paul's reference to conscience comes in connection with his

---

[8] Ernst Haenchen, *The Acts of the Apostles,* 643.

[9] Claude A. Pierce, *Conscience in the New Testament* (Naperville, Ill.: Allenson, 1955), 96.

statement "I have fulfilled my duty." As this could mean that he had "lived as a citizen," some would limit the thought to the apostle's public life,[10] but "to God" makes this conclusion somewhat doubtful. Prior to Paul's time the word had been used in the sense of *walk*[11] (i.e., live), with no necessary reference to the state or to public life. Here, however, there may be a glance at Paul's relationship to the Jewish nation (cf. his opening words, "My brothers").

No sooner had Paul made his opening statement than he was cut short by a crisp order, delivered by the high priest to those near the prisoner, to strike him "on the mouth" (cf. John 18:21–22). This was an obvious indication that the apostle had offended him by what he had said. Ananias the high priest held office for a decade or more and wielded considerable influence not merely by reason of his office but because of his great wealth. He was not averse to the use of violence when it served his purpose, so his command regarding Paul was in character.

Stung by the injustice of what Ananias had ordered, the apostle responded at once with the warning, "God will strike you." He may have had no particular event in mind, but some feel that he was prophesying the death of the high priest, which proved to be a violent one at the hands of Jewish rebels soon after the war with Rome began (Ananias was pro-Roman in his sympathies). The apostle's indignation can be measured by the epithet he hurled at the high-priest—"You whitewashed wall!" The language recalls somewhat the words of Jesus addressed to the scribes and Pharisees (Matt. 23:27). This was supposed to be a hearing "according to the law," but the order was contrary to the Law. Leviticus 19:15 may have been in Paul's mind. There was a saying that ran, "He who strikes the cheek of an Israelite strikes, as it were, the glory of God."

Over against the prophecy that God would strike Ananias, the bystanders posed a question that was also a complaint, "You dare to insult God's high priest?" The mention of God was deliberate, as though to contest the idea that God would move against His own servant.

This cooled off the aroused apostle, who apparently shifted abruptly to an apology for his sharp thrust, citing Scripture

---

[10] See F. F. Bruce, *Commentary on the Book of Acts*, 499. He points out that any contradition with Romans 7:7ff. can thus be avoided.

[11] Hermann Strathmann, *TDNT*, 6:526, 534.

(Exod. 22:28) that forbade speaking evil of the ruler of the nation. Although Paul had no respect for Ananias the man (and there were many who agreed with him), he was bound to respect his office. In the same way David had refused to touch Saul the king, though he had ample ground for finding fault with him as a man (1 Sam. 24:6; 26:9–11). Since Israel no longer had a king in Paul's day, the high priest was the ruler of the people.

There is a difficulty in Paul's statement that he was not aware that the one who had given the order was the high priest. Was it poor eyesight that accounts for his failure to identify Ananias? This is unlikely in view of the wording at the opening of the chapter—"looked straight at." It is tempting to take Paul's language as ironical (i.e., he could not bring himself to recognize such a man as high priest), but this is rendered doubtful by the past tense, "I did not realize." Likewise, it is awkward to find the word "brothers" put forward here, singularly out of place if the apostle was being caustic. Furthermore, can we really suppose that he would create prejudice needlessly and to his own detriment in such a delicate situation?

Perhaps the best that can be done is to fall back on the fact that Paul did not know Ananias personally. He had not had contact with the Sanhedrin for more than twenty years. The high priest may not have been wearing his official robes on this occasion, since he was not ministering in the temple and, in view of the fact that the meeting had been called by Claudius Lysias, may not have been presiding.

23:6–8. It may seem strange that Paul broke off his defense, which was scarcely begun, and sought rather to divide the Council by raising the issue of resurrection. But he evidently sensed that the interference of the high priest meant that no ordered defense would be tolerated and would be useless anyway, under the circumstances.

As to the propriety of driving a wedge between the Pharisees and the Sadducees, it must be realized that if this session should provide agreement by the Council that Paul was guilty of a religious offense, the commander might well conclude that his own responsibility was to turn him over to this body for formal trial. Paul's life and the possibility of any future ministry were at stake.

But was the apostle justified in declaring, "I am a

Pharisee"? There would be no ground for objection had he said, "I was a Pharisee" (cf. Phil. 3:5). However, on this occasion he was not saying that he was a Pharisee and therefore no longer a Christian, but that on the issues that divide Pharisees from Sadducees he stood firmly with the former group. Pharisaic theology, now crowned by his discovery of the Messiah in the person of Jesus, was still his possession (cf. 15:5). This was his spiritual heritage. The phrase "the son of a Pharisee" is probably intended to look beyond immediate parentage to a line of Pharisaic ancestors.

Now comes the bombshell: "I stand on trial because of my hope in the resurrection of the dead." Was this equivalent to the hope of resurrection such as Pharisaism maintained (cf. John 11:24)? It might appear so from Paul's reference to this very outcry when his case was being heard by Felix (24:21). One could point also to 24:15, and possibly to 26:6–8. But the latter passage seems to have latent in it the idea of the salvation to be brought to Israel by the Messiah. And certainly 28:20, in view of what follows in 28:23, does not permit us to think merely of the event of resurrection as being Israel's hope. The hope centered rather in the messianic salvation, which will indeed be crowned by resurrection, of which the resurrection of Jesus of Nazareth is the guarantee. So Paul was saying that the real issue in his case was not an alleged infringement of the sanctity of the temple but rather the theological issue of the nature of the hope of his people.

The announcement had the desired effect. Instantly the rift between the two parties became evident, the Pharisees rallying to Paul's support and the Sadducees opposing. It was on the same issue that the Sadducees had sought to trap Jesus (Matt. 22:23–33).

Because the word "all" at the end of verse 8 is literally "both," some interpreters conclude that "resurrection" is one item, and that the other is "angels" or "spirits," the latter two not being sharply distinguished. But the Greek word for both is sometimes used in the sense of "all" (see comment on 19:16). If "angel" and "spirit" are differentiated, what is the meaning of "spirit"? "Evil spirit," or "demon," is a possibility (cf. Matt. 8:16), but this sense will not fit in verse 9 of our passage; so it is best to take "spirit" in the sense of disembodied human spirit, as in Hebrews 12:23.

23:9–10. "We find nothing wrong with this man." The

Pharisees were ready to exonerate Paul on the spot, granting the possibility that he had been spoken to by an angel or spirit on this matter of resurrection. Perhaps the reference was to the vision that Paul had mentioned in addressing the crowd in the temple court (22:17–18). The tenor of the Pharisees' plea had much in common with the point made by one of their most prominent members, Gamaliel, that the danger of opposing God must be avoided at all costs (5:39). Proclamation of the resurrection was the background in both cases.

The commander, noting the ferocity of the dissension between the two parties, was afraid that the prisoner would be "torn to pieces" and consequently sent his troops into the fracas to whisk him away. It could be said that Paul was no safer in the presence of the highest court of his people than he had been in the midst of the mob in the temple area. In both cases he owed his preservation, humanly speaking, to the interference of the Romans.

23:11. Something better than the security provided by Rome became the experience of the prisoner that night. "The Lord stood near Paul" with a message that commended him for his testimony (which must include his word before the Council) up to this time and promised that his hope of bearing witness at Rome (19:21) would be realized. He could sleep in peace the rest of the night.

18

PLOT AGAINST PAUL AND TRANSFER TO CAESAREA
23:12–35

The apostle needed this assurance from a heavenly source, for his enemies lost no time in concocting a plot designed to end his life.

23:12–15. It is tantalizing that Luke does not identify the plotters beyond calling them "Jews." Perhaps the word is used here as in John, where rather often it carries the connotation of those who actively oppose Jesus. If so, there were Jews who saw in Paul the gravest danger to the continuance of Judaism in its pure and exclusive form. Since the Sanhedrin had let him slip through their fingers by their disunity, these men were prepared to offer themselves as a cohesive force pledged to kill Paul or be killed themselves in the attempt. They showed their seriousness by putting themselves under an oath, really a curse (anathema), committing themselves to abstain from food and drink until they accomplished their mission. In other words, they were inviting God to destroy them if they failed to fulfill their pledge.

Some writers (e.g., Schlatter and Jeremias) have identified them as Zealots, and S. G. F. Brandon is inclined to agree.[1] Schlatter concedes that there is difficulty involved in this identification when he writes, "The high priest consented, although there was an inexorable, bloody feud between the Sadducees and Zealots, and Ananias was especially obnoxious to them."[2] Apparently the Pharisees, due to the defense of Paul, were not approached, but it was felt that they would attend the

[1] S. G. F. Brandon, *Jesus and the Zealots* (New York: Scribner, 1968), 111 n.5.
[2] A. Schlatter, *The Church in the New Testament Period*, 216.

gathering if the high priest summoned the Council, and by the time they learned of the plot it would be too late to interfere on behalf of Paul as they had done before. As for the Zealots and the Sadducees, they would forget their differences for the sake of eliminating a common enemy, just as the Pharisees had joined with the Sadducees to seek the death of Jesus, becoming a party to treachery in the betrayal by Judas. They would justify their resort to violence by affirming that they were acting for the faith of their fathers and were doing God service (John 16:2). Paul had similarly justified his stern measures as a persecutor of the church (Acts 26:9).

The plan was to lie in wait for Paul and murder him before he reached the meeting place of the Council. If need be, the conspirators were prepared to die when they attacked the escort of soldiers, in order that some of their number might reach Paul to destroy him. It was a bold plot, quite in keeping with the fanatical spirit of the Zealot party. One need not picture these forty men as starving to death after the failure of their scheme, for Jewish lawyers skilled in the art of casuistry could readily be persuaded to find a way of relieving them from their oath.

The willingness of the leaders of the Sanhedrin to cooperate with the plotters rather than hold a bona fide trial reveals how conscious they were of the weakness of their case against Paul. The all-wise God permitted the plot to germinate that the evil intents of sinful men might be disclosed; yet He overruled in such a way that Paul was moved one stage nearer Rome, in accordance with His promise (23:11). How this was achieved is disclosed by what follows immediately.

23:16–22. An amazing story unfolds here, one that illustrates the sovereignty of God. At a time when the Jerusalem church was either too petrified by fear to lift a finger in Paul's behalf, or too concerned with its own future relation to Judaism to risk any attempt at intervention, from within the apostle's own kindred God raised up a helper for him in his time of need.

The problem is to do justice to two factors. On the one hand, if Paul's sister and her son were Christians, how would the son have learned of the plot? On the other hand, if they were not believers, would not the typical Jewish prejudice against the Nazarenes be so powerful as to smother the yearning desire to be of help to Paul? Luke has left us to our speculations, for he supplies no details. Perhaps the sister had become a believer through the testimony of Paul following his conversion (9:28).

It was the son who had the courage to enter the castle, once he had learned of the plot, and to seek out Paul to share the information about it. A centurion fell in with Paul's request that the young man be conducted to the commander. To the centurion, the apostle was "Paul, the prisoner." This was the label that identified him from this time on for years to come. In fact, he used the label several times when writing from prison (Eph. 3:1; 4:1; Philem. 1, 9). Paul made sure that people realized that this incarceration was not due to some criminal act but solely to his loyalty to Christ and His cause (Phil. 1:13).

The story of what went on in the Castle of Antonia is so vivid and circumstantial that it suggests Luke's presence with Paul on this occasion. It closes with a warning from the commander to the informant not to be loose of tongue, as someone had been in providing him with the information he bore. Secrecy was all-important, and so was time.

Verses 23–35 Immediately the commander set to work to remove the prisoner beyond the reach of the conspirators and to do it in such a way as not to attract notice. Even as verses 16–22 show to what great lengths the Jews would go to be rid of Paul, the present passage shows the lengths to which the Romans would go to protect a citizen of the Empire, even if he were a Jew.

23:23–24. The apostle was conducted out of the city under cover of darkness at nine o'clock, surrounded by 470 men. In the event of an attack on Paul resulting in his death, the commander would be held responsible. He might even be accused of working hand in glove with the conspiring Jews. So he supplied ample protection during this trip to Caesarea, the city where the Roman governor Felix had his headquarters.

23:25–30. Along with the troops went a letter from the commander to the governor. "The Roman law required that a subordinate officer, in sending a prisoner to his superior, should send along with him a written statement of the case."[3]

The term "Excellency" was reserved for important personages (cf. Luke 1:3). It is roughly equivalent to *honorable* used in reference to the mayor of a city.

The letter gave a summary account of the events surrounding Paul's arrest and detention in Jerusalem. There was an

[3]Paton J. Gloag, *A Critical and Exegetical Commentary on the Acts of the Apostles*, 2:324–25.

understandable desire to magnify somewhat the conduct of the writer in all of this, leading him to a misstatement or two, especially the claim that the rescue of Paul was due to the commander's knowledge that the threatened man was a Roman. This knowledge had not come until later. Again, no mention was made of the order for a flogging of the prisoner. The final statement about Paul's accusers is technically incorrect, for at the time of writing the commander had not yet informed the accusers of Paul's departure from the city and of their rights in the next development of the case; but by the time the letter reached the governor this contact had been made and the information imparted.

On the positive side, Claudius Lysias exonerated Paul of anything criminal (v. 29), and this was doubtless the main value of the letter as far as the historian was concerned. The verdict expressed concurs with that of Gallio at an earlier time (18:14–15) and of Festus and Agrippa later on (26:31–32).

23:31–32. Slipping out of Jerusalem when the city had become quiet, the force of foot soldiers and mounted men would attract little attention. Ahead of them lay Antipatris, forty miles away by a descending and somewhat winding road, where an ambush could be disastrous. The town, built by Herod the Great and named in honor of his father Antipater, was used by the Romans as a relay station for troop movements. Since the remainder of the journey to Caesarea, covering some twenty-five miles, was over the plain where the cavalry could make good time, the foot soldiers were no longer needed and could return to Jerusalem at a more leisurely pace.

23:33–35. At Caesarea the responsibility of the cavalry detachment was to present the letter and the prisoner to the governor, Antonius Felix, who governed from A.D. 52–60. He had been a slave, but like several others had gained the status of freedman under the emperor Claudius and was one of his favorites. This accounts for his elevation to the high post he now held, an honor that went to his head. At any rate, Tacitus in *Historiae,* describes him as "exercising the powers of a king with the disposition of a slave." His repressive measures only increased the restlessness of the masses in Judea, and his unscrupulous self-enrichment aroused their anger. According to Josephus, his use of brigands to assassinate objects of his dislike brought on a period of lawlessness that led up to the war with Rome.[4]

On reading the letter from the commander in Jerusalem, Felix inquired of Paul concerning his home province and was informned that it was Cilicia. Acting on that knowledge, he agreed to hear the case. Sherwin-White points out the unexpectedness of this, since Felix might well have preferred to avoid taking responsibility by returning Paul to his native area for trial, especially since Paul was a Roman citizen. The suggestion he makes is that Cilicia, like Judea, was an administrative district of the province of Syria, and "the Legate of Syria was not to be bothered with minor cases from Judea . . . and the status of Cilicia did not require that its natives should be sent back to it for trial."[5]

Ancient rulers could be temperamental when it came to listening to the complaints of their subjects. There is a story of Philip, the father of Alexander the Great, to the effect that when an old woman presented herself and begged him to hear her cause, she was repulsed by his impatient word, "I haven't time." Nothing daunted, she quickly replied, "Then stop being king." The story concludes with the observation that he not only listened to her but also to all the others—at once.[6]

There would naturally have been a slight delay until Paul's accusers could arrange to be present (cf. v. 30). Meanwhile the prisoner was detained in the governor's residence, which was evidently equipped with rooms suitable for such a purpose. This helps to explain Luke's comment in 24:26.

[4]Josephus, *Antiquities* XX.8.5.

[5]A. N. Sherwin-White, *Roman Society and Roman Law in the New Testament,* 55–56.

[6]Frederick Field, *Notes on the Translation of the New Testament,* 138.

19

DEFENSE BEFORE FELIX
24:1–27

While most of the chapter is properly described as a defense in the light of charges brought against Paul, it concludes with an account of further personal contacts between him and the governor.

Verses 1–9. This section deals with the charges brought against Paul by Tertullus on behalf of the Sanhedrin.

24:1–9. Before there could be a defense, the case against Paul had to be presented. For this purpose, some "five days" after the arrival of the prisoner a group appeared, representing the Sanhedrin, with Ananias at their head. Along with them came a certain Tertullus, who is called a "lawyer." This term, which occurs only here in the New Testament, basically denotes a public speaker, one with a good flow of words. But in this passage it has a more specialized meaning, attested by the papyri—namely, "attorney" or "advocate."

Tertullus was evidently engaged by the Sanhedrin to present their case against Paul. Tertullus is a Latin name, and "it is probable that Tertullus made his plea against Paul before Felix . . . in Latin, though Greek was allowed in such provincial courts by grace of the judge."[1] He could have been a Greek or even a Jew. Several times he identified himself with the Jewish people ("we"), but this is not decisive, since he could have adopted this stance for the sake of those who had asked for his services. More significant is the statement "We . . . wanted to

---

[1] A. T. Robertson, "Latin," in *ISBE*, 3:1841a.

judge him according to our law" (NIV footnote) but this is found in a portion of the text that is of doubtful authenticity. Verse 9 seems to distinguish between Tertullus and the Jews. Munck suggests that he was the regular legal consultant of the Sanhedrin. Favorable to this conclusion is the brief time available for securing and briefing a stranger.

About one thing there is no doubt—his command of the rhetoric requisite to such an occasion. While we probably have only a summary of his speech, it is evident that he gave almost as much attention to complimenting the governor as to the exposition of the case for the plaintiffs.

It is true that he spoke only in broad generalities of "peace" and "reforms," tracing these to the governor's foresight, for specific instances of benefit to the nation would have been hard to find. Even the reference to peace was a dubious compliment, for the ruthless way in which uprisings had been put down only made others inevitable as a protest. The meaning of "reforms" is doubtful, but the reference may have been to those very measures that were used to secure peace. Order was purchased at the expense of more strife in the future.

The advocate was careful to observe all the necessary expressions of respect, addressing the judge as "most excellent Felix" (cf. 23:26).

In voicing gratitude for the governor's alleged benefactions, Tertullus was certainly not speaking the mind of most Jews, for at the end of the two-year period mentioned in verse 27 Nero summoned Felix to Rome to give account for serious disturbances between Jews and Gentiles in Caesarea. When the investigation was broadened to include his administration as a whole, the evidence against him was so overwhelming that he was recalled. He would have been severely punished had it not been for the intercession of his brother Pallas on his behalf.[2]

The word "kind" must have been spoken with tongue in cheek, but this was conventional rhetoric not intended to be taken too literally and yet demanded by the occasion.

After asking for a hearing and promising to make it brief, Tertullus got down to the business at hand.

First, Paul was a "troublemaker" (v. 5). The full import of the term appears when one discovers that literally it means

[2]Josephus, *Antiquities* XX.8.9.

"pestilence" or "plague" (cf. Luke 21:11, the only other occurrence in the New Testament). What he had been to the church as its persecutor (Gal. 1:13), he had become in turn to the very body that had encouraged him in his persecuting role. But the argument was made more concrete by adding, "stirring up riots," and not here and there but "all over the world" (cf. Acts 17:6; 21:28), an obvious exaggeration.

By using the word "riots" Tertullus was putting in a prominent place a charge that he hoped would impress the governor as weighty. The term was intended to have political overtones, as in Luke 23:19, where it denotes a riot that in reality was an insurrection. Possibly the word was intended to be somewhat ambiguous, able to cover an overt revolt against the government but also capable of being used in the more restricted sense of upheavals (in this case, among the Jews) that were violent enough to create alarm for the state (see comments on 18:2). Sherwin-White points out (following Cumont) that the letter from Emperor Claudius to the people of Alexandria contains a close parallel to this charge. In this letter the monarch objects to certain politically objectionable activities of the Jews as "stirring up a universal plague throughout the world."[3] With reference to 24:5 the same author notes that the Jews "knew that the governors were unwilling to convict on purely religious charges and therefore tried to give a political twist to the religious charge."[4] In Paul's case the charge was untrue, as Roman officials had already ruled (18:12–16; 19:37–40).

In the second charge Paul was made out to be a "ringleader of the Nazarene sect." Of some interest is the fact that this is the only place where the plural is used (Greek, "sect of the Nazarenes"); in all other instances *Nazarene* is a reference to Jesus. It is not known to what extent Felix was informed about this group, but he could at least gather from the tone of voice and facial expression of Tertullus that it was thoroughly despised by the Jews as a whole. At a later time the word *sect* took on the meaning of "heresy." What was implied in this case was that the Nazarenes were a divisive force in Judaism that the Romans ought not to look on with favor, since it was so dissimilar as to lie outside the scope of being a permitted

---

[3] A. N. Sherwin-White, *Roman Society and Roman Law in the New Testament,* 51.

[4] Ibid., 50.

religion, the status enjoyed by Judaism. Paul was singled out as a "ringleader" of this sect. Rackham comments, "We also note that the preeminence of Paul in the church is no exaggeration of S. Luke's: his enemies, taking a figure from the army, acknowledge him to be a *front rank man* or head of the file."[5]

As a third item, Tertullus charged Paul with violating the sanctity of the temple (v. 6). The allegation was considerably modified from the original assertion (21:28), since here only an attempt at the desecration of the sacred place was claimed. Even in this softened form the charge was important for two reasons. First, it was more specific than the other two items mentioned by Tertullus and should have been capable of proof or disproof. Second, it concerned the Romans almost as much as the first charge did, since they were agreed that even if one of their own number violated the temple by seeking to go in, they would permit the Jews to put him to death (see comment on 21:27).

"We seized him" suggests that from the first the Jews had contemplated a trial. This is contrary to the narrative in chapter 21, where the mob is pictured as trying to kill Paul on the spot. "But it was essential to the case of Tertullus to maintain that Paul was legally a Jewish 'temple-prisoner' with whom Lysias had no right to interfere."[6]

At this point the listing of complaints against Paul ends, and the termination seems rather abrupt. Some manuscripts, particularly those of the Western type, supply a longer text, as follows: ". . . and wanted to judge him according to our law. But the commander, Lysias, came and with the use of much force snatched him from our hands and ordered his accusers to come before you," (NIV footnote). If this addition were to be accepted, the words that follow about "examining him" would refer to Lysias rather than to Paul. In other words, Felix was being challenged to corroborate the testimony of Tertullus by checking with Lysias. This is awkward, if not impossible, since the "him" at the beginning of verse 8 must be the same individual denoted by the "him" at the close of the verse, where the reference can be only to Paul. A further difficulty lies in the phrase, "about all these charges," for Lysias would not have been competent to bear witness on the first two charges. So the added material is rightly rejected and consigned to a marginal reading.

---

[5] R. B. Rackham, *The Acts of the Apostles*, 443.
[6] Kirsopp Lake and H. J. Cadbury, eds., *BC*, vol. 4.

Looking back over the allegations against Paul—a trouble-maker among the Jews who would bear watching by the Romans, a follower of the Nazarene (who had entertained messianic pretensions, only to be rejected by His own nation), and one who thought so little of the place his countrymen honored as most holy that he could try to bring a Gentile in and defile it—one can sense the cord of unity that runs through them all. It is neatly expressed by Munck as "an attempt to separate Paul and the Jewish Christians from the Jewish religion."[7] It is well to bear this in mind as one scrutinizes the apostle's reply in its various facets. Possibly T. W. Manson is right in saying, "It is probable that the strong desire of a large section of the early church to hold on to their Jewish affiliation was not unconnected with the wish to have the status of a *religio licita*,"[8] but this should be understood from the standpoint, not of expediency, but of conviction. In the case of Paul one need only point to Romans 11.

Verses 10–21. This section gives a report of Paul's defense, which was given after members of the Jewish delegation affirmed the correctness of the statements made by their spokesman.

24:10–21. Receiving a nod from the governor indicating that it was now his turn to speak, the apostle responded by taking up the charges in order. His opening statements, like those of Tertullus, were intended to take account of the dignity and capacity of Felix, but in Paul's case there was a brevity and restraint that were in marked contrast to the fulsomeness and flattery of the previous speaker. It was his earnest desire to remain within the bounds of truth (2 Cor. 13:8).

"A number of years" need not suggest that Paul was ignorant of the length of time Felix had been in office. He was not intending to be precise, but was indicating merely that the governor had had sufficient opportunity (over a period of five or six years) to become acquainted with the Jewish people and their situation (cf. v. 22). The same purpose underlies the choice of the word "judge" rather than *governor*. Felix had tried enough cases to have a store of information about the history, customs, and outlook of the nation, and Paul was counting on this understanding as he opened his defense.

[7] Johannes Munck, *The Acts of the Apostles,* 232.
[8] T. W. Manson, *Studies in the Gospels and Epistles,* 61.

Speaking to the first charge, the apostle intimated that his time in Jerusalem had been too limited to have organized a riot even if he wanted to. It is not easy to accommodate what happened to "twelve days." Meyer seeks to do it by supposing that the five days of verse 1 are to be reckoned from the organizing of the conspiracy and the departure of Paul from Jerusalem.[9] But this is hardly natural. Since Luke has not given a day-by-day account, one can only surmise how the time period was reckoned. In addition to the question of time, Paul brought in the matter of purpose. The reason he went to Jerusalem was "to worship." Probably this can be connected with his desire to arrive at the city for the celebration of Pentecost (20:16). Finally, he did not engage in public disputation or proclamation, much less stir up a riot (v. 12). His last visit, then, was in marked contrast to his first as a believer, when he had preached and debated at every opportunity (9:28–29; 22:18).

To meet the second charge, that he was a leader of the discredited sect of the Nazarenes, Paul conceded that he had such a connection, but his own preference was to speak of it as "the Way" (v. 14). *Sect* sounds negative and divisive; *way* sounds positive and purposeful. Further, he countered the sectarian allegation by asserting that his worship was directed to "the God of our fathers." He had not alienated himself from Israel's God any more than from her devoted saints. Also, he had not forsaken the sacred writings of his people. His faith was fully in line with what is found in the Law and the Prophets.

Despite the comprehensive nature of the language, it is likely that Paul had in mind more than anything else the promise of a Messiah (cf. Luke 24:44–46); for the hope of resurrection, to which he adverted immediately, was decidedly vivified and strengthened by the resurrection of Jesus Christ. But in this delicate situation Paul declined to turn aside and discuss the Messiah question directly, preferring rather to proclaim resurrection in terms familiar from the Old Testament, where a resurrection of "the righteous and the wicked" is set forth (Dan. 12:2). Proclamation of the resurrection as an item of faith had won him support from the Pharisees in the Council (Acts 23:6–9). Also it is probable that Felix, by virtue

[9]H. A. W. Meyer, *Critical and Exegetical Handbook to the Acts of the Apostles,* 443–44.

of his acquaintance with Judaism, would know that apart from the Sadducees, belief in resurrection was generally held among the Jewish people. In referring to "these men" (v. 15), Paul may have motioned with his hand to the Pharisees in the group from Jerusalem, especially if they were seated together. He must have ignored Ananias and the other Sadducees who were with him.

"So" (i.e., in view of the hope of resurrection), Paul sought to maintain a blameless conscience both Godward and manward (cf. 23:1). At the resurrection he would have to give account to God; meanwhile he must live uprightly before his fellows. He was fully aware of the extent to which spiritual convictions motivate conduct.

At length Paul injected the real reason for being in Jerusalem. It was to bring his people gifts for the poor and to present offerings (v. 17). This is the only time in Acts that the collection for the poor saints at Jerusalem is mentioned, though it is often referred to in Paul's letters to churches. Here again the language was carefully chosen—the people (*ethnos*) were stated as the beneficiaries rather than the church. This was a deliberate stroke to emphasize that the church in Jerusalem had not sundered itself from the people of God who made up the nation of Israel. But admittedly the church was the recipient.

J. E. H. Hull presents a plausible reason for the apostle's great concern over this fund.

> It was the fact of persecution (Acts 8:1) that initially led to the poverty of the Christian community in Jerusalem. It is possible that Paul was so concerned to relieve the destitution there (e.g., I Cor. 16:1ff) partly because he realized that he had contributed to it through his persecuting zeal.[10]

Somewhat uncertain is the meaning of the second statement of purpose, "to present offerings." He did present offerings in connection with the rites of purification (21:26), but apparently he had not had this in view when he went to Jerusalem. It may be, as some suppose, that the sentence is elliptical, Paul's meaning being on this order: "I came to Jerusalem to bring alms to my nation, and I entered into the Temple to make offerings."[11] Luke may have been compressing

[10]J. E. H. Hull, *The Holy Spirit in the Acts of the Apostles*, 76.
[11]Thomas Walker, *The Acts of the Apostles*, 509.

his narrative to save space. There is a possibility also that Paul had intended to present thank offerings at Jerusalem in gratitude for the successful completion of the trip and other blessings.

By this statement Paul indicated that he was moving into a discussion of the third charge, his alleged violation of the temple. He admitted to having been there and suggested the reason for it, namely, his purification after living so long among the unclean Gentiles. But there had been no crowd or disturbance, none, that is, of his making. What had developed along these lines was strictly because of "some Jews from the province of Asia" (cf. 21:27).

Here the apostle broke off without finishing the sentence. The technical word for this phenomenon of grammatical irregularity is *anacoluthon* (a Greek term meaning "lack of sequence"). Such constructions are fairly common in Paul's writings, so Luke may well have been reproducing his exact words here. The abruptness of the construction makes for suspense, which creates an atmosphere of expectancy that something weighty will follow. In this case it did, for the apostle was able to make the telling point that it was the duty of these Asian Jews, the ones who were responsible for the fracas in the temple, to be present for this trial. Their failure to appear could readily be interpreted as a demonstration that they could not substantiate their wild claim that Paul had brought a Gentile beyond the barrier into the inner confines of the temple area (21:28). Paul scored heavily on this item.

To round off his presentation he turned to the representatives of the Sanhedrin ("these who are here") to challenge them to make an accusation against him based on what he had said when he stood before them. The only thing he could suggest himself was his assertion that "the resurrection of the dead" was at issue (v. 21; cf. 23:6). No member of the Council was likely to challenge his statement of what had happened, for it was factual. Any challenge could only lead to the disclosure of a cleavage on this point between Pharisees and Sadducees, and this would have been an embarrassment to them in the present situation. So they remained silent. R. P. C. Hanson is of the opinion that this speech is substantially what Paul would have given before the Council had he not been interrupted.[12]

---

[12] R. P. C. Hanson, *The Acts,* 228.

Verses 22–23. These verses give Governor Felix's twofold reaction to what he heard. He delayed a decision on the case, meanwhile keeping Paul in custody.

24:22–23. Now all eyes were on Felix. What would the governor decide? His decision was to adjourn the proceedings. The trial was suspended, at least until he could confer with Lysias, the commander.

Rather strangely another factor is introduced here, the knowledge that Felix possessed of "the Way." Several questions need to be asked, the first of them being of a grammatical nature. How should the comparative adjective, used adverbially, be rendered? In the NASB the wording is "a more exact knowledge," meaning perhaps a more exact knowledge than people might suppose.[13] However, since the Koine period of the Greek language brought considerable flexibility into the use of the comparative, with fairly numerous examples of its use in a so-called elative or heightened sense best expressed by *very,* some grammarians prefer the translation "a very accurate knowledge" (Nigel Turner; Blass-Debrunner). An even stronger wording is "perfect knowledge" (*BC*). A decision between these is difficult. They all emphasize in some measure the knowledge Felix possessed of Christianity, and that was important to Luke. If a ruler was well acquainted with the faith and found himself unable to convict a leading representative of it, though he himself was not a believer, he became another Gallio (18:14–15).

A second question relates to the source of this knowledge. How was it acquired? To find the answer simply in the information provided by Paul in his speech is inadequate, for it was a defense against certain allegations rather than an exposition of the Christian faith. The answer may lie in the fact that the governor's wife was as Jewess (v. 24), but doubtless there were other contacts also. Felix had been in the country for several years and could hardly have failed to learn a great deal if he was at all receptive to information on the religious situation among the people he was expected to govern.

A third question relates to the bearing that this knowledge, however obtained, had on the decision to suspend the trial. Probably Felix was convinced of the innocence of Paul (cf.

---

[13] See A. T. Robertson, *Word Pictures in the New Testament,* 3:421.

Pilate's attitude toward Jesus) and so could not pronounce against him, yet felt a reluctance to incur the displeasure of the high court of Judaism. Already a course was being taken that continued to be followed as long as he had jurisdiction (cf. v. 27). So far so good. But then, how is the reference to Lysias to be explained? Clearly the governor gave the impression that no decision could be reached until his testimony was heard. After all, he had been an eyewitness of the turmoil at the temple, something that could not be said for the Sanhedrin. Yet the odd thing is that no further session of the court was held after the arrival of Lysias. For that matter, there is no record that he arrived at Caesarea at all.

What had started out ostensibly as a temporary thing—namely, that Paul was kept "under guard," with freedom to have visitors—became a drawn-out arrangement. We can only conclude that the Sanhedrin grew weary of waiting and withdrew to Jerusalem, where it had other business to attend to. For Paul, the long detention was alleviated somewhat by the ministration of friends in Caesarea who loved him dearly (cf. 21:8–14). Yet all the while the presence of a military guard reminded him that he was a prisoner. But he was a prisoner for the sake of Christ and for this reason was certain to see Rome in the Lord's good time. In this he was comforted. Human companions, including Luke, did their best to minister to his needs.

Verses 24–27. This passage describes the governor's changing attitude toward Paul. After his initial fear in response to Paul's presentation of the gospel, Felix's spiritual concern became a monetary one. In the end, self-interest prompted him to leave Paul in prison, though he was aware of the apostle's innocence.

24:24–27. The next contact between the governor and the prisoner occurred a few days later, when Felix came with Drusilla his wife. To speak of his coming is a bit strange, seeming to imply that the governor had been away in the meantime. This may well have been the case, and it would have served as a broad hint to the Sanhedrin representatives that they might as well go home. The meaning could be, however, that the couple arrived from their sumptuous quarters and came into the humble surroundings of the apostle (cf. 25:7).

Drusilla was the daughter of Herod Agrippa I, mentioned

in chapter 12, and the sister of Herod Agrippa II, about to be mentioned in chapter 25. According to Josephus,[14] Drusilla was given in marriage by her brother to the king of Emesa, a small domain on the Orontes River, but was lured from her husband and persuaded to marry Felix, who was attracted by her great beauty. This alliance, made when she was still in her middle teens, was contrary to Jewish law, seeing that Felix had not agreed to become a Jew.

Since this visit to Paul was not a part of the trial but only a private meeting, the apostle was free to discuss what was closest to his heart, "faith in Christ Jesus." According to the Western text it was Drusilla, rather than Felix, who expressed a desire to see and hear Paul. However, the remainder of the passage has nothing to say of her reaction, but concentrates on that of Felix.

The chances are good that in speaking of faith in Christ, Paul gave his personal testimony, including an account of his conversion. But Felix was not ready for faith, and Paul sought to make him aware of his sinful condition by speaking of those things that peculiarly fitted his character and conduct. What he needed was "righteousness," in contrast to the injustice that had characterized his regime thus far, and "self-control," especially in the area of passion (Felix was thrice married). And unless there was repentance, he would have to face the "judgment to come," which was inevitable for one whose life evidenced a lack of these qualities (Rom. 1:18; Eph. 5:3–6).

Such preaching, man to man, made Felix uncomfortable and fearful, if only for a short time, as the following verse indicates. But Paul had fulfilled his obligation as a witness for Christ. To speak thus frankly would not help his case in the eyes of the governor, but for that very reason it is an example of holy boldness, which those should consider who tend to berate him for dividing the Council to save himself (23:1–10) and for failing to preach Christ when the Council came to Caesarea for the trial before Felix (24:1).

Further meetings were held from time to time, probably by Felix alone in conference with Paul, but inspired by cupidity rather than by concern for his spiritual condition. Paul himself may have excited cupidity in the governor by his statement about bringing alms to his nation (24:17). Furthermore, the

---

[14]Josephus, *Antiquities* XX.7.1–2.

real purpose was to intercept Paul on the way and kill him. Observe the changed situation as compared with that noted in 23:13–15. Now the plot was no longer inspired by a few men but was the official plan of the leaders of the Jews. This seems to indicate that they had abandoned hope of getting a conviction against Paul under Roman justice. Judging from verse 24, there was pressure on Festus also from the populace of Jerusalem, who could usually be counted on to respond in the form of a demonstration when the Council requested it (cf. the manipulating of the crowd at the trial of Jesus before Pilate as reported in Luke 23:13–23).

However, Festus refused to be badgered, and indicated that he was about to return to Caesarea. There he would reopen the case, receiving testimony from the leading men of the Jews, and would try to determine the merits of their charges (v. 5). He did not relish having incompetent and unrepresentative persons pressing charges out of personal bias. Probably the group was roughly the same as the leading men referred to in verse 2.

25:6–12. True to his promise, Festus acted with promptness, taking up the case the very next day after his arrival. "The court" refers to the official judgment seat used during court proceedings (cf. 18:12). By this time the accusers were ready also, having made the trip from Jerusalem about the same time as the governor. So Paul was summoned to confront them, one against the many, but confident that the truth was on his side and that the Lord was with him. By their numbers and the vigor of their allegations they would browbeat and confuse him if they could. Paul was like a man doing battle for his life in a ring surrounded by ferocious animals.

One charge after another was voiced against him, and they were "serious." However, they had a fatal limitation—they could not be established. Proof was lacking. Luke does not bother to detail the accusations, for in the main they were what had been set forth in the presence of Felix, judging from what is reported of Paul's defense (v. 8). The mention of Caesar was new, but Paul sought to expose the underhandedness of the attack, namely, that it put forward the charge of creating disturbances (24:5) far and wide and was thereby calculated to give the impression of rebellion and of disloyalty to Caesar. Paul brought the motive of his accusers out into the open.

Festus was astute enough to realize that from the Roman standpoint there was no case against Paul, but he was prepared "to do the Jews a favor" in order to get his regime off on the right foot. The Jews were notoriously difficult for a foreigner to govern. His proposal was that the apostle be returned to Jerusalem for a continuance of the trial there. This does not mean that the governor had in mind to turn the case over to the Sanhedrin (the words "before me" exclude any such notion), but rather that he would have the Jews on hand as consultants. He contemplated no new developments, however. Paul was to stand trial "on these charges."

It was a strange request, unfair on the face of it. Paul's first experience before the Sanhedrin, plus the trial before Felix, had convinced him that he could not expect an impartial hearing. A hostile atmosphere would make a proper verdict more difficult to render in Jerusalem than in Caesarea. The very fact that the Jewish leaders had been willing to wink at a plot against his life and to cooperate in its execution was enough in itself to warn him about the folly of acceding to the proposal of Festus, which after all was but an echo of the request of the Jews themselves (v. 3).

It would help our understanding if we had some clue to Festus's thoughts at this time. C. F. D. Moule makes the following suggestion. He interprets the "favor" of verse 9 in these terms, that the governor

> wanted to give them a chance to assassinate Paul, yet without Festus appearing to play into their hands (for that might have endangered his reputation at Rome). He can prove no charge against Paul; neither can he hand him back to the Sanhedrin, from whom he has already been rescued by the Romans. All he can do is to see whether he can make it appear that Paul himself has asked for a transfer to Jerusalem: that will give the Jews a chance to get at him on the journey without Festus being responsible. It will be "just too bad" that the prisoner got assassinated on the way (after all, it was his own choice to be moved!)—and there will be an end of the Governor's "headache"![2]

This not improbable suggestion would become all the more plausible if Festus knew of the original plot of the Jews against Paul. On this Luke provides no information.

[2]C. F. D. Moule, *A Chosen Vessel*, 69–70.

21

DEFENSE BEFORE AGRIPPA
25:13–26:32

Though the legal assistants of the governor had counseled him about sending Paul to Caesar, they apparently provided no help in formulating a statement of explanation suitable to submit to the emperor. So Festus must have regarded the coming of King Agrippa as a highly fortunate circumstance, since this man had insight into Jewish matters that the governor lacked and could presumably help him in his dilemma.

Verses 13–22. This passage relates the conversation between Governor Festus and Agrippa concerning Paul. Agrippa's willingness to hear the prisoner opened the way for the hearing on the following day.

25:13–22. King Agrippa, a descendant of Herod the Great, was the son of that Agrippa who had imprisoned Peter (chap. 12). But he did not become king of the Jews as his father had been. His domain at this time included the territories to the north and east of the Sea of Galilee, formerly ruled by Philip and Lysanias (Luke 3:1), plus some cities in Galilee and Perea. He kept his hand in Jewish politics as much as discretion allowed and made trips to Jerusalem from time to time.

Accompanying him to Caesarea was his sister Bernice, who was also sister to Drusilla. Her relationship with Agrippa was morally suspect, as was much of her life—so much so that she shocked even the Romans by her conduct. The royal pair came to greet Festus, since he had recently arrived to take over the procuratorship of Judea. Their stay was long enough to prompt the governor to seek Agrippa's help on Paul's case.

In explanation of his predicament, the governor reviewed

out of the present session to illuminate the problem presented by an insistent nation demanding the death of an apparently innocent man. His perplexity was obvious.

> The complication and prolongation of the trial of Paul arose from the fact that the charge was political—hence the procurators were reluctant to dismiss it out of hand—and yet the evidence was theological, hence the procurators were quite unable to understand it.[2]

Since the governor had not found Paul guilty of the charges brought against him, he was not bringing Agrippa into the situation to have him pass on this very matter, but only to have his help in penetrating the mystery of a baffling case. He was looking for advice on how to inform Caesar of the basis for sending the prisoner to Rome. To send him without a clear statement of the charges would be unreasonable.

Of considerable interest is the way in which the governor referred to the emperor, calling him "my lord" (NASB; Greek, "the lord"; NIV, "His Majesty"). There was a time when scholars felt they could question Luke's accuracy at this point. The doubt was based on the well-known fact that both Augustus and Tiberius had refused the use of this title for themselves, because it exalted them unduly and hinted that those whom they ruled were virtually their slaves. However, there is ample evidence today, especially from the papyri, that in Nero's time this title was freely used. Adolf Deissmann observes that this change in the Roman attitude is to be traced to the influence of the East, with its tradition of despotism, to which the West gradually capitulated. He goes on to say,

> The fact that a New Testament writer well acquainted with this period makes Festus the Procurator speak of Nero simply as "the Lord" now acquires its full significance in this connexion. The insignificant detail, questioned by various commentators, who, seated at their writing-tables in Tübingen or Berlin, vainly imagined that they knew the period better than St. Luke, now appears thoroughly credible.[3]

[2] A. N. Sherwin-White, *Roman Society and Roman Law in the New Testament*, 51

[3] Adolf Deissmann, *Light from the Ancient East*, 354.

Chapter 26, verses 1–3. This chapter is almost entirely given over to Paul's defense before Agrippa. It is the most important of the apostle's statements on his own behalf.

Before following the remarks of Paul in his address to Agrippa, we must give attention to a few preliminary considerations. As noted above, Luke was probably present on this occasion. This impression is deepened by the description of Paul stretching out his hand (26:1). The movement registered in the memory of his friend.

The apostle's accusers were not there, so it was not necessary for him to speak to specific charges. This gave him greater freedom concerning the content of his address, allowing him to say something about his own spiritual pilgrimage and the nature of the message he had been commanded to communicate. Paul was very conscious, however, of the people who were before him, especially Agrippa. The words of Festus (25:26) prepare the reader for the prominence the Herodian had from start to finish. He, rather than Festus, invited Paul to speak, and Paul in turn acknowledged him as the one to whom he particularly directed his words (26:2). Toward the end the speaker gave repeated attention to his chief hearer (26:19, 26–28). When the address was finished, it was the king who rose first to declare the session terminated, and his was the final word on the case (26:32).

This occasion, including the speech itself and the verdict of the two rulers at its conclusion, was obviously of great importance to Luke. He has recorded the vindication of Paul given by Festus (25:25) and follows it now with the still stronger verdict of Agrippa, who, unlike Festus, was an acknowledged expert on Jewish matters (26:32).

The content of Acts 26 can be summarized as follows: Paul's introductory words (vv. 1–3), his early life in Judaism (vv. 4–11), his conversion and commission (vv.12–18), his Christian witness (vv. 19–23), his verbal exchanges with Festus and Agrippa (vv. 24–29), and the conference between the two officials (vv. 30–32).

Observe that the Ananias episode, which has such a prominent place in the first account of the conversion (chap. 9) and is mentioned in the second (chap. 22), is not included here. It would have been of only minor interest for a Gentile audience.

26:1–3. The word "defense" occurs twice here, which

raises a question as to the propriety of the language, seeing that this was not a trial and indeed could not be after the case had been appealed to Caesar. No witnesses were called against Paul or in his favor. Yet he spoke of making his defense, and Luke uses the same terminology (v. 24). The apostle maintained he was being judged (v. 6). One need only recognize that terms of this kind are not confined to a strictly legal situation but can be used more generally (cf. 19:33; 2 Cor. 12:19). Paul did indeed speak to clear himself; but more than that, he was intent on creating understanding in his hearers. He was aware of the things about which he had been accused by the Jews, but he was not speaking directly to these accusations.

He had a word of commendation for Agrippa's knowledge of Jewish matters. That the king should have such knowledge is not surprising, for he had spent several years in the land, in addition to his upbringing in Rome, where he undoubtedly had studied Jewish history and customs in preparation for his government service. Some years later Josephus claimed that Agrippa wrote sixty-two letters "testifying to the truth of the record" of events that the historian had put down in his *Jewish War*.[4] The same author noted also that Agrippa was "thoroughly conversant with Hellenic culture."[5] He would have been able to grasp much that eluded the comprehension of Festus.

Verses 4–11. Following his introduction, the apostle plunged at once into a recital of his life in Judaism. This was designed to lead to the conclusion that he had not been guilty of apostasy from the faith of his fathers but rather had seen the input of his early training fulfilled and expanded as the result of a crisis in his life.

26:4–5. An obscurity needs to be cleared up, if possible, concerning the description Paul gave of his life during his youth. Was a contrast intended between "in my own country" and "in Jerusalem"? If so, Paul was indicating that part of his youth had been spent in the Jewish community at Tarsus and rest of it in Jerusalem. This would conflict with his testimony in 22:3. But "from the beginning" is quite meaningless if it applies to separate times and places. Furthermore, not all Jews could have known of his life in Tarsus, when he had as yet not